Sex Offending

The LAW AND PUBLIC POLICY: PSYCHOLOGY AND THE SOCIAL SCIENCES series includes books in three domains:

Legal Studies—writings by legal scholars about issues of relevance to psychology and the other social sciences, or that employ social science information to advance the legal analysis;

Social Science Studies—writings by scientists from psychology and the other social sciences about issues of relevance to law and public policy; and

Forensic Studies—writings by psychologists and other mental health scientists and professionals about issues relevant to forensic mental health science and practice.

The series is guided by its editor, Bruce D. Sales, PhD, JD, University of Arizona; and coeditors, Bruce J. Winick, JD, University of Miami; Norman J. Finkel, PhD, Georgetown University; and Valerie P. Hans, PhD, University of Delaware.

* * *

Sex Offending

Causal Theories to Inform Research, Prevention, and Treatment

Jill D. Stinson
Bruce D. Sales
Judith V. Becker

AMERICAN PSYCHOLOGICAL ASSOCIATION
WASHINGTON, DC

Published by
American Psychological Association
750 First Street, NE
Washington, DC 20002
www.apa.org

To order
APA Order Department
P.O. Box 92984
Washington, DC 20090-2984
Tel: (800) 374-2721; Direct: (202) 336-5510
Fax: (202) 336-5502; TDD/TTY: (202) 336-6123
Online: www.apa.org/books/
E-mail: order@apa.org

In the U.K., Europe, Africa, and the Middle East, copies may be ordered from
American Psychological Association
3 Henrietta Street
Covent Garden, London
WC2E 8LU England

Typeset in Goudy by Stephen McDougal, Mechanicsville, MD

Printer: United Book Press, Inc., Baltimore, MD
Cover Designer: Berg Design, Albany, NY
Technical/Production Editor: Devon Bourexis

The opinions and statements published are the responsibility of the authors, and such opinions and statements do not necessarily represent the policies of the American Psychological Association.

Library of Congress Cataloging-in-Publication Data

Stinson, Jill D.
   Sex offending : causal theories to inform research, prevention, and treatment / Jill D. Stinson, Bruce D. Sales, and Judith V. Becker. — 1st ed.
      p. ; cm. — (The law and public policy)
   Includes bibliographical references.
   ISBN-13: 978-0-9792125-2-9
   ISBN-10: 0-9792125-2-9
   1. Sex offenders—Mental health. 2. Sex offenders—Psychology. 3. Psychosexual disorders—Etiology. I. Sales, Bruce Dennis. II. Becker, Judith V. III. American Psychological Association. IV. Title. V. Series.
   [DNLM: 1. Paraphilias—etiology. 2. Sex Offenses—psychology. 3. Men—psychology. 4. Models, Psychological.5. Psychological Theory. 6. Sex Offenses—prevention & control. WM 610 S859s 2008]
   RC560.S47S75 2008
   616.85'8306—dc22
                                                                                2007031798

British Library Cataloguing-in-Publication Data
A CIP record is available from the British Library.

Printed in the United States of America
First Edition

For Carl and my parents—JDS
For Mary Elizabeth—BDS
For my family—JVB

CONTENTS

ACKNOWLEDGMENTS

We would like to acknowledge the following people for their support and thoughtful comments on various drafts of this book: Hal Arkowitz, Connie Beck, Randy Garland, Bruce Hamstra, Scotia Hicks, Randy Oberhoff, Amy Olson, Ronda Oswalt Reitz, Sharon Robbins, Marika Solhan, and the faculty of Fulton State Hospital.

Sex Offending

1

INTRODUCTION

Even before sexual offenders were recognized as a unique population within the emerging fields of psychological science and criminology, those who committed unusual and deviant sexual acts were viewed as mysterious and frightening. As early as the late 19th century, Richard von Krafft-Ebing published his *Psychopathia Sexualis* (Krafft-Ebing, 1886/1997), detailing case studies of pedophilia, bestiality, and sexual sadism. The popularity of this work at the time reflected society's fascination with these offenders and a need to understand the causes of these behaviors. Since that time, not much has changed, and with good reason.

Official crime statistics collected from law enforcement agencies across the United States indicate that nearly 95,000 forcible rapes occurred in 2004 (U.S. Department of Justice, 2006). Victimization statistics reveal that only one third of sexual assaults are reported to police and other law enforcement officials (La Fond, 2005), which suggests that sexual crimes occur in the United States at a rate far higher than is represented in the official statistics. For example, data from the National Crime Victimization Survey for 2004 indicate that nearly 200,000 rapes occurred during this reporting period (Catalano, 2005). This statistic includes both child and adult victims. Nearly two thirds of victims of sexual assault are minors (La Fond, 2005; Snyder, 2000), and the majority of victims are female (Catalano, 2005; La Fond, 2005).

The number of sexual offenders in prison has dramatically increased over the past several decades, far surpassing the steady increase in the overall prison population (La Fond, 2005). It is estimated that almost 240,000 sex offenders are under the care or supervision of correctional agencies on any given day (Greenfield, 1997), with just under half of these incarcerated (La Fond, 2005) and the remaining percentage under supervision in the community.

Despite increasing professional interest in this population, and growing public fear of sexual violence, we still know relatively little about what drives these individuals to commit such unusual sexual acts. Several recent cases of convicted sexual offenders are illustrative:

> Randal Harty and Russel Harty are 23-year-old identical twin men from Gladewater, Texas. Since 2001, Randal Harty had been arrested for indecent exposure on two occasions, possession of child pornography on two occasions, child molestation, and suspicion of violating the conditions of his probation by going to a local junior high school (Bostic, 2004; Lynch, 2004a, 2004b, 2004c). He was convicted and sentenced to 10 years in prison and fined $10,000 on July 6, 2004 (Thompson, 2004). His brother, Russel Harty, had been arrested three times for voyeurism and once for indecent exposure (Evans, 2004; Lynch, 2004b). He was sentenced to 10 years in prison on January 5, 2006, after admitting to additional charges of possessing child pornography and multiple acts of voyeurism and public masturbation while on probation (Isaac, 2006). Both of these men focused on young women, primarily between the ages of 13 and 15, for their crimes.

> Over the course of 3 decades, Catholic priest John Geoghan of Boston was accused of molesting and sexually assaulting more than 130 young boys (Burge, 2002). Attention to these behaviors began as early as 1962, his 1st year in the priesthood (CNN, 2003), and continued until the late 1990s, when public outcry forced a response from the Catholic Church. During his trial in 2002, church documents revealed a lengthy history of concerned priests, cardinals, and parishioners who had questioned Fr. Geoghan's behavior with male children within his church. He also made statements regarding his connection with these youths, attributing his attention to their need for a father figure and as a way to resolve anger toward their fathers (Farragher & Paulson, 2003). Additional testimony by his treating psychiatrist indicated that Geoghan had engaged in sexual fantasies about children during this period of offending (CNN, 2002). He was eventually convicted of fondling a young boy in an offense that had occurred nearly a decade earlier and sentenced to 9 to 10 years in prison (Burge, 2002). He was killed by a fellow inmate on August 22, 2003 (Farragher & Paulson, 2003).

> James Allen Selby, a former war veteran in his mid-30s, was convicted of committing five sexual assaults in Tucson, Arizona, from October 2001 to May 2002 (Barrios, 2004b). He had a previous conviction from a rape that occurred in Colorado prior to his move to Arizona ("Extradition,"

2003) and was suspected of four additional rapes in San Diego and two sexual attacks on children in Oklahoma and Nevada (Newell, 2002a, 2002b). Media accounts presented Selby as an arrogant, violent, and narcissistic drifter, who threatened his victims and inflicted serious physical harm during the assaults and showed little remorse for his behavior (Newell, 2002a; Simonson, Machelor, & Pallack, 2004). By representing himself at his trial for sexual assault, murder, and kidnapping (Barrios, 2004b), he was able to question his victims, which was seen by some as sadistic (Barrios, 2004a). As in his earlier trials for sexual assault, Selby would claim that he and several of the victims had engaged in a consensual sexual relationship, despite evidence that he had choked and beaten a number of these women (Barrios, 2004c). After his conviction, Selby committed suicide in jail prior to his sentencing determination (Simonson et al., 2004).

These case studies illustrate several of the different ways in which sexual crime can be conceptualized. In the first example, the identical twins Randal and Russel Harty exhibit eerily similar sexually deviant behaviors. These men committed offenses against the same type of victims and used similar means of victimization. The fact that they are identical, not only in appearance but also in underlying genetic makeup, provides an observable and readily understood explanation for the similarity of their behaviors: their shared genetic code. This assumption is not new to criminology. For many years, researchers have attempted to demonstrate genetic predispositions for violence. Studies of twins, such as the Hartys, give us information about the extent to which genetic concordance contributes to similar behavioral and psychological outcomes.

However, twin research also considers the role of shared environmental characteristics during child rearing, in which a portion of the outcome is due to shared genetic material but another portion is due to what was learned in early childhood and adolescence. In the Harty cases, the men were not only identical twins but also were reared in the same environment, which could have simultaneously shaped their sexual desires and behaviors to produce like outcomes. Therefore, when faced with accounts of sexual crimes such as this one, we are left with many questions. Is there a genetic predisposition to sexual offending? If so, how does it manifest itself? Is there an added impact of the environment on this biological tendency? If so, what is it, and how does it interact with genetic makeup?

In the second example, church documents and trial testimony revealed early concerns with Fr. Geoghan's behavior, often noting his immaturity and his preference for spending time with young children. Beliefs and attitudes associated with relationships, the role of children, and one's own behavior with children may have strongly affected how an individual develops interests in children and acts toward them. For some individuals, their particular beliefs may vary significantly from the cultural norm and have enough influence over them to affect their cognitions (e.g., perceptions, decision making) and behavioral choices. Perhaps Geoghan maintained an elaborate belief system that drove this behavior and allowed him to justify or rationalize the appropriateness of his actions.

Further evidence presented at trial suggests that Geoghan engaged in extensive sexual fantasies involving young boys. His treating psychiatrist suggested that these fantasies were part of a larger illness and helped drive his appetite for sexual encounters with male children. But what role did these fantasies ultimately play? It is possible that they were manifestations or indicators of a larger psychological problem, but it is also likely that they helped reinforce his sexual interest in children and drove him to engage in future acts that were consistent with his imagined desires.

These cognitive and behavioral aspects of Geoghan's sex offending behavior could be generalized to other sex offenders. Individuals who commit these offenses perhaps have an unusual or deviant worldview that somehow justifies their behavior. Beliefs supporting sexual activity with children, or strong relationship attachments with children, might eventually lead to sexual activity with them. Behavioral reinforcements, such as sexual fantasy and masturbation, may also contribute to an individual's desire to engage in specific deviant sexual acts, with the hope of obtaining sexual gratification in the process.

The third example described the case of James Allen Selby, a sexual offender who committed numerous sexual assaults against women and children. Some of his offenses displayed remarkable violence and in one instance resulted in a charge of attempted murder. Consistent portrayals of Selby as narcissistic, arrogant, sadistic, and lacking in remorse suggest some etiological role of these personality characteristics. As with biological or genetic predispositions, the idea that personality traits contribute to criminal or otherwise antisocial behaviors is not new. Since the days of Freudian psychoanalysis, and some criminologists' conceptualization of criminal disposition (e.g., Caspi et al., 1994; Glueck & Glueck, 1950; Gottfredson & Hirschi, 1990), scientists have been intrigued by the prospect of isolating specific traits or characteristics that would help identify sex offenders or other violent criminals.

Several of the personality traits that have been ascribed to Selby are also associated with a lengthy tradition of research within the sex offender literature. Narcissism, arrogance, and a sense of entitlement have all been hypothesized as potentially significant factors in the expression of sexual violence. Perhaps Selby's insistence on representing himself and statements indicating that he had great confidence in his abilities and his innocence suggest the presence of some of these characteristics. Sadism has also been proposed as a relevant factor, not just in cases of sexual sadism but also in the occurrence of extreme violence, such as was noted with Selby's crimes. His desire to cross-examine his own victims and his theatricality in doing so (Barrios, 2004a) could be viewed as additional indicators of sadistic leanings in this individual. Finally, psychopathic traits such as lack of remorse or empathy and impulsivity have also been attributed to these sorts of crimes and were arguably evident in Selby's behavior.

These personality traits might have directly influenced Selby's decision to engage in sexually deviant behaviors. Or, these traits might have indirectly affected other relevant factors, such as learned behavioral responses, perceptions of the social world, or the expression of underlying biological propensities. An additional possibility is that they are a representation of some other underlying trait that not only causes certain behaviors but also shapes the way in which personality features are manifested across situations. In sum, personality may be the key to understanding why individuals commit sexual crimes.

The prior potential explanations for sexual offending are not the only ones that have appeared in the literature. Other etiological hypotheses, such as the idea that being sexually abused in childhood predisposes some male victims to become sex offenders in adulthood, or the assumption, popularized by Ted Bundy's final interview (Dobson, 1995), that pornography somehow negatively and irrevocably shapes one's sexual desire into deviant and sadistic fantasies, also have been explored by those wishing to comprehend the origin of sex-offending behaviors. More recent research has taken many of these single-faceted explanations and integrated them into more complex and comprehensive etiological frameworks, again with the hopes of improving our knowledge.

WHY ETIOLOGY IS IMPORTANT

Why is an understanding of etiology so important? One reason is prevention. We must know what causes the behavior in order to prevent it. This could be compared with early scientific efforts to identify the causes of disease. In 1876, Robert Koch and then, later that year, Louis Pasteur, definitively proved that disease was caused by bacterial infection and that specific organisms were responsible for different types of disease. In 1879, Koch again demonstrated and further substantiated this link between germs and disease (Prescott, Harley, & Klein, 2005; Simmons, 2002; Waller, 2002). With this new understanding of the etiology of medical illness, scientists were then able to focus on developing reliable and beneficial vaccines to protect individuals from contracting specific types of disease. In addition, a knowledge of disease causation helps people avoid those places and situations in which they are most likely to be exposed to deadly or harmful bacteria that could cause them to contract an illness.

Although prevention efforts within the social and behavioral sciences are perhaps more complex and multifaceted than medical inoculation procedures, the core concept remains the same: We must know the cause of a behavior before we can prevent its development in the individual and help others avoid its ravages. Much like medical science, psychological science must provide explanatory answers and apply this knowledge to prevention techniques.

A second reason for the importance of understanding the etiology of sex offending is the need to treat those offenders. Only with accurate knowledge of causation will we be able to develop treatments to assist those who have engaged in deviant sexual behaviors. Continuing with our earlier example, only when medical scientists had identified the cause of a disease were they able to develop successful cures or treatments that limit the effects of the disorder. The development and use of antibiotic medications that targeted a specific type of bacteria were entirely dependent on an etiological theory.

Much like this medical example, psychological treatments greatly rely on our understanding of the etiology of a mental illness, mental abnormality, or dysfunctional behavior. Without this understanding we are simply aiming in the dark and blindly hoping for the best when we develop intervention strategies. If, for example, research finds that cognitive–behavioral theories of sex offending are the most plausible explanation for sexual deviance, then treatment efforts should strongly emphasize these causal pathways and address cognitions, attitudes, and decision-making processes as the primary targets of treatment. However, if the research does not support this causal theory, then the use of cognitive–behavioral techniques in current clinical practice would be suspect.

Another use of sound etiological theory is for the prediction of future risk. This includes not only the prediction of how likely an individual is to engage in sex offenses or develop sexually deviant interests but also how likely he is to continue sex-offending behaviors beyond the initial offense. If the research literature demonstrates that personality characteristics are the underlying cause of sex offending, for example, then we would be able to (a) identify which traits would be most evident in an individual who eventually develops these behaviors; (b) identify what the threshold is for the severity or expression of these traits; (c) learn how to make reasonable predictions about age of onset, offending patterns, and response to prevention and treatment; (d) link these personality patterns with some level of future risk to the public; and (e) identify the offenders at highest or lowest risk with greater precision.

Prediction based on etiology would also allow for the identification of protective factors that would lessen the likelihood of engaging in sexually deviant behaviors. Thus, we would be able to additionally predict which factors promote positive or normative experiences over dysfunctional ones. Let us again turn to medical science for a close parallel to this concept. The knowledge that bacteria lead to infection allows scientists to more efficiently prevent and treat disease, but it also has contributed to the identification of protective factors, such as health or resilience factors that promote bacterial resistance or idiosyncratic responses to certain antibiotic medications that may enhance recovery from illness. Similarly, an accurate knowledge of the etiological basis for sexual deviance would lead us to discoveries of resilience factors or characteristics that would predict stronger treatment response for some individuals.

Finally, although prevention, treatment, and risk prediction are all important goals of clinical science and empirical research, we must also consider the value of etiology in informing our policy decisions. As we mentioned previously, public concern regarding the victims of sexual violence is quite high. The past decade has seen the proliferation of legislation related to this population, including laws that have established community notification requirements, mandatory sentencing for sex offenders, lengthier periods of incarceration and supervision, civil commitment laws for repeat offenders, and greater restrictions on community placement and employment for these individuals. These laws were born out of public fear, frustration with frequent media reports of sexual violence, and perceptions of the growing threat of sexual violence. Despite the well-intentioned efforts of policymakers, there is no literature to suggest that these policies were informed by etiological research. For example, in the case of civil commitment laws targeting sexually violent predators, etiology should play a key role in determining the ways of best treating these individuals so that they are unlikely to repetitively, violently offend.

GOALS FOR THIS BOOK

Given the importance of etiology, how refined and accurate is our etiological knowledge? Many explanations for sexual deviance have been proposed in both professional research literature and popular culture. Therefore, one goal of this book is to provide concise yet comprehensive summaries of the major classes of theories that have been proposed to explain sex-offending behaviors. Some of these theories, such as early psychodynamic conceptualizations of sexual deviance, are less frequently used by researchers and clinicians as a framework for understanding this problem. However, the contributions of these early etiological theories are still evident in treatment programs and later theoretical formulations. Thus, we will include not only the most recent theoretical approaches but also those theories that are historically influential. In presenting this literature, we describe the major assumptions and hypotheses of the various theories and discuss the research that has been used to support the tenets of these theories.

Another goal of this book is to identify critical flaws in logic, faulty assumptions, and research disproving causal relationships. In some cases, theoretical and empirical errors occur as the result of fierce loyalty to a theoretical viewpoint that has been adopted by proponents of the theory. For example, once a theory has been introduced into the professional consciousness, later research questioning its validity may not always be readily accepted. In other cases, errors may result from methodological flaws in the supporting research or in the way in which causal relationships are assessed. Regardless of the cause of such problems, it is important to have an understanding of the limitations of these theories in order to more accurately identify where future research and treatment efforts should focus.

A final goal is to introduce a new integrated theory of sexual deviance, which incorporates developmental, psychological, and behavioral components. It is our expectation that it will prove to be the most reliable and valid explanation of the etiology of repeated sexual offending and paraphilic sexual interests. Because it is a new theory, empirical support is limited at this time. However, we hope that future researchers will consider these ideas and work toward demonstrating their effectiveness in explaining harmful sexual behaviors.

To achieve these goals, in chapter 2 we discuss the major methodological limitations of current research practices that impact our ability to make valid and accurate assumptions based on the empirical literature. These limitations are evaluated in terms of how they might affect interpretations and uses of the etiological research.

In chapters 3 through 9, we address the major etiological theories and models of sex offending and analyze their limitations. In chapter 3, we consider the biological theories, which include genetic, hormonal, and neuropsychological bases for sexual deviance. This chapter also includes a discussion of the hypothesized role of developmental disability in the formation and expression of these behaviors. Chapter 4 focuses on cognitive theories of sex offending and includes information on attachment models, cognitive schemas, and information processing. In chapter 5, we address the more behavioral components of sex offending theory, such as conditioning paradigms, self-regulation research, and the addiction model of offending. Chapter 6, in which we discuss models based on social learning theory, provides a general discussion of the literature implicating social learning processes in the development of criminal behavior and the models devoted to sex-offending behavior (i.e., the abused–abuser hypothesis, and the role of pornography in the development of sexual deviance). In chapter 7, we present personality theories of sex offending, which are wide ranging in scope and influence on this field. This chapter includes an abbreviated look at psychodynamic conceptualizations of sexually inappropriate interests and behaviors, which have been largely abandoned in favor of cognitive–behavioral and other approaches in the United States and other English-speaking countries, as well as personality profiles that have been obtained through psychometric testing, and specific traits that have been proposed as mediators in this process.

In chapter 8, we consider evolutionary theories of sex offending, including hypotheses regarding sexual strategies and courtship disorder as potential explanations for sexual violence. Finally, in chapter 9, we discuss integrated models of offending, which include five theories of sex offending, all of which incorporate two or more of the etiological viewpoints discussed in prior chapters.

Then, in chapter 10, we present an original integrated theory of sex offending. In this chapter, we describe the theory's etiological framework, provide hypothetical examples to illustrate its hypotheses, and discuss relevant research drawn from related fields. We conclude the book with chapter 11, in which we discuss future directions for research, prevention, and treatment based on this new conceptualization of sex offending.

Two caveats are in order. First, the ideas presented in this book are derived from a combination of theoretical and empirical etiological research. In this scholarship, some researchers refer to their work as being based on a *theory*, whereas others use the term *model*. It is important to define these terms, because they are used throughout this book. A theory is a set of principles and propositions that are offered to explain the causal mechanisms underlying a phenomenon and predict future occurrences of that phenomenon. A model is a visual representation of a theory that allows for empirical testing. We will attempt to use these terms appropriately whenever feasible. However, there are instances in which an earlier author presented her or his idea as a model and named it as such, and despite later recognition of that work as a theory, it still maintains the original title of "model" (e.g., Finkelhor's precondition model or Malamuth's confluence model, discussed in chap. 9).

Second, although it was earlier believed that women were not capable of, nor likely to commit, sexual crimes, growing evidence suggests that they do commit deviant sexual acts (e.g., Becker, Hall, & Stinson, 2001; Christiansen & Thyer, 2003). Female offenders, however, may not be directly comparable to male offenders in some ways, such as recidivism and characteristics of risk (Cortoni & Hanson, 2005). In addition, we are unsure as to whether the two groups of offenders are etiologically similar, because the majority of sex-offender research, particularly that which addresses etiological theory, does not include substantial information on female sex offenders (e.g., Grayston & De Luca, 1999; Johansson-Love & Fremouw, 2006). Therefore, the focus of this book is limited to explaining the sexually deviant acts of men, although some of the theories discussed in this book, including our new theory of paraphilias and sex offending, could be easily applied to female sex offenders.

Moreover, it is our hope that this book will assist clinical scientists and practitioners in understanding exactly where we are and where we need to go in research to accurately understand the causes of sexual violence. Given that there are currently multiple possible explanations for sex offending, many of which have not been critically evaluated through research, and that the research that has been performed is often methodologically weak, the task of understanding, preventing, and treating this behavior is difficult today. In science, however, what is unclear one day can often become fact in the foreseeable future. We hope this book will stimulate sex-offender researchers to achieve this possibility.

2

METHODOLOGICAL LIMITATIONS
OF RELEVANT RESEARCH

Before starting the critical review of the existing theories that attempt to explain the causes of sex offending, we need to consider the major methodological limitations that can affect our understanding of the proffered theories and the development and maintenance of sex-offending behaviors. These limitations apply to the majority of empirical studies of sex-offending populations.

We start by considering a variety of sampling problems that have affected the conclusions drawn about sex offenders' psychological characteristics and behavior. We then review the problems associated with the use of self-report, a common and somewhat unavoidable practice in this area of research. Following this, we describe the use of inappropriate comparison groups, and we conclude with a discussion of the post hoc nature of this research.

SAMPLING EFFECTS

Sampling, or choosing the group that best represents the population of interest, is a critical feature of empirical research. For example, inclusion and exclusion criteria are very important in determining the validity of the results and whether those results can be generalized to other groups. It is not surprising, then, that research findings in the area of sexually deviant behavior are shaped by the samples that have been selected for study. Unfortunately, sampling effects are a notable methodological limitation in this area.

One such problem with sex-offender samples is that these are the offenders who have been identified and convicted for their sexual crimes. The use of this sample is unavoidable; if they have not been identified as sex offenders by either the mental health or criminal justice systems, then how would we know to include them in our research? It is likely rare for individuals who have never been identified as sex offenders to self-report this behavior to mental health professionals or legal authorities. The result is that we are dependent on research that in essence relies on convenience sampling.

Not only does this exclude those who have never been apprehended, but it also excludes those who have deviant sexual fantasies but who have not yet acted on them. This is important, because those who are not included in the research might be fundamentally different from those who are. Thus, any findings related to the identified group of sex offenders may not apply to those who are as yet unknown. It is also possible that many of these individuals have been identified later in their sex-offending careers, which may impact treatment approach, treatment success, risk factors, or cognitive beliefs related to offending. Results obtained using these offenders may not generalize to those who are in the early stages of developing sexually deviant interests or who have committed their first offense.

A second problem with current sampling methods is that many, if not all, studies require voluntary participation. Voluntariness of participation is a critical component of all research. Thus, the findings obtained from the study of sex offenders might be significantly biased because of the high number of individuals who refuse to participate in research related to sexual deviance. In addition, the sex-offender literature has consistently noted that many individuals identified as sex offenders deny or minimize their sexually inappropriate behaviors (e.g., Barbaree & Cortoni, 1993; Happel & Auffrey, 1995; Kennedy & Grubin, 1992; Nugent & Kroner, 1996). This denial often extends to any discussion of early sexual behaviors, sexually inappropriate behaviors or attitudes, and other criminal behaviors in addition to the primary sexual crime. Because of this, these individuals are less likely to voluntarily participate in any research aimed at understanding sexually deviant behaviors. The result is that sex-offender research excludes offenders who have not been identified by the criminal justice or mental health systems as well as those who have been identified but either refuse to participate or deny their offenses, further limiting the ability to generalize from these samples.

A third limitation is the use of rather rigid exclusionary criteria, which may challenge the validity and generalizability of the results. Although it is important to eliminate potential sources of bias for the sake of preserving internal validity, some researchers in this area have gone so far as to exclude individuals from the research that are a relevant population of interest. For instance, some researchers exclude psychopathic individuals or individuals with significant psychopathic features. In some ways, psychopathic individuals might be viewed as a necessary and understandable exclusion. They may be prone to greater rates of deception (e.g., Hare, Forth, & Hart, 1989; Rogers & Cruise, 2000; Seto, Khattar, & Lalumiere, 1997), and they may be fundamentally different from nonpsychopathic sex offenders in their motivations, cognitions, or response to treatment. However, by excluding these individuals, or even limiting their participation in treatment, researchers may be leaving out a substantial portion of sex-offending individuals. Not having complete data on a wide range of offenders limits our understanding of how these offense patterns and deviant sexual interests arise in a variety of individuals.

Those who deny their sex offenses are a second group that has not traditionally met inclusion criteria for sex-offender research. As discussed earlier in this section, many of these individuals may refuse to participate in research. Some, however, may be willing to offer information about their demographic characteristics, personality traits, or cognitive beliefs that would still be useful to researchers wishing to understand this population. Limiting our understanding of sexual deviance to only those who consistently and openly admit to their sexually deviant behaviors will not capture the full picture of offenders, especially given the high rates reported in the literature of offenders who do not readily acknowledge their sex crimes.

Other researchers exclude individuals who demonstrate certain psychological characteristics or severe psychopathology. In some cases, these exclusions make sense. For example, some researchers choose to exclude individuals in advanced stages of dementia who are simply unable to recall important details of their past, their sexual behaviors, or their belief structure at the time a sexual offense was committed. In this instance, it would be difficult to obtain reliable and valid data because of the nature of the individual's condition. An additional exclusion involves sex offenders who do not readily demonstrate sexual arousal on traditional physiological measures, such as the penile plethysmograph. Although this is typically explained as a means of homogenizing the sample to include only those with consistent and easily measurable deviant sexual arousal, it likely excludes a significant percentage of sex offenders. Because the role of sexual arousal in perpetuating sex-offending behaviors remains unclear, these exclusions may limit our knowledge of this complex offending process.

Other exclusions, however, make less sense and might have a greater overall impact on the research findings. Some studies have routinely excluded individuals who are psychotic. We grant that if these individuals are acutely psychotic at the time of data collection, it could impair the reliability of their self-report. However, it is often unclear as to whether the individual was psychotic at the time of the offense or at the time of the study. This is an important difference, because individuals who were psychotic at the time of the offense, but not during data collection, could still offer valuable insight into their thoughts, motivations, and behaviors leading up the offense. In another example, researchers interested in the impact of trait anger on the level of violence exhibited toward victims during a sexual crime excluded all men from the study who had killed their victims (Smallbone & Milne, 2000). One might logically assume that individuals who had actually committed murder during the course of a sexual offense (e.g., sadistic rape) might reliably demonstrate higher levels of anger than their nonmurderous counterparts. Here, it seems that the researchers eliminated an extremely relevant sample of individuals and thereby limited the findings from their study (this study and its limitations are discussed further in chap. 7, this volume).

Another concern with the way researchers have sampled the population of sexual offenders relates to their use of heterogeneous groups of offenders. In many instances, sex offenders are lumped together in a single category (e.g., "the sex offender group") regardless of real differences between them, including their sexually deviant arousal, victim selection characteristics, psychological functioning, level of cognitive capacity, and level of denial or minimization. This is not to say that it is never methodologically sound to use a heterogeneous mix of offenders. In some cases in which researchers want to know the effect of a general sex-offender treatment program or the overall impact of certain variables on sex-offending behavior, this can be justified. Nevertheless, this concern is typically not addressed as a potential limitation of much of the research, even though it should be considered in regard to how it could affect research findings.

Finally, the majority of the research in the area of sexual deviance, and certainly in the area of the causes of sexual deviance, is conducted with male offenders. Only recently has there been a recognition of female sexual offenders (e.g., Becker, Hall, & Stinson, 2001; Christiansen & Thyer, 2003; Cortoni & Hanson, 2005; Denov, 2003; Nathan & Ward, 2002). Because these female offenders have not been included in most of the research to date, we cannot say whether the same research findings that apply to men would apply to women. Unfortunately, however, this is not a simple problem to address, because we do not have large enough samples of female offenders at this point to conduct studies on the same scale as has been done with male offenders.

The critical message in this discussion is that researchers should be extremely cautious of potential methodological limitations relating to the selection of relevant participants for sex-offender research. Sampling effects could potentially affect the generalizability, validity, and the overall nature of the findings. Acknowledgment of these limitations will allow researchers to expand their research questions and direct future study toward neglected and often-excluded individuals who have committed sexually deviant acts.

SELF-REPORT

The vast majority of research conducted with sex offenders uses self-report as the primary method of data collection (e.g., Abracen, Looman, & Anderson, 2000; Blumenthal, Gudjonsson, & Burns, 1999; Connolly, 2004; Epps, Haworth, & Swaffer, 1993; Marshall, 1988; McKay, Chapman, & Long, 1996; Rice, Chaplin, Harris, & Coutts, 1994). This is perhaps one of the easiest and quickest ways to obtain information about past experiences, such as childhood family relationships, medical and psychiatric history, and past offending and nonoffending behaviors. It is also one of the few ways to gather information regarding an individual's thoughts, perceptions, fantasies, goals, or sexual preferences. Despite the ease with which researchers may gain information about a particular individual by using this method, there are specific problems associated with self-reported data that hinder our ability to draw conclusions from the research.

For instance, self-reported information is often biased to such an extent that the data may be unreliable for the purpose of prediction, explanation, or treatment. The problem of bias is inherent in any type of self-report, because individuals may feel pressure to present themselves in an overly positive or negative light, depending on the circumstances under which the questions are being asked. For example, during a job interview individuals often present themselves in an overly positive way, perhaps exaggerating certain characteristics that would be valued by a potential employer. Similarly, individuals who are seeking medical treatment in a crowded emergency room might exaggerate the severity of their symptoms to guarantee that they will be seen by a physician as quickly as possible. Although in the general population these biased self-reports may be relatively harmless and socially acceptable, with sex offenders these problems become more pronounced and have serious consequences for those who wish to learn from their self-reported statements.

Deliberate deception is one of the most obvious problems with self-reported information by sex offenders. These individuals might have a high motivation to deceive in order to enhance their standing among their criminal peers or to deceive those in authority. For example, many studies have attempted to address whether these offenders have committed other criminal or sexually deviant acts that are unknown to the authorities (e.g., Abel, Becker, Cunningham-Rathner, & Mittelman, 1988; A. J. L. Baker, Tabacoff, Tornusciolo, & Eisenstadt, 2001). Fear of prosecution or additional sanctions may provide these sex offenders with a clear motivation to deny additional offending. Similarly, offenders might be motivated to falsely report information in order to portray themselves as presenting minimal future risk of harm to others. It also is unlikely that many individuals would willingly report that they were planning future offenses.

Another potential source of deception is the tendency to provide information that rationalizes or explains the sexually deviant behavior. For example, an offender might exaggerate or fabricate information regarding childhood experiences. Telling someone that he was sexually abused as a child or neglected by his family provides him with a rationalization for inappropriate adult behaviors and allows him to offer some explanation for his deviations from social norms (e.g., "No one cared when it was happening to me, so why should they care now when it's happening to some other kid?"). From the offender's perspective, this type of deception might be necessary to explain the deviance as something unavoidable or out of his control, rather than a deliberate or calculated act.

Self-report may also be an unreliable indicator of past, present, and future thoughts and behaviors because of the offender's desire to create a socially desirable image. Social desirability is relevant when one is asking about cognitions, fantasies, or behaviors that might violate societal norms. Many indicators of psychological functioning that rely on self-reported information (e.g., personality instruments such as the Personality Assessment Inventory [Morey, 1991] or the Millon Clinical Multiaxial Inventory—III [Millon, Davis, & Millon, 1997]) have a measure of social desirability. For example, an assessment instrument might ask a question such as "Do you tend to be helpful toward others?" With this question, most individuals would probably respond affirmatively, regardless of whether they are helpful or not. An individual who demonstrates consistent disregard for others and causes distress for others rather than helps them might still answer affirmatively to impart the impression that he conforms to social norms and is not abnormal. This type of response style is particularly problematic because it allows sex offenders to deny or minimize their socially inappropriate behaviors.

Moreover, this population not only is motivated to give false information but also might use the opportunity to self-report as a way to manipulate the system (i.e., the criminal justice and mental health systems) or manipulate other individuals for some personal gain. Sex offending and other criminal populations have a higher likelihood of engaging in these deceptive behaviors (e.g., Gudjonsson, 1990; Happel & Auffrey, 1995; Sewell & Salekin, 1997), so wariness toward self-reported information is warranted.

Another issue with self-report is that some sex offenders might have beliefs that represent significant distortions of reality. We are referring not to delusions per se but instead to cognitive distortions that impact the way the offender interprets and rationalizes his own behaviors as well as the actions of others. Pedophiles or child molesters might agree with statements such as "Children benefit from sexual activity" or "I've never really hurt a child" and firmly believe that these things are true. Asking them whether they have ever caused harm to a child will result in a denial, not because they are motivated to deceive or because they are responding in a socially acceptable manner but because they believe that they have never hurt a child. The offender's self-report is significantly distorted because of distortions in his cognitive schemas, thought patterns, or information-processing abilities.

A final concern with the validity and reliability of self-report is that many sex offenders are remarkably poor historians (e.g., Simon, 1999). The individual's inability to recall such information will distort the reliability and accuracy of the self-report. For example, they might be unable to accurately or completely recall events or emotional experiences that occurred in childhood. They also might have difficulty recalling details of crimes they have committed, especially if they were intoxicated by alcohol or another illicit substance at the time of the crime. Finally, a large number of similar crimes (e.g., multiple voyeuristic acts over a period of years) might lead to confusion when specific information is required to assess each incident.

There are a number of reasons for this poor historical accuracy. For one, many of these individuals have a long history of substance abuse (e.g., Abracen et al., 2000; Kafka & Prentky, 1994; Langevin & Lang, 1990; Mio, Nanjundappa, Verleur, & de Rios, 1986). The individual might have used the substance either just prior to, during, or immediately after the event of interest. The intoxication or withdrawal effects of the drug might significantly interfere with the individual's ability to encode and then later recall specific details of the event. For example, the excessive use of alcohol prior to the criminal act could cause a blackout, whereby the individual lacks memory for that period in time. Another effect of substance abuse would be more indirect, in that long-term abuse of some substances (e.g., marijuana; McKim, 2000) could cause general memory impairments over time. In such a situation the substance abuse may not directly cause forgetting in regard to a specific event but instead cause more general memory impairments.

A second explanation for poor recall ability in this population relates to childhood experience. Clinical and empirical studies have noted varying estimates of childhood sexual, physical, and emotional abuse in juvenile and adult sex offenders (e.g., Graham, 1996; Haapasalo & Kankkonen, 1997; Jonson-Reid & Way, 2001; Seghorn, Prentky, & Boucher, 1987; Worling, 1995). These abuses might impact an individual's ability to remember important childhood events or interpret his own and others' behaviors during that time period. A direct effect of physical abuse, for example, might be the occurrence of head injuries that are severe enough to cause lasting memory impairment. Other effects of childhood trauma might be more indirect. A child who has been neglected or emotionally abused, for example, might have difficulty recalling information about family relationships or parental behaviors in an unbiased manner (e.g., Haapasalo & Kankkonen, 1997). Research on autobiographical memory suggests that individuals who have undergone significant traumatic events have deficits in remembering specific personal events; memories of childhood and other relevant developmental periods tend to be overgeneral and vague (Berntsen & Rubin, 2002; de Decker, Hermans, Raes, & Eelen, 2003; V. Edwards, Fivush, Anda, Felitti, & Nordenberg, 2001; Meesters, Merckelbach, Muris, & Wessel, 2000; Parks & Balon, 1995; Raes, Hermans, Williams, & Eelen, 2005). This is not to say that individuals who have experienced traumatic childhood abuse have suppressed these memories but rather that memories of these and other childhood events may be less specific or detailed in nature, thereby creating difficulty for one who is hoping to gather information about early childhood development and behavior.

Another important factor that may be related to poor recall and unreliable description of significant historical and autobiographical events in sex-offender research is lowered intellectual functioning. Research with nonoffending individuals with lower intellectual functioning has demonstrated that they exhibit higher rates of acquiescence in interviews and are more likely to endorse behaviors or beliefs that they do not hold than are individuals with higher intellectual functioning (e.g., Beail, 2002; Finlay & Lyons, 2002; Heal & Sigelman, 1995; Sigelman, Budd, Spanhel, & Schoenrock, 1981). Several explanations have been offered for this effect, including difficulty with understanding questions that are grammatically or structurally complex (Finlay & Lyons, 2001, 2002), problems with responses that require abstraction or complex judgment (Finlay & Lyons, 2001), response formats that may lend themselves to more yea-saying (e.g., yes–no questions vs. open-ended questions; Finlay & Lyons, 2001), memory deficits (Beail, 2002), and differences in status between the interviewer and interviewee (Heal & Sigelman, 1995).

In addition to problems of acquiescence, some researchers have noted increased instances of denial among sex offenders with lower intellectual functioning (e.g., Baldwin & Roys, 1998; Simon, 1999). Heal and Sigelman (1995) noted that this increased nay-saying among individuals with intellectual disabilities occurs when questions involve taboo topics. This research suggests that sex offenders with lower intellectual functioning may be more likely to deny behaviors and beliefs involving taboo topics, such as sexually inappropriate behaviors.

Some individuals may also be poor historians because of the effects of institutionalization. After a long period of institutionalization, whether it be in a hospital or a prison, the individual may have difficulty recalling specific events prior to being placed in a long-term facility. For example, a sex offender who has spent 15 or more years incarcerated for a sex crime might have difficulty accurately remembering minute details during a postincarceration interview. Aging effects, as well as effects of living in an austere environment that offers little cognitive stimulation, could interfere with the offender's ability to relate specific behavior details and cognitive processes that may have been at work at the time of the crime. In addition, individuals who have been placed in hospitals for significant periods might have had poorer cognitive functioning at the outset, limiting their ability to later recall facts about their criminal behavior as well as important early life events that may have been critical to the offending process.

Frequent disruptions in childhood or adulthood due to either hospitalization or incarceration may also interfere with the individual's ability to accurately recall important life events. Behaviors or symptoms that necessitated institutionalization of some kind also could impede memory formation or storage. For example, a youth who evidenced significant externalizing problems might have been placed in a juvenile detention facility, a group home, or a mental institution for an underlying mental illness. Marked symptoms of such an illness may result in his inability or difficulty in articulating the events leading up to his placement. Extreme stress, cognitive confusion, or withdrawal may prevent him not only from understanding the world around him at that time but also from accurately remembering it at some later point.

Moreover, all of these factors are important when we consider their combined impact on the accuracy of research driven by self-reported data. Much of what we know about sex offenders comes from what they tell us. Unfortunately, this is a problem that is not easily remedied. To understand and make predictions from an individual's internal world, including cognitive processes, motivation for behavior, and perceptions of interpersonal relationships, we must get the information from the individual. So although the problem of bias in self-report is perhaps unavoidable with sex offenders, researchers must be aware of the limitations of self-reported data, attempt to find reliable corroborating information whenever possible, and clearly identify these sources of bias in their research. Although corroborating resources present their own problems (e.g., official records may be underestimates of the total number of offenses, other individuals may be unaware of internal or unique factors that contribute to offending), researchers must acknowledge these problems and make efforts to resolve them if we hope to gather the most reliable and accurate information available for our research.

SELECTION OF COMPARISON GROUPS

A third overarching methodological concern with sex-offender research is the use of inappropriate or uninformative comparison groups. In this section, we address the types of comparison groups that most commonly appear in this area and how the selection of these groups can impact the results.

The most traditional comparison groups, matched according to age, ethnicity, or other relevant demographic variables, consist of participants who are nonoffending, non–sexually deviant, and non–mentally ill. These types of comparison groups, when compared with sex offenders, isolate variables that are attributable to the individual's status as a sex offender. However, the field has advanced to the point where these comparison groups are less useful because more specific differences must be identified within sex-offender subpopulations to develop and refine theories of sex offending, treatment for deviant sexual behaviors, and risk prediction. For example, when a researcher intends to use sexually deviant behavior or some variable related to sexually deviant behavior (e.g., cognitive distortions in child molesters) as the outcome variable, traditional comparison participants will most likely not exhibit the dependent variable to any significant degree, making them uninteresting as a comparison group.

A second type of comparison group includes individuals who are similar in either criminal behavior or psychological functioning. These samples originally consisted of violent or nonviolent offenders who had not been arrested or convicted of sex crimes or psychiatric patients who had not evidenced deviant sexual arousal. For example, a researcher might select a group of non–sex-offending psychiatric inpatients to examine whether an adverse childhood environment predicts general psychological dysfunction in adulthood or something more specific in a group of sex offenders. Although early researchers used these comparison samples to isolate variables that would uniquely contribute to sexually deviant behaviors, the results showed that there often were marked similarities between these groups (e.g., Caputo, Frick, & Brodsky, 1999; Grier, Clark, & Stoner, 1993; Happe & Frith, 1996; Herkov, Gynther, Thomas, & Myers, 1996; Langevin, Wortzman, Dickey, Wright, & Handy, 1988; Marshall & Mazzucco, 1995; Moody, Brissie, & Kim, 1994; Nussbaum et al., 2002; Oliver, Hall, & Neuhaus, 1993; Yanagida & Ching, 1993), which leads us to consider that sex offending is just another manifestation of underlying mechanisms that lead to deviancy or disorder in general.

This finding is not surprising, because some research demonstrates that sex offenders engage in a wide variety of criminal activities in addition to sex offending (e.g., Simon, 1997b, 2000). Given this fact, we should expect sex offenders to share a number of characteristics with non–sex offenders who have committed other crimes. In addition, sex offenders may have psychological disorders or symptoms that are unrelated to deviant sexual interest. Therefore, it would make sense that they share psychological or developmental characteristics with other individuals with mental illness who have not committed sexual crimes.

It is important to note, however, that we do not know whether these overlapping characteristics or traits substantially contribute to sex-offending behavior or whether they simply are part of the etiology of more general deviant tendencies. Future research should not be content with simply looking for similarities between sex offenders and other groups. Research with sex offenders needs to identify causal mechanisms that uniquely lead to sex offending. Stated another way, why don't all offenders and all people with mental illness commit sex crimes?

A third type of research compares different groups of sex offenders according to offense type or treatment status. As previously discussed, many research efforts merely combine sex offenders into one large, heterogeneous group, which presents its own set of problems. Others, however, do divide sex offenders according to offense type or sexually deviant interests and seek to discover meaningful differences between groups. This also poses problems. For instance, many sex offenders demonstrate multiple sexually deviant interests or acts (e.g., Abel et al., 1988), and it is therefore difficult to cleanly divide them into different groups. A second concern is the inherent assumption that these different types of offenders are fundamentally different from one another and that we are dividing them in appropriate ways that reflect true differences. For example, perhaps the primary differentiating factor is not in the type of victim but in the purpose that the sex offense serves for the individual. These considerations must be evaluated to accurately identify and compare different subpopulations of sex-offending individuals.

Moreover, whether a comparison group is methodologically appropriate and can provide useful results largely depends on the implicit and explicit goals of the researcher. These goals must be stated when the justification for the use of a comparison sample is unclear or when concerns regarding the group's appropriateness is in question. Again, like many of the other limitations noted in this chapter, the problem with finding a useful comparison group may be somewhat unavoidable and should be openly addressed by the researcher.

POST HOC NATURE OF THE RESEARCH

A final methodological consideration is the post hoc nature of most sex-offender research. First, the research uses information that is obtained sometime after the original offense occurs, which allows for subsequent events to critically alter the variables of interest. One example is that, over time, offenders are able to develop justifications, rationalizations, and excuses specific to the sex offense of interest, even though these cognitive beliefs might not have been present before or at the time of the actual offense. Research being conducted at some later point might erroneously give these rationalizations greater weight as explanatory constructs. Similarly, if an offender comes to believe that his substance use or impulsivity were largely responsible for his sexually inappropriate behaviors, then he might discount other critical factors that also contributed to the crime. Therefore, post hoc research may not accurately identify the relevant causal antecedents for the offender's behavior. One solution is to conduct longitudinal research that examines the evolution of cognitions and behaviors in a large sample of individuals with sexually deviant fantasies, some of whom might later turn to sex offending. Despite some of the problems inherent with this solution, such as limited funding, time constraints, and the need for large samples of individuals, longitudinal research has been successfully applied to a number of developmental concerns, including sex-offending behaviors (e.g., Nisbet, Wilson, & Smallbone, 2004; van Wijk et al., 2005), and it offers more informative results than the traditional post hoc methods.

Another related limitation of post hoc designs is that offenders who are studied long after their crimes have occurred have typically participated in treatment for their sexually deviant interests or behaviors, even if only for a limited time. It is possible that treatment influenced the offenders on a number of important variables, including cognitive distortions, attitudes toward victims, deviant arousal patterns, and overall levels of psychopathology. If these variables were altered prior to research and assessment, then the researcher is not getting an accurate picture of the factors in the individual's cognitive and interactional world that led up to and caused the offense.

Second, much of the existing empirical research was designed to explain, treat, or predict the behaviors of individuals who commit sexually deviant acts without any clear theoretical basis. The theories and hypotheses are developed after the research findings are known. When one's goal is to simply describe the population or some specific characteristic of a population, then atheoretical research may provide an unbiased way to uncover the information. However, for researchers whose goal is either to explain the behaviors of sex offenders or to make predictions regarding their behaviors, an atheoretical approach is problematic. Some theoretical underpinnings are necessary to identify relevant variables, operationally define variables, identify potential confounds and interaction effects, and select appropriate assessment instruments to detect the phenomenon.

For example, research on cognitive distortions should have some inherent supposition about how those distortions are formed, how they function for the offender, and how they affect the offense process. Without a theory, how do we know which cognitive beliefs are relevant and important in the sex-offending process? Are we going to limit our study of distortions to beliefs that relate to sexual behavior, or do we expand our definition to include all distorted beliefs about interpersonal interaction? Do we include beliefs about personal responsibility? Are they cognitive distortions if they are beliefs held by individuals in the population who are not sex offenders (e.g., rape myths)? How do we distinguish the effects of pre-offense beliefs and postoffense justifications in determining the risk of future crimes, and how would we measure them in any meaningful way without some understanding of which ones are important?

The field has advanced to the point where researchers must ask theory-driven questions and evaluate the data with that purpose in mind, even if the results do not support the original hypotheses. Even disconfirming data is useful if it helps us refine our theory. Research that is designed to evaluate specific hypotheses and theoretical ideas is needed at this stage to contribute to our understanding of sex-offending behaviors and our next steps regarding prevention, treatment, and public policy. Without theory-driven methods, resulting conclusions may be unhelpful in our efforts to deal with this problem.

SUMMARY AND CONCLUSIONS

In this chapter, we have discussed several problems inherent in the current etiological literature addressing sexually deviant behaviors. Sampling effects, or who is included or excluded from the research, largely shape the ways in which we investigate sex-offending populations. The extensive use of self-report fosters potential bias, whereby individuals may present information that is unintentionally distorted, deliberately untrue, or only partially remembered. Selection of comparison groups, whether they are nonoffending matched control participants, criminal offenders without known sex offenses, or psychiatric patients with similar backgrounds and mental health needs, impacts the strength and significance of our results. Finally, the post hoc nature of much of our sex-offender research limits the extent to which we may apply our findings. Post hoc bias and treatment effects, an inability to examine causal antecedents as they occur, and atheoretical research are all issues that must be addressed to improve our understanding of etiological factors.

We admit that these problems are daunting; some of them may be inevitable realities of research in this field. However, being aware of these limitations and striving to decrease their collective impact on research validity and reliability will only strengthen our scientific knowledge and empirical conclusions. And just as we would have future researchers consider these sources of methodological bias, it is equally important to critically evaluate the existing theories of sex offending and their specific limitations. Our next chapter begins this task.

3

BIOLOGICAL THEORIES

Technological advances in the way scientists measure biological and psychological phenomena have led to a growing interest in perfecting biological explanations for human behavior. The introduction of advanced brain scanning and neuroimaging techniques; gene sequencing; and more precise measures of bodily chemicals, such as hormones, have allowed scientists to more accurately determine human biological processes. It is not surprising that psychological theory has reflected a growing belief in the strong contribution of biological processes to the development and manifestation of a variety of human behaviors. These theories focus on specific biological predispositions that may have direct and predictable effects on an individual's cognitive and behavioral makeup.

In this chapter, we examine the role of these biological predispositions and processes in the development of sexually deviant thoughts, impulses, and behaviors. A number of biological theories are considered, and each is explained in terms of its possible relationship with sex-offending behavior. We first address biological theories of brain structure, which claim that sexually deviant behaviors emanate from some impairment or abnormality in certain structures of the brain. Second, we consider theories that look to the balance of hormones in the body, as well as neurotransmitter levels within the brain. Third, we analyze the idea that sex chromosome abnormalities or genetic traits may play some role in the development of sexual deviance. Fourth, we review biological theories that suggest that mental retardation plays a primary role in the development sex offending. Although intellectual impairment and mental retardation are sometimes considered in the cognitive and developmental realms rather than exclusively in the biological, the fact that these conditions are due to physiological factors supports their inclusion in this particular chapter. Finally, we address the limitations of each of the theories.

STRUCTURAL EXPLANATIONS

Structural explanations for male sexually deviant behavior have evolved from interest in the brain's role in sexual functioning (i.e., physiological tasks, such as erection and ejaculation) and sexual drive, desire, or motivation (Kafka, 1995, 2003). Research into the neuropsychological aspects of desire has revealed that the temporal lobe and structures of the limbic system (e.g., the thalamus) play an important role in the regulation of sexual drives (Berlin, 1988; Kafka, 1995, 2003) as well as mood and aggression, which also may play a role in sexual offending (Kafka, 1995). Consequently, damage or injury to these areas of the brain might result in abnormal behaviors in the realms of sex, mood, or violence.

Structural brain impairments are perhaps one of the most common foci for biological research relating to sex-offending and sexual deviant behaviors. A great many researchers have used postmortem examinations and current neuroimaging techniques (e.g., magnetic resonance imaging) to examine the brains of sex-offending individuals to determine whether there are, in fact, any inherent structural differences that might explain their deviant behavior.

Early studies focused on two specific variables that were said to correlate with structural impairment: (a) intellectual functioning, which is discussed in a later section of this chapter, and (b) the presence of any brain abnormality as indicated by neuropsychological tests or brain examinations. Such studies found rates of brain abnormality among sex offenders ranging from 33% to 100%, as compared with matched control participants, whose rates typically ranged from 0% to 17% (Aigner et al., 2000; Corley, Corley, Walker, & Walker, 1994; Galski, Thornton, & Shumsky, 1990; Hucker et al., 1986; Langevin, Bain, et al., 1988; Langevin, Wortzman, Wright, & Handy, 1989; Wright, Nobrega, Langevin, & Wortzman, 1990). These findings suggest that there is some link between structural brain abnormality and sex-offending behaviors. The most common way in which this relationship, and hypotheses surrounding it, are described is according to the area of the brain that is affected (i.e., right and left temporal lobe, frontal lobe, and cerebral blood flow) and the type of sex offense that results from said impairment.

Temporal Lobe Abnormalities

A number of studies indicate that when sex offenders are divided into groups according to their deviant sexual interests, they show significant differential impairment in the temporal lobes. This is to be expected given that temporal lobe structures play a number of roles in human behavior, including regulating emotional response, verbal learning, and sexual interest and drive (Lang, 1993; Langevin, Wortzman, Dickey, Wright, & Handy, 1988; Purves et al., 1997).

Left temporal lobe abnormalities, which are most often associated with individuals who are sexually attracted to children (Galski et al., 1990; Lang, 1993; Langevin, Bain, et al., 1988; Langevin, Wortzman, et al., 1989; Wright et al., 1990), differentiate pedophiles from most other types of sexual offenders. This finding suggests that left temporal lobe abnormalities might explain the development of pedophilia. However, one study of men who had committed incest-only offenses against children found fewer neuropsychological abnormalities overall (Langevin, Wortzman, et al., 1988), indicating that these offenders have a different etiological basis for their behavior. This finding is supported by research that incest offenders do not evidence arousal to the same cues that nonincest child molesters do on the penile plethysmograph (e.g., Kaplan & Becker, 1992).

Left temporal lobe damage also is associated with more difficulty with speech, verbal understanding, and ability to learn new verbal information (Lang, 1993). Such deficits could hamper an individual's ability to process and interpret verbal or interpersonal stimuli as well as limit the ability to retain new or unfamiliar information. Left lobe dysfunction could also lead to difficulties in self-regulatory processes in these individuals, interrupting the various emotional feedback systems that drive behavior (Galski et al., 1990). A combination of these factors—poor verbal skills, conceptual difficulties, emotional dysregulation, and deviant sexual interest in children—could drive an individual to commit sex offenses against a specific victim group. For example, an individual with impairments in verbal understanding and emotional regulation might have significant difficulties in learning to relate the verbal speech cues (e.g., the child-victim saying that she is frightened; saying that she likes the offender) with emotional response cues (e.g., the child-victim showing fear; showing nonsexual interest). The result is that the offender might misinterpret emotional cues from the child or conceptualize the child as a potential sexual partner. Thus, it is hypothesized that pedophiles sustained left temporal lobe impairment prior to the initiation of their sexual activity (Galski et al., 1990; Langevin, Bain, et al., 1988; Langevin, Wortzman, et al., 1989; Wright et al., 1990). These communication difficulties might also have an indirect effect on sex offending in terms of peer interaction. If the individual has profound verbal deficits, then he might have extreme difficulty communicating with age-appropriate peers and might instead turn to others, such as children, for support. Many child molesters, for example, form inappropriately intimate relationships with children as substitutes for the relationships they lack with adults (Murray et al., 2001). This is discussed in more detail later in the chapter. However, it is important to note that these interpersonal deficits might stem from this type of biological abnormality.

Right temporal lobe abnormalities, specifically, temporal horn dilations, are most often found in persons who have committed violent or sadistic sexual offenses (e.g., rape; Aigner et al., 2000; Hucker et al., 1988; Lang, 1993; Langevin, Bain, et al., 1988). Studies have noted that right temporal lobe abnormalities are found in rapists and sexual sadists at significantly higher rates than in control participants or in other types of sex offending individuals. Similar rates of abnormality in this region are also found in murderers and other highly violent offenders, suggesting that there may be a specific aggressive component to the functional impairment caused by this structural abnormality. Thus, right temporal lobe impairment could trigger violent and aggressive behaviors and increased sexual drive or arousal, with the combination leading to more violent forms of sex offense, such as rape (Langevin, Bain, et al., 1988).

For many sexual sadists, the location of the abnormality in the temporal horn suggests that there could be a disruption of communication between the temporal and frontal lobes, resulting in more aggressive and disturbing behaviors (Aigner et al., 2000). One set of researchers also argued that there is a deficient communication process between the two temporal lobes that interacts to enhance deviant sexual behaviors (Flor-Henry, Lang, Koles, & Frenzel, 1988). According to these researchers, the left temporal lobe is most associated with sexual interest, which is part of the cognitive component of the sexual process, whereas the right temporal lobe is associated with sexual arousal or drive, which is part of the physiological component. A failure of the two lobes to appropriately and effectively communicate could lead to mixed signals, resulting in a lack of behavioral inhibition for deviant sexual interests or a lack of control over violent sexual tendencies.

Finally, it has been hypothesized that right temporal lobe impairments are responsible for more general deficits in these offenders, including spatial, attentional, and perceptual abnormalities, which may moderate deviant sexual behaviors. For example, deficits in attentional processes may impair an individual's ability to disengage from one stimulus and devote his attention to another. In the case of a sexual offender, he might be unable to disengage his attention from sexual thoughts of a child and devote his attention instead to the consequences of offending or the negative impact of his behavior on the victim. If this hypothesized relationship is valid, then offenders with right temporal lobe deficits (i.e., rapists and sadistic sex offenders) should show the general deficits noted previously. Although researchers have not yet compared rapists with non–sex offenders and nonoffenders on these variables, several studies have thus far failed to demonstrate significant differences in the spatial performance abilities of rapists when compared with other sex offenders (e.g., pedophiles; Langevin, Wortzman, et al., 1989; Ponseti, Vaih-Koch, & Bosinski, 2001). This finding can be interpreted in two ways. First, these data could be used to argue that the right temporal lobe abnormalities do not play a significant role in this type of sexual offending. This conclusion seems inappropriate, however, given the research reviewed earlier in this section. Second, an impairment of this type may independently affect behaviors that are indirectly related to sex offending (e.g., aggression), but there is no research to confirm this hypothesis. Finally, research has not explored the hypothesized attentional or perceptual difficulties that would result from right temporal lobe abnormalities in these individuals.

Frontal Lobe Abnormalities

The frontal lobe of the brain is responsible for many of the behaviors that make us human, such as reasoning, problem solving, abstract thinking, and behavioral inhibition. Early evidence of a link between frontal lobe dysfunction and sexual deviation came from research on individuals with frontal lobe brain tumors or frontal lobe epilepsy. It was found that abnormalities in this region were associated with a higher prevalence of sexually deviant interests (Cummings, 1999), which was theorized to expressively lead to sexually deviant behaviors.

To explain this hypothesis, Raine and Buchsbaum (1996) argued that deficits in frontal lobe functioning might create a loss of inhibition in certain areas of the brain designed to reduce aggressive behaviors, and such dysfunction could then increase the likelihood of aggressive or antisocial tendencies. In addition, they argued that frontal abnormalities are highly correlated with increased risk-taking, antisocial behaviors, emotional instability or unpredictability, and argumentative behaviors. These various traits and behaviors could increase the chances of violent behavior. Also, Raine and Buchsbaum posited that damage to the frontal lobe structures could lead to impulsivity, poor self-control or self-regulation, and poor social understanding (e.g., the inability to correctly interpret social stimuli). Again, this could have detrimental effects on the behavior of the individual and, if these factors are combined with some inappropriate sexual urges, it could lead to sex-offending behaviors.

Cerebral Blood Flow

Low or abnormal cerebral blood flow has been implicated as a risk factor for a number of different psychopathological conditions, including the paraphilias (Hendricks et al., 1988). Studies that have examined the cerebral blood flow of various typologies of sex offenders have demonstrated that child molesters have significantly lower cerebral blood flow levels than rapists or non–sex-offending groups (Hendricks et al., 1988; Raine & Buchsbaum, 1996). The exact etiological significance of this finding, however, is unclear. Although the areas of lowered blood flow are within the left temporal lobe and the frontal lobe, suggesting that the lowered amount of cerebral blood and oxygen contained in the blood might contribute to the findings of neuropsychological impairment of these areas, it may just as well be a product of them. In addition, because lowered cerebral blood flow is a risk factor for nonsexual psychopathology, it may simply be an indicator of overall neurological dysfunction in more severe and psychiatrically disturbed sex-offender groups.

HORMONES AND NEUROTRANSMITTERS

Hormones and neurotransmitters are two of the body's primary mechanisms to maintain homeostatic functioning. *Hormones*—chemical secretions from a variety of glands throughout the body—control a wide range of bodily functions such as blood pressure, the reproductive cycle, body temperature, and the release of other hormones. *Neurotransmitters* are chemical agents within the brain that help control many aspects of cerebral functioning as well as mood and autonomic reactions. These two types of bodily chemicals are often interrelated and have been linked to numerous behaviors and emotional states, including sexual deviance.

Hormones

Several different types of hormones are hypothesized to relate to sexually deviant behavior. Perhaps the most frequently studied hormone in relation to violence and sex offending is the male hormone testosterone. In men, testosterone production begins in the Leydig cells of the testes. Testosterone is then spread throughout the body and controls a number of bodily functions, including the creation of spermatozoa, sexual maturation in pubescent boys, and the maintenance of sexual arousal (Bain, Langevin, Dickey, & Ben-Aron, 1987). It has been speculated that testosterone plays a role in enhancing feelings of aggression and in facilitating aggressive tendencies in males (Bradford, 1983), including sexual violence (Bain et al., 1987; Hucker & Bain, 1990). Researchers reason that testosterone may not just affect a male's tendency toward aggression but that its effects on sexual functioning (e.g., sexual arousal, sex drive) may interact with aggressive tendencies to result in sexual violence.

Bain et al. (1987) cited early research indicating mixed results for the testosterone hypothesis. They concluded that although testosterone may play some role in facilitating the development of sexual aggression and deviant sexual arousal, it has not been conclusively proven that testosterone itself may be implicated as a causal mechanism in this process. Furthermore, their research suggested that there is not a clear link between testosterone and generalized aggression, much less sexual aggression. Hucker and Bain (1990) supported this conclusion in their summary of the literature, suggesting that more work needs to be done to determine the extent to which testosterone is specifically involved in sexually violent behavior.

Despite the lack of clear evidence for a link between testosterone and sexual aggression, some researchers have postulated that other hormones that work in the formation and regulation of testosterone may play mediating or even causal roles in the development and maintenance of inappropriate sexual behaviors. Two related possibilities have been raised. First, a variety of hormones that stimulate the production of testosterone may appear at higher levels in sexual offenders, thus indicating a problem in the regulation of testosterone. This could explain the mixed findings of earlier studies in which testosterone levels and sexual offending could not be linked. Second, disorders in hormone production and distribution mechanisms may cause problems not only in hormone regulation but also more broadly in abnormalities in sexual drive, interest, and arousal (Lang, Flor-Henry, & Frenzel, 1990).

One such hormone that has been implicated in the biological explanations of sex offending discussed in this section is the luteinizing hormone (LH), which increases the production of testosterone in males through stimulating secretion by the Leydig cells of the testes (Lang et al., 1990). Other hormones that have similar effects, in that they increase the production of testosterone in males and enhance overall testosterone levels, include the follicle stimulating hormone (FSH), dehydroespinandrosterone sulfate, androstenedione, prolactin, and estradiol (Marieb, 2001). Hypersecretion of these six hormones could result in abnormally high levels of testosterone, which would have the hypothesized effects described previously. Finally, cortisol, a "stress hormone," also has been discussed in relation to sex-offending behavior. Cortisol affects a wide range of somatic systems and primarily affects the immune system and increases production of glucose in the body. It is regulated by a negative feedback system to keep the body functioning properly under high levels of stress. The body will essentially "shut off" cortisol's releasing mechanism (adrenocorticotropin hormone) when levels of cortisol remain high, so that the body is not injured or harmed by high levels of this hormone (Marieb, 2001). Researchers have not specifically hypothesized the mechanisms by which this hormone may cause sex offending, but there is a continued belief that cortisol will be abnormally elevated in sex offenders (Lang et al., 1990).

In summary, several hormones have been identified as possible contributors to sexually deviant behaviors, with increased levels of these hormones hypothesized to have an impact on aggression and sexual drive. Abnormal levels of these specific hormones in sex-offending individuals would lend support to the idea that these chemicals play a role in the development of sexually deviant interests and behaviors. It is also probable that there is a defect in the underlying regulatory processes of these hormones, and this wider abnormality within the endocrine system would have far-reaching effects on sexual drive and the responsiveness of target organs (e.g., other hormone-producing glands) and would impact other hormones within the body. This might in turn have effects on biological processes, such as sexual drive, as well as affect the moods and behaviors of the affected individual.

Several lines of research address these hypotheses, but the results have been mixed, and it still remains unclear whether there is a relationship, causal or not, between hormone levels and sexual drive and sexually aggressive behaviors. Lang et al. (1990) failed to find clinically significant elevations of FSH, LH, estradiol, and testosterone in their sample of sex offenders. They also failed to find support for their prediction that prolactin, cortisol, and androstenedione would be significantly elevated in incest offenders and pedophiles, compared with control groups, suggesting that it is unlikely that these hormones play a major role in sex-offending behaviors. Bain et al. (1988), however, concluded that there were in fact significant group differences in LH, FSH, and testosterone levels between sex offenders and control participants. No differences were found between groups for dehydroespinandrosterone sulfate, cortisol, and estradiol. Despite the researchers' assertions that the differences were significant, the sex-offending group as a whole averaged within a normal range of hormone functioning, suggesting that there were in fact no significant differences between groups or notable elevations within the sex-offending sample. Furthermore, in the cases of testosterone and cortisol, there was a greater number of control participants with abnormally elevated levels than there were in the sex-offending group. These findings support the conclusion that the hormones affecting testosterone production are not a likely causal source of sexual deviance or sexually aggressive behaviors.

There is still the question of whether the hormone-secreting mechanisms of the endocrine system are functioning properly in sex-offending samples. One such relevant hormone secretion mechanism involves the role of gonadotropic releasing hormone (GnRH). GnRH is responsible for the secretion control of a variety of hormones, including LH and testosterone. GnRH acts on the hypothalamic–pituitary hormone secretion mechanisms and determines when and in what amount these hormones should be secreted. Gaffney and Berlin (1984) found that there was a significantly increased rise in LH levels in pedophiles after an injection with GnRH compared with control participants. The implication of this finding is that pedophiles may be hypersensitive to GnRH and therefore release more LH in response to it, thus leading to greater testosterone production overall. Bain et al. (1988) similarly tested this hypothesis by using GnRH to detect abnormal changes in the hormonal systems of pedophiles versus control groups.

Again, it was found that despite similar baseline levels of LH in both pedophiles and normal control participants, the pedophiles, when injected with GnRH, exhibited significantly increased levels of LH over the control participants. Although Gaffney and Berlin believed this finding was significant only in terms of testosterone production, Bain et al. (1988) argued that this dramatic increase in LH can be attributed to an exaggerated secretion response in the hypothalamus–pituitary regulation systems of pedophilic men. This could have implications for organ sensitivity to hormone secretion and decreased hormone production throughout the system, in addition to increased testosterone synthesis. Why this specific hormonal regulation defect would cause pedophilic sex offending, however, remains unclear.

Neurotransmitters

Abnormalities in neurotransmitter activity also have been hypothesized to relate to sex offending. Although the research regarding the role of neurotransmitter function or dysfunction in sex offenders is currently in its infancy, a large body of research exists concerning the relationship between certain neurotransmitters and violent, impulsive behavior. Several of the theoretical models explaining the relation of neurotransmitter levels to violent behavior may be extended to include sexual violence.

Serotonin, a neurotransmitter that operates as a behavioral inhibitor (Coccaro & Kavoussi, 1996), is hypothesized to affect acting-out behaviors. The assumption is that lower levels of serotonin in the brain lead to less behavioral inhibition, with the resulting failure of the inhibitory mechanisms contributing to acting out in an aggressive and impulsive manner. This model also suggests that the aggressive responses of individuals with decreased overall serotonin levels will be more markedly severe than in someone with normal serotonergic functioning. In other words, when this inhibitory system is operating at significantly diminished levels, the individual will be less apt to deal with threat or frustration in socially acceptable ways, and aggressive outbursts and impulsive violence will be more likely to occur. Research supports this model. Lower levels of serotonin are strongly correlated with impulsive aggression (e.g., suicide, unplanned assaultive behaviors) rather than generalized aggression (Coccaro & Kavoussi, 1996; Kafka, 1997; Klinteberg, 1996; Stoff & Vitiello, 1996; Virkkunen & Linnoila, 1996).

Stoff and Vitiello (1996) proposed a model that includes not only serotonergic dysfunction but also the effects of lowered serotonin levels on related peripheral proteins and hormones. They postulated that this is indicative of a systematic abnormality in the processing of hormones and neurotransmitters in the inhibitory systems of the brain. This particular model is somewhat supported by evidence that impulsive–aggressive criminal offenders are more likely to have significantly lowered levels of monoamine oxidase and tryptophan, enzymes that are precursors to serotonin production

(Klinteberg, 1996; Stamps, Abeling, Van Gennip, Van Crutchen, & Gurling, 2001; Stoff & Vitiello, 1996). The evidence also suggests that other enzymes are lowered as well, thus leading to decreased serotonin production, which would result in decreased behavioral inhibition. The literature raises the possibility that these types of systemic abnormalities might be due to some genetic factor (Stamps et al., 2001; Stoff & Vitiello, 1996), which is addressed later in this chapter.

Other neurotransmitters that have been linked with violent as well as sexual behaviors are norepinephrine and dopamine. These are said to play a role in the regulation of a wide variety of behaviors, including attention, goal-directed behavior, and sexual appetite (Kafka, 1997). In the case of these two particular neurotransmitters, increased activity in the brain may facilitate aggressive tendencies. Stimulation of the norepinephrine and dopamine receptors in the brain has been linked with aggression in animal and human studies (Coccaro & Kavoussi, 1996). The hypothesis that increased dopamine and norepinephrine are responsible for aggression is also supported by the fact that narcotics that affect these certain neurotransmitter receptors, such as cocaine and methamphetamine, have also been shown to increase aggressive behavior.

The ultimate issue for our purposes is whether these models of impulsive–aggressive behavior and neurotransmitter dysfunction can be used to explain sex-offending behaviors. It is possible that because these processes increase an individual's impulsive and unplanned violent behaviors, sex offending might be one of them. If combined with some other predisposition toward sexually deviant or inappropriate interests, abnormal neurotransmitter levels could lead to impulsive sexual violence. Research, however, must be conducted to validate this theory (Stamps et al., 2001).

GENETICS AND SEX CHROMOSOME ABNORMALITIES

Early criminologists and psychologists largely adhered to the concept of *biological determinism* (Brennan, Mednick, & Volavka, 1995), believing that certain personality or behavioral characteristics were genetically transmitted from parent to child, which resulted in the child's behaviors not being completely within his control. Thus, when biological explanations for criminal and violent behaviors were in their infancy, researchers looked to what they believed were specific genetic traits (e.g., intelligence, aggression) to establish a link between genetics and sexually deviant or violent acts (Carey, 1996; Goldman, 1996). This model of sex offending supposes that a sex offender may have some genetic defect that makes him more likely to engage in deviant sexual practices. This form of biological sexual determinism also makes the individual less likely to be able to effectively and consciously change his behaviors.

Although researchers discovered that it was possible to control the breeding of certain animal species to select for more aggressive offspring (e.g., Gariepy, Lewis, & Cairns, 1996), it was unclear as to whether such results were likely with human beings. To test the possibility of specific genetic traits determining one's deviant sexual or violent proclivities in humans, researchers used twin and adoption studies. The primary intent of such research was to ascertain whether the biological offspring of violent parents became violent adults, regardless of whether their parents were present during the child-rearing process. These studies also explored whether the rates of genetic concordance between identical and fraternal twins were significantly related to their rates of violent and criminal activity. The general findings of these studies were that genetics alone did not play a major role in the development of such behaviors; genetic predisposition combined with a highly criminal or dysfunctional environment was the most likely cause of resulting criminal or deviant behaviors in the offspring (Brennan et al., 1995; Carey, 1996; Goldman, 1996; see also Gaffney, Lurie, & Berlin, 1984). In fact, a recent compilation of the results of hundreds of such studies indicated that, overall, genetic factors account for approximately 41% of the variance in resulting antisocial behavior, with both shared and unshared environmental factors accounting for the remaining 59% (Rhee & Waldman, 2002). Although genetic influences are strong, environmental influences are also critical in the development of such behaviors. Because these and other results did not support the hypothesis that general antisocial behaviors or specific ones, such as sex offending, were genetically transmitted disorders or dysfunctions, research in this vein was subsequently abandoned for different theories, biological or otherwise, that might more accurately explain the initiation of sexually deviant or inappropriate behaviors.

Sex chromosome abnormalities have also been considered viable explanations for sex offending. Harrison, Clayton-Smith, and Bailey (2001) discussed the three primary chromosomal abnormalities that are related to violent and sexual offending. The first of these is XXY, also known as *Klinefelter's syndrome*, in which male babies are born with an extra female chromosome. These individuals tend to be more passive, withdrawn, and quiet compared with normal XY males. Although these individuals display normal, average intelligence, as a whole this group is likely to exhibit speech and language difficulties and later academic challenges. Relevant to sexual functioning, sexual interest is typically limited. A second karyotype is XXXY, which is a variant of Klinefelter's syndrome. These males tend to have significant IQ impairment, often with mental retardation, and exhibit behaviors that are immature and infantile (e.g., temper tantrums). Finally, XYY males manifest significant problems with temper tantrums, hyperactivity, and behavioral and interpersonal problems.

Because of the generalized problems with impulsivity, immaturity, and a lower than normal frustration tolerance that are associated with these chromosomal abnormalities, researchers have suggested that they may contribute to an increased likelihood of delinquency and sex offending (e.g., Beckmann et al., 1974; Harrison et al., 2001). Because of their interpersonal and behavioral problems, individuals with these particular karyotypes may demonstrate significant difficulties in peer relationships and coping strategies, which further predispose them to inappropriate criminal actions. For instance, Beckmann et al. (1974) researched a group of forensic inpatients and discovered that the number of individuals with sex chromosome abnormalities was significantly higher in this sample than in a population without sex chromosome abnormalities. In fact, these researchers found that the number of XYY individuals alone was nearly 50 times higher than in a nonpsychiatric and nonforensic sample without karyotypic abnormalities. The results suggested that the individuals in this sample who displayed abnormal karyotypes were more behaviorally unstable, had higher rates of mental retardation, and were more impulsive than the rest of the forensic inpatients. As far as this model applies to sex offending, Harrison et al. (2001) examined a small sample of boys with sex chromosome abnormalities within a sample of sex-offending adolescents. Again, there was a much higher prevalence of boys with karyotypic abnormalities in a sex-offending sample than in a normal sample of adolescent boys (4% vs. 0.1%). The researchers concluded that their difficulties with appropriate peer functioning, behavioral problems, and impulsivity made them more likely to sexually offend than karyotypically normal individuals because of their inability to efficiently cope with environmental and interpersonal stressors.

Because of the paucity of studies addressing chromosomal abnormalities and sex offending, and limited sample sizes in the extant studies, more research is needed before conclusions about causal mechanisms can be drawn. For example, it is difficult to say with any certainty whether individuals with chromosomal abnormalities are more or less likely to commit sex offenses because of an actual genetic predisposition or because of environmental factors that shape their learning processes. The studies mentioned here were all conducted on forensic inpatients, who notably have a very different living environment and history than many others who many exhibit these chromosomal abnormalities. Also, some of the underlying assumptions about the behavioral processes of karyotypically abnormal individuals may be flawed. Historically, much attention has been paid to the XYY individuals, because many early criminologists supposed that the extra Y chromosome and excess testosterone also implied higher levels of masculinity and aggression. However, this assumption has not held up under empirical scrutiny (Brennan et al., 1995).

MENTAL RETARDATION

Deficits in intellectual functioning have been implicated as a precursor to sex-offending behaviors. By *mental retardation* or *intellectual impairment*, we refer to deficits in skill or adaptive functioning that may be manifested by individuals with brain injury or damage or lifetime developmental disability. A number of studies have demonstrated that sex offending is largely overrepresented among persons with intellectual disabilities (Day, 1994; O'Callaghan, 1998), even though there are not consistent significant differences between the prevalence of sex offending in a population of individuals with mental retardation and a population of individuals without mental retardation (Murray et al., 2001). In other words, sex offending happens at a much greater frequency among samples of persons with significant intellectual impairments.

There are two major theories that link mental retardation with sex offending. The first focuses on the characteristics of individuals who are mentally disabled and how those specific factors might contribute to sexually deviant behaviors. The second attributes a link between mental retardation or other developmental disorders and sex offending by examining the role of the actual mental age relationship between offender and victim. Each of these theories is addressed here.

Regarding the first theory, numerous researchers have postulated that sex offenders who demonstrate significant intellectual impairment have four types of characteristics that may predispose them to sexually aberrant behaviors: (a) impulsive behaviors and poor judgment, (b) aggression and acting out, (c) poor interpersonal skills, and (d) poor coping skills and self-esteem.

Sex offenders with developmental and intellectual deficits display greater impulsivity and poorer judgment than other sex-offending individuals (Cox-Lindenbaum, 2001; Schoen & Hoover, 1990), which may lead some individuals with mental retardation to engage in sexually inappropriate behaviors. They may also evidence poor judgment in selecting sexual partners or initiating sexual behaviors (R. Blanchard et al., 1999; Stermac & Sheridan, 1993). Finally, deficits in rational judgment or behavioral inhibition, which are part of this category, might further increase the likelihood of impulsive sexual behaviors.

Closely related to this impulsivity is the finding that some individuals with intellectual deficits may demonstrate a greater tendency toward aggression and acting-out behaviors, often sexual in nature (Cox-Lindenbaum, 2001; Schoen & Hoover, 1990). These aggressive and acting-out sexualized behaviors may appear as early as adolescence in some mentally disabled sex offenders (Cox-Lindenbaum, 2001), and this may be due to functional brain impairments in the areas of anger control and behavioral inhibition. However, the majority of mentally disabled sex offenders are not overtly aggressive; instead, they commit "nuisance" sex offenses, such as exhibitionism and voyeurism. So although aggressive behaviors have been attributed to the overall intellectual and developmental limitations of offenders with mental retardation, aggression is not the norm in this particular population (H. Brown & Stein, 1997; Day, 1994; Stermac & Sheridan, 1993).

Poor or limited interpersonal skills as well as deficits in verbal skills are an important component of this etiological view. These offenders manifest marked deficiencies in verbal abilities, including conceptual understanding, which may affect their ability to function appropriately in interpersonal relationships (Murray et al., 2001). Mentally disabled sex offenders, therefore, are more likely to misinterpret the interpersonal "signals" of others or display a much wider range of inappropriate behaviors when interacting with others, some of which might include sexual behaviors (Schoen & Hoover, 1990). This is consistent with the earlier stated research finding that many individuals in this category commit noncontact sex offenses, which may be more likely to occur in the context of poor interpersonal understanding or lack of knowledge of appropriate behavioral expression. And although a "misinterpretation" explanation also would encompass contact-based sex offenses, such as rape, the interpersonal skill deficits might occur at such a level as to inhibit direct or overt approach of others, instead leading to more distant, noninteractive offenses.

Finally, mentally disabled sex offenders demonstrate significant coping skill deficits and lowered self-esteem (Cox-Lindenbaum, 2001; Schoen & Hoover, 1990), so dealing with frustration or stress may be particularly difficult for these individuals because of their limited intellectual abilities. They may also tend to act out in inappropriate or seemingly bizarre ways as a result of an inability to cope with stressors. For example, there is the possibility that sexual acts may somehow restore a feeling of self-confidence (Cox-Lindenbaum, 2001). However, as with many of the other behavioral categories mentioned here, there is most likely some other factor or combination of factors that would lead specifically to sex-offending behaviors in these situations, because sex offenses are still relatively rare in this population.

The second theoretical approach postulates that it is the mental age and skill levels of the individuals that cause them to commit sex offenses at abnormally elevated rates compared with a population without mental disabilities. The first component of this theory is that adults with mental disabilities might commit sexually inappropriate acts because they are making crude or imitative attempts at what they perceive as normal sexual interests (Day, 1994). Because of their intellectual deficits, they might not fully understand what others mean by sexual behavior, and their resulting attempts to imitate such behavior or to satisfy their own sexual urges may fall short of what is considered normal or appropriate sexuality.

The second component of this theory considers the mental age or level of development of the offender and the victims. Some researchers have hypothesized that offenders who are mentally retarded may be overrepresented among pedophiles because the offenders have the same approximate mental age of the victims (O'Callaghan, 1998). According to this view, an adult who is mentally disabled may think in terms of a young child yet still has the sexual urges of an adult. Because of limited mental capacity and understanding, the individual might relate conceptually better with small children and might often associate with them. Also, because of the frequent lack of sexual education among populations of persons with mental disabilities (Schilling & Schinke, 1989), the individual might not fully appreciate the sexual interest or arousal that he experiences. This could then lead to the individual acting out on his sexual urges with these children. Day (1994) further supported this hypothesis through research suggesting that sex offenses among persons who are mentally disabled are generally crimes of opportunity, committed against victims close at hand, rather than planned or deliberate acts of sexualized aggression. In other words, some mentally disabled child molesters may be acting out on their sexual urges with victims with whom they are often in contact, which may frequently be children. This could also be used to explain the number of mentally disabled sex offenders who victimize other individuals who are mentally disabled (H. Brown & Stein, 1997). However, other research suggests that this observed link between developmental disability and pedophilic offending is far more complex and that the concept of mental age does not accurately represent the interpersonal or social functioning of individuals who are intellectually disabled (National Clearinghouse on Family Violence, 1998).

LIMITATIONS OF THE BIOLOGICAL EXPLANATIONS OF SEX OFFENDING

Despite the current interest in biological explanations, the various theories and hypotheses that have been presented using a biological framework are still in their infancy. These theories also manifest a number of problems, ranging from making relatively unfounded assumptions about the normal functioning of certain biological systems to inconsistencies in the methodology used in the studies to investigate such explanations. In this section, we address the most important limitations of these biological explanations.

First, a majority of the these hypotheses, including the structural explanations and those using hormones and neurotransmitters, rely heavily on current knowledge of brain and bodily functioning, and that knowledge is still very limited; we are only at a stage where we understand gross functioning of certain systems. For example, although serotonin is given such importance in many areas of psychopathology, its exact role continues to elude researchers. Also, much of the knowledge we do have about brain functioning comes from brain dysfunction, which may not be a reliable or consistent source of information. One individual with damage to a certain area of the brain may exhibit behaviors very unlike another individual with the same type of impairment. So although researchers have gathered interesting data regarding the role of neuropsychological impairment and chemical agents that may play a role in the development and maintenance of sex offending, the theories and hypotheses about the role of human biology in sex offending have yet to be proven.

Second, the methodology used by researchers to provide empirical support for these theories is not always consistent. Use of varying samples of sex offenders and other groups, as well as different forms of testing, limits the types of information that can be obtained from the research. This could explain why a number of studies seem to contradict each other and why researchers fail to agree on the origin of the neuropsychological impairment demonstrated by the participant. Until researchers design their studies in such a way that they will add incrementally to the existing knowledge base, progress in this area is likely to remain slow.

A third limitation is that researchers often assume that a link or correlation between the presence or absence of certain biological phenomena implies that they played causal roles in the individual's sex offending. The research to support the hypotheses outlined in this chapter has been performed after the person has committed a sex offense, and this fact is consistent throughout sex offender research. However, researchers also assume that the biological factors under consideration, whether they be temporal lobe abnormalities or mental retardation, occurred before the sexually deviant interests and that these biological factors directly caused the sexual deviance. In some cases, such as chromosomal abnormality, it is obvious when the biological deviance occurred. With other factors it is not so simple. Even if such a chain of events can be established, there is a large number of nonoffenders who have similar impairments with no deviant sexual interest, as well as sex offenders with no impairment. Therefore, it is not reasonable to automatically assume that any presence of abnormality will suggest a root cause of the behavior.

Fourth, biological theories fail to take into consideration the large social impact of the impairment on the offender. For example, when examining the traits or behavioral factors associated with mental retardation (e.g., impulsivity), the biological theorists do not appear to give much credit to the environmental impact on the formation of this trait. Individuals with certain biological characteristics, such as mental or intellectual disability, are often treated differentially within society, and this might have significant impact on their behavior. Although biological predispositions play some role in shaping behavior, societal reactions and environmental impact on behavior also are likely to be significant. Biological theories would be more powerful if they included a greater emphasis on the interaction between biological abnormality and environmental or social stressors and other psychological features of the individual.

Finally, the most prominent limitation of the biological theories of sex offending is the lack of research to support them. A large percentage of the studies that rely on these theories simply provide a link between biological phenomena and sex-offending behavior rather than establishing a clear causal pathway. For example, in the research regarding the temporal lobes, theorists have suggested a disconnection between the left and right temporal lobes that may contribute to sex offending, but these theorists do not explain how this miscommunication or feedback error between the two temporal lobes would invariably lead to sexually deviant behaviors. In other cases, such as the genetic hypothesis and frontal lobe impairment, the research has not been supportive of the theoretical views of the researchers (e.g., Raine & Buchsbaum, 1996). Also, as noted previously, some studies contradict one another because of their differences in methodology. Until a more sound body of research exists, it will be difficult to know the impact of biological factors on the development of sexually deviant interests, arousal, and behavior.

SUMMARY AND CONCLUSIONS

The biological theories encompass a variety of physiological systems, from the anatomical and chemical structures of the brain to the basic genes that make up each individual. Research involving the structure and function of specific areas of the brain has suggested that the temporal and frontal lobes are potential sources of impairment or dysfunction in sex-offending individuals. Although many researchers have speculated as to the role of hormones and neurotransmitters in sexually deviant behaviors, the research has not proven a causal link. Similar findings have resulted from research into potential genetic contributions to sexually deviant interests and behaviors, including sex chromosome abnormalities that affect broad areas of development and functioning. Finally, we discussed the role of intellectual and developmental deficits, including the impact of these deficits on impulse control, adaptive behavior, interpersonal functioning, and coping skills. Also, although there is evidence to suggest that sex-offending behaviors may be overrepresented in some populations with developmental disabilities, it remains unclear how cognitive and developmental disabilities may contribute to this behavior.

Despite the limitations noted in the preceding section, the biological theories as a whole have been valuable in conceptualizing and guiding etiological research. First, the theories described here have emphasized the importance of the biological precursors that shape learning and behavioral adaptation and expression. Although it may be tempting to simply discredit early attempts at identifying singular biological substrates, these approaches are useful in that they have drawn attention to the need to consider biological predispositions, systemic abnormalities, and other genetic factors that likely play a role in the development of these complex behaviors.

Second, these theories have highlighted the impact of biological or genetic abnormality on a variety of systems. We may not adequately understand the intricacies of the brain or its systems, and we may lack the considerable knowledge that would be required to understand the full effects of hormone or neurotransmitter imbalances, but we can see from this research that maladaptive functioning in any of these domains can have lasting and varied effects on behavior, cognitive functioning, and interpersonal relationships.

Third, although these theories may not always adequately address the role of environmental and interpersonal factors, the implicit assumption is that biological realities interact with the individual's environment to produce the behaviors of interest. For example, the effects of neurostructural abnormalities on sexual behavior are discussed in terms of verbal comprehension, cognitive perception, and regulatory feedback from the environment. This recognition of the interaction between biology and the environment is a positive feature of these theories that must be included in future theory development and research.

4

COGNITIVE THEORIES

Cognitive processes have been advanced to explain a variety of psychological disorders, such as depression, anxiety, and sexual deviance (Barlow, 2002; Beck, 2002; Marshall, Laws, & Barbaree, 1990). Early cognitive explanations, some of which are still in use today, focused on the role of repetitive and automatic thought patterns in shaping emotions and behaviors (Beck, 2002). Most later cognitive theories postulated that various mental processes, including emotion interpretation, cue perception, and information processing, drive these emotions and behaviors. Despite their shared interest in the influence of these cognitive processes on behavior, the different cognitive theories vary in terms of how they explain the progression from thought to behavior.

Cognitive theories of sex offending also vary in their hypotheses about the cognitive processes that are critical in explaining and understanding this form of deviant behavior. Although researchers recognize that the basic components of cognitive processes are the same (e.g., cognitive distortions, self-esteem, empathy), they differ in their interpretation of the role of each component and how significant the components are in contributing to sex offending.

In this chapter, we address the major cognitive theories as they relate to the perpetration of sex offending and the maintenance of sexually deviant interests. The first type of cognitive theory concerns early attachment and loneliness. Here, it is believed that sex offenders gained insecure attachment styles stemming from childhood and act out in deviant ways to confront their deep-rooted feelings of loneliness. Second, we describe how cognitive schemas are hypothesized to affect the sex offender's underlying beliefs about the world, which can lead to, and be used to justify, sex offending. The third type of theory addresses the role of information processing and cue perception in the facilitation of sex offending and sexually deviant thoughts. This part of the chapter includes discussions of the theory of mind and social cognition and how each relates to an offender's ability to process interpersonal cues. In the last section, we address the limitations of these theories.

ATTACHMENT THEORY

Attachment theory was first introduced by Bowlby (e.g., 1958, 1988) as an explanation of the relationship between a child and his primary caretaker (e.g., the mother) and how that early relationship would impact functioning in adulthood. Bowlby (1979) suggested that abnormalities within the attachment relationship could impair the child's capacity for interpersonal bonding and emotional attachment to others in adulthood. He further believed that many forms of adult psychopathology could be related to disturbances in these early relationships. Attachment was further defined by the development of specific attachment styles, including secure, anxious, and avoidant attachment (e.g., Ainsworth, Bell, & Stayton, 1974; Ainsworth, Blehar, Waters, & Wall, 1978). In studies of children's behavior on being separated from their mothers or encountering a strange and anxiety-provoking situation, the child's behavior was strongly impacted by the relationship with the mother. For example, children who exhibited anxious attachment cried inconsolably when separated from the mother and explored the environment very little when faced with a strange stimulus, even in the presence of the mother (e.g., Ainsworth, 1963, 1967).

In the context of this early relationship, childhood attachment behavior serves the purpose of teaching children role expectations in relationships. The young child learns what is expected of him and what he should expect from others in interpersonal interactions (e.g., Bowlby, 1977, 1988; Burk & Burkhart, 2003; Ward, Hudson, Marshall, & Siegert, 1995). The way that children perceive interpersonal roles will influence their overall cognitive conceptualization of the world and the way that they interpret incoming information. Once this has been established in childhood, it will be fairly stable across the life span (Bowlby, 1977).

Marshall (1989, 1993) hypothesized that poor parental attachments in childhood lead to either emotional or social loneliness, with the latter having greater implications for social interaction processes, and to lowered self-esteem or anxiety regarding perceived self-worth. These two types of deficits in later functioning are said to result from the child not learning the appropriate "rules of behavior" and the typical role expectations for interpersonal relationships. The resulting feelings of chronic loneliness and low self-worth may lead to other problems in adult relationships and interpersonal functioning, including intimacy deficits and extreme frustration. Mediators in this process (e.g., emotional or cognitive deficits) may exacerbate an already-existing problem, with the individual being unable to fully function in and derive satisfaction from intimate relationships. It perhaps is not surprising that the literature on sex offenders and their early childhood experiences suggests that a disproportionate percentage of sex offenders had poor parental attachment and greater perceived parental rejection (Marshall, 1989, 1993).

To fully understand why poor parental attachment has been theorized to lead to sex offending, we first need to consider two possible dysfunctional attachment styles in adulthood that may be specifically related to sexually deviant behaviors: (a) the anxious–ambivalent attachment style and (b) the avoidant attachment style (Ward et al., 1995).

Anxious–Ambivalent Attachment Style

It has been argued that individuals who have developed an anxious–ambivalent attachment style in response to poor parental attachment are low in self-esteem and self-confidence, dependent on others for approval, easily frustrated by interpersonal relationships (Ward et al., 1995), more likely to experience negative emotional states after interpersonal rejection (Marshall, Anderson, & Champagne, 1997), and unfulfilled by interpersonal relationships that they perceive lack depth and understanding from the other person (Beech & Mitchell, 2005). In the case of sex offenders, this extreme discomfort with one's self and with intimacy with adult partners may lead the individual to turn to other ways to alleviate the underlying anxiety. Attributions and beliefs about others may lead the individual to engage in more self-serving sexual behaviors and see others as deserving of his sexual abuse (Marshall, 1993). This has been argued to be particularly true of child molesters because they see children as submissive and nonthreatening, as compared with adults, whom they find overbearing and anxiety provoking (Marshall & Mazzucco, 1995; Segal & Stermac, 1990).

It has also been argued that people who have an anxious–ambivalent attachment style seek out relationships and fixate on their failure to form satisfying bonds with others. Because these individuals have unsatisfying or uncomfortable relationships with adult peers, they turn to relationships with children. The person may then become needy and dependent on his relationship with a young child; try to create an inappropriate intimacy; and believe that the child feels the same way about him in this relationship, possibly because of a misinterpretation of role expectations (Ward et al.,

1995). A relationship with a child, which closely models what the offender believes an adult relationship should be like (e.g., sexual relations), may temporarily relieve the anxiety that he feels and increase his self-confidence. A larger literature exists exploring this concept more fully, focusing primarily on the intimacy deficits described here (e.g., Marshall, 1989; Ward, Hudson, & Marshall, 1996; Ward et al., 1995; Ward, Polaschek, & Beech, 2006) and their proposed relationship between abnormal childhood attachment, deficits in the formation of adult interpersonal relationships, and sex-offending outcomes. We discuss this further in chapter 9 of this volume, within the context of integrated models of sex offending.

Avoidant Attachment Style

An individual with an avoidant attachment style is likely to be detached from interpersonal relationships. Instead of seeking out relationships and fixating on his failure to form satisfying bonds with others, the person with an avoidant attachment style is likely to place little value on relationships, have poor empathy skills, and be hostile toward others (Ward et al., 1995). It is theorized that beneath the avoidant exterior lies a deep-rooted fear of rejection that causes the person to create distance and avoid intimate relationships, leading to prolonged emotional and social loneliness. This chronic loneliness will increase overall hostility and aggression, because the individual feels that he has been cheated out of peer intimacy (Marshall, 1993; Ward et al., 1995).

The avoidant attachment style may lead to sex offending in some cases. The hostility and resentment that these men experience, when combined with sexual and aggressive urges during puberty, may result in feelings of entitlement and desire for power and may facilitate the initiation of sex offending. Sexually deviant behaviors will then be maintained as a way to alleviate frustration and remain distant from intimate relationships with other adults (Marshall, 1993).

Another way in which this attachment style may lead to sex offending is through the interaction of poor or nonexistent empathy, which results when a functional emotional attachment is not formed with early caregivers or when one has a desire to remain detached from peers (Ward et al., 1995). When combined with an arrogant desire for control or power and aggressive impulses, the lack of empathy and related detachment make it unlikely that the person is willing to invest the time in establishing an intimate relationship. The result is that the man desires impersonal sex and treats sex partners as objects. Collectively, all of these characteristics can lead to rape or other types of violent sexual assault.

Some people with an avoidant attachment style are less violent while still remaining hostile toward others. They, too, have a strong fear of rejection, but rather than being aloof regarding relationships they are simply more fearful. Men with these characteristics might commit noncontact sex offenses, such as exhibitionism and voyeurism, to fulfill their sexual desires.

COGNITIVE SCHEMAS

From infancy, human beings are constantly categorizing the objects they encounter in the world around them. Early developmental and cognitive theorists hypothesized that the brain organizes these categories of learned information and perceived experiences into meaningful patterns, or *schemas* (e.g., Piaget, 1977; see also Fiske & Taylor, 1991). Schemas, which serve a variety of functions for cognitive understanding, knowledge acquisition, and information processing, affect perceptions, attitudes, and beliefs. One of the primary purposes of a schema that we consider here is as a behavioral and conceptual *script*.

Because a schema contains an organized pattern of past experiences, we as humans draw from these experiences to interpret incoming information and determine an appropriate course of action under our newly revised schema (Fiske & Taylor, 1991). In other words, a schema helps us identify and interpret perceptions that should be important to us, allows individuals to make sense of what is going on around them by placing information in a meaningful order, facilitates interpretation of interpersonal events and interactions, and allows us to predict future events on the basis of a specific situation or various components of the situation (Fiske & Taylor, 1991; Ward, 2000b; Ward, Fon, Hudson, & McCormack, 1998). For example, if a child grows up in a conflict-filled environment with negative messages about interpersonal interaction, it will shape the way that the child, as an adult, will view social interactions. On the basis of that child's schema, he may be more likely to interpret social situations negatively and label them as conflictual. The adult is relying on his childhood interpretations and past patterns of events to understand the current situation and make certain predictions about what is likely to occur next in any given situation.

Schemas are ultimately exhibited in the form of automatic thought patterns, so that people are generally unaware of any specific schemas they are using. Early research with sex offenders concentrated on the automatic but maladaptive thought patterns, or *cognitive distortions*, as they have come to be known, presumably generated by dysfunctional cognitive schemas. A number of researchers have also looked at other concepts related to cognitive schemas in sex offenders, such as blame attributions and bias. We describe these concepts in the sections that follow and evaluate the overall schemas that have been proposed to explain various types of sex offending.

Cognitive Distortions

As stated previously, research on schemas indicates that the salient product of a cognitive schema is an automatic thought. Cognitive distortions, or maladaptive thoughts, are consistent thinking errors that occur outside of the individual's conscious awareness (Abel, Becker, & Cunningham-Rathner, 1984; Geer, Estupinan, & Manguno-Mire, 2000; Murphy, 1990; Neidigh & Krop, 1992). For sex offenders, these distortions are thoughts that generally refer to various aspects of the offending process, such as victim selection, justification, or minimization of the act itself. The distortions of sex offenders have been identified fairly frequently in diverse samples (e.g., Blumenthal, Gudjonsson, & Burns, 1999; Neidigh & Krop, 1992; Sahota & Chesterman, 1998). For example, child molesters might believe that the victim "is too young to remember this or know what I am doing" (Neidigh & Krop, 1992, p. 212), whereas adult rapists might argue that "women who are [raped] are somehow partly to blame" (Segal & Stermac, 1990, p. 163).

Researchers have offered multiple hypotheses to explain the presence of these cognitive distortions in sex offenders. Although some suggest that these thoughts reflect personal beliefs and attitudes, and are techniques for denial and rationalization to minimize the seriousness of an offense (Ward, 2000b; Segal & Stermac, 1990), others have studied these thought distortions as signs of pervasive thinking errors or maladaptive cognitive schemas (Geer et al., 2000; Ward, Fon, et al., 1998). Whether sex offenders' maladaptive cognitive beliefs are related to more deeply held ideas about victims and deviant sexual preferences still needs to be demonstrated through empirical study (Blumenthal et al., 1999; Neidigh & Krop, 1992).

Causal and Blame Attributions

One way to understand how an individual interprets and explains his behavior and the behavior of others is to examine his cognitive attributions. Two types of attributions that have been studied in individuals with sexually deviant interests and behaviors are (a) *causal attributions* and (b) *blame attributions*.

Causal attributions comprise a broad category of cognitive justifications or rationalizations, three of which are theorized to be significant in the sex offending process. The first of these, *locus of control*, describes whether the offender views his behaviors as controlled by internal or external forces (e.g., mental disorders, seduction by the victim). The second attribution, *stability*, describes behavior as either stable and consistent, or unstable and unpredictable, across time. Finally, the attribution of *controllability* refers to the sense of control that the offender feels he has over his behavior (e.g., "I just couldn't stop myself"; Geer et al., 2000; McKay, Chapman, & Long, 1996; Weiner, 1986). The important question is whether offenders endorse consistent patterns of causal attributions. The use of these attributional styles to describe an offending process would be limited if an attributional pattern could not be identified.

Researchers have suggested that each type of sex offender uses consistent attributions. Child molesters endorse internal, stable, and uncontrollable causes for their behaviors, whereas rapists endorse external, stable, and uncontrollable causes for their behaviors (McKay et al., 1996). This research indicates that child molesters have a tendency to internalize their reasons for offending, attributing it to either a mental disorder or excessive anxiety, for example, whereas rapists focus on external factors, such as victim availability or outside pressures. Both groups have also demonstrated consistent behaviors across time and a seeming inability to control their sexual impulses (McKay et al., 1996). These attributions provide evidence as to the nature of the cognitive schemas of these individuals and how they perceive the offending process. This is discussed in greater detail later in this section.

Whereas causal attributions look at how the offender perceives the world and evaluates his own behavior, blame attributions indicate the extent to which an offender blames himself or others for his actions. However, blame attributions are somewhat similar to causal attributions in that they attempt to define how offenders think about their behavior and the behavior of others. There are three primary components to blame attribution, the first two of which are very similar to causal attribution. *External attribution* looks to whether the offender blames external factors for his offense, and *mental element attribution* looks at the offender's tendency to blame mental factors (e.g., mental illness, anxiety) for his behavior. These are similar to external and internal locus of control. However, a third factor, *guilt feeling attribution*, considers whether an offender admits to feelings of guilt or remorse over his behavior (Blumenthal et al., 1999). The placement of blame is mediated by this third factor. For example, an offender who blames internal processes for his behavior would be more likely to feel guilt, shame, or remorse related to his behavior than an offender who blames outside factors. A test of this theory revealed that rapists made more external attributions for their behavior than did child molesters and that child molesters had significantly higher guilt feeling attributions than rapists (Blumenthal et al., 1999). This research suggests that there is a potential relationship between causal and blame attributions and that there might be different schemas operating to create these attributions in the two types of offenders.

Bias

The empirical literature suggests that sex offenders exhibit a number of cognitive biases in thought content, suggesting that they have a more deeply rooted belief system that contributes to their feelings of resentment and justification for their behaviors. For example, Marshall et al. (1997) hypothesized that sex offenders may be more likely to engage in a self-serving and self-protective biases because of their low self-esteem, poor attachment to others, and social anxiety. This type of bias operates by protecting the individual against perceived slights or criticisms that are potentially damaging to the individual's self-esteem or sense of self-worth. When confronted with the possibility of failure or criticism, the individual will interpret the situation, or perceive his own behavior, in a biased and self-serving way to protect feelings of self-worth.

A second bias, a belief in sexual entitlement or a kind of sexual narcissism, is characterized by the offender's belief that "satisfying his own [sexual] impulses is more important than the negative consequences for the . . . victim" (Hanson, Gizzarelli, & Scott, 1994, p. 189). In this instance, the offender feels that he is entitled to fulfill his deviant sexual desires, despite the wishes of the victim or society. Hanson et al. (1994), finding that incest offenders endorsed strong feelings of entitlement to sexual fulfillment, hypothesized that this strong sense of entitlement could lead to decreased self-control during a period of sexual arousal.

Another bias commonly found in sex offenders is in their goal-setting behavior. Ward, Fon, et al. (1998) suggested that during the offense process, sex offenders become more concrete and rigid in their thinking; are more likely to focus on narrow, lower level cognitive goals; and exhibit lesser self-awareness than when they are not in a state of deviant arousal. In other words, the sex offender, once engaged in the victimization process, is likely to bias his goal-setting behaviors by focusing on more immediate, lower level goals (e.g., preventing the victim from crying out) rather than concentrating on higher level cognitive inhibitory goals (e.g., learning to control sexual impulses without offending). The offender in this state is also likely to act impulsively and pursue somewhat thoughtless goals because of this goal-setting bias. Although the goal-setting bias may not then lead to the onset of sex-offending behaviors specifically, it can lead to the perpetuation of impulsive and aggressive acts, which for some individuals may include sex offending, or contribute to specific behaviors (e.g., coercion) during a sexually deviant act.

Finally, there is a bias among sex offenders in attentional processes. Presumably because of their underlying cognitive schemas, sex offenders are likely to pay attention to belief-consistent information and ignore information and knowledge that is inconsistent with their beliefs (Ward, Fon, et al., 1998). A sex offender exhibiting this biased thinking style will selectively attend to behaviors of potential victims that are consistent with his beliefs and ignore any incoming stimuli that would contradict them. For example, a child molester might notice a child hugging him as a sign of sexual interest and not pay attention to the child's crying because that is not consistent with his belief that this child loves him. Because of this attentional bias, sex offenders may not easily, or even be able to, internalize new information that challenges their distorted beliefs.

Cognitive Schemas in Sex Offenders

On the basis of sex offenders' cognitive distortions, blame and causal attribution styles, and types of biases, researchers have proposed that sex offenders have underlying schemas that are very different from those of non–sex offenders. For example, researchers agree that sex offenders have maladaptive attitudes or beliefs that disinhibit them (e.g., Segal & Stermac, 1990; Ward, Fon, et al., 1998) and justify their behaviors (Hanson, 1999). The beliefs and attitudes that are part of sex offenders' justificatory schemas focus on the self, the victim, and their ability to control the victimization situation or act itself (Hanson, 1999; Ward, Fon, et al., 1998; Ward, 2000b).

Ideas about one's self will impact how the offender processes or interprets incoming information about himself. The sex offender will be fairly egocentric, which is evidenced by a strong self-serving bias, with his needs and desires being paramount in driving his behaviors (Hanson, 1999; Hanson et al., 1994). This egocentricity or self-interest allows the offender to justify his deviant sexual behaviors because they satisfy his needs or build his self-esteem.

The sex offender will also see victims as deserving of their victimization (Hanson, 1999), or he may have maladaptive views of what the victim wants from the offender (Hanson, 1999; Ward, 2000b). For example, child molesters endorse a number of cognitive distortions and beliefs that are consistent with the idea that children are sexually motivated, are the ideal relationship partners, and would ultimately want to have sex with the offender (Abel et al., 1984; Hanson, 1999; Hanson et al., 1994; Segal & Stermac, 1990; Ward, 2000b). In this case, the victim is portrayed, through the lens of the offender's schema, as someone who wants to have sex with him. These beliefs disinhibit the offender and nullify evidence to the contrary, such as fear or hesitancy on the victim's part. It also allows the offender to ignore other knowledge that contradicts his schema, such as the knowledge that having sex with children is illegal. Because of the thoughts and attitudes generated by the schema, the offender may believe that his victim wants to engage in a sexual act.

The final component of the cognitive schema relates to the offender's beliefs in the controllability of the event and the extent to which internal or external factors were responsible for the sex offense (Ward, Fon, et al., 1998). A consistent tendency to blame others for the offense or to make self-statements such as "I just couldn't help myself" indicates that the offender's schema functions to negate his responsibility in making the decision to commit a sexually deviant act.

INFORMATION-PROCESSING MODELS

An information-processing model explains how an individual cognitively manipulates information, whether it be from internal cues or the environment. Such models encompass a wide range of cognitive functions that allow the individual to begin with incoming stimuli and end with a set of behaviors. The individual receives some sort of stimuli into the cognitive system, paying attention to certain stimuli more than others because of other factors such as a cognitive schema. The newly acquired information is encoded into memory, compared and contrasted with previously stored information that is relevant to the situation, and put through a complex process of matching the new information with the knowledge and beliefs contained in his cognitive schemas. Finally, the information is accessed and interpreted in such a way as to guide future behavior (Fiske & Taylor, 1991).

Two types of information-processing theories have been applied to sex offenders. The first theory posits that sex offenders have different and dysfunctional ways of interpreting social cues and lack an ability to make rational choices based on the information they receive. The second type examines the theory of mind of sex offenders and attempts to explain the oft-cited lack of empathy in sexual offenders. A *theory of mind* refers to the understanding that an individual has about his own mental states and those of others and how we perceive others and understand their perceptions during social exchanges (e.g., Keenan & Ward, 2000; Ward, 2000b). This theory suggests that sex offenders have difficulty in recognizing and interpreting the emotional states of others and cannot consider their emotional perspective when making decisions. Both of these theories are closely related to one another, but they have been separated here for ease of understanding their components.

Social Information-Processing Dysfunction

Theorists argue that the social information processes of sex offenders differ from those of non–sex-offending individuals (McFall, 1990) and that the information-processing mechanisms at work change throughout the offense cycle as sexual arousal and affective states fluctuate (Johnston & Ward, 1996; Ward, Hudson, Johnston, & Marshall, 1997). For example, the first step in a social information-processing model involves the perception and understanding of the individual. Johnston and Ward (1996) suggested that a number of biases and motivational factors are involved in determining what information is actually perceived by the individual and that limited cognitive resources force the person to use shortcuts (e.g., schemas) to perceive or acquire the incoming information. In other words, what the individual is likely to perceive is highly affected by his own previously held beliefs and attitudes, or schemas. For a sex offender, a specific belief about the sexual behavior of children might then affect how he perceives the behaviors of a child and cause him to notice things that are consistent with his own beliefs.

The second stage of the social information-processing model is the use of previously stored information in memory. Thoughts that are more important to the individual, such as sexually deviant thoughts in the case of a sex offender, will be more easily retrieved (Ward et al., 1997). Once information has been retrieved from memory, it is compared with the current incoming stimuli. The stored information can strongly bias interpretation of new information at this stage. The stimuli are likely to be interpreted according to previously formed expectancies, with ambiguous information being interpreted to align with what the individual already believes (Johnston & Ward, 1996). This process explains why sex offenders misinterpret ambiguous or innocuous information in a sex offense–supportive way. A sex offender is assumed to have certain sex-related expectancies, or sexually deviant schemas. New information is selectively attended to and interpreted in an expectancy-consistent manner. An offender against children thus might incorrectly interpret a child's affectionate hug as a sign that the child wants to engage in sexual activity, because this is consistent with his beliefs about sexual expression in children. This process may also help the offender to ignore expectancy-inconsistent information, such as the child crying or struggling to escape. The information is perceived and interpreted in a way that confirms his previously held beliefs.

The final stage of social cognition, the use of learned behavioral patterns that are consistent with the person's perceptions and interpretations of others' behaviors, explains why a pedophile, who believes that a child wants to engage in sexual activity, is likely to initiate sexual behaviors with the child. This thought pattern contributes to the sex offender thinking that sexually deviant behaviors are appropriate responses to the same or similar situations. These behaviors will themselves be integrated into the schema and social information-processing system and become automatic patterns for the offender (Johnston & Ward, 1996).

The initiation of this third step, sexually deviant behavior, involves several other skills and competencies that are inherent in the social information-processing model. Decision skills are used by the offender to generate alternatives, choose a behavioral option, and evaluate the potential outcome resulting from such behavior (McFall, 1990). These decision skills, activated during the stage at which the individual is interpreting the information, are then implemented to allow the person to choose a course of action given all of the information. However, the selection of the behavioral response depends largely on the individual's beliefs and interpretations of an event, with sex offenders' prior experiences leading them to believe that sexually deviant behaviors are appropriate.

Enactment skills, used during the behavioral response stage, allow the individual to evaluate the impact of his behavior and adapt to a changing situation (McFall, 1990). A sex offender might use these skills to interpret the victim's continuing reaction to the sex offense or make changes to his behaviors to avoid detection. These skills represent the continued interpretation of social and interactional information and the ability to adapt to a changing social interaction in a way that benefits the offender. Enactment skills have been found to be deficient in sex offenders. Racey, Lopez, and Schneider (2000) compared sex-offending and non–sex-offending adolescents and found that whereas the non–sex-offending adolescents had impairments in their abilities to interpret and perceive emotional facial expressions, sex offenders were more noticeably impaired and were more likely to misinterpret nonverbal cues. Malamuth and Brown (1994) obtained similar findings with adult rapists, confirming that they had underlying suspicious schemas that interfered with their abilities to appropriately understand the emotional expressions of women. Research also suggests that physical and sexual arousal in sex offenders lead to differential processing and cue-reading abilities. While in a sexually aroused state, the offenders' abilities to accurately read females' cues were significantly impaired (McFall, 1990), implying that there might be a relationship between processing abilities and sexual arousal. The logic is that sex-related beliefs and biases are more easily accessible in the interpretation process when the individual is in a sexually aroused state. This would affect the sex offenders' cue interpretation, decision making, and behavioral responses when sexually aroused.

Empathy and Theory of Mind

The theory of mind is central to the concept of *empathy*, the extent to which an individual can understand and relate to the emotions of another. Without empathy, the individual is likely to engage in highly egocentric and selfish behaviors (e.g., sex offending) and fail to understand the emotions and mental states of the victim (e.g., Geer et al., 2000; Marshall, Hudson, Jones, & Fernandez, 1995). According to the theory of mind, limitations in the ability to understand and perceive the emotions of others probably reflect overall limitations in understanding others' mental states.

Marshall et al. (1995) suggested that there are four stages at which empathy can be displayed: (a) emotion recognition, (b) perspective-taking, (c) emotion replication, and (d) response decision. The first two stages are crucial, because the individual must be able to recognize or acknowledge the emotional state of another person and be able to take that person's perspective, in order for the latter two stages to occur. For example, to have a mutually satisfying romantic encounter, the individual must be able to simultaneously recognize and internalize the corresponding emotional needs of others, such as what emotional responses a partner would desire (Keenan & Ward, 2000).

A great deal of evidence suggests that sex offenders have specific and marked deficiencies in the first two stages (Geer et al., 2000; Hanson &

Scott, 1995; Hudson et al., 1993). Because sex offenders might not have the ability to recognize certain emotional cues in potential victims or interpret them appropriately, their subsequent actions will not reflect empathic thinking. This will lead to the selfish or egocentric behaviors that are expected of an individual who lacks an appropriately developed theory of mind. The sex offender will be unable to relate to what his victim is feeling or experiencing, which will contribute to continued sex-offending behaviors because the offender is unable to engage in emotion replication or a rational decision-making process. As stated previously, there has been some evidence to support the supposition that sex offenders lack sufficient emotion recognition and perspective-taking skills. A theory of mind has also been tested in children with conduct disorder. These children were more likely to attribute hostile intentions to others than were children without conduct disorder (Happe & Frith, 1996), which suggests that sex offenders might also misattribute emotional states.

LIMITATIONS OF THE COGNITIVE THEORIES

Cognitive theories not only have provided a means for explaining sexually deviant behaviors but also have provided a foundation for devising some of the more successful treatments for sex-offending behaviors (e.g., Barker, 1993; Becker & Kaplan, 1993; Marques, Day, & Nelson, 1994; Marshall & Eccles, 1996; McGrath, Cumming, & Livingston, 2003; McGrath, Hoke, & Vojtisek, 1998). Despite its value for these treatment innovations, and its wide use in explaining other forms of psychopathology and problematic behavior (Barlow, 2002; Beck, 2002), there are a number of limitations when trying to rely on them for understanding sex offending.

First, the cognitive theories substantially overlap in terms of the assumed role of varying cognitive processes. Theories that focus on cognitive schemas, attachment, and information processing consider separate etiological pathways but all rely on underlying cognitive schemas or beliefs. It so far has been impossible to independently measure the components of these theories to test which best represents the appropriate cognitive causal mechanism behind sex offending. For example, regardless of whether attachment style or processing style is the key variable, our understanding of this would depend mostly on the ability to empirically measure cognitive schemas. This problem is compounded by the fact that the variables associated with information processing and cognitive schema formation (e.g., thought content, perceptual organization) have not been clearly defined. Some authors use these terms almost interchangeably (e.g., Ward, 2000b; Ward & Hudson, 2000).

Second, although there is a large body of literature speculating on the various applications of cognitive theories to sex offending, there is relatively little empirical research on sex-offender samples to support theorists' claims. It may not be accurate to assume that because non–sex-offending individuals have a specific way of processing information or rely on certain schemas that sex offenders do these things in substantially different ways. It is possible that their cognitive processes function in similar ways to those of normal individuals but that the thought content driving these processes is fundamentally different. Without research directly assessing sex offenders, it is impossible to identify whether their cognitive schemas are dysfunctional and, if so, how they are dysfunctional, or whether their information processing is fundamentally different. It also is impossible to identify which components of cognitive processing should be labeled "dysfunctional" in sex-offending samples and how these components interact with each other.

Third, because of the nature of cognitive theories, one has to rely a great deal on self-report in research. Although there are methods that would allow for indirect assessment of cognitive constructs (e.g., the Stroop task), self-report is still generally considered to be the best and most direct way to ascertain what an individual is thinking. It is not surprising, then, that the research used to test cognitive theories to date has relied almost exclusively on self-reported measures of beliefs, attitudes, and perceptions. This is a major problem because, as discussed in chapter 2 of this volume, sex offenders may be motivated to fabricate information for legal reasons (e.g., exaggerating their cognitive distortions or uttering offense-supportive statements because they wish to present themselves as having diminished responsibility for their behaviors), or social acceptability, or because of psychological dysfunction (e.g., sex offenders with little empathy might also have high rates of psychopathy, which will likely compromise the accuracy and reliability of responses). For these reasons, researchers using sex-offender samples and cognitive measures should be particularly cautious regarding conclusions based on self-reported cognitions.

Fourth, cognitive theorists assume that sex offenders have offense-supportive beliefs and attitudes, or cognitive schemas, that lead to sex-offending behaviors. However, they conclude this on the basis of knowledge that the person committed a sex offense and statements that the offender uses to explain the offense. Even if the offender believes that what he is reporting is an accurate representation of his cognitions, how do we know whether the explanation led to the crime or the crime led to a justificatory rationalization? Without longitudinal data on people who subsequently become sex offenders, we have no way of discerning the causal sequence.

Fifth, cognitive theories do not attempt to explain where the sexually deviant schemas or information-processing strategies originated. These theories make the implicit assumption that the deviant arousal and the acceptance of sexually deviant behaviors were already present in the individual. So although the theories might be useful in explaining how these deviant schemas or processing strategies can contribute to or reinforce sex offending, they do not adequately address the issue as to how the sexually deviant motivations arose in the first place. How these cognitive schemas and processes came to be sexually deviant is essential knowledge, if the goal is to understand the etiology of the sexually deviant behaviors.

Sixth, cognitive theories rely on the supposition that sex offenders have sex offense–supportive beliefs and that nonoffenders do not have these beliefs. However, literature examining negative attitudes toward women in terms of rape have not reliably demonstrated that only rapists hold these negative beliefs or endorse rape-supportive statements (e.g., Epps, Haworth, & Swaffer, 1993; Forbes & Adams-Curtis, 2001; Johnson, Kuck, & Schander, 1997). There are individuals who hold the so-called sex offense–supportive beliefs but do not commit sex offenses or engage in negative behaviors toward women. This implies that there is some other variable or set of variables driving the behavior. This finding needs to be incorporated into any cognitive theory of sex offending.

Seventh, many of the cognitive hypotheses are difficult to empirically test. This is best illustrated with the attachment models, which assume negative effects of poor childhood attachment. The primary obstacle to testing them is that, without longitudinal studies, one can measure the strength and nature of childhood attachment only through post hoc self-report or indirectly deduce the likely effect of attachment problems on deviant, sexual behaviors. An example of the latter problem can be found in Marshall's (1997) and Marshall and Mazzucco's (1995) studies. They concluded from their research that improved levels of self-esteem or self-worth and decreased levels of sexually deviant arousal were fundamentally related. It is erroneous to assume that posttreatment changes in these two variables imply a causal relationship between them. Because the treatments administered focused primarily on lowering sexual deviance, concomitant changes in self-esteem cannot be assigned a causal role without some experimental manipulation of this variable as well. They further assumed that self-reported histories of poor attachment are to blame for the pretreatment low self-esteem, with little evidence to support this idea. In addition, they did not collect control data to determine whether the relative measures of self-esteem are consistently lower than the self-esteem of people who have not committed sex offenses, which again limits the causal assumptions we can make from this research.

Eighth, early research, especially that which tested attachment theory and theory of mind, showed few differences between sex offenders and non–sex-offending inmates on cognitive measures of attributional and attachment styles (e.g., E. Baker & Beech, 2004) and the processing of socially generated interaction cues (Happe & Frith, 1996; Marshall & Mazzucco, 1995). This indicates that different cognitive styles or social processing abilities might be an artifact of offender status rather than specifically related to sex offending. In other words, it might be that certain beliefs, attitudes, and perceptual processes are different in sex offenders because they are different in all criminals. General offenders as well as sex offenders are a heterogeneous group, and many of them engage in criminogenic and antisocial thinking. For example, attachment theory might explain general aggressive patterns and hostile cognitive attributions in interpersonal relationships, but it might not explain why some aggressive individuals commit specifically sexually aggressive interpersonal acts, or even differentiate between specific sex acts among a group of offenders (e.g., Lyn & Burton, 2004). Researchers must clarify whether the cognitive processes they have identified are characteristic of sex offenders, or of offenders in general, before suggesting that they can explain sexually deviant acts.

SUMMARY AND CONCLUSIONS

Thus far, we have examined three primary classes of cognitive theories. The first of these is attachment theory, which focuses on early childhood attachments to important individuals and the later consequences of those attachments on interpersonal relationships. Researchers have proposed that sex offenders are likely to demonstrate two primary attachment styles related to their offending: (a) anxious–ambivalent attachment and (b) avoidant attachment. The next group of cognitive theories involves cognitive schemas and their relationship with behavior. Cognitive distortions, causal and blame attributions, and bias were considered as evidence of underlying schemas related to sexual offending. The last set of cognitive theories relates to information-processing models, in which social information processing and theory of mind (empathy) are discussed in relation to sex-offending individuals' ways of perceiving and interpreting incoming social information.

Several critical limitations to these theories have restricted their use and application to sex-offending samples in empirical research. Despite these limitations, the cognitive theories are useful in shaping our understanding of this population and their behaviors. Perhaps one of the most salient and basic contributions of the cognitive theories is that they bring attention to the role of individual thoughts, beliefs, and attitudes. Traditional views of offending introduced by criminologists and psychologists focused on strictly biological drives and genetic predispositions (see chap. 3) and the reinforcing properties of the offenses (see chap. 5). Here, however, we see an emphasis on the role of the self and conscious thought in the offense process, taking etiological research in a direction different from that which was inspired by other theories, such as biological and evolutionary views (see chap. 8). It allows for consideration of the individual and idiosyncratic mental processes that drive behavior.

Another positive contribution is the developmental viewpoint that is introduced in attachment theory. Few etiological conceptualizations of sex offending incorporate developmental perspectives into the formation of adult behavior. Although attachment models of sex offending may lack the complexity that is needed for a comprehensive explanation of this behavior, the idea that early and ongoing development in childhood and adolescence can critically alter adaptive (or maladaptive) interpersonal functioning in adulthood is an important one.

Last, the cognitive theories introduce the idea that core cognitive concepts, such as the cognitive worldview or schema, have the capacity to drive both deviant and nondeviant behaviors. Here we see that processes that are at work in normal, non–sex-offending individuals are also at work in sex-offending ones. These theories provide some explanation of how "normal" processes may be changed in such a way as to create deviant interests and behaviors. Deviant behaviors therefore develop in a way that is parallel to nondeviant ones, which provides a parsimonious explanation that is more appropriate for empirical examination.

5

BEHAVIORAL THEORIES

Behavioral theories, which originated with the classical and operant conditioning paradigms, initially focused on behavioral learning in animals (e.g., Pavlov, 1927; Skinner, 1932). Later research extended these theories to explain a wide range of human behaviors (e.g., Melton, 1964; Seligman & Johnston, 1973) when it was found that human learning processes could be parsimoniously explained by learning contingencies.

One such behavior is sexual deviance (Marshall & Eccles, 1993), which is generally defined in terms of *paraphilias*, or recurring fantasies, urges, or behaviors regarding sexual activity that is nonconsensual, with an age-inappropriate, nonsexual stimulus (American Psychiatric Association, 2000). This definition is based on behavioral principles, given the implied relationship between frequent thoughts and behaviors and the development of patterns of sexual arousal. There is an assumption that sexually deviant arousal plays a pivotal role in the commission of sexual crimes and that individuals who maintain sexual relationships with or sexual feelings toward inappropriate stimuli (e.g., children, animals, inanimate objects) are more likely to commit acts of sexual violence than those with appropriate sexual desires (e.g., Becker, 1998; Hunter & Becker, 1994; Lalumiere & Quinsey, 1994). Behavioral theories have been used to explain the emergence and maintenance of deviant sexual arousal and its relationship to sex offending.

In this chapter, we first explore the potential role of classical and operant conditioning in the early formation and maintenance of deviant sexual arousal and sex offending. The availability of reinforcement for sexually inappropriate behaviors and the perceived lack of aversive or negative consequences for those who engage in such behaviors are considered. We then address self-regulation and its role in establishing a pattern of sexual deviance. Behavioral self-regulation mechanisms can either facilitate or inhibit deviant sexual behavior and have been used to explain relapse or recidivism in sex offenders. When self-regulation fails, the result is the commission of sex offenses as a persistent and rewarding behavioral pattern. For this reason, some behavioral theorists suggest that sex offending has numerous similarities to other addictions (e.g., gambling, substance abuse). We conclude the chapter with a discussion of some important limitations to the use of behavioral theories to explain sexual deviance as a learned and reinforced behavior.

CLASSICAL AND OPERANT CONDITIONING EXPLANATIONS OF DEVIANT SEXUAL AROUSAL AND OFFENDING

Classical conditioning is a behavioral learning process in which a stimulus that automatically elicits a particular response is paired with a previously unrelated stimulus so that both will produce the same behavioral response. *Operant conditioning* uses reinforcement and/or punishment to strengthen or weaken a desired behavior. A specific event or stimulus that increases the desired behavior is viewed as a reinforcer of that behavior, whereas punishment results in a decrease of the behavior.

As applied to deviant sexual arousal, classical conditioning theorists posit that the nonsexual stimulus (e.g., a child, an animal) is paired with sexual arousal and then later elicits that arousal. In the operant conditioning paradigm, the theorist would argue that the behavioral response (e.g., sexual arousal) rewards the association with the nonsexual stimulus, leading to the nonsexual stimulus increasing the probability of sexual arousal. Behavioral theorists believe that classical and operant conditioning processes, begun in early childhood or adolescence, may lead to the development and maintenance of deviant sexual arousal and sex offending through a "complicated and repetitive [sequence] of desensitization, reinforcement, pairing, and generalization to become sexually aroused to deviant stimuli" (Lockhart, Saunders, & Cleveland, 1988, p. 9).

The conditioning of deviant sexual responses may occur through early sexual victimization or happenstance. In the former etiological sequence, a child who is sexually abused by an adult learns to pair sexual arousal and activity with having sexual contact with an adult as a child, or with a child when he becomes an adult. An example of the conditioning of deviant sexual responses through happenstance is when a young boy knows that his mother was watching him masturbate but experienced no negative consequences as a result. In that situation, he might pair the sexual arousal and behavior with someone watching him engage in sexual activity. This reinforcement sequence could lead to exhibitionism in later life.

Role of Reinforcement

Even though behavioral processes can create learned behaviors, the reward and punishment contingencies of operant learning will affect the success or failure of the conditioning process, including the acquisition, maintenance, or removal of inappropriate sexual desires and behaviors (Bootzin, 1975). It was originally hypothesized that the primary, and possibly only, reinforcing process behind deviant sexual arousal was sexual satisfaction itself (Marshall & Fernandez, 1998). Early masturbatory activity was paired with inappropriate fantasies, which led to the formation of deviant sexual habits as these inappropriate fantasies became strongly associated with sexual gratification (McGuire, Carlisle, & Young, 1964). In other cases, innocent early sexual experimentation that included deviant arousal to inappropriate or unusual sexual objects served as a sexual release for the individual. Thus, the child learned that he could use deviant stimuli to gain sexual satisfaction. The more these deviant behaviors continued, the more they became strengthened (e.g., Abel, Osborn, Anthony, & Gardos, 1992; McGuire et al., 1964).

These early theories were limited by the assumption that sexual release was the only salient reward for engaging in sexual deviance. Yet research has shown that many other reinforcements exist. This idea arose from a more socially constructed idea of sexual victimization, specifically in situations of rape (Herman, 1988). Men were said to gain more satisfaction from the control over their victims, or from humiliating or subjugating their victims, than from the sexual act itself. In this view, it was less a sexual need that drove the offender to commit rape than a desire to gain control over a helpless victim (e.g., Groth & Hobson, 1997; Herman, 1988).

Removal of a negative mood state, such as anxiety, depression, or low self-esteem, is another factor that can serve as a reinforcement for some sex-offending individuals. The presence of a negative mood state in offenders who have limited ability to cope with strong emotions or stress may precede the commission of a sexually deviant act (e.g., Nelson, Miner, Marques, Russell, & Achterkirchen, 1989; Ward & Hudson, 1998). The act then provides elevated mood, as a result of either sexual stimulation or increased self-esteem due to maintaining control over the situation, as discussed earlier. In this scenario, the likelihood of sexual activity being perceived as reinforcing is related to the ability of the individual to successfully cope with a negative mood state and his reliance on that ability. If alternative coping strategies are not present, then the individual will learn to rely on deviant sexual behaviors as a release mechanism (Marshall & Marshall, 2000). Generalization of the use of the deviant sexual strategy to increase one's mood can sometimes lead to the development of multiple paraphilias (Abel, Becker, Cunningham-Rathner, & Mittelman, 1988; Maletzky, 1993).

Immediate gratification has been suggested as another important reinforcing tool for the sex offender. Normal forms of sexual gratification may not provide the immediate satisfaction and mood enhancement that the individual seeks. Deviant sexual acts, if more rewarding to the person (Nelson et al., 1989), often occur in sex offenders who participate in crimes of opportunity rather than crimes that require extensive thought and planning. For these persons, it is the immediacy and excitement of the moment that are reinforcing and that make continued sexual deviance attractive (Gottfredson & Hirschi, 1990, 1993, 1994; Gottfredson & Polakowski, 1995; Hirschi & Gottfredson, 1995).

Role of Punishment

During this learning process, reinforcement of the developing sex offender can be tempered by a fear of negative consequences for engaging in deviant sexual practices. This fear should lead the individual to weigh the value of the reinforcement he is guaranteed to achieve from the deviant act against the possible negative consequences that can result from engaging in that act. Perhaps one of the most obvious concerns for a potential sex offender is the fear of being caught or punished as a result of the deviant sexual act. If a sex offender believes he will most likely be caught and subsequently punished, this may outweigh any of the reinforcing possibilities and prevent the behavior. Unfortunately, sex offenders use numerous strategies to disrupt this punishment contingency, which can account for the more than 200,000 juvenile and adult sex offenders under correctional care or supervision on any given day in the United States (Greenfield, 1997).

First, the impact of the fear of negative consequences will be affected by the offender's perception of the likelihood of being caught and punished for the offense. If the offender perceives that he has only a 50% or less chance of the sexual violence being discovered and the offender being identified, then he is unlikely to be inhibited by thoughts of negative consequences from the authorities. Such probabilistic perceptions do not have to be accurate to guide the offender's behavior. In addition, when there is not a swift negative reaction to offending behavior, regardless of the age of the offender, it may send a message to the offender that the behavior is unlikely to be noticed by the authorities. This contingency can severely limit the offender's ability to recognize the seriousness of the act and the potential societal consequences of it (Roshier, 1989; Wilson, 2003).

Second, potential offenders can increase their perceived probability of not being caught by intimidating or coercing their victim into silence with threats of future harm to the victim or his or her family (e.g., Kaufman, Hilliker, Lathrop, & Daleiden, 1996). Such intimidation or coercion is often successful with child victims (Kaufman, Hilliker, Lathrop, & Daleiden, 1993). This may include anything from verbal threats to actual demonstrations of physical harm that would be continued if the crime were reported to authorities. In doing this, the offender perceives he has safely guaranteed the silence of his victim, which would limit the possibility of detection and prosecution.

Third, fantasy may be a significant contributor to the either real or perceived lack of negative consequences for sexually deviant desires or behaviors. For example, sexual fantasy can allow the individual to successfully engage in deviant sexual impulses (e.g., masturbating while fantasizing about young children) without engaging in the corresponding deviant and criminal act of child molestation (American Psychiatric Association, 2000). Because the sexual interactions are limited to the imagination of the offender, they are unknown or unavailable to concerned others and therefore are not subject to negative appraisal (Dwyer, 1990). In addition, when the individual fantasizes about inappropriate sexual behaviors, he may discontinue the fantasy after the reward (e.g., sexual satisfaction) and not consider the negative consequences (e.g., victim harm, legal action) stemming from such behavior (Dwyer, 1990). In other words, not only has the individual reinforced his sexual desires, but also the narrow content of his fantasy may make him less cognizant of the negative consequences resulting from such behaviors.

Fourth, individuals with deviant sexual arousal may be able to desensitize themselves to the upsetting feelings associated with sexual offending, such as guilt, remorse, or victim empathy (Lockhart et al., 1988). Whereas normal individuals show concern for the feelings of others, many sex offenders become less sensitive to the suffering of the victim over time and no longer experience guilt or suffering as aversive contingencies that follow the deviant behavior (Rice, Chaplin, Harris, & Coutts, 1994). This lack of empathy may be further exacerbated by the degree to which the individual is psychopathic or has antisocial personality disorder, which is discussed at greater length in chapter 7 of this volume.

Fifth, prevailing social conditions may decrease the probability that sexually deviant individuals will receive harsh punishments or consequences for their behaviors. Greater societal tolerance of male antisocial behavior may lead to greater acceptance of an early offender's behavior, thereby distorting the offender's perceptions of the likelihood of negative consequences (Herman, 1988). This early societal permissiveness is rationalized under the logic that the juvenile deviant behavior was harmless experimentation that the juvenile will grow out of. Dismissing possibly harmful sexual behaviors with a "boys will be boys" explanation could have serious consequences for the future, because youth need to be reinforced or punished for their behaviors. Because of these prevalent societal perceptions of youthful sexual behavior, even recent legislative changes aimed at this offender population (e.g., juvenile registration, community notification) may not be sufficient to deter offending behaviors. Without proper correction early on, it is possible that young male offenders will see this behavior as acceptable and less likely to be punished by society at large.

In sum, the occurrence of continued deviant sexual behavior depends on the importance of reinforcement and punishment contingencies relevant to both deviant and normal behaviors. For example, a significant number of reinforcements for deviant sexual behavior, paired with a lack of reinforcements for appropriate behavior and further complicated by the perceived lack of negative reprisal or aversive consequences for the deviant behavior, will increase the likelihood that sex offending will continue. Fantasy and masturbation may strengthen the reward value of the sexual deviance and at the same time shield the individual from public scrutiny. Other reinforcers may also play a large role in maintaining the sexually deviant behavior. However, if the negative consequences of the behavior are sufficiently strong and salient that they do present great risk to the offender and/or lead to empathy for the victim, then the deviant sexual behavior is less likely to reoccur.

SELF-REGULATION PROCESSES AND DEVIANT SEXUAL AROUSAL AND OFFENDING

Self-regulation theory has been applied to sexually deviant behaviors because the goals of sexual satisfaction, mood regulation (Erber & Erber, 2001), or other reward systems related to sexual deviance can affect recall, judgment, and information processing. According to self-regulation theory, sexually deviant goals and corresponding strategies will be incorporated into the automatic behavioral processes of the sex offender because they have been successful in eliciting reinforcements in the past. Self-regulation processes can enhance, maintain, elicit, or inhibit certain behaviors (Ward & Hudson, 1998).

Self-regulation involves the selection of goals by the individual and the search for ways to achieve those goals through a series of cognitive and behavioral processes. These internal and external processes allow the individual to participate in goal-directed behavior consistently over time and across situations (Ward, 2000a). Specifically, self-regulation is a process through which an individual recognizes the need for approach or avoidance goals relevant to specific situations or contexts, modifies his or her behavior to be consistent with achieving these goals, and then adopts the resulting behaviors through a feedback loop as an automatic behavioral process that soon operates without conscious control. Carver and Scheier (2001) viewed these new behaviors as the embodiment of feedback processes.

In the learning process, there are two primary feedback loops through which one may acquire information or ways of behaving. One of these is a *negative feedback loop*, in which deviations from the normal system are minimized and internal behavior recognition mechanisms reorganized to restore the system to a state of proper functioning. In a *positive feedback loop*, the deviation or behavior is amplified by the perceived mechanism of change rather than corrected by it (Watzlawick & Beavin, 1967). In this process, the positive feedback loops will maintain the system and its deviations or present states of learning and response, whereas the negative feedback loop will operate to change some process and bring about a new learned response. To accomplish one's goals, the individual engages in goal setting at various levels of a hierarchy of positive and negative feedback loops (Nelson, 1993).

These feedback loops often use reinforcement contingencies similar to those in a conditioning learning model. These reinforcements may affect not only the direction of the feedback loop but also the intensity of the learning or self-stabilization process. For the behavior to be internalized in a self-regulatory manner, the person's perception of the reward affects behavior (Carver & Scheier, 2001). If a reward is perceived as more likely after a specified goal-oriented behavior, then the behavior is more likely to be included in self-regulatory learning. The same process applies to perceptions of negative consequences. This will occur regardless of whether the goal is related to approach or avoidance of certain situations. However, regulatory failure may be attributed to the failure of these feedback mechanisms to shape involuntary behavioral responses (Tomie, 1996).

Although self-regulation was first used to explain fairly basic learning and response patterns, the theory has been broadened to include more complex behaviors. Recent literature has considered the behavioral learning process behind sexual deviance as a self-regulatory one, with the sex-offending individual modifying his behavior and internalizing sexually deviant automatic behavioral patterns in a number of ways.

Three different pathways have been proposed to explain the incorporation of sexual deviance into an individual's self-regulation mechanisms: (a) underregulation, (b) misregulation, and (c) intact regulation (Ward, Hudson, & Keenan, 1998). The first of these, *underregulation*, suggests that the offender lacks the ability to incorporate avoidance or inhibitory goals into his behavioral patterns. Thus, the regulation system is not fully successful. The research literature suggests that inhibitory goals are much more difficult to achieve (Ward, 2000a; Ward & Hudson, 1998), because the positive reinforcements for sex offending behaviors are more prevalent or salient than the negative consequences. In other words, because the behavior is more likely to be seen as an effective mechanism through which to achieve a goal, it is more difficult for the offender to maintain avoidance or inhibitory goals toward the deviant behavior. The underregulation of avoidance or inhibitory goals will lead to the development and implementation of approach goals, or the inappropriate desires to commit sexually deviant acts.

Misregulation involves the use of effective strategies to achieve specified goals, but the goals have somehow backfired and resulted in a loss of control for the individual (Ward, 2000a). Here, the offender tries to use his coping mechanisms to achieve appropriate sexual satisfaction or an appropriate means of mood stimulation, but these methods fail, and the offender then turns to practically anything that will return him to homeostasis. Stress has a major impact on the self-regulatory process (Ward, Hudson, & Keenan, 1998), in that high levels of stress paired with poor coping abilities will make appropriate self-regulated responses less likely to occur. For example, a pedophile may know that society disapproves of his sexual desire for children, and he has learned that adult partners are a more appropriate outlet for sexual desire. However, in times of stress, he may not be able to successfully approach an adult partner, and the system fails. Therefore, the offender knows that he will remove a negative mood state as well as achieve sexual satisfaction if he commits a sexual crime against a child. Here, the self-regulatory system has not been strong enough to withstand the emotional or sexual desire. So although the appropriate mechanisms and knowledge exist in the individual, they are not always successful and may lead to regulatory failure.

In the third sexual-offense pathway in this model, *intact regulation*, the self-regulatory system is working, and there does not appear to be any failure of the process, but the individual has internalized inappropriate approach and avoidance goals. This may involve the conditioning or autoshaping of involuntary sexual responses (e.g., arousal at an inappropriate stimulus) and the use of these responses as approach goals (Tomie, 1996). The use of sexually deviant goals may create a warped self-regulatory system in which the offender believes maintaining arousal at any cost is an appropriate approach goal and avoiding detection by authorities is an appropriate avoidance goal. In this process, the offender has an intact self-regulatory system, but the goals have been poorly and inappropriately defined.

ADDICTION PROCESSES AND DEVIANT SEXUAL AROUSAL AND OFFENDING

The addiction model has been broadly applied to a number of psychological and behavioral responses that occur in a repetitive and compulsive manner. A great deal of research literature in the past several decades has attempted to explain the mechanisms behind addiction and clarify how behavior can reach a point where it appears uncontrollable and compulsive (Shaffer, 1994). One of the most common explanations involves a variety of behavioral factors such as artificial removal of negative states and response expectancies linked to the substance of abuse. In this explanation, the individual is confronted by a negative emotional state (e.g., anger, stress) with which he is unable to cope (Lundy, 1994; Marlatt, Baer, Donovan, & Kivlahan, 1988). A foreign substance, such as a narcotic, may be used initially to artificially remove this negative mood state. Once this occurs, the individual experiences a subjective feeling that the negative emotional state is removed, which is followed by pleasant associations. These associations are then paired with the substance of abuse, leading to a conditioned response (Marlatt et al., 1988).

Another important factor in this addiction formation process is the interpretation of certain cues to form expectancies. If an addict believes that the substance abuse will continue to reduce negative emotional states, this belief will help shape his response toward his ability to self-regulate emotional states as well as toward the substance's ability to change a negative emotional state (Marlatt et al., 1988). Addiction decreases the person's ability to rely on internal self-coping mechanisms to solve psychological distress (Pearson & Little, 1969) and drives him to use substances for rapid relief. This further contributes to the strengthening of the association between the substance of abuse and release from anxiety or stress.

Because the addiction process seems centralized around a behavioral conditioning process in the individual, rather than a specific addictive property of substances themselves, the concept of addiction has expanded to include not only illicit substances but also other areas of concern such as overeating, gambling, and excessive sexual behavior. It is not surprising that sex addiction mirrors addiction to illicit substances in a number of ways.

First, sexual addictions or compulsions are marked by the lack of control that is noted in the addictive processes for alcohol and other drugs. This loss of control is often central to defining a sex addiction (Barth & Kinder, 1987; Carnes, 1983, 1990; Gold & Heffner, 1998; Herman, 1988). Second, sex addicts often continue their behavior despite the negative consequences that often stem from it, such as deterioration of close relationships, unwanted pregnancies, sexually transmitted diseases, or involvement with the legal system (Carnes, 1990; Gold & Heffner, 1998; Lundy, 1994). Third, much like persons addicted to other substances or activities, sex addicts use sexual behavior to escape from negative emotional states such as loneliness, anger, and stress (Earle, Earle, & Osborn, 1995; Goodman, 1992; Lundy, 1994). Finally, sex addicts may become habituated to their sexual behaviors, needing an increased "fix" to maintain the same arousal pattern from the behavior over time (Carnes, 1983, 1990, 1994; Gold & Heffner, 1998; M. F. Schwartz & Brasted, 1985).

This last feature explains why sex addiction can lead to repeated sex offending. A study conducted by G. Blanchard (1990; cited in Carnes, 1994) reported that 55% of sex offenders overall were defined as having features of sex addiction, with 71% of pedophiles and 38% of rapists reporting the symptoms associated with sex addiction. Not all sex addicts commit illegal sexual acts, but because a substantial number of sex offenders merit labeling as sex addicts, there might be a link between these patterns of behavior (Carnes, 1990).

Some researchers believe that sex offenders who are also sex addicts use and internalize these deviant behaviors as a way to cope with distressing emotions (i.e., removal of negative emotional states; Barth & Kinder, 1987; Earle et al., 1995; Gold & Heffner, 1998; Lundy, 1994). However, because not all sex addicts engage in such behavior, there must be more to it than simply a desire for increased emotional regulation. The tolerance effect observed in some sex addicts may lead to an increase or escalation in sexual behavior, with each sex act becoming progressively worse and more disruptive to functioning, eventually leading to illegal sexual activities. Carnes (1983) proposed three progressive levels of sexual behavior: (a) *victimless sexual behaviors* such as excessive masturbation, use of pornography, and intense use of sexual fantasy; (b) *illegal yet anonymous sexual behaviors* such as exhibitionism, voyeurism, telephone scatalogia, and use of prostitutes or prostitution; and (c) *victimizing offenses* such as child molestation and rape. Proponents of these steps advocate the idea that sex addiction can evolve into sex offending when appropriate or current patterns of sexual behavior are no longer sufficient to elicit prior levels of sexual or emotional satisfaction (Carnes, 1983, 1990; Herman, 1988; M. F. Schwartz & Brasted, 1985). These researchers further hypothesize that, over time, conventional intercourse or sexual behaviors at lower levels of the continuum will be perceived as undesirable, and the individual will be conditioned to prefer deviant stimuli.

Finally, several additional factors relate to the individual's functioning prior to this behavior addiction process that may mediate his progression through the levels of sexual behavior mentioned previously. First, dehumanizing sexual attitudes and the sexualization of others are important (Earle et al., 1995). When the individual already has the tendency to view others as sexual objects, it can speed his progression from victimless sex acts to sexual victimization of others. Second, when sexual obsession and fantasy are used as primary coping strategies, the individual is less likely to have other available alternatives to deal with stress, anxiety, or anger (Carnes, 1990; Shaffer, 1994). This lack of alternatives and dominance of inappropriate coping strategies limits the individual to sexual behaviors as a primary coping strategy. Finally, some sex addicts are characterized by a persistent desire for self-destructive or high-risk behaviors, which will increase the likelihood that they will receive consistent stimulation from inappropriate sexual behaviors (Carnes, 1990; Gold & Heffner, 1998).

In sum, because of the behavioral learning processes behind addiction, it is reasonable to assume that sex addiction follows a behavioral conditioning process. The individual copes with negative emotions by engaging in risky and excessive sexual behaviors. Furthermore, there is some evidence to support the idea that certain traits or symptoms of sex addiction might increase the likelihood of sex offending, creating an addiction to sexually inappropriate behaviors over time.

LIMITATIONS OF THE BEHAVIORAL THEORIES

There are a number of limitations to these behavioral theories. First and foremost, although the theories might explain how the behaviors are reinforced over time, there is little discussion in the literature as to how the deviant stimuli were presented initially and why interest in them occurred. Although it has been theorized that sexually deviant interests result from sexual experimentation or even early sexual victimization, this is not characteristic of all sex offenders' backgrounds. Behavioral theories also do not adequately explain why some individuals with early deviant sexual experience fail to be reinforced by the event. Furthermore, they exclude any explanation as to why so many sex offenders lack deviant sexual arousal patterns on measures of sexual interest or share arousal patterns similar to those of normal, non–sex-offending men (e.g., Looman & Marshall, 2005). This also limits our ability to generalize the deviant arousal patterns of some sex offenders to broader mechanisms of reinforcement in all such offenders.

Second, we do not know what combination of reinforcers or negative consequences are necessary to either maintain or eliminate deviant sexual behavior. Post hoc explanatory analyses do not necessarily provide accurate causal explanations for the deviant behavior; neither do they provide accurate predictive models. Although the literature supplies possible learning contingencies to explain the deviant behaviors, this research has been based on post hoc analyses once the sex offense has already been committed. There is no research that has predicted which reinforcing or punishing contingencies are likely to be causally predictive of sex offending in any given situation. For example, prison might serve as a very powerful negative consequence for some persons but be irrelevant for others. Behavioral theories do not explain why.

Third, there is limited discussion in the behavioral literature on the effect of mediators and moderators on the development of sexually deviant arousal and behavior. *Mediators*—factors that may change throughout the course of learning, such as social support for nonoffending behavior, level of supervision, and access to victims—are likely to play a significant role in learning or avoiding sexually deviant behavior. *Moderating variables*—pre-existing conditions that might affect the offending, such as cognitive processes, victim empathy, and conflict between physical desires and moral values—play a significant role in determining the extent of one's likelihood to engage in deviant sexual behavior patterns. For example, some individuals have more empathy or emotional feeling for victims than others. The extent of victim empathy or capability of remorseful feelings will affect an offender's likelihood of adopting patterns of sexual offense. If an individual has no empathy, as occurs with severe psychopathy (Hare, 1999), then that person will be more likely to engage in or continue sexually inappropriate behaviors than someone who felt immensely remorseful over his sexually deviant proclivities and sorry for his victims. The behavioral paradigm disregards the important role that these mediating and moderating factors play in the learning process and the continuance of sex offending behaviors.

Fourth, there is an assumption that individuals are susceptible to and influenced by the threat of negative consequences. Beccaria (1764/1963) first proposed the idea of punishment as a deterrent in the 18th century. Much like the behavioral theorists of today, he and many later criminologists assumed that the presence of a punishment would serve as specific deterrent for an individual's criminal propensities. However, the empirical research has not supported this notion, which is what we should logically expect. The three elements necessary for deterrence to work (i.e., swiftness, certainty, and severity), are not always present in the today's legal system. Therefore, a sex offender may not consider the punishments to which he would be subjected as a deterrent. A behavioral learning explanation that uses correctional punishment as a learning contingency is unlikely to be accurate.

Fifth, cognitive explanations of sexually inappropriate behaviors and deviant arousal have received recent attention in the sex-offender literature (see chap. 4). The idea that automatic thought processes and cognitive rationalizations significantly contribute to sex offending cannot be discounted. Expectancy and motivation explanations, such as those that focus on self-regulatory processes, are also underestimated in many of the behavioral models even though, as we argued earlier, they are logically related. If some individuals are more cognitively motivated to offend or to not offend than others, then it is an obvious failing of the behavioral theories to ignore these processes.

Sixth, there is criticism related to the definitions provided in current views of self-regulation in the offense process. Various researchers have conceptualized self-regulation theory only in terms of establishing behavioral goals (e.g., Ward, 2000a; Ward & Hudson, 1998). However, an extensive literature describes self-regulation in terms of its impact on emotional responding, development of adaptive or maladaptive strategies, and interpersonal functioning (e.g., Baumeister & Vohs, 2004; Gross, 1998, 1999a, 1999b; Linehan, 1993a). Within this literature, establishing regulatory goals is seen as only one of several components of self-regulation. Furthermore, this literature also adopts a developmental perspective on self-regulatory strategies, providing a more comprehensive explanation for how individuals learn and incorporate environmental stimuli over time to drive their goal-setting and regulatory behaviors. Any etiological theory incorporating self-regulatory mechanisms must include this developmental perspective and broaden its definitions of self-regulatory functioning in order to adequately explain the phenomena of interest.

Finally, addiction-based explanations of sexual deviance contain some degree of associational error. Not all sex addicts escalate to the point where they are sex offenders, and not all sex offenders are sex addicts. Although some factors may predispose certain sex addicts to engage in sexually inappropriate and deviant behaviors, we are unsure of protective or aggregating factors that may affect this process, and we are unaware of all the underlying processes that might affect such behavior. Additionally, sex addiction is not recognized in the research or clinical literature as a valid or reliable psychological diagnosis of behavior. Until the term and the reported symptoms of this construct are better defined, our understanding of the possible relationship between sex offending and sexual compulsivity will remain limited.

SUMMARY AND CONCLUSIONS

Behavioral theories of sex offending fall into several categories. The first theories discussed here are based on the principles of classical and operant conditioning. This includes the roles of reinforcement and punishment contingencies in the formation and maintenance of behavior. We have addressed a number of potential outcomes that may be viewed as either reinforcing or punishing, depending on the context. A second type of behavioral theory involves self-regulatory functioning and the achievement of behavioral goals. Last, we described the way in which addiction models have been applied to the development of sexually deviant behaviors.

The criticisms outlined in the preceding section of this chapter identify important limitations to the etiological application of these theories. However, efforts to use stringent behavioral explanations for sex offending have presented several advantages, which cannot be ignored. For one, the powerful role of reinforcement is undoubtedly at work in this process, just as it is to some extent in nearly all learned or continued behavior. The biological and cognitive theories, as well as others discussed later in this book, do not give sufficient credit to the reinforcing properties of sexual satisfaction, interpersonal interactions, and other internal or external stimuli that may be seen as a desirable consequence of sexual behavior. Future etiological theories must include the role of reinforcement and provide explanations that differentiate the potential reinforcements present at each stage of development of sexually deviant interests and behaviors.

A second and related point that we gain from the behavioral theories is that a critical balance of reinforcement and punishment is a necessary component of the process. It is not enough that the behavior is reinforcing; we know from operant conditioning models that potential reinforcement must be considered in light of potential punishment. Also, although we are able to identify a number of punishments as well as reinforcements that may be related to sex offending, we are unable to predict which reinforcements will outweigh the punishments, and vice versa. Despite our inability to pinpoint these relationships in the current etiological and empirical literature, they should be included and addressed in future theoretical efforts.

A final advantageous component of the behavioral theories is related to the self-regulation model presented earlier. Recent literature has implicated self-regulation and self-regulatory mechanisms in the development of a variety of adaptive and maladaptive behaviors, including emotional modulation, achievement, interpersonal functioning, eating, crime, and self-injurious behavior (e.g., Baumeister & Vohs, 2004; Linehan, 1993a). Although we have described several limitations of the current self-regulation literature in relation to sex offending, recognition of the role of this fundamental human process is vital to our understanding of complex processes such as sexual interest and behavior.

6

SOCIAL LEARNING THEORIES

Social learning theory first appeared in the psychological and socio-logical literature in an attempt to explain the process through which indi-viduals may model or imitate observed actions and then incorporate these actions into their own behavioral repertoire (Akers, 1985; Bandura, 1969a, 1977). According to this theory, the individual observes certain behaviors in others, learns the reactions to and consequences of such behavior, and then later imitates these behaviors to achieve the same desired result (Bandura, 1969a).

Social learning theory has been used to explain conforming, appropri-ate behaviors as well as criminal and sexually deviant ones. We open this chapter with a discussion of social learning theory as it applies to a broad spectrum of behaviors and then address the two primary social learning hy-potheses that have been advanced as potential explanations for sex-offending behaviors. The first, the *abused–abuser hypothesis*, posits that some sexually abused children model the actions of their abusers and become sex offenders themselves in later life. The second hypothesis assumes that violent sexually explicit materials serve as models for deviant sexual behaviors for budding sex offenders and reinforce their deviant sexual impulses. The chapter con-cludes with a critical analysis of each of these social learning hypotheses and a discussion of the limitations of the research.

SOCIAL LEARNING THEORY

As just noted, the basic premise underlying social learning theory is that particular behaviors can be acquired through vicarious observation and subsequent modeling of the observed behavior. Early evaluation of this theory demonstrated that young children learned both positive and negative moral judgments and behavioral patterns through modeling or imitating others whom they trusted and respected (Bandura, 1969b). These effects were consistent across learning scenarios and developmental levels, implying that the initiation of behaviors could be attributed to viewing and internalizing the actions of others.

The social acquisition of learned behaviors depends on a variety of factors, however. Bandura (1977) postulated that three components affect the primary internalization of a given behavior and the later likelihood of an individual actually initiating the behavior. First, the *characteristics of the models* play a significant role. In general, the models must be trusted or revered figures or in some way close to the observing person (e.g., parents of the child). In other words, individuals are more likely to imitate the behavior of a model to whom they strongly relate. Second, the *actual behavior observed* plays an important role. The behavior that a person observes must be in some way similar to other previously learned behaviors. A very obedient and conforming child, for example, might not respond to very aggressive and inappropriate modeled behavior. More moderate behaviors, or those that are not overly extreme in either direction, are most likely to be adopted by the observer. Third, the *observed consequences of the behavior* also impact the probability that the behavior will be imitated later. We expand more on this idea throughout the chapter. Behavioral learning principles (see chap. 5, this volume) are helpful in understanding whether the observed behavior will be learned. If the individual views immediate negative consequences for the modeled behavior, then he will be less likely to engage in that behavior at some later point. However, if there are positive consequences, or simply a lack of negative reaction, then the modeled behavior might appear more attractive or beneficial. The combination of these three factors—model identity, type of behavior, and observed reactions—determines whether the modeled behavior will later be initiated by the target individual.

Social learning approaches have been extensively applied to learned criminal behaviors (Akers, 1985, 1998). Akers (1998) suggested that there are criminal models for deviant behaviors and conforming models for appropriate or noncriminal behaviors. Because they share the same learning pathway, the same principles mentioned previously therefore apply to learned criminal behaviors. The characteristics of the observed models, the extremity of the behavior, and observed consequences all play a role. However, some additional factors must also be considered in the social learning process for deviant behaviors. Specifically, some criminal behaviors may be learned and imitated through four mechanisms: (a) the incorporation of criminal definitions, (b) the differential effects of reinforcements for criminal versus conforming behaviors, (c) peer associations and family interactions, and (d) stimulus discrimination or generalization (Akers, 1998).

First, an individual who chooses to engage in a specific behavior will generally acknowledge certain beliefs or definitions that are favorable toward or in support of that behavior. If an individual holds strong beliefs or definitions that would oppose some specific activity, he will be less likely to perform the behavior or approve of others who support that activity. One who strongly believes that stealing is a reprehensible act is less likely to engage in shoplifting than one who believes that he is entitled to take things from others who are more fortunate. The definitions learned through contact with others or observation of others' behaviors will thereby shape the later actions of that individual.

Second, if the observed incentives for criminal behavior outweigh or appear more salient than the observed incentives for conforming to noncriminal standards, then it is more likely that criminal behaviors will be internalized and imitated. Even someone who believes that stealing is morally reprehensible might agree to it if guaranteed a substantial benefit greater than can be obtained through legitimate means. However, it is not only the negative or positive consequences of criminal behavior, or the consequences or outcomes of conforming behavior, that singly shape a person's behavior. It is the balance between them in the immediate situation, including the relevance of the goals, salience of the consequences, and importance of the outcome, that determines the individual's response.

Third, somewhat related to the identity and characteristics of the observed person are the roles of family and peer interactions. Theories of differential association (Sutherland & Cressey, 1966) posit that associating with criminals or deviant individuals will lead one to adopt criminal or deviant definitions, values, or behaviors. In essence, watching a trusted peer or family member would lead one to engage in activities similar to those of that person and to approve of that person's actions. If those activities are deviant or criminal, then the observer is more likely to adopt similar tendencies.

However, there may be another learning component to family or peer associations. It might be that an individual in a highly deviant or dysfunctional family may not learn other, nondeviant ways of behaving in response to the environment. If a young child becomes accustomed to violence as a response to frustration, then he might never learn other ways of coping with frustration or negative emotional states. The behavior of the family is thus the only source of information that the individual has, early on, from which to learn appropriate responses. Others that are introduced later might not be as powerful as these early childhood models.

Finally, stimulus discrimination and generalization play a role in the learning process (Akers, 1998). *Stimulus discrimination* is the mechanism through which an individual is able to differentiate separate characteristics of two or more stimuli. *Stimulus generalization* is the process through which an individual learns to apply the rules of one situation or stimulus to similar situations or stimuli. A young child may display stimulus discrimination when he learns that not all animals are called dogs, that some are cats, bears, and so on. Stimulus generalization may be shown by that same child when he observes that slapping a dog may lead it to bite, and he then infers that slapping other dogs may lead them to bite in the same manner.

For criminal or deviant behaviors, social learning theory incorporates stimulus discrimination and generalization processes as well. For example, a delinquent youth may observe that his friends are more or less likely to be caught robbing a house in one neighborhood than another. That same youth may also generalize the knowledge that his friend carries a weapon in one robbery and uses it as an effective threat, so that now he knows that carrying a weapon can be used as a threat in any situation.

Social learning theory can therefore be successfully used to explain the acquisition and maintenance not only of conforming or appropriate behaviors but also of deviant and inappropriate ones. Through relationships with others, an individual may learn certain ways of behaving and use this knowledge to shape his own values, beliefs, and actions. Peer and family associations also dictate how a person will learn to conduct himself in the world. If the observed actions of others are negative or deviant, then the resulting behaviors of the observer will likely be the same.

THE ABUSED–ABUSER HYPOTHESIS

Some researchers have taken social learning hypotheses of criminal learning and applied them to more specific types of learning, such as sexual deviance. Given the large number of children who are sexually abused each year in the United States (e.g., Becker, 1988; Berliner & Elliot, 2002; Finkelhor, 1994), it is not surprising that some have considered the impact of the abuse on social learning processes and sexually deviant interests. In accordance with the *victim-to-victimizer* or *abused–abuser hypothesis*, some researchers have surmised that a small percentage of children, after being sexually abused, will go on to sexually abuse others as adults or as older adolescents, because they have now learned sexually deviant patterns of arousal (Burgess, Hartman, & McCormack, 1987; Burton, Miller, & Shill, 2002; Freeman-Longo, 1986; Freund & Kuban, 1994; Garland & Dougher, 1990; G. Ryan, 2002). However, although there is fairly good evidence to support the fact that most children who are sexually abused do not go on to become offenders as adults (e.g., the disproportionate number of women who were victimized as children; Berliner & Elliot, 2002; Putnam, 2003), there is still a large percentage of sex offenders who report that they were sexually abused as children (Becker, 1988; Craissati, McClurg, & Browne, 2002; Graham, 1996; Jonson-Reid & Way, 2001; Seghorn, Prentky, & Boucher, 1987; Veneziano, Veneziano, & LeGrand, 2000; Worling, 1995; Zgourides, Monto, & Harris, 1997), implying that some sexually abused children do become sex offenders in adolescence or adulthood. It is interesting that the numbers of victims who later become perpetrators are disproportionately male.

Researchers have focused on these particular offenders, suggesting that something in the way that they interpreted or perceived their own abuse impacted them differently as adults. So although some victims of sexual abuse may learn deviant sexual behavior patterns from their own abusive experiences, perhaps the more relevant question in regard to social learning theory is, What aspect or aspects of the abusive experience contributed to this learning pathway?

The abused–abuser hypothesis has been advanced by a number of researchers to explain this process. Using a social learning framework, these researchers have identified not only the process through which this learning occurs but also several key variables that help to determine whether sexually deviant behavioral patterns will likely be adopted or learned by the individual victim.

The first stage in this process is understandably the occurrence of sexual abuse and the resulting cognitive explanations devised by the victim. A sexually abusive act occurs against a child or adolescent, and he makes various cognitive inferences about the event and its causes and may create a belief system or cognitive schema to help explain his abuse. Several different types of thought patterns might be more conducive to the vicarious learning of sexual arousal related to sexual abuse, such as (a) "This must be normal"; (b) "This isn't harmful, because someone I trust is doing this to me"; or (c) "This is pleasurable in some way" (Briggs & Hawkins, 1996; Burton et al., 2002; Eisenman, 2000; Freeman-Longo, 1986; Hummel, Thomke, Oldenburger, & Specht, 2000). A child who views his abuse experience as normal is more likely to adopt a belief system or definitions that are favorable to sexually deviant interests. The child may grow into an adult who views sexually abusive acts as less harmful and more pleasurable to the victim. Thus, how the child or adolescent victim initially perceives the abuse significantly shapes whether he learns sexually inappropriate behavioral patterns and later acts on them.

The second stage of this process includes a number of factors that are vital to the social learning of sexually deviant behavior. Burton et al. (2002) and Garland and Dougher (1990) addressed each of these factors in detail, and their findings are briefly summarized here. The first of these is the *age of the victim*. If the victim is very young at the initiation of the sexual abuse, then he might be more impressionable and easily adopt observed behaviors through social learning. Furthermore, the child might not be fully aware of normative customs or socially accepted behaviors at a very young age, and therefore he would be less likely to understand the sexual abuse as harmful, especially if the perpetrator of the abuse normalizes the experience.

A second factor is the *relationship between the victim and the offender*. As mentioned earlier in this chapter, the relationship between the observer and the behavioral model plays an important role in the learning process. A similar rule applies in the case of sexually deviant learning. If the victimizer or abuser is someone known to and trusted by the victim, then the abusive behavior has a greater chance of being examined, learned, and later enacted by the victim. This process may also interact with cognitive explanations or normalization of the abuse (e.g., "If my dad is doing this, and he loves me, it is probably okay"). Consequently, sexual abuse by someone unknown to the child or someone whom the child does not trust or respect is less liable to result in modeled sexual deviance.

A third factor is the *type of sexual act* and the *amount of force* used also assist in the learning or modeling of the abusive behavior for some victims. The force or brutality involved in the sexually abusive act may shape the imprinting or learning of the behavior, in that the victim is simply more likely to pay attention to and have strong emotional reactions toward physically harmful or forceful experiences. Researchers in this area have suggested that because some sexually abused youth lack appropriate ways of resolving especially traumatic abuse experiences, they resolve it through reenacting the abuse itself and inflicting similar harm on others (Burton et al., 2002; Graham, 1996). This is somewhat supported by research evidence indicating that many sex offenders who report childhood histories of sexual abuse are more likely to commit sex acts (e.g., sodomy) that were part of their own abusive experience (Veneziano et al., 2000).

A fourth factor is the *sex of the perpetrator*. Victimization by a male offender seems to increase the likelihood of learning sexually deviant interests or behaviors (Burton et al., 2002; Garland & Dougher, 1990; Kobayashi, Sales, Becker, Figueredo, & Kaplan, 1995). A male victim of sexual abuse may be more likely to model his own sexual behaviors after the patterns demonstrated by men in his life, including the perpetrator of the abuse. The effects of victimizer sex on social learning mechanisms may be due to several underlying factors, such as the use of more force by male offenders; the societal shame associated in cases of male–male sexual abuse, which may prevent victims from reporting their abuse and thereby dealing with it; or more excessive and harmful types of sexual acts, which might have a greater traumatic impact. Regardless of the reason, sexual victimization by a male adult against a male victim increases the strength of sexual deviance as a learned behavior when combined with these other factors.

A fifth factor is the *duration of the abuse* understandably plays a large role in the reinforcement and learning of sexually deviant behaviors. If the abuse occurs over a more extended period of time, then the victim has more opportunities to observe the abusive behaviors and the rewards (or punishments) experienced by the offender. Furthermore, the abused child may develop emotional or social ties to the offender (Garland & Dougher, 1990; Hummel et al., 2000), thus increasing the normalization of the abusive acts. In other words, if the victim becomes emotionally attached to the offender, then the victim may gradually learn to accept the offender's behavior as appropriate or justifiable in some way.

Finally, the number of perpetrators may also play a role in the victim's understanding of and reactions to the sexual abuse. Victimization by more than one person may reinforce the belief that this is a normal experience or that the victim has somehow asked for or deserved the abuse (Freeman-Longo, 1986). If the abuse occurs by multiple perpetrators, then the victim may begin to model or imitate these behaviors, not simply because of their frequency but also because of these beliefs associated with them.

The third stage of the process in terms of the abused–abuser hypothesis is the initial response of the victim and of others in whom the victim confides. If the victim does not tell anyone of the abuse, this could be indicative of two things: (a) that the victim is afraid to tell or does not think it would help or (b) that the victim may already be affected by changes in cognition that tell him that the abuse is probably deserved or understandable. In this second instance, the victim may already have normalized the experience because of, for example, age or relationship to the offender. However, failure to report the abuse in either case may reinforce social learning, because the victim will not have the opportunity to receive negative outside messages regarding the abuse or to resolve his feelings about the experience. Over time, dealing with the abuse by oneself may lead to learned behaviors consistent with abuse, such as sexual arousal in inappropriate situations or unusual beliefs about what constitutes sexual relationships.

If the victim does tell others, their response is very important as to whether the abusive patterns may be internalized. An indifferent reaction, or disbelief, may lead the victim to feel that he is not being listened to. More important, however, the victim may feel that maybe he overreacted to the abuse and that it was not as bad as initially perceived. If this occurs, it is reasonable to assume that the victim would interpret the abuse in a different and more normalized way. A reaction that would not lead to socially learned deviant patterns would be a case in which the victim observed the offender receiving punishment or some negative sanction for his actions. Unfortunately, though, this does not always occur. So, even if the reactions of others are appropriate and express understanding or sympathy for the victim, whether the offender receives negative sanction for the abuse is also important.

Most, if not all, of the research to date in support of social learning theory has examined the experiences of sex offenders who report childhood or adolescent sexual abuse. Focusing on these particular offenders, some interesting findings have emerged that may offer partial support for social learning theory as an explanation for sex offending. Sex offenders who report that they were sexually abused as children report many of the abuse characteristics noted in the abused–abuser hypothesis, such as multiple perpetrators of the abuse, longer duration of the abuse, coercion or force, a previously established relationship with the perpetrator, and age at the time of abuse (Burton, 2000; Burton et al., 2002; Hummel et al., 2000; Seghorn et al., 1987).

Many research findings support the idea that certain cognitive traits, such as lack of empathy, sexually deviant interests, distorted attitudes, and some degree of sexual preoccupation or excessive sexual fantasy, are evidenced to a greater extent by sex offenders who report childhood histories of sexual abuse (Briggs & Hawkins, 1996; Burton et al., 2002; Craissati et al., 2002; Simons, Wurtele, & Heil, 2002). Furthermore, sex offenders who were sexually abused also demonstrate higher levels of deviant arousal and certain victim characteristics (e.g., being male children) that differentiate them from other sex offenders. Many of these offenders show higher rates of sexual arousal toward children (Becker, Hunter, Stein, & Kaplan, 1989; Freund & Kuban, 1994), a preference for male victims (Barbaree, Marshall, & McCormick, 1998; Burton, 2000; Cooper, Murphy, & Haynes, 1996; Worling, 1995), and a higher total of victims (Cooper et al., 1996).

This suggests that sexual abuse may have some impact on the learning of sexually deviant behavior patterns, but how that abuse specifically is modeled and later manifested is still somewhat unclear. Researchers have compared sex offenders with abuse histories to non–sex-offending prisoners with similar childhood histories and sex offenders without a history of abuse and found no significant differences in their abuse histories (Benoit & Kennedy, 1992; Haapasalo & Kankkonen, 1997; Jonson-Reid & Way, 2001). These samples of offenders failed to differentiate among any of the groups on characteristics of childhood abuse, thereby suggesting that there is not a clear link between childhood abuse experiences and specific sexual offense patterns. However, it is still important to note that these groups consisted of offenders, both sex and non–sex offenders, so there may have been a ceiling effect in terms of outcome variables. Additionally, self-report of abuse scenarios might significantly confound these results, limiting our ability to make assumptions about the impact of childhood sexual abuse on these individuals.

SEXUALLY VIOLENT PORNOGRAPHY AND SOCIAL LEARNING

For many years, researchers have attempted to establish a connection between pornography and violent sexual acts. Social learning theorists suggest that viewing pornographic materials may serve as a model to some individuals and encourage them to engage in behaviors that the pornographic films or photographs have portrayed. To the extent the pornographic materials depict sexual violence, viewers may internalize deviant sexual role expectations or certain deviant attitudes about women because of the pornographic presentations (Itzin, 2002; Masterson, 1984).

Although there is some mixed evidence that men's attitudes or expectations may change after viewing pornographic materials, there is scant evidence that these attitudes will lead to noticeable behavioral change (Bauserman, 1996; Masterson, 1984). This is likely due to the fact that only certain types of pornography have any significant impact on the viewer. In this section, we address the types of pornography that have been more firmly linked to sexual aggression—namely, (a) violent sexual pornography, or rape pornography, and (b) child pornography. Pornographic films and pictures that do not contain violent or inappropriate sexual content (e.g., children, fetish items) are not discussed here because of a research consensus that these types of materials do not significantly contribute to the development of sexually deviant behaviors. For a review of the effects of nonviolent forms of pornography, see Donnerstein, Linz, and Penrod (1987); Donnerstein and Malamuth (1997); Itzin (2002); Mann, Sidman, and Starr (1973); Masterson (1984); and Zillman and Bryant (1989).

Two primary types of pornography have been linked to sexually aggressive behaviors. The first of these is usually labeled as "sexually violent pornography," and it more generally falls under the category of rape pornography. In this type of material, women are portrayed in humiliating or degrading situations and are often the victims of forced or coerced sexual interactions (Marshall, 1988). Using a social learning framework, an individual who views rape pornography might experience a change in his attitudes toward women and, more specifically, toward rape myths (Cramer et al., 1998) and might experience increased perceptions of reward for and societal acceptance of sexually aggressive behaviors. This might lead the viewer to later engage in rape or other sexually coercive behaviors, using the sexually violent pornography as a model or example.

Evidence indicates that there is some increase in hostility toward women or acceptance of rape myths following viewing of sexually violent pornography. A number of studies have reported that repeated exposure to sexually violent images decreases empathy and compassion toward female victims, increases the acceptance of physical violence and sexual coercion, and may desensitize the viewer to anxiety or arousal provoked by viewing these materials (Check & Guloien, 1989; Knudsen, 1988; Linz, Donnerstein, & Penrod, 1988; Malamuth & Check, 1980, 1981, 1985). After prolonged exposure to sexually violent pornography, male participants in these studies empathized less with female victims of rape and endorsed agreement with significantly more rape myths (e.g., "She was asking for it," "She enjoyed it"). K. A. Lahey (1991) outlined several specific attitudes that men endorsed after increased viewing of sexually violent films: violence does not hurt, abuse does not matter, women like rape, women lie, women do not know what they like, and women are not worth much. An individual who strongly endorses these particular attitudes might be more likely to find sexually coercive behaviors an acceptable way to obtain sexual gratification. But how do these beliefs develop in some viewers of rape pornography? Perhaps the more important question is, Will viewing rape pornography lead to rape?

From a social learning perspective, the strength of the belief and the subsequent likelihood that the belief will lead to behavior (e.g., rape) depend largely on the reinforcements observed in the learning process. One such reinforcement is the response of the female character in the pornographic film. Women in these films are often portrayed as enjoying the sexually violent acts inflicted on them and are also shown seeking out sexual violence or abuse (Check & Guloien, 1989; Knudsen, 1988; Norris, 1991; Sinclair, Lee, & Johnson, 1995). The female character–victim in rape pornography films may show a positive reaction to the rape and the rapist, so that the viewer receives a conflicting message about the rape. On the one hand, it is a violent sexual act, but on the other hand, the woman does not seem to mind and, in fact, appears to enjoy it. The naive viewer might come to believe that women are not substantially harmed by rape and enjoy sexually violent interactions.

A second reinforcement comes from social cues of others, whether it be other characters in the pornographic film or others with whom the viewer is watching the film. Social cues send important messages to the individual about the acceptability of certain types of behavior, including sexual behavior (Dienstbier, 1977; Norris, 1991; Sinclair et al., 1995). It is not only the observed behavior but also the reactions of other observers that help reinforce socially learned activities. The responses of other characters in the sexually violent film are important in how the viewer will interpret the rape or other aggressive sexual behavior. If the perpetrator of sexual violence in the pornographic film is rewarded for his behavior, the viewer may use this as a social comparison and may further assume that this behavior would be rewarded in reality (Norris, 1991). Additionally, the reactions of others viewing the same materials are a possible source for social comparison feedback. If others watching the film are excited by it and seem approving of the sexually violent behaviors, then the individual viewer might be more apt to see the sexually aggressive messages of the film as both positive and rewarding (Sinclair et al., 1995).

Finally, there is some evidence that sexual abusers of adult women used pornography prior to their offense and requested that their victims act out certain components of the violent pornography they had viewed (Bergen & Bogle, 2000; Marshall, 1988). This might indicate that these offenders have learned specific arousal sequences from observing the actions of characters in violent pornography. However, there seems to be a regular use of nonviolent pornography by these offenders as well (Langevin, Lang, Wright, et al., 1988), which limits the conclusions we can make regarding the impact of one specific type of pornography. Additionally, researchers have been unable to consistently link rapists' specific offense behaviors with the content of the pornography they viewed prior to the offense (Fisher & Grenier, 1994).

The second type of pornography believed to play a role in the etiology of socially learned sexual aggression is child pornography. This is different from rape pornography in that the victimized character is a child rather than a woman, but there may still be a considerable level of sexual violence or aggression toward the victimized character. Social learning theory proposes that a select group of individuals may view or read child pornography and subsequently develop sexual interest in children similar to those portrayed in the pornographic material. These individuals would observe models engaging in the sexual abuse of young children and would internalize this behavior as an acceptable form of sexual interaction.

Research on the applicability of child pornography to social learning theory has been somewhat limited, however. Unlike studies using rape pornography, child pornography has not been shown to research participants to elicit sexual arousal. Instead, researchers have relied on child molesters' reports of their use of various pornographic materials. Child molesters have reported increased usage of child pornography prior to committing their offenses (Howitt, 1995; Marshall, 1988, 2000). Recent research has suggested that use of child pornography is a reliable indicator of sexual interest in children, perhaps more so than previous offenses against children or other sexually deviant behaviors (Seto, Cantor, & Blanchard, 2006). Across these studies, offenders have reported the use of pornography to desensitize themselves, overcome their inhibitions, and arouse themselves in preparation for the sexual victimization of a child (Knudsen, 1988; Marshall, 1988, 2000). Child pornography also appears to reduce empathy toward child victims (Knudsen, 1988; Simons et al., 2002), much in the same way that rape pornography reduces empathy or compassion for female victims. Portrayals of enjoyment on the part of the child victim, or a lack of negative consequences for the perpetrator, may help reinforce the pedophile's views of children as an obtainable or appropriate sexual target.

LIMITATIONS OF SOCIAL LEARNING THEORY AS APPLIED TO SEX OFFENDING

Despite preliminary evidence suggesting that modeled or imitated learning does play a role in the development of sexually deviant interests and behaviors, several limitations restrict the usefulness or appropriateness of this theory to explain sexual offending. Some of these critiques refer to social learning theory in general, whereas others may be applied to the specific hypotheses mentioned in this chapter.

First, there is the assumption that internalized attitudes or beliefs will lead to corresponding behaviors. Although it sounds plausible that a belief would lead to a particular corresponding action, research in social psychology and criminology has failed to demonstrate a clear connection between pre-existing attitudes and observable action (Ajzen & Fishbein, 1980; Akers, 2000; Fishbein & Ajzen, 1975; Fishbein, Hennessy, Yzer, & Douglas, 2003; Hirschi & Stark, 1969). The translation from thought or perception to action is critical in the social learning process. One observes behavior, makes some judgment of it, internalizes that judgment as a belief, and then later acts on that belief to produce behavior similar to the previously observed actions. In this case, observing some form of sexual violence would lead to attitudes or definitions consistent with sexually deviant interests, which would in turn lead to inappropriate sexual behaviors. However, without clear evidence that attitudes and beliefs do in fact lead to behaviors, the accuracy of this process is called into question. The relationship between attitude and behavior must be proven before sex offending can be explained in this manner.

Second, if modeling has as great an impact on human behavior as suggested by this theory, then why haven't more people engaged in these behaviors? As mentioned previously, large numbers of children who were sexually abused do not go on to commit sexually inappropriate acts as adults (e.g., Berliner & Elliot, 2002; Rind, Tromovitch, & Bauserman, 1998). Similarly, the vast majority of people who view violent sexual pornography or child pornography, including research participants, do not become sex offenders (e.g., Donnerstein & Malamuth, 1997; Fisher & Grenier, 1994; Linz et al., 1988). This is typically explained by referring to the importance of reinforcers and potential punishments (e.g., Check & Guloien, 1989; Dienstbier, 1977; Knudsen, 1988; Norris, 1991; Sinclair et al., 1995), but no one has proven that this is the key in preventing some individuals from engaging in the observed behaviors. The fact is that we do not know why so many people are able to observe a given behavior and refrain from participating in it. It is easy to suggest that these unknown factors, which understandably rely heavily on individual perception and experience, are responsible for a person's interpretation of events and the impact that it has on them. However, without research documenting these facilitating and inhibiting factors, we are left without an understanding of why most people who observe these inappropriate sexual behaviors do not act on them.

Third, there is the problem of applying a very general theory to an extreme, rare type of behavior. Social learning theory and its related hypotheses may fare well when explaining relatively common behaviors, such as aggression or affection (Akers, 1998), but behaviors with extremely low base rates (e.g., sex offending) are not so easily explained. For example, research demonstrates a link between exposure to excessive media violence and aggressive behavior in children (e.g., Donnerstein, Slaby, & Eron, 1995; Huesmann, Moise-Titus, Podolski, & Eron, 2003), but the success of social learning theory in explaining this phenomenon is largely due to the relatively frequent occurrence and implicit social acceptability of aggressive behavior. However, it becomes difficult to explain sexually deviant behaviors in this same manner, because they are extreme occurrences that are rarely socially condoned. Although exposure to sexually deviant messages may occur through some types of pornography or through sexual victimization, it is unlikely that such extreme behaviors will be quickly and easily internalized. So although the tenets of social learning theory may be applicable to a broad array of behavioral outcomes, it might not be so easily applied to very specific, rare types of behavior. Because these behaviors seldom occur, and because they are on such an extreme end of the behavioral continuum, theories meant to explain all behavior may not adequately explain them.

Fourth, most of the research relies heavily on self-reported past experiences of the offenders themselves. Unfortunately, some of these offenders might be motivated by secondary gain to falsely report either a past history of abuse or their use of violent pornography. There are instances in which identified sex offenders might wish to garner sympathy by falsely claiming to be victims of childhood sexual abuse, or they might see violent pornography as an excuse for their inappropriate behaviors. Additionally, these offenders may simply not remember the exact sequence of events that preceded their own offenses or understand links between past experiences and their own behaviors. Studies based on self-reports from these offenders might not accurately represent the role of these past modeled behaviors in the lives of sex offenders. Because these past experiences are difficult to verify using official sources, this particular problem might continually plague the research in this area.

Fifth, and finally, although some rape pornography research has shown that nonoffending research participants, after being shown significant amounts of rape pornography, are more hostile toward women and endorse more rape myths, the studies of child pornography rely on the reports of child molesters rather than controlled experimentation with nonoffending participants. The difficulty here is that child molesters who used child pornography are a self-selecting group. It may have been their deviant interests in child pornography that led them to sexually offend rather than the other way around. This is somewhat supported by Howitt's (1995) finding that most of the pedophiles in one study reported using child pornography for sexual arousal long after they had committed their first pedophilic offense. It may be that sex offenders who use sexually violent pornography were already demonstrating or internalizing sexually deviant interests prior to ever viewing the pornography. Also, because a great many studies examine the pornography use of offenders rather than the effects it has on nonoffenders, it is thereby difficult to establish a causal link between the pornography itself and sexually deviant acts.

These five concerns call into question the validity of social learning theory as an explanation for sexually deviant behaviors. Although there is some support for the idea that these behaviors, like many others, may be learned through observation and internalization, the theory does not yet adequately explain why so many individuals refrain from these behaviors, or why some offenders report that their behaviors started before the observed experience (e.g., pornography). More research is needed to explore the full extent to which these particular behaviors may be learned from observation of sexually deviant acts, the factors that facilitate or inhibit these behaviors, and the way in which cognitive definitions or beliefs regarding this behavior are acquired.

SUMMARY AND CONCLUSIONS

Social learning theory was developed to explain the relationship between observed experience and behavior. In this chapter, we have discussed the important factors that contribute to the likelihood of observed phenomena becoming learned behaviors. We also addressed two ways in which this theory has been applied to sex-offending behaviors. The first of these is the abused–abuser hypothesis, whereby researchers have suggested that early experiences of childhood sexual abuse predispose some individuals to later patterns of sexually deviant behavior. The second refers to the role of sexually violent pornography in the development of beliefs and behaviors that facilitate sexually violent offending. We further discussed the research on child pornography and the reported association between this type of pornography and offenses against children.

As in previous chapters, we have presented a number of limitations, which should be addressed in future etiological and empirical research. Still, there are aspects of social learning theory and the social learning theories as applied to sexual deviance that can inform this future research. The first of these is the emphasis on environmental factors that may contribute to the development of certain types of behavior. Theories that focus on strictly biological or even cognitive factors often exclude influences that occur in the individual's environment. We know from the behavioral theories and other psychological and social research that the environment and important events during development play a critical role in shaping later behaviors. Social learning theories are valuable in that they not only emphasize environmental factors but also provide an explanation for how they may lead to specific, learned behavior.

A second related advantage is that, within this context, sex offending is viewed as a learned behavior. This contradicts earlier views of sex offending that assumed inherent biological or genetic causes, which were not only viewed as predetermined but also perhaps unchangeable. Viewing sexually deviant interests and behaviors as learned gives us a new perspective that incorporates childhood experience, other developmental events, and cognitive factors such as attitudes and beliefs. This of course allows for different possibilities in assessment, prevention, and treatment, which might not have been possible with other etiological views.

Last, social learning theory—particularly the abused–abuser hypothesis—considers the role of childhood experience in the development of these behaviors. Specifically, the theory details potential effects of childhood sexual abuse that may be related to problematic behaviors in adolescence and adulthood for some individuals. Despite the limitations that would prevent the broader application of this theory to a sex-offending population (e.g., the lack of sexual abuse histories for some sex-offending individuals, poor reporting of prior childhood experiences), it is useful to consider childhood events and examine them for any potential link to offending or other maladaptive behaviors. Although they may not lead to sex offending as directly as is posited by this theory, early experience may shape cognitions, emotions, interpersonal relationships, or other related behaviors that are predictive of offending.

7

PERSONALITY THEORIES

Theories of personality and personality development are perhaps the earliest means through which clinicians and researchers attempted to explain deviant or abnormal behavior in human beings. Early theorists in this area, such as Sigmund Freud (1905/1962) and Krafft-Ebing (1886/1997), suggested that something in the development of the self or person significantly contributed to the development of sexually deviant interests and behaviors. As more formal assessments of personality were developed, scientists speculated not only as to the types of personality present in these individuals but also as to the origins of their specific personality traits.

In this chapter, we explore this area of research and consider the findings that have contributed to our understanding of sex-offending behaviors. First, we briefly discuss the early psychodynamic formulations of sexuality and personality development. Second, we address more recent conceptualizations of personality as applied to sex-offending populations. We evaluate various sex-offender personality types that were derived from personality testing and discuss how these suggested typologies would contribute to sex offending. Third, we look at personality traits as mediators of behavior and discuss several that have important implications for sexually deviant behaviors. Finally, we examine limitations of the current personality literature in providing a complete picture of the etiology of sex offending.

PSYCHODYNAMIC PERSONALITY CONCEPTUALIZATIONS

Psychodynamic theory broadly refers to an approach in which internal feelings, drive states, and the conflicts between them motivate behavior at both conscious and unconscious levels. In this section, we introduce several of the major psychodynamic modes of thought that have been applied to the phenomena of sexual deviance and sex offending. We begin with Sigmund Freud's classical psychoanalytic view, which expands to the broader area of ego psychology, as described by Freud and his psychoanalytic successors. Next, we consider sexual deviance from the viewpoint of object relations theory and describe the psychodynamic components of Bowlby's (1958, 1969, 1979) original conceptualization of attachment theory. Finally, we include hypotheses introduced by Stoller (1975, 1987, 1991) to explain sexual deviance.

Classical Psychoanalysis and Ego Psychology

Sigmund Freud's (1905/1962) original psychoanalytic hypotheses included various stages of psychosexual development, which he believed would significantly impact later adult functioning. The classical view holds that children develop according to five observed psychosexual stages: (a) oral, (b) anal, (c) phallic, (d) latency, and (e) genital. Each of these stages associates certain behaviors (e.g., the sucking reflex in the oral stage) with pleasurable sensations for the child. The child learns to associate specific activities with physiological needs and sexual pleasure. Freud's initial ideas regarding sexually deviant behaviors were that the individual had become fixated in an earlier stage of sexual development and was acting out the behaviors of that particular stage. The deviant sexual act became a ritual through which sexual pleasure could be achieved (Gabbard, 1994), thereby reliving the sensations of pleasure that were associated with a more immature stage of sexual development.

However, certain anxieties also accompany each of the stages of psychosexual development, and some of these anxieties were hypothesized by Freud to relate to significant sexual perversion in adulthood. For example, Freud (1905/1962) hypothesized that castration anxiety, or the male fear of being castrated and thereby losing one's male identification, occurs during the phallic phase of development. He suggested that perverse or deviant forms of sexual behavior and sexual fantasy served the purpose of alleviating castration anxiety. Gabbard (1994) described exhibitionism in these terms, noting that the exhibitionist can reassure himself that he has not been castrated by publicly displaying his genitals to unsuspecting victims.

Classical psychoanalytic views of personality and sexual development also included the role of sexual and aggressive drives, which Freud believed to be crucial to the inherent behavioral tendencies of the individual, and the formation of an unconscious tripartite personality structure: (a) the *id*, which is the more fundamental and animalistic drive; (b) the *superego*, which consists of learned morality; and (c) the *ego*, or the mediator between the forces of the id and the superego. A later expansion of Freud's original formulation, called *ego psychology*, highlighted the conflicts between inner drives and the role that the conscious and unconscious features of the ego played in mediating these conflicts.

These psychodynamic hypotheses ultimately suggested that personality and human behavior are largely shaped by mental mechanisms operating outside of conscious awareness (Larsen & Buss, 2002). These unconscious mechanisms develop primarily during early childhood and define adult interaction styles and motivation. Some researchers have suggested that Freud's theory labels human nature as inherently "violent, self-centered, and impulsive" (Larsen & Buss, 2002, p. 193), which led psychoanalytic theory to be applied to the more deviant and base forms of human behavior, such as sex offending.

Freud (1905/1962) posited that various aspects of the personality (viz., the ego and superego) develop to regulate the sexual and aggressive feelings generated by the instinctual and pleasure-seeking id that is innately part of all humans. He described a sexual instinct that is natural to humans, and he believed that certain mental forces and resistances that develop during normal personality maturation serve to adapt and normalize the sexual impulse. The development of moral understanding and internalization of the ego and superego lead an individual to temper his or her natural sexual drives into manifestations of sexuality that are appropriate given learned societal norms. Freud used the example of sexual sadism to demonstrate this innate capacity for sexual abnormality or impulsivity. Freud stated that just as sexual expression is a natural human tendency, so is aggression or violence. He posited that because cruelty and sexuality are both fundamental human traits, it is not unusual that these basic human instincts might come to be associated. Believing the association between these two instincts is deviant and unthinkable, society has evolved moral standards that forbid the co-occurrence of violence and sexual activity. A person who does not conform to these norms, or who simply does not learn them, is at increased risk of abandoning himself to these two competing drives (i.e., sexuality and aggression), which may result in sexually aggressive or sadistic acts.

Freud (1905/1962) further hypothesized that some individuals fail to adequately internalize these social norms in the form of the ego or superego and that these individuals are more likely to act impulsively on innate sexual urges and engage in socially taboo sexual acts. Sexual aberrations that occur beyond mere sexual impulsiveness are due to an unconscious pairing of a nonsexual symbolic fetish object (e.g., a specific part of the body or item of clothing) with innate sexual desire (Freud, 1905/1962). This fetish object then automatically elicits a state of sexual arousal without the earlier established association between the object and sexual pleasure being obvious or consciously known to the individual.

Freud also addressed the behavior of people who are primarily sexually attracted to children, suggesting that these individuals may have experienced some degree of trauma in their childhoods that led them to associate more strongly with children, either because of a desire to compensate for neglect in their own childhoods or because they identify with the child as a projection of the idealized self (e.g., Palermo, 2002; see also Howells, 1981). Here, a person develops pedophilic interests as a means to address the internal conflicts (e.g., lack of love) that stem from his own childhood experience. Freud posited that the individual attaches sexual value to children because he was unable to adequately or sufficiently resolve psychosexual conflict in early childhood.

Palermo (2002) added to the dual-drive model of sexual deviance, noting that the differences between individuals in ego strength and fundamental ego formation create differences in their fantasies and expression of their sexual and aggressive drives from the id. Because of these idiosyncratic features of the ego, the individual will manifest various forms of sexual deviance (e.g., pedophilia, fetishism, voyeurism).

Object Relations Theory

The fundamental idea behind object relations theory is that the individual, as a young child, internalizes relationships between himself and important objects (e.g., caretakers) in the environment (Leguizamo, 2002). The development of the ego and identification formation includes the consolidation of the sense of self, the identification of others as objects in the environment, and the realization of important relationships between the self and objects (e.g., mother–child relationship; Kernberg, 1976, 1995). Kernberg (1995) additionally suggested that these object relations that form with the development of the ego drive cognitive schemas regarding interpersonal interactions throughout the life span. In other words, what an infant or young child learns about his relationships with important objects in the environment helps determine his ability to recognize and engage in interpersonal interactions in the environment later in life. The child not only internalizes his perceptions of the self and others but also internalizes the concept of a relationship (see Gabbard, 1994).

Another important component of forming and internalizing representations of the self and objects in the environment is affect. Instinctual drives from the id (e.g., sex, aggression) emerge in the context of relationships. The connection between the drives of the self and the relationship with an object is linked by an affective state (e.g., Gabbard, 1994; Kernberg, 1976, 1995). Intense affect, both positive and negative, helps define these early relationship and object formations. Later, the child will integrate these positive and negative affective experiences into his cognitive definitions of the self and others. These affective feelings, triggered by drive states, are then related to specific relational experiences and expectations for the child. These cognitive and social expectations are integrated into the development of the ego and the superego and are continually shaped and modified through social and interpersonal experiences (Fonagy & Target, 1996; Gabbard, 1994).

The tenets of object relations theory have been applied to the development of deviant sexual interests in three primary ways. First, it is possible that early childhood relationships involving trauma or mistreatment could lead the child to internalize maladaptive self–object relations. Some theorists have observed that traumatic events in a child's early life, such as childhood sexual victimization, may substantially alter how the child perceives sexual relationships and his role in the sexual relationship with another object (Leguizamo, 2002). According to this hypothesis, a child who experiences intensive negative affective states in relationship to an important object (e.g., a caretaker) must adapt to the negative state to survive the experience. However, this temporary adaptation to a harmful relationship with the object may in turn irrevocably alter the way that the child will view relationships with others in the future. In other words, a child who is faced with negative or dysfunctional object relationships will perhaps internalize that relationship as the norm, which will impact his relational development in the long term. Internalization of these maladaptive templates whereby a child is subject to the sexual drive of an adult, for example, could lead him to seek out similar sexual relationships with children on reaching adulthood himself (Leguizamo, 2002).

Second, it is possible that an individual who commits deviant sexual acts has selected an inappropriate or abnormal object to which to transfer sexual excitement. In defining relationships between the self and other objects, the child typically will select a sexual object that reflects past experiences and observed relationships between others, forming a dominant object choice (Kernberg, 1995). For example, a young child who observes the relationship between his parents will then internalize sexual expectations from the observations of that relationship. According to this hypothesis, it is possible that a child will develop sexual interest in some other object, should he be exposed to that object in a sexual way during critical phases of development. Once this dominant object choice has been established, it will be internalized as the subject of erotic desire and sexual excitement, perhaps regardless of societal or cultural views that might contradict the sexual nature of such an object (e.g., a fetish object).

Finally, it is possible that deviant sexual interests may form through the perversion or misperception of crucial components of the sexual relationship or sexual functioning. Kernberg (1995) specifically addressed this possibility by discussing the role of teasing and the development of exhibitionism and voyeurism. He hypothesized that sexual teasing, or the withholding of a sexual object, is likely to increase sexual or erotic desire because of the inherently forbidden nature of sexual drive and sexual activity. Acts that hint at but do not explicitly demonstrate sexual activity are those that are more likely to frustrate an individual and increase his desire (Kernberg, 1995). Individuals who are sexually aroused by watching others (i.e., "voyeurs"), or those who expose themselves to others for sexual pleasure (i.e., "exhibitionists"), have taken the concept of being sexually teased or teasing to a maladaptive extreme. The belief that exhibitionism will entice another into sexual activity and satisfy his or her erotic desire, or that watching someone without that person's knowledge is an appropriate stage of the sexual relationship, is a perverse misperception of the sexual relationship.

Attachment Theory

Attachment theory was initially developed by John Bowlby (1958) in an attempt to combine object relations and ethology to explain the development of personality and interpersonal relationship patterns in young children. Although the theory originated in the context of psychodynamic thought, Bowlby himself doubted many of the fundamental tenets of psychoanalysis proposed by Freud (see Bretherton, 1995; Holmes, 1995) and in his later works described attachment theory as a developmental–cognitive model (e.g., Bowlby, 1988). In chapter 4, we described current applications of attachment theory to sex offending as a cognitive theory, given that Bowlby's final formulations and recent attachment research have focused on the role of attachment in the development of cognitive schemas in young children. However, in this section we describe attachment theory as it was first introduced, a psychodynamic theory of personality development, and relate it to other contemporary psychodynamic models. Because early attachment work was conducted to explain general psychopathology rather than specific deviant acts, such as sex offending, we do not discuss attachment research with sex offenders in this section (for more information regarding how recent attachment research has been applied to this population, see chap. 4).

Bowlby (1958) introduced attachment theory as a means to explain a child's primary object relation (e.g., relationship with the mother) as the foundation of personality. Here, he described certain behaviors of young children that would serve to bind or attach the child to his mother, including sucking, clinging, following, crying, and smiling. He viewed these behaviors as independent instinctual activities that shared a common goal—binding with the primary caretaker. Over time, these behaviors would become integrated and recognized as attachment behavior. Bowlby (1979) later added emotional response to this equation, noting that the attachment bond and behaviors associated with it occurred in the presence of intense emotions, such as joy or frustration.

However, Bowlby's (1969, 1977) concept of attachment and the instinctual behaviors driving the attachment bond were becoming more removed from the original Freudian concepts of instinct (i.e., sex and aggression) and more directed toward other motivational factors, such as emotion, a desire for security, and behavioral associations of pleasure or happiness with the presence of the primary caretaker. Furthermore, Bowlby (1988) rejected the fundamental selfishness assumed in Freud's models of development. Instead, he relied more on the object relations viewpoint and saw attachment as something that fostered the development of the child's representation of the self, objects in the environment, and relationships with those objects.

One of the early goals of attachment theorists was to explain the development of pathological personality features, including psychopathy, in adulthood. Bowlby and Ainsworth (Ainsworth, Blehar, Waters, & Wall, 1978; Bowlby, 1977) developed a typology of attachment styles, noting features of secure, insecure, and avoidant attachment (see chap. 4 for more information on these constructs). The different attachment styles were attributed to different experiences with attachment in childhood, with a maladaptively attached child forming persistent patterns of detachment toward others, hostility, and anxiety (e.g., Bowlby, 1969, 1979). Therefore, children faced with distant, inconsistent, or unloving primary caretakers could develop maladaptive interactional expectations and biases that would significantly impact their adult functioning. These concepts were later incorporated into cognitive views of childhood development.

Still, despite Bowlby's (1988) later rejection of many psychodynamic concepts in favor of cognitive, behavioral, and developmental contributions to the theory, his original model of childhood attachment (Bowlby, 1958) and its later impact on personality shared some commonalities with contemporary psychodynamic thought. For example, the primary role of the mother and maternal experience in the child's development, his descriptions of unconscious representations of the self and how they are formed by these early experiences, and the idea that psychopathology results from failures within the early environment are all central to current psychodynamic as well as attachment models (Eagle, 1995).

Stoller's Psychodynamic Contributions

Robert Stoller (1991), a psychoanaltically influenced theorist, made numerous observations regarding the development of sexually deviant behavior. Stoller noted that the original psychodynamic term for sexually deviant fantasies and behaviors—*perversions*—is necessary because it connotes a sense of sinfulness and humiliation that is the core of the deviant act. Stoller viewed the motivation behind perverse sexual activity as one of hostility and revenge.

Stoller (e.g., 1975, 1987) described a process in which an individual commits perverse sexual acts in response to a childhood trauma that threatened the development of gender identity. Specifically, Stoller referred to early stages of development in which male children must develop their own gender identity separate from that of their primary caregiver—the mother. He feels that this process of separation may be particularly difficult or incomplete for some individuals, leading to a sense of "rage at giving up one's earliest bliss and identification with mother, fear of not succeeding in escaping out of her orbit, and a need for revenge that she put one in this predicament" (Stoller, 1975, p. 99). This hostility is carried into adulthood, with the individual forming a perverse fantasy of revenge in which the trauma of separation is relived and then converted into a sense of triumph. The man will seek to harm his sexual partner, to reverse the role of pain and humiliation and instead emerge victorious from the perverse sexual situation. Although orgasm would be equated with this feeling of victory, the individual would need to relive the perverse and humiliating sexual act repeatedly over time, because he will not be able to permanently banish the danger to his gender and sexual identity that was created in childhood (Stoller, 1975).

Also inherent in this theory is the idea that a critical component of the perverse sexual fantasy or act is dehumanization of one's sexual partner (e.g., Stoller, 1975). This is necessary to more easily humiliate and degrade the object of sexual attention. It is this act of humiliation and degradation that is significant, allowing the individual to experience psychological revenge for the earlier trauma. Stoller further noted that it is not necessary for the victim to suffer physical harm for the act to be harmful and humiliating. Acts such as exhibitionism and voyeurism are still manifestations of hostility toward the sexual object of interest, as long as the intended victim experiences shock, outrage, or a feeling of having been offended (Stoller, 1987). This expression of hostility against an unsuspecting victim reinstates the gender or sexual identity that was challenged in early childhood by separation from the mother.

Another important aspect of Stoller's theory regarding the development of perversion is how objects of sexual interest are chosen. Stoller (1975) posited that certain sexual acts, such as voyeurism, exhibitionism, and fetishism, arise from the hidden or mystical nature of sexuality in our current culture. Therefore, much like Kernberg (1995), Stoller suggested that forbidden sexual desires are somehow transformed into forbidden sexual acts (e.g., voyeurism), in which individuals sexualize the indirect components of sexual behavior (e.g., particular items of clothing, the act of disrobing) into a perverse sexual framework.

A final consideration regarding Stoller's explanations for sexual deviance is that he suggested that all individuals have perverse sexual fantasies, if not outright perverse sexual actions. In fact, believing that perversion is simply a hostile and sexual form of neurosis, he made a statement indicating that because everyone is neurotic, everyone is also perverse (Stoller, 1991). Stoller (1975) stated that perversion represents a character disorder for some persons and that these individuals are likely to continually engage in sexually perverse behaviors and are inclined toward hostility in sexual acts. For others, the perversion is merely an underlying mechanism that varies in terms of severity, influence, and likelihood of expression. In other words, Stoller hypothesized that nearly all individuals are inherently perverse but that they may not exhibit their perversions in overt ways.

SEX OFFENDER PERSONALITY TYPES

After this early theorizing, researchers turned to formulations of personality development based on the results of psychometric assessment. After the introduction of several major self-report inventories of personality, such as the Minnesota Multiphasic Personality Inventory (MMPI; Butcher et al., 2001) and the five-factor model of personality traits (Costa & McCrae, 1992), attempts were made to develop sex-offender personality profiles or traits that would differentiate sex offenders from nonoffenders and from offenders who do not commit sex offenses. These personality inventories relied on the individual's ability to accurately characterize his or her personality traits across a range of behaviors and situations, including views of the self, responses to hypothetical situations, and endorsement of certain psychological symptoms. Researchers hoped to find evidence that sex offenders would be markedly different on dimensions of personality functioning and that these distinguishing facets of personality specific to deviant sex offenders would lend clues as to the causes of their sexual deviance.

The testing instruments used to classify sex offenders by their personality types fall into two main categories. The first of these includes measures such as the MMPI and the Millon Clinical Multiaxial Inventory (MCMI; Millon, Davis, & Millon, 1997), which provide characterological assessment through items measuring various psychological symptomotology. These instruments require respondents to provide a consistent and coherent description of their psychological traits (e.g., narcissism, psychopathy), and they report these results as a personality profile (i.e., a combination of psychological traits, such as psychopathy, and specific psychological symptoms, such as posttraumatic stress). The end result is an evaluation of an individual's level of psychological distress and some interpretation of how that distress would impact his or her overall ability to function.

A great many studies have evaluated responses on the MMPI and MCMI for adult and adolescent sex offenders. Studies comparing sex offenders with either non–sex offenders or nonoffender control participants have provided mixed results. For example, Langevin, Paitich, Freeman, Mann, and Handy (1978) found that although the MMPI profiles of some sex offenders (i.e., exhibitionists) were indistinguishable from those of normal control respondents and did not manifest any distinctive personality features, these results did not match the findings of earlier studies that used the MMPI. However, they also noted that other sex-offender groups (e.g., pedophiles, incest offenders) did manifest distinct and abnormal personality characteristics across a range of personality dimensions when compared to the profiles of nonoffending control participants. Although this evidence suggests that more pathological, contact sex offenders have meaningful personality differences as demonstrated by the MMPI when compared to each other and control groups, the question remains why exhibitionists, who also have sexually anomalous behavior, do not manifest similar profiles.

Cohen, Gans, et al. (2002) and Cohen, McGeoch, et al. (2002) reported that outpatient pedophiles manifested significantly higher rates of personality pathology on the MCMI than did nonoffender, control participants who were not mentally ill. These researchers cautioned, however, that the personality symptoms reported by the sex offenders might not be singularly related to their sex-offender status, because an offender control group was not included in the research. In other words, their profiles may reflect offenders in general and not just sex offenders. Some studies that have compared sex offenders to sexually normal psychiatric inpatients have found that some sex-offender groups do not significantly differ in terms of personality pathology (e.g., Curnoe & Langevin, 2002; Hall, Shepherd, & Mudrak, 1992; Herkov, Gynther, Thomas, & Myers, 1996; Yanagida & Ching, 1993), whereas other researchers have found that some sex offenders can be significantly distinguished by their personality profiles on the MMPI when compared to other offending or psychiatric groups (e.g., Curnoe & Langevin, 2002; Herkov et al., 1996; Losada-Paisey, 1998). The latter findings, demonstrating differences between sex offenders and other offenders, identify the sex offenders as being more socially withdrawn, higher in psychopathic deviance, and more likely to endorse items suggestive of paranoia and thought disorders (Curnoe & Langevin, 2002).

In an attempt to explain the diversity in findings, additional researchers have used personality inventories to focus on potential personality differences between types of sex offenders. Studies using cluster analysis found that the personality profiles of diverse groups of adult and adolescent sex offenders cluster into three to four types, characterized by varying levels of psychopathic traits, neurotic symptoms, and social maladjustment (Anderson, Kunce, & Rich, 1979; Heersink & Strassberg, 1995; Langevin, Lang, Reynolds, et al., 1988; Lussier, Proulx, & McKibben, 2001; Smith, Monastersky, & Deisher, 1987; Worling, 2001). Other studies have demonstrated that rapists tend to show higher rates of hostility, resentfulness, and social alienation than child molesters, who endorse symptoms more consistent with passivity, emotional disturbance, and avoidance (Armentrout & Hauer, 1978; Carpenter, Peed, & Eastman, 1995; Chantry & Craig, 1994b; Duthie & McIvor, 1990; Shealy, Kalichman, Henderson, Szymanowski, & McKee, 1991). Finally, McCreary (1975) found that child molesters with frequent arrests showed higher levels of personality pathology than child molesters with no prior arrest histories.

However, the findings just reviewed are not consistently supported in the literature. There is considerable research suggesting that there are no significant differences between sex-offender groups in terms of personality pathology when divided according to sex-offense type (e.g., Chantry & Craig, 1994a; Hall, Graham, & Shepherd, 1991; Valliant & Blasutti, 1992). Although sex offenders may cluster into specific personality types on these personality inventories and similar instruments, the personality types that are obtained on these measures divide the offenders into classes on the basis of either demographic or psychological variables and not by offense type or type of sexually deviant interest (see S. M. Dwyer & Amberson, 1989; Hall et al., 1991).

Because the findings from these studies are so diverse and contradictory, it is difficult to discern how the results obtained from sex offenders on these inventories can inform us about the origins of sexually deviant behaviors. These findings conservatively suggest that some sex-offender groups manifest personality pathology that is notably different from individuals in the normal population but that this might indicate a wider range of behavioral problems, antisocial acts, and poorer coping skills overall. However, these same profiles do not consistently distinguish sex offenders from psychiatric or criminal populations, suggesting that the combination of high psychological distress with characterological problems might predispose these individuals to commit a number of abnormal or inappropriate behaviors but does not specifically and invariably predispose them to commit sexually deviant behaviors.

The second main class of personality assessment instruments uses a trait-based approach rather than focusing primarily on profiles of symptoms of psychological distress. For example, Eysenck (1971) divided personality traits into extroversion versus introversion and neuroticism versus psychoticism, in the hope of explaining some types of behavior (e.g., sexual abnormality). Many other subsequent theories and corresponding measures of personality have used the trait model as a basis for defining different personality types. Perhaps the most well-known of these personality assessments is the NEO Five-Factor Inventory (NEO-FFI; Costa & McCrae, 1992), based on the proposed five factors of personality: (a) Neuroticism, (b) Extroversion, (c) Openness to Experience, (d) Conscientiousness, and (e) Agreeableness. Instruments based on the personality trait approach report on the significance of specific personality traits in an individual or group of individuals, thereby providing a summary of the personality traits that might drive the behavior of interest.

Other researchers have used trait inventories to identify unique or particularly salient traits in sex-offender populations. Research comparing the overall personality traits of sex offenders compared with normal control participants finds that sex offenders are markedly different from normal individuals on some traits (e.g., impulsivity, dominance) but are not significantly different on others (e.g., anger, novelty seeking; Cohen, Gans, et al., 2002; Cohen, McGeoch, et al., 2002; Dalton, 1996). Dennison, Stough, and Birgden (2001) compared incest offenders to normal control participants and found that the incest offenders were higher in Neuroticism and lower in Extroversion and Conscientiousness on the NEO-FFI, similar to findings by Fagan et al. (1991) that pedophiles demonstrated markedly higher Neuroticism and lower Agreeableness and Conscientiousness. However, when sex offenders have compared to other non–sex-offending inmate groups or psychiatric patients, there no longer are any significant trait differences between the groups (Grier, Clark, & Stoner, 1993; Moody, Brissie, & Kim, 1994; Nussbaum et al., 2002; Oliver, Hall, & Neuhaus, 1993). Finally, Gingrich and Campbell (1995) used the Eysenck Personality Questionnaire (Eysenck & Eysenck, 1975) to distinguish various sex-offender groups and noted that significant profile differences were obtained for pedophiles, rapists, and exhibitionists in that the rapists were higher in extroversion, the pedophiles were higher in neuroticism, and the exhibitionists demonstrated significantly low levels of extroversion.

As with the studies that use personality inventories such as the MMPI and MCMI, those that use trait-based measures of personality provide limited explanation as to the relationship between these traits and sexually inappropriate behaviors. Although they demonstrate differences between sex offenders and normal individuals, they fail to show consistent and meaningful differences between sex offenders and psychiatric inpatients or incarcerated criminals. Again, for these measures to explain motivations for offending and to identify personality moderators that substantially drive deviant sexual behaviors, they must provide evidence of how personality characteristics relate specifically to sex-offending behavior as opposed to how they explain general criminal or inappropriate behaviors.

PERSONALITY TRAITS AS MEDIATORS

Personality research that attempts to describe the relationship between a personality trait and behavior often focuses on personality as an independent variable, hypothesizing that a certain personality characteristic is singly and directly related to a behavioral outcome. However, one can also conceptualize a personality trait as a mediator of behavior. Here, the trait is indirectly related to the behavioral outcome and interacts with other personality, biological, cognitive, or social variables in predictable ways to produce a behavioral response.

Current research into the link between personality and deviant behavior considers the role of specific traits, both personality disorder traits and non-personality disorder traits, that may mediate the behavior of interest, such as sex offending. According to this view, an individual may manifest specific personality traits that are generally considered exaggerated or disordered. Here, the deviant or exaggerated trait mediates the individual's behavior, whether by limiting his ability to generate a range of normal interpretations for interpersonal stimuli or by impacting the view of the self in relation to others in the surrounding environment. In this section, we address several of the major traits that are believed to strongly mediate sexually deviant behaviors and discuss the role of personality disorders in general in sex-offending trajectories.

Antisocial and Psychopathic Traits

A number of traits have been associated with antisocial personality disorder or the construct of psychopathy that might influence the development and behavioral manifestation of deviant sexual interests. Psychopathy and antisocial personality disorder are characterized by such traits or symptoms as impulsivity, lack of remorse or guilt, callousness, manipulativeness, marked affective and interpersonal deficits, and egocentricity (American Psychiatric Association, 2000; see also Hare, 1991; Porter, Campbell, Woodworth, & Birt, 2001). A history of research demonstrating that psychopathic or antisocial personality traits are disproportionately related to sexual deviance led to an interest in the role that these traits play in the sex-offending process. In the sections that follow, we address several of the major traits of these disorders that have been considered in the sex-offending literature.

Impulsivity

Impulsivity, which refers to a lack of impulse control and need for instant gratification, is seen in a variety of adult and juvenile offenders. Impulsivity is thought to be in direct contrast to behavior that is planned and deliberate, and it may be either a general behavioral trait or specific to certain situations (e.g., sexual impulses; Coles, 1997). Because of this, impulsivity is related to a variety of mental disorders as a symptom of a larger problem regarding behavioral and cognitive control. Individuals characterized by significant levels of impulsivity may engage in behaviors that are harmful to the self or others, with little thought to the consequences or meaning of behavior. Psychopathic individuals or other individuals with personality disorders who manifest high levels of impulsivity, however, still maintain the ability to selectively act in very deliberate and intentional ways, but with disregard to the consequences of these controlled actions.

Impulsiveness has been linked with aggressive and violent behavior in a number of studies (e.g., D. W. Edwards, Scott, Yarvis, Paizis, & Panizzon, 2003; Hart & Dempster, 1997; Reid, 1995). In many chronically violent offenders, such as certain psychopathic subgroups (e.g., those characterized more by a glib or superficial interpersonal style, those who evidence deficient affective experience), impulsivity and a corresponding irresponsibility have been identified as major personality features that drive their behavior (Cooke & Michie, 2001). Psychopathic individuals or individuals with antisocial personality disorder who are also quite impulsive are therefore more likely to engage in violent offending and have an increased probability of being involved in sexually violent behaviors.

Impulsivity as personality pathology is often linked to sexual deviance in certain sex-offender subgroups, such as psychopathic rapists who commit a number of sexual assaults in an impulsive and indiscriminant fashion as part of a generally impulsive and disinhibited lifestyle pattern and engage in numerous criminal and violent activities (Eher, Neuwirth, Fruehwald, & Frottier, 2003; Porter et al., 2001; Prentky & Knight, 1991). These psychopathic sex offenders largely commit these acts as crimes of opportunity rather than as the result of sexually deviant arousal or paraphilias (Porter et al., 2001; Prentky & Knight, 1991). They have difficulty refraining from opportunities that might enhance sensory stimulation or provide immediate gratification. Therefore, they have a tendency to engage in acts of sexual violence when the opportunity presents itself, and they have poor abilities to inhibit such sexual or pleasure-driven impulses. Because these offenders have a high threshold for sensory stimulation and are sensation seeking in nature, sexual violence is, to them, another means through which to gain a diverse range of sexual experience (Porter et al., 2001). Impulsivity, therefore, may mediate the relationship between other personality characteristics (e.g., sensation seeking) and sex-offending behaviors. An impulsive and violent nature will create a scenario in which any situation perceived as a potential for sexual gratification or any other rewarding interaction will be approached in an impulsive way, with limited cognitive consideration of the probable consequences of sexual coercion or other available alternatives for similar sensory stimulation.

The literature on impulsivity as a mediator for sex offenders has been mixed. Although some of the sex-offending literature has identified a certain group of psychopathic sex offenders who are mostly characterized by lifestyle impulsivity and a wide range of sexual and nonsexual crimes (e.g., Eher et al., 2003; Porter et al., 2001; Prentky & Knight, 1991), others have failed to find that impulsivity differentiated sex offenders from other nonsexual violent offender groups (Caputo, Frick, & Brodsky, 1999). These results imply that although impulsivity may be a significant contributing factor in the commission of criminal acts, we still do not understand the specific role that impulsiveness plays in mediating the relationship.

Anger

A second trait of psychopathy and antisocial personality types is trait anger or aggressiveness. Anger and aggression are commonly thought to be either one of two types: (a) *instrumental,* which implies that there is an incentive or reward for the angry or aggressive response, or (b) *reactive—*

expressive, which indicates that the anger or aggression is an uninhibited reaction to perceived provocation. Instrumental aggression is often planned and has a specific purpose. For example, threatening a victim with a weapon during the course of a robbery might more effectively secure the victim's cooperation and intimidate him or her into compliance. Reactive or expressive aggression is thought of as more of a personality trait, in that the anger or aggression results from a particular perceptual style that the individual has. Someone with reactive anger (trait anger) tends to become angry or hostile more easily, interprets situations in an angry way, and reacts impulsively with aggression or violence in response to perceived threat. It comes as no surprise, then, that an individual with a personality style that easily lends itself toward anger and aggression should be affiliated with higher levels of violence.

Knight and Prentky (1990) proposed a number of rapist typologies, two of which are characterized by their expression of trait anger. The *pervasively angry* rapist is described as a persistently angry and easily provoked individual. This type of sex offender often engages in both sexual and nonsexual violence with very little provocation. The *vindictive* type of rapist is seen as angry toward women and uses a great deal of violence during the sexual assault, often more than is deemed necessary to gain victim compliance. In these instances, the presence of anger or readiness to aggress in the personality makeup of the rapist determines the level of violence used during sexual assault and the readiness to engage in sexual violence.

Joireman, Anderson, and Strathman (2003) suggested that there is a complex relationship among aggression, impulsivity, and sensation seeking among individuals high in these traits (e.g., psychopathic individuals) that might lead to specific violent offense patterns. These researchers hypothesized that individuals high in sensation seeking are disproportionately attracted to risky and aggression-inducing situations. Because they are more apt to engage in these aggressive scenarios, there are more inherent provocations for their anger. So, not only are these individuals more easily angered, but also they are attracted to situations in which anger is a likely result. This model may be related to sex offending, although it was originally intended to explain nonsexual violent acts. For example, men who find risky or deviant sexual behaviors particularly stimulating have a higher likelihood of engaging in sexual behaviors that will more easily spark their anger or aggression. Being rejected by a potential sexual partner may make them more angry and hostile toward that partner. Finally, their impulsivity, combined with their reactive anger, will lead to hostility or violence toward the targeted individual.

Unfortunately, as Prentky and Knight (1991) noted, the differentiation between expressive and instrumental anger and aggression has not withstood empirical scrutiny. Research has failed to discriminate between the two types of anger in samples of psychopathic individuals and sex offenders (e.g., Eher et al., 2003; Hart & Dempster, 1997; Porter et al., 2001), and it is therefore difficult to determine whether trait anger plays a direct or indirect role in the instigation of sex offending. Additionally, measures of trait anger have failed to differentiate offender groups on the basis of the levels of aggression displayed in their offense patterns (Smallbone & Milne, 2000). In other words, regardless of how aggressive sex offenders have been in the course of their offending (e.g., sadistic rapists vs. verbally coercive child molesters), the measures of traits and the traits themselves have failed to distinguish between these groups.

Callousness and Lack of Empathy

Finally, individuals with strong psychopathic and antisocial traits are noted for a number of interpersonal deficits, such as their callousness in interpersonal relationships and lack of empathy for others. These traits are considered hallmarks of the psychopathic personality cluster, because many psychopathic individuals are characterized by not only their antisocial and impulsive behaviors but also their lack of emotional depth and callousness in dealing with other individuals. Among psychopathic individuals, callousness has been reported as a significant predictor of violent and nonviolent recidivism (e.g., Porter et al., 2001; Salekin, Ziegler, Larrea, Anthony, & Bennett, 2003), and sex-offending psychopathic individuals have had notably higher rates of callousness on psychopathy measures than violent and noncontact offender groups (Caputo et al., 1999).

Caputo et al. (1999) and Porter et al. (2001) suggested that callousness and a lack of empathy play an important role in the sex-offending process. They examined a sample of youthful sex offenders and found that early victimization and abuse experiences in the home, combined with difficulty inhibiting impulses, likely caused these youth to inadequately internalize social norms regarding guilt and empathy. Consequently, these young offenders adopted a callous and unempathic personality style that makes them more likely to victimize others. A sex offender with a callous attitude toward the well-being of others is less apt to hesitate and consider the potential impact of sexual coercion on his victim. This offender will seek to satisfy his own desires with little concern for the negative impact on the victim.

These antisocial or psychopathic traits—impulsivity, expressive anger or aggression, and lack of emotional depth and empathy—all increase the probability that an individual might engage in sexually deviant behaviors. Although not directly causal, each of these traits interacts with other aspects of the offender's personality and his immediate situation to increase the chance that a sexual assault or sexually coercive behavior can occur.

Narcissistic Traits

Narcissism, as described by Baumeister, Catanese, and Wallace (2002), is an interpersonal response style characterized by unrealistically inflated self-esteem or ego, grandiosity, dominance over and hostility toward others, lack of shame or guilt, and a general feeling of superiority and entitlement. Individuals high in narcissism are therefore more likely to perceive themselves as deserving of attention or praise from others and to react to interpersonal rejection with hostility or resentment.

Narcissism as a personality disorder trait has been linked with increased rates of violence and aggression (e.g., Nestor, 2002). Individuals with narcissism are characterized by their self-centeredness, exploitation of others in interpersonal situations, and hostility toward critical others (American Psychiatric Association, 2000; Barnard, Hankins, & Robbins, 1992). A significantly narcissistic individual could be more violence prone because of his or her inflated ego and sense of superiority and entitlement. A narcissistic or egocentric view of the world would leave the individual with the belief that violent action is justified as a response to interpersonal conflict (Salekin et al., 2003). Additionally, an individual with narcissism would be easily threatened or insulted by others because he expects an inordinate amount of praise or admiration. When this does not occur, someone high in narcissism is more likely to react with anger or hostility. He may then lash out violently toward the source of distress to relieve the feelings of insult or threatened ego (Nestor, 2002). In other words, individuals with narcissism have an inflated but fairly unstable sense of self-worth. Despite their assertions that they are superior, their past actions often do not support their inflated egos. When their self-worth is challenged, they will manifest an extremely negative and potentially violent response.

Baumeister et al. (2002) and Bushman, Bonacci, van Dijk, and Baumeister (2003) developed a narcissistic reactance model to explain rape or sexual coercion in a select group of narcissistic sex offenders. In these individuals, higher than normal rates of narcissism significantly contribute to their commission of sexually violent acts. This theory posits that those with narcissism feel substantially entitled to admiration from others. Specifically, some men who are high in narcissism might feel sexual entitlement as well, believing that they are special somehow and that they deserve sexual favors.

This particular type of man will attempt to gain sexual access to a woman seen as "unattainable" (Baumeister et al., 2002) to further the idea that he is deserving of admiration and favor from desirable others. However, if this man is rejected by the woman he has chosen, he will experience anger and narcissistic injury over the slight. The narcissistic reactance theory of rape suggests that one or more of three things will then occur: (a) The forbidden object will be seen as more desirable than it was before, (b) the injury will be repaired by attempting to engage in the forbidden behavior, and (c) the person who removed the desired object or caused insult will be attacked or become the target of some other form of aggression (Baumeister et al., 2002). In terms of sexual refusal, the narcissistic features of the rejected man may cause him to behave aggressively to prove that he can and will have what he desires.

For example, a man high in narcissism may approach a woman and proposition her for sex, feeling that he is entitled to sex and having greater expectations for sexual access to any woman he wants. She rejects him, and he feels that his ego and self-worth have been unfairly challenged. He may then react aggressively toward the woman to prove that he can have the sex that he wants and feels he rightly deserves. By engaging in this sexually violent act, the man perceives that he has reestablished his ability to have any woman that he desires. Additionally, completing the sexual act will allow the individual with narcissism to establish his perceived sexual prowess with peers, because he will be able to boast of sexual conquests without his peers knowing that he used force to obtain sex from the woman.

Empirical study of the narcissistic reactance theory of rape has suggested that men high in narcissism are more likely to endorse rape myths and other statements displaying hostility toward women, to feel less empathy for female victims of rape, to react more negatively when refused or rejected by a female, and to react aggressively when faced with sexual disappointment (Bushman et al., 2003). This evidence suggests that the presence of significant levels of trait narcissism might very well predispose these men to behave aggressively or in a hostile manner toward women when they feel they have been insulted or slighted sexually. In this case, the narcissistic cognitions and interpersonal patterns generated by an inflated ego may contribute to an increased likelihood of sexual coercion or violence.

Walker, Rowe, and Quinsey (1993) examined one facet of narcissism, authoritarianism, in relation to sex-offending behaviors. They found that a high degree of authoritarianism was significantly related to past sexually aggressive behaviors and future risk of sexual violence (but see Hunter & Figueredo, 2000). Walker et al. posited that high authoritarianism mediates sexually aggressive behavior by predisposing the person to traditional sex role beliefs, including the belief that men should be sexually dominant over women. Furthermore, these men would be easily able to justify using force to obtain sexual gratification because they feel dominant and deserving of sexual attention.

Some offenders may also manifest high levels of narcissism in violent ways to restore self-esteem or because they lack appropriate coping skills or self-sufficiency in the face of negative life events (e.g., Hunter & Figueredo, 2000). For these men, their narcissistic characteristics may limit their ability to deal positively or appropriately with rejection from others. Their grandiose and inflated feelings of sexual entitlement might also drive them to engage in coercive behaviors to garner the sexual attention they feel they deserve. They might also have marked impairments in their ability to empathize with others, which, as discussed previously, would decrease their willingness to desist from aggressive or violent sexual acts. In sum, the presence of high narcissism in a sex-offending individual might substantially contribute to his history of sexually aggressive behaviors because of the perceptual and cognitive implications of this particular personality trait.

Sadistic Traits

Although the *Diagnostic and Statistical Manual of Mental Disorders* (*DSM–IV–TR*; 4th ed., text rev.; American Psychiatric Association, 2000) describes a paraphilic disorder known as *sexual sadism*, in which an individual fantasizes about or engages in sexual activity aimed at inflicting pain, humiliation, or degradation on an unwilling victim, there are also individuals who may exhibit sadism as a general personality characteristic or trait without any specific sexual interest in sadistic behaviors. A type of personality disorder focusing exclusively on sadism was included in an earlier edition of the *DSM* as warranting further research or study (3rd ed., rev.; American Psychiatric Association, 1987). This disorder recognized the existence of individuals who engaged in cruel and sadistic acts on a regular basis and who seemed to have consistently sadistic features incorporated into their personality structure. Hare, Cooke, and Hart (1999) defined the crucial component of sadistic personality disorder as "a cruel, demeaning, and aggressive approach to interactions with other people" (p. 572). Other hallmarks of a sadistic trait cluster include intimidating or terrorizing others for personal gain, taking pleasure in the obvious suffering of others, extreme dominance or control in interpersonal relationships, and a fascination with violence or torture (Hare et al., 1999).

Sadism as a pathological personality trait has been noted for quite some time in the psychological literature, mostly in connection with sexual murder or other violent sexual crimes (e.g., Berger, Berner, Bolterauer, Gutierrez, & Berger, 1999). Rates of sadistic personality disorder and trait sadism reported in the sex-offender literature indicate that approximately one third of sex offenders meet criteria for significant sadism (Berger et al., 1999; Berner, Berger, Gutierrez, Jordan, & Berger, 1992). This implies that for some offenders sadism may play a causal or mediating role in their sexual offenses. Prentky and Knight (1991) also hypothesized that a certain type of sadistic rapist may exist who can be differentiated from more angry and impulsive rapist groups, suggesting that the sadistic desires of these rapists may play a special role in the types of sexual crimes that they commit.

Because sadistic individuals have a greater than normal desire to inflict pain and humiliation on others, this internal driving force to commit such acts may contribute to their sexual crimes. For example, if a male sadist desires to hurt or humiliate a female, he might force her to engage in demeaning and humiliating sexual acts, because this is likely an effective way for him to not only impose his will on an innocent victim but also to subject her to unnecessary pain and humiliation. Sexual homicide may also be related to sadistic impulses in this type of sex offender, given that his desire to inflict torture or great pain on a victim might culminate with the victim's death.

The relationship between sadism and sex offending is also strengthened by the research on sexual sadism as a paraphilia. Sexual sadistic individuals are individuals who engage in a variety of acts so that they may witness the psychological or physiological suffering of their victims and thereby achieve sexual pleasure or gratification. With this particular disorder, the relationship between sadism and sexual violence is more clear. In this instance, sadism has a specific goal (i.e., sexual gratification) and a specific target (i.e., sexual violence). It is therefore understandable that one who would meet criteria for sexual sadism would engage in sexually deviant and violent behaviors.

However, the relationship between sexual sadism and sadism as a general personality trait is less clear. A study by Holt, Meloy, and Strack (1999) failed to differentiate sex-offender and violent-offender groups with multiple sadism measures. Their research also indicated that psychopathy and sadism were very strongly related. Another study, by Berger et al. (1999), found similar results in that sadistic sex offenders could not be successfully differentiated from psychopathic, nonsadistic sex offenders. Additionally, these authors found a strong relationship between sexual sadism and sadistic personality disorder in their sex-offending sample. Overall, these results imply that sadism is not necessarily a discrete personality trait, and any relationship between trait sadism and sex offending may be highly confounded with psychopathy or a paraphilic diagnosis of sexual sadism. Therefore, although sadism may still mediate the actions a sex offender takes once he has engaged in an act of sexual violence, there is a complex relationship among psychopathy, deviant sexual interest, and sadistic impulses that drives the resulting behavior.

Disordered Personality Traits

Numerous diagnostic studies of sex offenders in correctional and mental health settings have demonstrated that sex offenders display significant personality pathology, with many of them displaying significant symptoms of personality disorders in Cluster B of the Axis II categories, as defined by the DSM–IV–TR (Barnard et al., 1992; Berner et al., 1992; Bogaerts, Vervaeke, & Goethals, 2004; McElroy et al., 1999). These disorders are characterized by a number of common traits, including egocentricity, impulsivity, erratic or unstable mood, difficulties with self-identity, and unpredictable behaviors with harm to self or others (American Psychiatric Association, 2000). Additional research has suggested that sex offenders may also have relevant personality problems relating to social detachment and emotional withdrawal (Cohen & Galynker, 2002; Fazel, Hope, O'Donnell, & Jacoby, 2002).

The important question is whether these elevated levels of personality pathology contribute to sex offending and sexually deviant interests. Emotional instability, as seen in many of the Cluster B personality disorders that characterize some sex-offender groups, may decrease the individual's ability to appropriately cope with negative emotional states. As mentioned in chapter 5, sex offending may become an acquired mood stabilization tool. Whenever negative emotions become unbearable for the offender, he learns that sexually deviant behaviors may increase mood and stabilize emotions.

Self-esteem difficulties, which may also be associated with personality pathology of this type, may mediate the relationship between sexually deviant interests and sexually deviant behaviors. Offenders with chronic self-identity and self-esteem problems may attach to inappropriate others (e.g., children) to feel loved and wanted. Because they have a strong need to feel good about themselves or to know who they are, they may be at risk of engaging in inappropriate behaviors that have satisfied these needs in the past. Much like fluctuating emotional states, poor self-image may be bolstered through sexual activity that promises mood stabilization and self-regulation.

Differences among sex-offender groups may emerge when one considers the role of personality pathology in the offending process. Rapists, who are typically higher in psychopathy, narcissism, and trait anger or aggression, may initiate violent sexual behaviors that reflect these characteristics. Child molesters, who are viewed as more passive and socially detached, may be more attracted to children because of their perceived nonthreatening or compliant nature. Sex offenders who engage in mostly noncontact sexual offenses, such as exhibitionists or voyeurs, may be similarly passive and socially avoidant, leading them to engage in these more withdrawn and less interpersonally detached types of sexually deviant behavior.

Finally, the primary concern regarding sex offenders with clinically significant levels of personality disorder symptoms is that these offenders are clearly troubled in terms of interpersonal relationships. Personality disorders are defined by the interpersonal distress caused by their related symptoms, and many of the symptom clusters seen in sex offenders indicate that these men have substantial difficulty with appropriate interpersonal relations. The social and cognitive problems that arise from these personality symptoms lead these offenders to become involved in inappropriate social relationships, to misinterpret the motivations and desires of others, and to become overly focused on certain aspects of the self or interpersonal interactions that may lead to aggressive and violent behaviors. Therefore, the personality traits of some sex offenders predispose them to violent or inappropriate sexual exchanges.

LIMITATIONS OF THE PERSONALITY THEORIES

Although the personality theories are attractive as potential explanations for deviant sexual behaviors, they are limited in several ways. For instance, a number of problems proscribe the use of the psychoanalytic theories as explanations of sexual deviance. Although these ideas were the prevailing etiological explanations for nearly a century, difficulty generalizing from Freud's original sample of patients, concerns regarding test validity with instruments used to establish unconscious sexual processes and desires, and the inability to make accurate and useful predictions about future sexually deviant behaviors have led to the near-abandonment of these theories as valid explanations for this type of behavior. Freud developed his ideas of internal drive states and resulting conflicts between them, and his conceptualizations of personality and psychosexual development, through his work with female "hysterics," who were substantially different from the male pedophiles and sexually sadistic or fetish-prone individuals that he later described. His use of case studies to develop a wide-reaching theory is also questionable, because the developmental pathways for one specific individual cannot be generalized to a diverse group of people.

Freud's use of clinically invalid instruments to identify sexually deviant unconscious desires is particularly problematic (Garb, Lilienfeld, & Wood, 2004; Hunsley, Lee, & Wood, 2003; Lilienfeld, Wood, & Garb, 2000). Freud's initial psychoanalytic work with his patients relied on projection as a clinically valid means to elicit personality-based responses or to establish unconscious motives and drives (Howells, 1981). Freud hypothesized that unconscious feelings or conflicts could be identified through *projection*, which relies on the impulsive actions or feelings of the id to occasionally break through the barrier of the ego or superego. For example, an individual with a strong sexual attraction to a fetish object or to children will frequently be able to suppress such drives through the actions of the ego. However, under conditions that weaken the boundaries of the ego or challenge the individual's coping mechanisms, the unconscious desires of the id may be behaviorally manifested. One such projective technique used by many psychoanalysts is the Rorschach Inkblot Test (Exner, 1974), which is said to draw forth unconscious feelings and motivations through an individual's interpretation of ambiguous stimuli. Unfortunately, this and many other projective techniques based on psychoanalytic theory have been difficult to validate as true measures of internal processes, have questionable reliability among clinicians, and are generally thought to be inappropriate for many types of clinical evaluation (Garb et al., 2004; Hunsley et al., 2003; Lilienfeld et al., 2000).

Other psychodynamic models have been similarly plagued with conceptual difficulties. Stoller's (1975, 1987, 1991) work, for example, makes assumptions regarding the development of deviant sexual interests whereby he stated that all individuals have some degree of perverse sexual interests but failed to adequately describe the mechanisms that would prevent the majority of the population from engaging in sexually deviant acts, if they do in fact have these underlying fantasies of a perverse nature. Bowlby's (1958, 1969) early work with attachment models and the development of a disordered personality lacked explanation of the relevant cognitive mechanisms that have been recently included in attachment research. Additionally, many of the psychodynamic theorists have remained true to Freud's original conceptualizations of the basic personality structure (e.g., Kernberg's, 1976, 1995, object relations model and Stoller's hostile perversion model), even though they lack empirical validation.

Another serious limitation of psychodynamic theoretical conceptualizations is their inability to generate predictive behavioral hypotheses that can be empirically tested. If it is true that all human beings possess innate drives propelling them toward sexual deviance, how do we know when they will manifest these drives in the form of sex offending? Furthermore, how do we know what level of socialization is appropriate to suppress these drives?

Finally, the overall theory did not consider the role of other psychological variables that impact and reflect personality development, such as cognitive or social factors, and the psychodynamic hypotheses that were applied to sex offending did not adequately explain other, broader types of human behavior, which substantially limits their explanatory power for very extreme or rare behaviors. For example, the psychosexual developmental stages initially described by Freud have been largely discounted as comprehensive or accurate explanations of human psychosexual development since the introduction of newer cognitive and developmental models (see Marshall & Barbaree, 1990; Ward & Hudson, 1998; Ward, Hudson, & Keenan, 1998). If Freudian psychoanalytic theory is considered inadequate to explain normal sexual development, then it is difficult to support Freudian explanations of deviant sexual development.

The second wave of personality theories used a number of testing methods to develop profiles of sex-offender groups. These profiles were often inconsistent in the testing literature, with sex offenders demonstrating a vast mixture of traits and profiles that were sometimes different from those of control participants and sometimes not. Given that many of these instruments were originally developed on normal, nonoffending, and not psychologically disturbed groups, it is therefore not surprising that a heterogeneous group of sex offenders would obtain varying scores. Applying instruments that were developed and normed on normal populations to extreme groups that demonstrate low base-rate behaviors provides invalid results. How are we to really know whether the traits or symptoms believed to be significant for sex offenders or other marginal groups could be identified using normal, nondeviant samples? Perhaps the greatest limitation of these instruments, however, lies within their construction. As many researchers have noted, the MMPI, MCMI, and similar testing instruments were developed as personality inventories using items almost entirely based on psychological symptomology (e.g., Levin & Stava, 1987). These measures are more accurate at assessing states of psychological disorder and dysfunction according to affective and behavioral signs rather than offering a useful personality profile. The results are reported in terms of how pathological the individual is rather than what type of personality he has. The use of these instruments as measures of personality traits is severely limited, because they tell us only whether the person exhibits clinically significant psychological symptoms. Therefore, the profiles or scores obtained on these personality inventories should not be applied to personality-based etiological explanations of deviant behavior. These results are more effectively used to link psychological distress or impairment with deviant and inappropriate behaviors as a whole.

Another limitation is that the trait-based theories of personality often assume traits to be stable across time and situation. However, some personality research demonstrates that behaviors deemed to be trait based may significantly vary according to characteristics of the situation. Bem and Allen (1974) found that an individual's behavioral consistency varies across situations and that personality traits are not as predictable as once supposed. Instead, personality traits interact with differing people and environments to shape behavior in seemingly inconsistent ways. In other words, instead of saying that a person is an extrovert (a trait), he may instead engage in a variety of extroverted or introverted behaviors, depending on who is present in a given interaction, what the consequences of certain behaviors may be, or the impact of other situation-based variables. Where this becomes problematic in terms of etiological theory is in trying to determine which situational variables then interact with which personality features to create a specific outcome. If these traits cannot be viewed as stable, then we will be less able to accurately and effectively predict behavior, at least until a detailed science of personality–situation interactions develops (Hicks & Sales, 2006).

A related problem arises when one considers the stability of personality traits across the life span. Some evidence suggests that with the more extreme and even pathological personality traits or dysfunctional syndrome patterns, there is a clear aging-out effect (e.g., Coolidge, Segal, & Pointer, 2000; Foster, Campbell, & Twenge, 2003; Kenan, Kendjelic, & Molinari, 2000; Molinari, Kunik, & Snow-Turek, 1999). Not only are traits situational, but also the strength of adherence to these particular traits depends on the age and life experience of any given individual. For example, psychopaths are seen as less psychopathic as they age. Individuals with extreme impulsivity and dramatic behaviors, such as those with borderline personality disorder, act in less dramatic and pathological ways from mid- to late life. This is an important consideration when evaluating the personality traits or diagnoses of personality disorder in sex-offender samples. Much of the research evaluating incarcerated sex offenders looks at men who have been incarcerated for some period of time, and many of them are relatively advanced in age. Studies that report significant age differences in their sex-offending populations are therefore limited in that older offenders may show a less dramatic personality pathology pattern than younger offenders, regardless of the sexually deviant interests, victim type, or even criminal history of the offender. Henn, Herjanic, and Vanderpearl (1976) conducted a study with rapists and child molesters and found significant age differences between the two groups. Perhaps it is not surprising that the rapists—who were significantly younger— also manifested more personality disorder traits than the child molesters. Because we cannot be sure as to what truly caused these personality differences— age or sex-offender type—these data do not contribute to our understanding of what causes these offenses. Additionally, the results of studies such as the one conducted by Fazel et al. (2002), which used only elderly sex offenders, may not be applicable to groups of juvenile or young adult offenders, given that low rates of personality pathology are likely due to age of the sample rather than any reliable personality differences.

An additional problem concerns how researchers and theorists define their terms and define personality pathology across studies. There is a significant degree of definitional overlap, not only in the research but also in our diagnostic nomenclature. For example, many of the Axis II, Cluster B personality disorders seen at elevated rates in sex-offending samples share many of the same symptoms. Impulsivity is common to borderline personality disorder as well as antisocial personality disorder or psychopathy. Egocentricity is a hallmark feature of psychopathy or antisocial personality disorder and narcissistic personality disorder. With many features in common, it is therefore difficult to say with certainty which constellation of dysfunctional personality traits is most significant in the causal explanation of deviant behavior. Unfortunately, many of these clusters also include a mix of recognized personality traits as well as attitudes and behaviors which, although related to the original personality formulation, may be only secondary to the actual trait. Including behaviors as part of personality may cloud the picture and confound our understanding of what outcomes may accurately be attributed to the original trait.

Furthermore, many researchers define their variables in such a way as to possibly exclude relevant groups from studies of personality pathology and its relationship to violence and deviant sexual behaviors. In Smallbone and Milne's (2000) study of trait anger and aggression, for example, the authors excluded any sex offenders with a psychiatric diagnosis and those who had murdered their victims. Although these exclusions were likely made to increase internal validity and for ease of comparison with non–sex-offending groups, it seems that excluding the psychologically disturbed and murderers, who likely would show high rates of anger, would decrease the findings of pathological anger. The findings of wide variations of trait anger and its expression among sex-offender groups, and the finding that trait anger and physical aggression are unrelated, are confounded by the exclusion of groups who are perhaps highest in anger and physically aggressive actions (i.e., murderers). Methodological shortcomings such as this are prevalent in the literature on sex offenders (see chap. 2, this volume), and this creates problems in defining personality constructs. When important groups are excluded from the studies, or when concepts are not clearly defined, the resulting conclusions may not be generalizable to the sex-offending population as a whole.

Another limitation concerns the assumptions underlying many of the theories regarding personality traits as mediators of sexually deviant behaviors. Most of these theories assume that the propensity for sexual violence exists. With these theories, certain personality traits are a mediating link between sexually deviant thoughts and behaviors. The sexually deviant thoughts are a given in this particular equation. Although this mediational approach may provide a promising lead in our efforts to understand sex offending, there are no corresponding explanations of how these deviant sexual thoughts came to be. And although it is important to know that certain traits may increase the probability of acting on deviant impulses, without knowing where these deviant impulses originated we do not have a clear understanding of what causes, or how to proactively prevent, sexual violence.

Furthermore, the mediational trait theories of sex offending describe many personality traits that are common to a wide range of offenders, not just sex offenders. The majority of psychopathic individuals are not sex offenders. Similarly, many impulsive, sadistic, or narcissistic individuals do not also engage in sex-offending behaviors. So although these traits may play an important role in the sex-offense process for individuals with sexually violent proclivities, it is not the case that these traits are specific to sex offenders. Because of this, we are unsure of how sex offenders are uniquely different from other offender groups. If these traits even indirectly cause sex offending, shouldn't there be more sex offenders than there are? Why don't all impulsive and egocentric individuals engage in sexual assault for the purposes of immediate sexual gratification? A review of this literature leaves the reader with the impression that something more is there and that something vital has been overlooked. It seems as if more than the mere presence of these personality traits, combined with some propensity toward sexual deviance, is probably required. Even sex offenders with deviant interests do not always engage in sex offending when the opportunity presents itself. Something else needs to be added to the explanation to make it more plausible as an specific explanation for sex offending.

In addition, the theorists using this model have not provided a complete picture of the many components of the process. The contributing factors (i.e., sexually deviant interests) are somewhat vague. Does having a sexually deviant interest mean a paraphilia? Does it imply a desire beyond the individual's control? These are not explained by the mediational trait models. Many of the variables are also hopelessly confounded. As mentioned earlier, many of the concepts or constructs within these personality clusters overlap or mean different things to different people. For example, is it the egocentricity that is the key, or is it the lack of empathy for others (which likely results from egocentricity to some extent) that is the most important component? Etiological theory and related research need to specify all of the parts of the process and how they interact.

Finally, as with many of the hypotheses and theories proposed to explain sex offending, the research is limited to the sex offenders of whom we have become aware, either through the mental health or criminal justice systems. This is important for personality theories in particular, because those whom we have identified may manifest more personality pathology or psychological problems than those whom we have yet to find. These theories may not apply equally to other, more high-functioning and perhaps psychologically stable sex offenders who have yet evaded capture. It is always the case that those offenders in custody and available for study are those who are incapable of eluding authorities or who have many other problems that prohibit them from functioning appropriately within society. This problem limits our understanding of sex offenders and their personality structure to those who have been caught and identified as sex offenders. Therefore, the theories presented thus far, which rely on the elevated rates of personality pathology found among adjudicated offenders, may apply to only a select group of sex offenders and may not accurately represent what causes sex offending for a more general group of offenders.

SUMMARY AND CONCLUSIONS

Given that personality theories, like biological theories, represent some of the earliest attempts at explaining sexually deviant behaviors, it is difficult to describe them succinctly while doing justice to their contribution to the field. In this chapter, we have examined the psychodynamic theories, including Freud's psychoanalysis and ego psychology, object relations theory, Bowlby's original version of attachment theory, and Stoller's psychodynamic conceptualizations of deviant sexuality. These theories address the impact of early childhood experiences on ego formation and personality development and how these processes may affect adult sexual functioning. Later personality theories focused on personality types derived from assessment instruments such as the MMPI, MCMI, and NEO-FFI, as well as others, which might be predictive of inappropriate sexual behaviors. Other theories focus on specific personality traits as mediators. Antisocial–psychopathic, narcissistic, and sadistic traits, in addition to personality disorder traits, may mediate important relationships between biology and environment or between thoughts and behaviors. Despite the breadth of these theories, each emphasizes the role of personality functioning in determining behavior, particularly behavior associated with sexual interest and expression.

Personality theories, like the other theories described in this book, have provided us with new ways of understanding sex-offending behaviors. Perhaps one of the most important contributions is a focus on the self and the way in which individual traits or characteristics may form a predictable pattern of behavior. Theories that acknowledge the existence of an idiosyncratic self may provide greater depth to our understanding of human beliefs, behaviors, and emotions than those that view behavior in an isolated, impersonal way. In addition, personality researchers have given personality traits a more specific role in complex behaviors; specifically, some researchers suggest that personality mediates the relationships between other variables. For example, narcissistic traits may interact with perceptions and interpersonal relationships to potentially create aggressive responding. Inclusion of the self in these ways makes inherent sense when considering the complexity of sex-offending behaviors.

A second and related beneficial component of these theories is the consideration of early experience—how it impacts the self, personality development, and later behavior. As with social learning theories (see chap. 6), there is a focus on developmental antecedents that may play a role in the process. Attachment theory, for example, places primary importance on the child's relationship with the primary caregivers. This relationship has been implicated in a variety of theories of psychopathology and may logically extend to theories of sex offending. So, although we do not always agree with psychodynamic views of childhood experience and personality development, we do agree that childhood experience is likely important in the process and should be included in future research efforts.

Finally, some of the personality theories are commendable for their efforts to include empirically driven research in theory formation. Personality types or traits derived from psychological assessments represent an effort to quantify and measure the critical etiological variables. A great deal of research has gone into the trait- or type-based personality theories, which gives us a more informed and scientific view of the phenomenon. Even though this method of creating theory has its problems (see chap. 2 as well as the section titled Limitations to the Personality Theories earlier in this chapter), the inclusion of empirical constructs may provide a more valid premise on which to develop our theoretical understanding of sex offending.

8

EVOLUTIONARY THEORIES

Evolutionary psychological theory considers human behavior to be the result of millions of years of adaptive changes designed to address specific challenges within the environment (Kennair, 2003; Siegert & Ward, 2002). Through evolution, the human mind has developed into a system of specialized modules and information-processing pathways that respond to environmental challenges or problems with distinctive adaptive behaviors (Siegert & Ward, 2002). Specific environmental stimuli are processed according to the functional adaptive responses that were most successful for early humans. However, because our current environment differs from that of our human ancestors, some behaviors will be perceived as dysfunctional or abnormal (Kennair, 2003). Because of this, evolutionary scientists have generated a number of hypotheses regarding the impact of evolutionary processes on both normal and abnormal sexual behaviors.

In this chapter, we explore a number of evolutionary theories that attempt to explain sexually deviant behaviors as the result of evolutionary processes. We begin by discussing evolutionary contributions to our understanding of sexual development and the dichotomy between male and female sexual behavior. Next, we describe four theories that rely on evolutionary postulates about sexual selection and sexual strategies to explain deviant sexual behaviors: (a) sexual coercion as a conditional sexual strategy, (b) the competitively disadvantaged male hypothesis, (c) sexual aggression as a direct adaptation, and (d) sexual aggression as a by-product of other adaptations. We then consider Freund's work (e.g., Freund, 1990; Freund & Kolarsky, 1965) with his theory of courtship disorder, which suggests that certain paraphilic behaviors are the result of faulty courtship behaviors in men. The chapter concludes with a discussion of the limitations of evolutionary theories for understanding sexually deviant behaviors.

EVOLUTION AND SEXUAL SELECTION

To ensure the survival of their species and the heritability of their individual genes, animals and humans are driven to maximize reproductive success and work toward the survival of their offspring. To accomplish these goals, organisms must not only select an appropriate mate but also successfully copulate with the chosen partner. In doing so, a number of obstacles must be addressed. The organism must consider the biological factors related to successful reproduction (e.g., physical health, genetic quality), the availability of resources needed to rear the offspring, competition for these resources, competition for desirable sexual partners, and the willingness of mates to invest the needed amount of time in parenting (Barrett, Dunbar, & Lycett, 2002; Buss, 1998).

Evolutionary scientists have hypothesized that because of fundamental differences in male and female reproductive capacities, both humans and animals evolved over time with critical differences in gender-specific mate selection preferences. Because women carry the responsibility of pregnancy, childbirth, and the nursing of offspring, they incur greater reproductive costs than do men, whose minimum reproductive contribution is the provision of genetic material via copulation. Additionally, female reproductivity is limited by length of the gestation period, age, and other relevant biological factors that do not similarly apply to males of the same species. Therefore, women not only face greater reproductive costs in their efforts to further the survival of the species but also have greater biological constraints that limit the number of offspring they can produce in a lifetime. Women must therefore be more selective when choosing mates, because they will ultimately have more to lose from poor mate choice. Men, however, can impregnate multiple women in a short period of time and are not limited by gestational period or age, so they can produce far more offspring in a lifetime and are not forced to make the same critical mate choice decisions.

This disparity between male and female reproductive capabilities and mate selection needs creates a situation in which one sex (females) has greater reproductive value and is therefore more sought after than the other sex (males; Barrett et al., 2002; Buss, 1998). Because this sex-driven difference is relatively stable in animal and human species over time, both species have developed a number of adaptations designed to maximize reproductive success in this environment. These selected-for adaptations were then passed along to the next generation in that species. Those who were unsuccessful in mate selection and reproduction therefore did not pass on their genetic traits. The sexual selection strategies that were most successful are believed to still be present in animal and human sexual behavior today (Buss, 1998).

A number of hypotheses regarding sexual selection and evolutionary adaptation have been derived from the theory of sexual selection. Women, as the more selective half of the sexual pair, will base their mating decisions on two factors. In their efforts to bear offspring that are most fit and most likely to survive, they will select mates on the basis of either their genetic fitness or their ability to provide critical resources (Buss, 1998; Miller, 1998). Desired physical traits denoting good genetic fitness have been evolutionarily selected in human species to include such factors as physical attractiveness, body symmetry, and overall strength, which suggest that the man is free from disease or genetic defects that would compromise the survival of his future offspring (Barrett et al., 2002). Additionally, women would seek men who were able to succeed in physical challenges, such as male-to-male competition, to further demonstrate their strength and genetic deservedness. A more important selection factor typically is the ability to provide resources for offspring. A man's ability to supply food, protection from predators, and other material necessities predicts a woman's willingness to copulate with that man. If he is able to provide for the offspring and ensure their survival into adulthood, it would help alleviate the costs to the woman associated with childbirth and child rearing (Buss, 1998; Miller, 1998).

Men also use a number of strategies to identify potential mates that have proven evolutionarily successful in producing viable offspring. Men seek out women who appear to be capable of reproducing, using such indicators of fertility as age, physical appearance, and general health. Men, for example, would not benefit reproductively from mating with women who are incapable of conception or who appeared to have serious disease or physiological defects that might indicate poor fitness (Barrett et al., 2002). However, because men are biologically able to invest less in the reproductive process, they may not have to attend to such factors as rigidly as do women. The cost for men for copulating with a reproductively undesirable woman is far less than for a woman who copulates with a reproductively undesirable man.

Because men are attempting to copulate with sexually selective women, they must use a variety of tactics or strategies to gain mate access. These may include physical displays of strength or prowess to demonstrate genetic quality or the ability to protect young, displays of resources or wealth to indicate an ability to assist in the rearing of offspring, or any other tactic designed to guarantee that the woman will mate with the man in question. One of these possible tactics is sexual aggression and rape.

SEXUAL SELECTION, HUMAN SEXUAL AGGRESSION, AND RAPE

Evolutionary psychologists have noted that the human ability to adapt to changing environmental conditions is an evolutionary adaptation that furthers the survival of our species (Gangestad & Simpson, 2000; Jones, 1999; Thornhill & Thornhill, 1992). Quick response to rapid change allows humans the flexibility to judge a situation and decide from a number of alternatives which behavior would be most appropriate for enhancing success or survival. This selected-for adaptiveness applies to a wide range of human behaviors, including sexual and reproductive activities. Those who were most successful in terms of adapting their behavioral choices to environmental demands were those most successful in gene propagation (Malamuth & Heilmann, 1998).

In this way, reproductive strategies could be conditional in nature, with the organism demonstrating remarkable flexibility in his or her attempts to obtain access to a desirable mate. Given that the male of the species must expend more effort in securing a mate, males will show greater adaptability in their efforts to attract females. Human males, like males of other species, display a variety of healthy reproductive strategies and related tactics to secure a mate, including demonstrations of genetic fitness, direct male competition, and provision of necessary resources. Sexual coercion or aggression has also been argued to be a reproductive strategy (Gangestad & Simpson, 2000; W. M. Shields & Shields, 1983; Thornhill & Thornhill, 1983, 1992).

Conditional Sexual Strategies

Evolutionary theorists have noted, on the basis of both animal and human research, that female compliance is not a necessary condition of copulation and reproduction. Males may successfully impregnate unwilling females. Researchers have examined this fact in relationship to sexual violence committed by males against females to explain the existence of rape and other sexual offenses. These behaviors lie on a continuum, with rape representing a more primitive sexual strategy; culturally learned strategies, such as acquisition of resources, represent a more recent and acceptable adaptational strategy (Bailey, 1988). Regardless of whether rape is necessarily an adaptational strategy today, the success of this strategy in past generations in primitive environments created a genetic pattern that may still exist (Bailey, 1988; Malamuth & Heilmann, 1998; Thornhill & Palmer, 2000).

Within this theory of conditional sexual strategies, a number of factors are particularly relevant. Blocked opportunity may be important, in that when men are somehow prevented from finding adequate mating opportunities they may switch to alternative strategies that involve mating by coercion or direct force (e.g., Figueredo, Sales, Russell, Becker, & Kaplan, 2000; Lalumiere,

Chalmers, Quinsey, & Seto, 1996; Malamuth & Heilmann, 1998; Quinsey & Lalumiere, 1995). Another factor that may drive the man to switch mating strategies is the degree of risk he is willing to take to secure mate access (Lalumiere, Harris, Quinsey, & Rice, 2005). If a man views the potential consequences of sexual coercion as acceptable risk, it will increase his likelihood of acting in a coercive manner. This variable, typically referred to as *mating effort*, strongly influences the amount of time and energy that a man will expend in pursuit of sexual partners (Lalumiere et al., 2005; Lalumiere & Quinsey, 1996). Although the direction of the relationship is not entirely clear, evidence has shown that sexually coercive men engage in a higher degree of mating effort than non–sexually coercive men (Lalumiere et al., 2005). These men also engage in other risky behaviors, including criminal and antisocial activity, suggesting that their high degree of mating effort and sexual coerciveness may be related to a more general willingness to take risks to achieve some desired goal. Sexual offenses such as rape may result from the man's drive to engage in sexual activity and his willingness to engage in high risk behaviors to do so.

The potential cost of sexual coercion or rape is also a critical factor in the selection of a sexual strategy, because behaviors with the least costs will be viewed as the most viable alternatives. For example, features such as infrequent punishment of rape, societal acceptance of coercive sexual behavior, and a low likelihood of detection indicate that the man will incur few personal costs in selecting a coercive sexual strategy. Another important factor is the man's perception of rape as an important contributor to lifetime reproductive success (W. M. Shields & Shields, 1983; Thornhill & Palmer, 2004). Because men face fewer reproductive costs than women (e.g., time, physical constraints), they can produce a greater number of offspring over the course of a lifetime and can have multiple partners using multiple mating strategies (e.g., rape, deception) to maximize mating success. The men's perceptions of lifetime reproductive potential and life span (Thornhill & Palmer, 2004) influences how they will view their need to reproduce in the immediate environment.

Finally, a number of other psychological and developmental factors are involved in determining the conditions under which alternatives may be selected. Gene–environment interactions during development, specific psychological adaptations activated throughout the life span, and the interaction between relevant psychological mechanisms and static environmental conditions all relate to the man's propensity to select coercive versus noncoercive, appropriate sexual mating strategies (Thornhill & Palmer, 2000, 2004). When potential benefits of coercive sexual behavior exceed the costs of such behavior, then it becomes adaptive for that particular organism or species (W. M. Shields & Shields, 1983; Thornhill & Thornhill, 1983, 1992). From an evolutionary perspective, men who use a conditional approach to selecting a viable reproductive strategy will be the most successful at gene propagation.

The basic premise of the conditional sexual strategies hypothesis is that men use a number of conditional sexual strategies to secure mate access, some of which may involve coercive or inappropriate behaviors. Central to this hypothesis is the idea that all men are equipped with multiple strategies by which they can either attract or secure potential mating partners. Over time, each man will develop alternative tactics that represent preferred mating behaviors. Whether they will use a certain tactic or rely on a specific strategy is largely conditioned on personal experience and factors within the environment.

W. M. Shields and Shields (1983) divided human male conditional sexual strategies into three primary groups: (a) honest courtship, in which the man uses reproductive strategies that emphasize either genetic fitness or the ability to provide resources in a socially and culturally condoned manner; (b) deceitful or manipulative courtship, in which the man deceives the woman in such a way that she falsely believes that he is willing to invest in potential offspring; and (c) coercive or forcible rape tactics, in which the man denies the woman mate choice and copulates with her against her will.

These authors as well as others (e.g., Jones, 1999) note that men may be capable of all three of these strategies and will use them, or move back and forth on the continuum proposed by Bailey (1988), depending on conditions within the environment and the costs and benefits that would result from selecting one particular strategy over another. In other words, underlying this hypothesis is the assumption that all men will posses very similar strategies in their potential behavioral repertoire, including those that involve rape and sexual coercion. What motivates men to rape or engage in other inappropriate sexual behaviors depends on environmental conditions that drive behavior choice, such as female vulnerability, availability of mating opportunity, and the potential costs of certain sexual behaviors.

Evolutionary researchers have gathered evidence from sexual behavior patterns in animal species to support the idea of rape and other sexually coercive behaviors as an evolved, adaptive sexual strategy for men. Much as has been proposed for human rape, animal rape is said to occur under certain conditions, such as male dominance (Nadler, 1988; Smuts, 1996; Smuts & Smuts, 1993), female inability to escape or resist male sexual attention (Nadler, 1988; Smuts & Smuts, 1993), and intense male competition for mates (G. R. Brown, 2000; Crawford & Galdikas, 1986; Smuts, 1996; Smuts & Smuts, 1993).

Animal models have been used therefore to explain the conditional sexual strategies model proposed by W. M. Shields and Shields (1983), positing that all males are in some way capable of sexual aggression. Evidence from insect studies—specifically, studies of scorpionfly mating strategies—demonstrates that males may engage in a variety of tactics to successfully attract a female sexual partner. These males will then use whichever strategies are most successful for them, which may involve engaging in forced copulation (e.g., Crawford & Galdikas, 1986; Thornhill & Palmer, 2004; Thornhill & Sauer, 1991).

Competitively Disadvantaged Males

This hypothesis, also sometimes referred to as the *mate deprivation hypothesis*, was derived from the idea that not all males will have access to normal or appropriate sources of reproductive opportunity. Certain characteristics of the male or of his environment may make him a less desirable reproductive partner. Because he is unable to find a suitable mate in socially acceptable ways (e.g., providing resources for potential offspring), he will turn to sexual coercion to secure mating opportunities to propagate his individual genes (Figueredo et al., 2000; Lalumiere et al., 1996; Malamuth & Heilmann, 1998; Quinsey & Lalumiere, 1995). Sexually coercive tactics, such as verbal threats and physical force (e.g., rape), allow the male to secure a mate in spite of his relative disadvantage. Despite the female's unwillingness to engage in sexual activity with this male, she may still conceive and rear his offspring. Therefore, men who use sexually coercive tactics to reproduce are successful in passing on their genetic material and indirectly passing on sexually coercive mating strategies as an adaptive means to an end.

There are environmental and interpersonal variables that can be used to explain sexual coercion from a competitive-disadvantage standpoint, as well as research that supports this theory. In our earlier discussion of available tactics that men may use to gain access to fertile women, a number of factors emerged that are significant in the mating process. First, men use a variety of alternatives to demonstrate their reproductive worth to potential mates. Second, the alternatives that they use depend largely on an interaction between the needs of the woman and the demands of the environment. Under some conditions, women may desire a mate who demonstrates resources that will provide materially for the offspring. In other instances, in which perhaps offspring require more care or supervision during infancy, the woman may choose a mate who is likely to assist in the day-to-day tasks associated with child rearing. Finally, a woman may seek a mate who demonstrates an exceptionally strong genetic makeup. There are instances in which a man is unable to meet the requirements of the woman or the demands of the mating environment and therefore may be excluded from the potential pool of acceptable mates.

Three general categories of disadvantage may apply to this last group of men. First, a lack of physical attractiveness or relative strength may convey poor genetic quality, poor nutritional status, or a history of disease or parasitic infection (Figueredo et al., 2000). Women may view men in this category as undesirable mates because poor genetic material or an inability to ward off disease or infection could be passed on to the offspring. Other features of the man aside from physical appearance also may suggest genetic unsuitability to the woman, such as poor behavioral control or limited intellectual capacity. Although research has not directly evaluated the physical attractiveness or relative strength and health of sex-offending men compared with non–sex-offending men, some findings have demonstrated that sex offenders who used coercive strategies in their sex offenses demonstrated high rates of learning disabilities and overall intellectual deficit (e.g., Awad & Saunders, 1989).

Second, the man may lack the ability to provide resources for the woman and potential offspring. Men who are socioeconomically disadvantaged within their social group might not be able to offer the material goods and support necessary to rear offspring to an independent adulthood. In a social group in which women place high value on these resources, men of low social status or material wealth might be excluded from a woman's pool of potential male partners (Figueredo et al., 2000; Lalumiere et al., 1996; Palmer, 1992; Thornhill & Thornhill, 1983). These men are therefore deprived of the opportunity to gain mate access because of their limited ability to offer the desired resources. Some support for this assertion has been noted in the literature by researchers who attest that the vast majority of rapists are young, economically disadvantaged men who would lack the resources historically associated with evolutionary models of reproductive competition (Thornhill & Thornhill, 1983, 1992).

Third, social skills or general interpersonal competency would affect a man's ability to compete for mating opportunities. Men who are unable to competently interact with potential sexual partners are less likely to obtain sexual mating opportunities (Figueredo et al., 2000; Lalumiere et al., 1996; Thornhill & Thornhill, 1983) and thus will need to use an alternate means of securing mate access. Once again, using coercive sexual tactics will allow these men to engage in the reproductive process from which they have been excluded. Thornhill and Thornhill (1983) noted that research supports this idea that rapists have greater social and interpersonal deficits, citing rapists' low self-esteem, poor self-motivation, interpersonal submissiveness, and poor social skills.

Animal models of behavior have also been applied to the competitively disadvantaged male hypothesis, with researchers positing that certain behaviors by animals, within certain groups, reflect the assumptions of this theory. For example, rape within various primate species is more likely to involve subadult males who are unlikely to successfully challenge dominant adult males for female access (e.g., Crawford & Galdikas, 1986; Smuts, 1996; Smuts & Smuts, 1993). These males are therefore unable to compete for mating opportunities and will use subversive coercive strategies to reproduce. However, research on primate sexual aggression reveals that sexually coercive behaviors are characteristic of nearly all males in several primate species, suggesting that it is not only competitively disadvantaged males who are capable of rape (Crawford & Galdikas, 1986; Nadler, 1988).

Rape as Adaptation

Some evolutionary researchers have suggested that the presence of coercive sexual behavior—specifically, rape—results from a direct evolutionary adaptation. Those who adhere to this theory note that rape and other coercive sexual behaviors likely evolved in response to certain environmental conditions in order to influence reproductive success (Thornhill & Palmer, 2000; Thornhill & Thornhill, 1992). These adaptations were purposefully designed to solve certain evolutionary problems, namely, limitations or barriers to successful mating. Thornhill and Thornhill (1992) suggested that men's ability to detect vulnerable victims, select women of child-bearing age, and engage in sexual activity in the absence of female desire are all evidence that men have a specific adaptation for rape and sexual coercion. From this perspective, rape was specifically designed as a viable alternative in environments that limited a man's ability to reproduce.

The theory that rape is a specific adaptation can be applied to other evolutionary ideas, including the conditional sexual strategies and mate deprivation hypotheses. Individuals who are successful in gene propagation by means of forced copulation will pass along their genes and reproductive techniques to future generations of men. Sexual coercion as a direct adaptation can then be applied to conditional sexual strategies, so that we could expect all men to have purposefully inherited sexual aggression as a successful mating technique. It can also be applied to the mate deprivation hypothesis, according to which men who are unsuccessful using appropriate mating strategies will directly adapt to use coercive mating strategies.

Rape as a By-Product

Others, however, believe that sexually coercive behaviors are a by-product of other male adaptations, such as a greater desire for sexual activity and sexual variety, the willingness to engage in impersonal sex, and the use of aggression to satisfy desires and demonstrate fitness (Malamuth & Heilmann, 1998; Palmer, 1991; Thornhill & Palmer, 2000). Sexual aggression is then an indirect effect of other evolutionary adaptations. For example, an adaptation for greater sexual desire or motivation allowed for the genetic survival of men who sought out more mating opportunities but also likely created situations in which men engaged in sexual activity against the will of their female partner(s). Similarly, an adaptation favoring aggressive behavior might also increase the use of aggression in multiple areas, perhaps including sexual activity.

If one applies this hypothesis to the earlier described evolutionary theories of sexual coercion, sexually aggressive behavior could have evolved as a by-product of other conditional sexual strategies, thereby increasing the likelihood that numerous men will be capable of committing sexually aggressive acts. For example, an evolved sexual strategy favoring mate variety, whereby men seek out multiple women with whom to mate, might also result in men being less concerned with the desires or willingness of each individual female partner. Similarly, coercive mating tactics might be used by disadvantaged men as a by-product of other evolved tactics, such as the use of aggression to fulfill needs and desires.

In support of the rape-as-by-product hypothesis, Palmer (1991) cited research evidence from interspecies rapes by marine animals. In these situations, the rape would not result in viable offspring, therefore making it unlikely that the rape was driven by a directly adapted sexual strategy. If it does not produce offspring, it would not be adaptive. However, using the rape-as-by-product perspective, the rape may be attributable to other male adaptations, such as a low threshold for physiological arousal. From this view, the rape is the result of the male becoming easily sexually aroused. Palmer (1991) further noted that the occurrence of rape in primate models is not limited to males who are incapable of securing a willing mate, again supporting the idea that noncompetitively disadvantaged males are capable of rape because it is a by-product of general male aggressiveness in the species.

Courtship Disorder

Courtship disorder was initially formulated and proposed by Freund (1990; Freund, Scher, & Hucker, 1983, 1984) as an explanation for a variety of sexually inappropriate behaviors, including exhibitionism, voyeurism, frotteurism (i.e., the nonconsensual rubbing against another person for the purpose of sexual arousal), and preferential rape. Freund and other researchers suggested that humans, much like animals, have appropriate courtship patterns that assist them in attracting and securing a suitable mating partner. These courtship patterns may be linked to evolutionary theory in that they represent successful mating strategies that have been selected for over time and across species. A variety of sexually coercive and inappropriate behaviors, therefore, may be attributable to deviations from normal courtship practices.

Early work by Freund and Kolarsky (1965) postulated that individuals, once interested in finding a potential mating partner and engaging in sexual activity, seek out sexual partners by engaging in a courtship pattern consisting of four phases: (a) location and appraisal of a partner; (b) pretactile interaction, including looking, smiling, or talking to the potential partner; (c) tactile interaction; and (d) sexual union (Freund, 1990; Freund & Blanchard, 1986; Freund, Scher, & Hucker, 1983; Freund & Watson, 1990). In this way, humans interact in a predictable manner regarding sexual attraction and mating. A human male will attempt to locate a mating partner and appraise the potential value of this partner. He then will use a variety of nontactile methods of attracting or demonstrating interest in the identified individual. Finally, the man will engage in intimate tactile contact and then sexual contact with the selected partner.

Deviations from the typical courtship patterns include exaggerations, distortions, or complete omissions of any of the four phases noted here (Freund, 1990; Freund & Blanchard, 1986; Freund et al., 1983; Freund, Seto, & Kuban, 1997; Freund & Watson, 1990). In addition to suggesting that some paraphilic behaviors result from deviations from the normal patterns of courtship interaction, these researchers also have hypothesized that some individuals perhaps develop a specific preference for moving directly from the early sexual interest to sexual union or orgasm, thereby in effect bypassing the typical stages of the sexual mating process (Freund et al., 1997; Price, Gutheil, Commons, Kafka, & Dodd-Kimmey, 2001).

Freund (1990) outlined ways in which each of a number of paraphilias could be linked to these distortions or exaggerations of the four phases of sexual interaction. He hypothesized that voyeurism is perhaps a distortion of the first phase, in which a man would be seeking out a potential sexual partner. Voyeuristic behavior represents a deviation from the appropriate behaviors involved in looking for and subtly appraising the value of a potential mate. Exhibitionism and telephone scatologia were regarded as deviations from the pretactile phase, in which an individual would typically use verbal and expressive means of attracting a partner or expressing sexual interest. Frotteurism or "toucherism" was regarded by Freund as an example of a gross exaggeration of the tactile phase (see also Freund et al., 1997), and rape was seen as a deviation in the fourth phase, with the three earlier phases being entirely omitted (see also Freund & Seto, 1998). Freund and Blanchard (1986) suggested that all men have the potential to distort these phases to achieve sexual goals, though possibly as only a vestigial remnant of ancestral mating strategies.

One important finding related to the concept of courtship disorder is the high rate of comorbidity between the paraphilic disorders related to inappropriate courtship. Individuals who show behavioral patterns consistent with deviation from one phase of the courtship process are likely to show other deviations or distortions as well (Freund, 1990; Freund & Blanchard, 1986; Freund et al., 1997; Freund & Watson, 1990). In other words, individuals who prefer exhibitionist behavior, a distortion of the pretactile phase, are also likely to engage in deviant behaviors related to the other phases, such as voyeurism (looking and appraisal phase) or frotteurism (tactile phase). This high rate of co-occurrence is said to result from an underlying disruption in the ability or desire to engage in the appropriate courtship behaviors in the normative or typical sequence. Numerous studies have demonstrated consistent and significant links among these various disorders, again primarily including exhibitionism, voyeurism, frotteurism, telephone scatologia, and preferential rape (Freund & Blanchard, 1986; Freund et al., 1983, 1984; Freund & Seto, 1998; Freund et al., 1997; Freund & Watson, 1990). This evidence supports the conclusion that there is likely an underlying causal disturbance, namely, courtship disorder, that explains the significant relationship between these particular disorders.

LIMITATIONS OF THE EVOLUTIONARY THEORIES

The introduction of evolutionary theories of sex offending and sexual coercion into the psychological literature has sparked a great deal of controversy. Many researchers have noted the limitations of these theories, critiquing their underlying assumptions, their focus on only a narrow group of individuals (i.e., male sexual deviants), and the problems that occur when trying to extend animal behaviors to human motivations. Given that such a large literature on the limitations of evolutionary hypotheses exists (e.g., Travis, 2003), we identify here only the major criticisms of these models.

Perhaps one of the most oft-cited criticisms of evolutionary explanations for rape and sexual coercion is that only a small proportion of sexual victimization is explained. Work by Thornhill and Thornhill (1992) and Thornhill and Palmer (2000) suggested that proof of the assumption that sexually inappropriate behaviors are reproductively motivated may be found in the demographic characteristics of rape victims (i.e., predominantly females of child-bearing age and victims not so severely harmed as to prevent conception and successful childbirth; the majority of these rapes occur vaginally to maximize reproductive benefit). However, despite these demographic statistics, there is still the matter of other sex offenses that do not fall into these categories and that are not adequately explained by the supposition that sexual assault results from a desire to reproduce. Many victims of sexual offenses are incapable of bearing children (e.g., male victims, child victims, postmenopausal women, and victims who are murdered during the course of the sexual offense; e.g., Brownmiller & Mehrhof, 1992; Coyne, 2003; Koss, 2003; Lloyd, 2003). Vaginal penetration is not the only type of sexual assault, and it may not even be the primary means of sexual penetration used against victims. In addition, this model explains only a small portion of sexually deviant behaviors, namely, forcible rape. It does not explain pedophilia, zoophilia, and other sex offenses committed for nonreproductive purposes. A final instance of nonreproductively driven sexual assault is incest: Mating within the family would likely be selected against in an evolutionary context, because any offspring produced might be challenged in terms of their survival.

Although some researchers have claimed that sexual assaults against potentially child-bearing females are the majority, perhaps fewer than 50% of actual sexual victimizations meet the necessarily criteria for reproductive viability (Coyne, 2003). Furthermore, although some authors (e.g., Thornhill & Palmer, 2000) have assumed that evidence of reproductive motivation demonstrates adaptation, they failed to note what percentage of sexual assaults would have to be reproductively successful to prove this assumption (Coyne, 2003). Finally, this theory presupposes a sexual, reproductive motivation for rape, which is not supported by the research on victimization and deviant sexual interests (Coyne, 2003; Kimmel, 2003; Koss, 2003).

A second major limitation of the evolutionary explanations has two components. The primary concern is related to the assumption that the individuals perpetrating these offenses are male and that their predisposition toward rape or other sexual assaults is a common, almost universal male trait. Although the majority of known sex offenders are male, there is a growing consensus that females are also responsible for a significant amount of sexual crime (e.g., Becker, Hall, & Stinson, 2001; Grayston & De Luca, 1999; Lewis & Stanley, 2000; B. K. Schwartz & Cellini, 1995). If, according to evolutionary theory, women have different motivations and methods for engaging in sexual activity, then it also stands to reason that they likely have different motivations than men for engaging in sexually deviant activities. Evolutionary theories of sex offending, even more gender-neutral ones such as courtship disorder, have not addressed the potential role of gender in the context of sex offending.

A secondary yet more important concern, though, is the claim that the likelihood or the ability to commit sexually coercive acts is common to all men and merely requires the appropriate environmental or social conditions to evoke sexually violent behavior. It is contradictory to say that sexually coercive acts developed as a specific, evolved strategy to perpetuate the genes of a select few who used this strategy and to say that it is common to all males in our species. If there is an evolutionary, selected-for advantage for those individuals to commit sexually coercive acts, it would make sense to assume that this trait or inherited characteristic would be present in a majority of men, because anything guaranteeing survival of an individual's genetic characteristics increases the likelihood of those characteristics appearing in the population. However, it is not possible to say that this trait is universal and at the same time differentially inheritable—affecting only a few men within the population (e.g., Bixler, 1992; Lloyd, 2003). If this theory were accurate, then we would expect to see more rapists and higher rates of sexual victimization occur in our society. The conditions that proponents of evolutionary theory have described as those that are necessary to evoke rape (e.g., limited mating opportunity, presence of vulnerable victims) are not rare and therefore do not explain the relatively low rates of sexual assault.

A third limitation relates to the evidentiary basis of the evolutionary theories. Researchers developed explanations of certain human sexual behaviors as adaptational in nature on the basis of observations made in the animal kingdom. Although humans and animals share certain fundamental motivations (e.g., food, survival) that would link them in terms of functional adaptiveness, it is questionable whether complex human behaviors can be quickly and easily explained by relying on animal analogs. There are many important differences between humans and animals that limit the comparability of their behaviors. One such problem is assigning a human label, such as rape, to an animal behavior. The definition of *rape*, in human terms, relies on an understanding of will and consent. *Submission* and *instinct* may be better concepts to describe animal behavior than *consent* (e.g., Kimmel, 2003; S. A. Shields & Steinke, 2003). An additional problem is that researchers have successfully described instances in which sexual coercion appears in animal species, but they have not explained how some animal species seem to be characterized by the absence of forced sexual behaviors (Kimmel, 2003). Finally, comparisons made between human sexual behavior and the reproductive behaviors of animals cannot account for the role of such important concepts as reasoning, judgment, and problem solving in sexual behavior and offending.

A fourth criticism of the evolutionary explanations relies on this last point. These models typically exclude, or only briefly address, the role of important cognitive and psychological variables that likely play a role in the development of sexually deviant behaviors and interests. For example, human sexual behavior is closely tied with various cognitive and affective processes, including the interpretation of emotions, perceptions of the behaviors and emotional needs of others, social norms, and attitudes about sexual and other behaviors (Akins & Windham, 1992; Ward & Siegert, 2002a). Even in a conditional model of sexual strategies, psychological mechanisms, such as perceptions of environmental conditions, are vital to understanding how behavioral choices are made (Smuts, 1992). Additionally, the human ability to use language to communicate goals and desires is also relevant for understanding multiple forms of human interaction, including sexual behavior (Futterman & Zirkel, 1992). The role of these and other important cognitive and affective processes is largely ignored by evolutionary theories that focus almost entirely on rote reproductive processes and an unconscious drive to reproduce.

A fifth concern is that although these theories may seem appealing on a theoretical basis, they present significant challenges to researchers interested in empirically testing them. According to evolutionary theory, many of these adaptational processes began very early in the development of humanity, when the behaviors were adaptive, but these same behaviors may be maladaptive in current environments. How are we to know whether they were ever adaptive to begin with? We lack the ability to test things that happened thousands and perhaps millions of years ago, leaving us to conjecture about how humans and other animals developed and interacted with one another in earlier times. Furthermore, to test current ideas of how humans select mates or engage in typical courtship patterns we must rely heavily on self-report, and not only must we use self-report from a potentially unreliable population (i.e., sex offenders), but we must also ask them about cognitive processes and motivations that are likely outside of their own awareness (e.g., why they selected vulnerable yet fertile victims; S. A. Shields & Steinke, 2003).

A sixth concern has been expressed by many authors who have criticized Thornhill and Palmer (2000) and other evolutionary theorists for their use of sexual assault statistics and other relevant data to support their claims. The myriad definitions of *rape* used in this research (e.g., rape between adults, in which consent is an issue, vs. rape between animals, in which consent is impossible to assess) limit the ability of researchers to accurately test and explain this phenomenon (Lloyd, 2003; S. A. Shields & Steinke, 2003; Ward & Siegert, 2002a). Other authors suggest that evolutionary psychologists in favor of an adaptational explanation for sexually aggressive behaviors have used only those statistics or data that support their ideas, perhaps excluding relevant but conflicting victim and perpetrator information (Allgeier & Wiederman, 1992; Coyne, 2003; Koss, 2003). The use of self-report information in various studies reinforces this concern, given that men in these samples may have motivation to minimize or exaggerate their typical sexual practices (S. A. Shields & Steinke, 2003). Similarly, the claims that the majority of men who commit these offenses are young and economically disadvantaged— and therefore competitively disadvantaged—use selective statistics and fail to account for significant biases in reporting of offenses and processing in the legal and judicial system.

A final criticism is that there is a logical fallacy in the reasoning process of evolutionary theorists. Scientists identified a behavior (i.e., sexual coercion) and labeled it as a solution to some ancestral, evolutionary problem. From that, evolutionary researchers inferred the cause and the function of sexually inappropriate behaviors as a means by which to propagate the species. One cannot assume the cause of a behavior based on the mere existence of the problem (S. A. Shields & Steinke, 2003). Stating that men rape because it is or at one time was in their best interests to do so does not truly explain the existence of sexual aggression. And being unable to verify the existence of the early problem leaves us unable to verify the existence of this set of theoretical propositions.

SUMMARY AND CONCLUSIONS

Evolutionary theories have been proposed to explain a variety of human and animal behaviors, including sexual aggression and rape. In the first part of this chapter, we reviewed the basic premises underlying human sexual interaction from an evolutionary perspective. This included a discussion of the differential reproductive capabilities of men and women and the impact that this difference had on successful strategies for human reproduction and gene propagation. We then explored several hypotheses that have emerged from this research, focusing on the outcome of sexually aggressive or coercive behaviors (i.e., rape). The first of these looked at rape as one of several conditional sexual strategies, whereby environmental demands and interactional experiences dictate which of several potential strategies may be selected. The second hypothesis explained rape as an outcome of competitive disadvantage for some men, whereby they lack the resources or genetic fitness to secure mate access through other, more appropriate means. The next two views considered rape as either a direct adaptation or a mere by-product of other, related adaptations. Finally, courtship disorder described rape and other inappropriate sexual behaviors as interruptions of a normal mating process, with potential deviations occurring in any of four sequential stages.

Evolutionary theories have provided us with a unique perspective on the development of sexually deviant behaviors. Although there are considerable limitations to this approach, several important features must be emphasized to inform future research. One of the most significant features of these theories is that sex-offending behaviors are viewed as adaptations for environmental or interpersonal events. As we have mentioned in earlier chapters, some theories have excluded environmental contingencies and learning processes or have given them only a minor role in the development of sexually deviant behavior. Evolutionary theories place environmental demands, even if remote, at the forefront of the process. Like social learning theories or behavioral models, evolutionary theories describe responses from the environment as critical determinants of behavior.

Although we do not necessarily agree with the nature of the adaptation that is described in this line of research, it is interesting to consider that sexual behaviors may serve some purpose for the individual and not simply result from blind coincidence or some predetermined abnormality within the individual. Viewing sexual deviance as functional, whether adaptive or maladaptive in the given context, takes us in a different direction for research into the etiology and treatment of these behaviors.

A final point is that evolutionary theorists examining sexual deviance have conducted theory-based research, which is less often seen in the etiological research as a whole. Using previously developed models to test their primary hypotheses demonstrates the way in which other theories should be devised and empirically tested.

9

INTEGRATIVE THEORIES AND MODELS

Thus far, we have discussed single-faceted theoretical explanations for sexually deviant interests and behaviors. However, given the complex nature of human behavior and human thought, it is too simplistic to conceptualize sex offending as the result of actions in only one domain. It is not surprising, then, that many researchers have used the basic components of the theories reviewed in chapters 3 through 8 to create multifaceted, integrated models in the hopes of achieving a better understanding sexual deviance. In this chapter, we consider the major integrated theories and models of sex offending, including those by Finkelhor (1984), Marshall and Barbaree (1990), Hall and Hirschman (1991, 1992), Malamuth (1996, 1998a, 1998b), and Ward and Siegert (2002b). Because these authors presented their theories in a single article or book chapter, we are able to critically review all of them in this chapter.

FINKELHOR'S PRECONDITION MODEL

In 1984, Finkelhor introduced the *precondition model*, which integrated a variety of internal and external variables to explain sex-offending behaviors. This model is notable for the fact that it combines a number of theoretical orientations into a comprehensive etiological structure—a first in the area of sex offending, which until this point had exclusively relied on univariate etiological approaches—and because it introduces potential interactions between internal psychological vulnerabilities and external or situational factors that are often associated with the commission of a sex offense. The resulting theory is relatively straightforward, with four preconditions that Finkelhor theorized were necessary for a sex offense to occur. Because this theory specifically refers to child sexual abuse, throughout this section we refer to *child victims* and describe the perpetrators of the sex offense as *child molesters*.

The first precondition is the *motivation to sexually abuse*. Finkelhor (1984) noted that motivation is a necessary component of any behavioral process and that motivation to sexually offend had not yet been exhaustively examined by researchers. He suggested that there are three components to motivation, the first of which is *emotional congruence*. This refers to the emotional role the victim plays for the offender and the impact of the sexual act itself. For some offenders, it is likely that relating sexually to a child serves an important emotional function. For others, the mere act of sexual release or satisfaction will serve that need, and a child merely fills the role of sexual partner. In this case, the potential emotional ramifications of the sex offense will motivate sexually deviant behavior. The second motivator described by Finkelhor is *sexual arousal*. If an offender views a child as sexually arousing, that by itself could motivate him to commit a sexually inappropriate act with a child. Finally, *blockage* is a motivating factor behind sex-offending behaviors. This occurs when other sources of sexual gratification (e.g., adult partners) are unavailable or do not carry the same potential for sexual gratification. Finkelhor listed several examples of each of these motivators, including arrested emotional development; a need for power and control; inadequate social skills; and psychodynamic factors, such as narcissistic association with young children or castration anxiety. He also described cultural factors that may play a role in driving the offender, such as the erotic portrayal of children in advertising or prevalence of child pornography. He combined these factors without regard to their theoretical underpinnings; the important point to note is that Finkelhor described this process as highly idiosyncratic, so that each offender has a unique combination of needs and desires that will determine his ultimate behavior.

The second precondition involves *overcoming internal inhibitors*. Finkelhor (1984) stated that this one factor by itself is not enough to initiate abuse but that it is crucial for the offender to somehow overcome inhibitions in order to commit a sexually inappropriate act with a child once motivated to do so. Internal inhibitions may include such factors as social norms or learned moral values. Examples of these disinhibiting factors on an individual level would be alcohol or other drug intoxication, mental disorder, or poor impulse control. An example of cultural disinhibitors would be weak or ineffective legal sanctions against child molesters. These factors would therefore increase an offender's likelihood of acting on his motivation to sexually abuse a child.

The third precondition is that the offender must *overcome external inhibitors*. These are factors that would essentially make it more difficult for an offender to find a suitable victim, such as good parental supervision, strong social networks, and strong maternal bond between mother and child. Therefore, for an offender to successfully select and victimize a particular child, he must rely on factors such as poor supervision of the child or increased opportunity to be alone with the child (e.g., babysitting).

The fourth and final necessary precondition is *overcoming the resistance of the child*. This in particular refers to the vulnerability of the victim. Offenders typically seek out children who are emotionally deprived or who are unaware of sexual abuse and sexual boundaries. Furthermore, the offender might take advantage of situations in which he and the child share a great deal of trust. In these instances, the offender cannot only commit a deviant sexual act but also decrease the likelihood of being caught and sanctioned for such behavior.

Finkelhor's (1984) model presupposes that all four conditions are necessary for an offense to occur. A motivated offender who overcomes internal inhibitions but who cannot find and effectively isolate a child from a capable guardian (i.e., an external inhibitor) or who cannot groom the child to engage in a sexual act (i.e., resistance of child) cannot complete the sex-offense process. From this we can infer that the sex-offense process could be stopped at any one point if only a single precondition is not met. Finkelhor additionally hypothesized that an offender moves through the four preconditions sequentially, beginning with a state of motivation and ending with finding a potential victim who is unlikely to resist. Each step in the process is dependent on the previous one. If the offender is adequately motivated but is unable to overcome internal inhibitions against sexually deviant behavior, the offense will not occur. Finkelhor discussed this facet of the theory in terms of treatment of sex offenders and the prevention of sexual crimes against children, believing that interrupting the process at either the stage of motivation or the stage of internal disinhibition would effectively reduce sex offending against child victims.

There are many limitations to this early integrative theory, which we briefly summarize here (see Howells, 1994, and Ward & Hudson, 2001, for additional relevant commentary). The first and most obvious difficulty with this theory is that it fails to explain how someone initially reaches the first precondition—the motivation to sexually abuse a child. The model begins with the assumption that some individuals will inherently find children sexually appealing or will find children to be a reasonable potential alternative to an adult sexual partner. The presence of deviant sexual interests at the outset is assumed. However, the goal of an etiological theory of sex offending should be to explain the development of such sexual interests, and although it is important to consider how an individual would move from sexual motivation to the sexually deviant act, it still leaves us wondering where the deviant sexual interest might have come from initially.

Similarly, the theory fails to explain why certain psychological vulnerabilites are ultimately manifested in deviant sexual behaviors. Ward and Hudson (2001) suggested that an etiological theory of sex offending must explain why certain factors result in sexual behaviors as opposed to other, nonsexual types of behavior. Finkelhor's (1984) precondition model does not address this. So, beyond the problem of assuming that the individual already has deviant sexual tendencies, this theory also assumes that the given psychological vulnerabilities will be invariably expressed in terms of inappropriate sexual behaviors.

A second limitation is the use of multiple theoretical orientations and causal mechanisms without truly integrating them into a whole. Various psychodynamic constructs (e.g., castration anxiety) are used with competing explanations such as classical conditioning or social learning theory (e.g., social skills deficits), which leads to inconsistency and theoretical confusion (Ward & Hudson, 2001). Finkelhor's (1984) model also fails to specify which of these mechanisms would be most relevant for different individuals, which increases the incoherence of the theory's basic tenets. How do we know when an offender is most affected by naracissistic identification with a child, for example, as opposed to a strong need for power and control? Not only may these two concepts be incompatible within the same individual, but also we are given no framework for determining which is most applicable to any given offender.

A third limitation to Finkelhor's (1984) theory combines a number of psychological and social factors without a clear empirical justification for doing so. Psychodynamic constructs, for example, have not been extensively tested or empirically validated in this context (Howells, 1994). And although some constructs may demonstrate greater empirical validity than others (e.g., social skills deficits vs. acting out traumatic experiences), these are assigned no greater weight or explanatory power. Furthermore, Finkelhor does not explain how these variables are theoretically related to one another (Ward & Hudson, 2001), which should also be determined empirically to test the accuracy of this theory.

A fourth limitation is the exclusion of a number of factors that may be important in the offending process, many of which have empirical support in the etiological literature. For example, this theory does not consider the role of empathy as a potential inhibitor (Howells, 1994), which may in fact prevent a number of motivated individuals from victimizing a child. Also, cognitive factors, which have been addressed in numerous other theoretical conceptualizations of sex offending, are virtually absent (Ward & Hudson, 2001). These cognitive factors could serve a number of functions, including motivation and disinhibition. Additionally, cognitive processes may bias the way offenders process information, thereby altering their perceptions of external inhibitors (e.g., threat of sanction) or child vulnerability (e.g., assessment of the child's emotional state). Developmental factors, which would explain the emergence of deviant sexual arousal or impaired interpersonal skills, are excluded as well. These developmental factors are vital in explaining how one initially becomes motivated to see children as sexual objects (Ward & Hudson, 2001).

A fifth limitation to theory is that some of the factors identified by Finkelhor (1984) may not contribute to the offending process in the way that he initially envisioned. Howells (1994) noted that poor social skills may not be causally important but may only be a factor in determining which sex offenders are identified and sanctioned. Of course, this would be a limitation of many theories, because most etiological formulations are based on identified sex offenders. However, Howells (1994) made an important point in that several of Finkelhor's proposed etiological characteristics may not be necessary causal conditions. For example, consider the assumption that motivated offenders lack appropriate sources of sexual gratification. It is not probable that all sex offenders lack appropriate social and sexual contacts, so blockage and emotional congruence may not be relevant in all cases. In addition, not all child molesters show deviant sexual arousal, thereby suggesting that it is not a necessary condition for motivation (Howells, 1994). Similarly, deviant sexual arousal may not be a precursor to the initiation of sex offending but instead may develop over time as the result of deviant sexual fantasy, which is not considered in any of the four preconditions (Howells, 1994; Ward & Hudson, 2001). If it does develop over time, which is supported by early research on sexual fantasy and classical conditioning (e.g., McGuire, Carlisle, & Young, 1964), then it cannot be a primary motivator prior to the initiation of sexually deviant behavior. It would perhaps explain the maintenance of deviant sexual behavior instead.

Finally, the most important precondition in the theory is the first one, motivation to sexually abuse another person. Ward and Hudson (2001) argued that internal inhibitors are irrelevant if an individual is already motivated to commit an offense. We would go even further to suggest that a truly motivated offender who is seeking to commit a deviant sexual act will find a way to overcome external inhibitors and will locate a vulnerable victim. Although still necessary conditions, these last two preconditions should not be given as much consideration as motivation. Another potential explanation is that motivation is a critical but later stage of the offending process, because other variables (e.g., developmental and psychological vulnerabilities) have already predisposed the individual to act in certain ways and to consider deviant sexual behaviors. What a model should explain is how the offender ultimately reaches this motivation stage, when he decides that it is time to commit a deviant sexual act.

MARSHALL AND BARBAREE'S INTEGRATIVE THEORY

In 1990, Marshall and Barbaree introduced an integrative theory of sex offending that combines biological influences and childhood experience in a sociocultural context. Later, Marshall, Anderson, and Fernandez (1999) and Marshall and Marshall (2000) expanded this earlier conceptualization to include more specific cognitive and behavioral factors that exerted an influence on the developmental process. We briefly describe the components of the original model and then include the new additions.

Marshall and Barbaree (1990) noted that there is a genetic basis for aggression and that aggression is a trait that is likely an adaptive human behavior and was therefore selected for in our ancient environments. They made the important suggestion that despite any possible genetic underpinnings of aggressive behaviors, biological factors merely contribute to the learning process and the development of behavioral patterns. These biological features assist the individual in the ability to both learn and inhibit new behaviors. Rather than stating that aggression is purely hereditary, they suggested that genetic propensities shape the way that individuals adapt to and navigate within their environments.

An important biological connection made in this theory is that between sex and aggression. Marshall and Barbaree (1990) referenced the neuropsychological literature to demonstrate that sex and aggression are mediated by similar neural substrates and neural networks and that they share similar hormonal and endocrine pathways throughout the brain and body. Marshall and Barbaree cited the importance of puberty and adolescence, when an individual is learning to identify, separate, and appropriately express sexual and aggressive impulses.

The basic underlying assumption of this theory is that males have a "biologically endowed propensity for self-interest associated with a tendency to fuse sex and aggression" (Marshall & Barbaree, 1990, p. 257). In other words, these authors posited that human males are biologically set to pursue self-interested goals and in doing so are highly likely to use both sex and aggression to achieve these goals. Given this assumption, Marshall and Barbaree (1990) then stated that males must therefore learn and implement inhibitory controls that will limit their reliance on sexual and aggressive self-interested behaviors. These inhibitory mechanisms will allow them to interact with others, within the context of larger social constraints. In addition to learning these controls, some biological structures (e.g., hypothalamus, amygdala) may mediate this relationship and lessen the influence of potentially harmful biological propensities.

The second important component of Marshall and Barbaree's (1990) original formulation includes *childhood experience*. After reviewing the developmental literature, these authors concluded that some particular features of a negative childhood experience may in fact contribute to later antisocial and aggressive behaviors, including sexual aggression. Negative parental interactions, poor socialization, limited information regarding appropriate sexual behavior and development, and poor overall attachment may lead to problems with adolescent and adult socialization; modeling of violent behaviors; as well as a failure to develop and internalize behavioral controls, appropriate problem-solving strategies, and norms for social interaction. These developmental outcomes result in insensitive and hostile adults who feel a sense of social inadequacy and use aggression as a means to solve problems. Marshall and Barbaree further posited that the emotional loneliness in these individuals increases stress and anxiety, which may disinhibit sexual impulses and produce attitudes consistent with sex offending. For example, a man who feels a great deal of social inadequacy and relies on violent behaviors to meet social goals (e.g., affection) might develop fantasies of power over or contempt for women. In his efforts to receive affection from a desirable woman, he might resort to violence to secure sexual compliance. Through this hypothesized developmental pattern, some men will fail to learn the necessary inhibitory controls and will instead develop traits and attitudes that facilitate sexually aggressive behaviors in adolescence and adulthood.

The third feature of this theory is *sociocultural context*. Although sociocultural messages are omnipresent and will affect every individual to some degree, children with poor parental models may be more susceptible to them because they have not received adequate modeling and attitude formation in their home environment. Marshall and Barbaree (1990) were most concerned with the three cultural factors that they most strongly relate to sexual violence: (a) interpersonal violence, (b) male dominance, and (c) negative attitudes toward women. Here Marshall and Barbaree relied on the idea of social learning and the modeling of important behaviors; children who are not receiving appropriate and healthy messages about socialization at home will model those that they see portrayed in the larger culture, including messages from violent media presentations and pornographic images.

Finally, Marshall and Barbaree (1990) discussed what they called *transitory situational factors* that also play a role in the process. These represent both internal and external factors that disinhibit the prosocial controls that are present, including use of alcohol or other substances, anger toward females, sexual arousal, and permissive or facilitative attitudes toward sexual violence. They also called for research on other potential transitory situational factors such as the condition of anonymity, a low chance of detection or discovery, the dehumanization of the victim, and the role of stress and anxiety.

Marshall et al. (1999) and Marshall and Marshall (2000) later added to this original conceptualization by expanding the role of cognitions; behavioral learning; and specific childhood experiences, such as childhood sexual abuse. The focus of these updates was still on certain characteristic psychological vulnerabilities hypothesized to affect the development of sexual interests and aggressive behaviors. These authors suggested that because of the poor and insufficient parenting and dysfunctional attachment patterns noted in the original theory, some individuals will develop inadequate coping styles. These youth have failed to learn appropriate strategies to deal with negative internal and external states and will therefore adopt self-indulgence as a strategy by which to solve their problems. Later, they may rely on sex as a coping strategy, given that self-stimulation and sexual activity will improve their mood state in a fairly reliable and consistent way.

Additionally, Marshall and Marshall (2000) believed that childhood experiential variables contribute to lowered self-esteem, which may expose children to specific vulnerability for sexual abuse because they may seek out affection and attention from adults in their environment. Failure to feel loved by their parents and important others may lead these children to become close to others who are displaying inappropriate affection for a child or adolescent, which could lead them to be involved in sexually abusive relationships with adults.

Marshall and Marshall (2000) hypothesized that the combination of poor coping skills, vulnerability for abuse, and low self-esteem leads to heightened sexual activity and masturbation during the juvenile years. They suggested that young sex offenders will also engage in a fair amount of deviant sexual activity in an attempt to cope with internal and environmental experiences, and they will fantasize about certain rewarding behaviors, which will lead to behavioral reinforcement and the development of permissive cognitive distortions. These cognitive distortions (e.g., "Sex with a child doesn't hurt anyone") will also serve as disinhibitors for future deviant sexual behaviors. This predisposition toward sexually deviant interests, combined with disinhibition and the opportunity to offend, then leads the individual to commit sex offenses against others and will condition and entrench these behaviors over time.

Although this theory offers a balanced and well-integrated view of how sexually deviant interests develop over the life span, there are a number of important limitations. Here we discuss some of the broader ones, followed by the more specific limitations (see Ward, 2002, for further discussion of the theory's limitations for clinical practice).

First, one of the major problems associated with this theory is that it applies to only a very specific subset of sex offenders. Ward (2002) noted that Marshall and Barbaree (1990) included only early onset, preferential offenders in their explanation, limiting it to those who begin their sex offending early and have deviant sexual interests driving their offending behaviors. Perhaps more important, though, is that it also applies to offenders who have low self-esteem, abnormal juvenile sexual behaviors, and a childhood history of sexual abuse. So what we have is a theory that may explain the behaviors of preferential pedophiles with low self-esteem, childhood sexual abuse histories, early onset of sexually inappropriate behavior, and poor coping skills. Unfortunately, that is only a fraction of the sex offenders who must be addressed for prevention and treatment.

A related concern is that Marshall and Barbaree (1990) largely ignored the issue of different offender typologies. Their theory implies a number of offense pathways but never specifically states which pathways are important for which offenders; furthermore, Marshall and Barbaree did not outline the potential offender typologies that are implied by the various components of the theory. The authors need to specify relevant mechanisms that lead to or invoke sexually deviant pathways (Ward, 2002) and clearly outline the precursors of offending that correspond with each different offender type. Without this critical component of the model, the reader is left with a multitude of variables that may or may not be significant or relevant for any one offender or offender type.

Second, Ward (2002) criticized the assumption that sex and aggression are fused at either the biological or the learned psychological level. He noted that although sex and aggression may rely on similar neural pathways and structures in the brain, this does not necessarily imply that these two behaviors are intricately linked. These neural substrates are responsible for a wide variety of behavioral and psychological processes, and it would be incorrect to assume that these behaviors are phenomenologically similar or may become "confused" in the brain. Ward (2002) further argued that the observational and self-reported finding that aggressive and sexually inappropriate behaviors are frequently linked may be due not to biological similarities but instead to instrumental necessities—for example, aggression may be used as a tactic or strategy to gain compliance during the course of a sexual act. There may not be some implicit biological or learned association between the two drives beyond this. Furthermore, not all sexually inappropriate acts involve violence, which would also imply that they are not invariably linked in our behavioral makeup (Ward, 2002).

There also is a problem with the general assumption of how one learns to discriminate between and inhibit sexual and aggressive impulses. Marshall and Barbaree's (1990) theory assumes that sex and aggression are not only intricately intertwined but also that humans must learn to identify each of these impulses and inhibit them or they will thoughtlessly act in sexually aggressive ways. The natural human tendency will be toward aggressiveness and sexual satisfaction. Although this idea was introduced and endorsed by Freud (see chap. 7, this volume), many believe that the natural human state is not one of uncontrolled libidinous desire that one must constantly strive to inhibit. If this assumption were correct (i.e., that all humans were naturally predisposed toward violence and sexual violence and could learn to control it only through rigorously learned inhibition), then it would be logical to assume that there would be a greater abundance of sex-offending and sexually violent behavior. Placing the burden on the individual to learn inhibition may not be entirely accurate, because some means of inhibition through neural substrates and genetic predispositions is likely in place prior to learned contingencies.

Third, there are several conceptual gaps in the explanations of childhood experience and vulnerability and their contribution to eventual sexual and interpersonal difficulties. A general assumption of this theory is that various childhood experiences result in poor attachment and vulnerability. From here, however, Marshall and Barbaree (1990) posited that the child is more vulnerable to childhood sexual abuse, which they believed is pivotal in the development of deviant sexual interests. There is not sufficient evidence from developmental literature that poor attachment in and of itself significantly contributes to the occurrence of child sexual abuse. Many other variables are likely involved in this process. A second problem with this assumption is one of directionality. Perhaps not all victims of abuse manifest poor attachment patterns prior to the abusive experience. Marshall and Barbaree and Marshall and Marshall (2000) suggested that the dysfunctional attachment preceded the abuse in cases in which both are present. In cases in which a child has been sexually abused by a family member or trusted friend at a very young age, it may be impossible to establish a strict timeline in which a dysfunctional attachment style formed prior to the abuse.

Another conceptual difficulty is the reliance on negative childhood experiences and the potential for child sexual abuse as causal factors for inappropriate juvenile sexual behavior. As discussed in chapters 4 and 6, not all children who are sexually abused or have dysfunctional attachment will evidence clear patterns of inappropriate sexual arousal or behavior in adolescence. In addition, not all sex offenders have histories of childhood sexual abuse. The supposition then that vulnerability and the occurrence of abuse are both necessary and sufficient conditions leading to problematic sexual behavior in adolescence is not consistent with known cases of sexual deviance.

Fourth, the evidence Marshall and Marshall (2000) presented in support of inappropriate juvenile sexual history is inconsistent with their hypothesis. They stated in the original model and its revisions that a critical step in the process is the manifestation of deviant sexual interests in adolescence. However, the empirical research presented to support this claim (see Cortoni & Marshall, 2000, cited in Marshall & Marshall, 2000) instead shows that rapists and child molesters were normative in the relevant areas of sexual development, including onset of sexual behaviors, numbers of sexual partners during the teenage years, and content of sexual fantasies. So rather than demonstrating that different groups of sex offenders did in fact manifest unusual or deviant sexual behaviors in adolescence, as would be predicted by the theory, the research presented by Marshall and Marshall shows that these offenders could not be differentiated from their nonoffending counterparts on the relevant sexual variables.

The final limitation discussed here is the dearth of information given to explain the use of sex as a coping strategy, as opposed to other potentially reinforcing activities. Marshall and Marshall (2000) stated that sex is a highly reliable means of reinforcement for these individuals. Although this is likely true, they did not explain why other reliable forms of reinforcement (e.g., illicit substances) are ignored in favor of sexual stimulation. This reasoning also leads to the problem of frequency—if sex is used as a coping strategy by males with negative childhood experiences and vulnerability, there should be far more individuals using sex in this manner, thereby creating more sex offenders. The authors' failure to adequately address other means of coping that may be available, or why it is so significant for only a select few individuals who do go on to commit sexual offenses, limits the explanatory power of the early hypotheses of the theory.

HALL AND HIRSCHMAN'S QUADRIPARTITE MODEL

Hall and Hirschman (1991) took evidence from the literature regarding sex-offender characteristics and grouped them into four factors that they believed were not only related but also were most significant in the etiology of the sex-offending process. The first of these components is *physiological sexual arousal*. Many theorists and treatment providers traditionally have focused on the role of deviant sexual arousal as an important contributor to sexually deviant behaviors (e.g., Hall & Hirschman, 1991). However, these authors noted that whereas deviant sexual arousal may be more pivotal for sexual aggression toward inappropriate stimuli (e.g., children), the role of deviant arousal in other sexual crimes (i.e., rape) is less clear. They suggested that "similar physiological processes may underlie sexual arousal that results in appropriate sexual behavior as well as sexual arousal that results in sexual aggression" (Hall & Hirschman, 1991, p. 664). In other words, the same mechanism may control arousal for both deviant and nondeviant sexual behaviors. From this, they determined that it is not the sexual arousal alone that is driving the deviant sexual behavior and that cognitive appraisals of the arousal play an important role at this step in the process.

Their theory's second component, *cognitive appraisal*, refers to a variety of mental processes involved in the understanding of emotions and behavior and the prediction of consequences. Specifically, Hall and Hirschman (1991, 1992) described both justifications and myths that may disinhibit an individual to such an extent that the behavior seems acceptable or appropriate. For example, believing in rape myths (e.g., "Women secretly enjoy being raped") allows an offender to justify his act of sexual aggression. They made the important point that these cognitive appraisals do not need to be accurate or truthful for them to be believed by the individual (Hall & Hirschman,

1992). They suggested that these cognitive beliefs are conditioned over time through cultural messages of acceptance and social learning processes.

Another form of cognitive appraisal that is significant is the belief in the morality or wrongness of an act. If an offender does not believe that he is committing an immoral act, it is unlikely that he will have internal inhibitions in place to prevent such an act from occurring. Additionally, one's beliefs regarding the likelihood of being detected and punished are relevant factors in the decision to engage in a specific behavior. This type of cognitive appraisal involves more complex features of processing, including appraisal of the situation, the victim, potential threat to self, and the value of perceived benefits. When these perceptual and interpretive factors combine with strong physiological arousal, the individual may have a greater likelihood of committing a deviant sexual act.

The third feature of Hall and Hirschman's (1991, 1992) theory is *affective dyscontrol*. The authors noted that negative affective states are often antecedents to sex offending, with anger being an important aspect of negative emotion for rapists and depression being the same for child molesters. This component is hypothesized to primarily affect the inhibitory control of offenders, with some negative emotional experiences becoming so powerful that the individual is unable to inhibit inappropriate or predatory behavior. For example, a man who is sexually attracted to children may be able to inhibit his desire for sexual intimacy with them because of guilt, anxiety about harming the child, and empathy. However, when he becomes significantly depressed, these inhibitory cognitive appraisals may no longer be salient enough to prevent him from acting in accordance with his sexual arousal.

The fourth feature of this theory consists of a more enduring set of characteristics, namely, *personality problems or disorders*. Hall and Hirschman (1991) described adverse childhood and adolescent experiences (e.g., poor socialization, harsh punishment) and developmental variables (e.g., impaired social skills, low level of education) that contribute to the development of trait variables more highly associated with personality disorders. They include characteristics such as selfishness, exploitative style, lack of remorse, and unstable or antisocial lifestyle, which Hall and Hirschman noted are common for many criminals as well as men who are sexually aggressive toward others. These traits interact with the other three components of the theory by potentially intensifying the impact of affective dyscontrol, deviant arousal, or cognitive appraisals that facilitate offending.

The first three factors are described by Hall and Hirschman (1991, 1992) as largely state and situation dependent. These variables are viewed as vulnerabilities that are activated only in certain situations that may result in sexually aggressive behavior. From this, one can assume that these components are not only idiosyncratic but also highly variable across environmental contingencies. For example, an individual may be subject to transient anger or depressive states that are triggered by life events. However, the authors presented a contradiction in which they acknowledged the importance of these environmental situations in triggering the first three factors but at the same time downplayed the role of environmental variables in the sex-offending process, referring to environmental contingencies as "tangential" (Hall & Hirschman, 1991, p. 665). So although the state variables mentioned are dependent on environmental factors, the environmental conditions necessary to trigger the relevant internal states are not described. According to the authors, the most important contributor to inappropriate sexual behavior depends not on the environment but instead on the motivational precursor (i.e., the most potent of the four factors). What initially drives sexually aggressive behavior is the one factor that is most problematic for the individual. This one factor will activate the others and thus lead to a sex offense. They believed that it is the factors, specifically the one factor that serves as a motivational precursor, not the environmental triggers, that should be the focus of our interest.

Hall and Hirschman (1991, 1992) then identified four sex-offender typologies based on the four potentially different motivational precursors. For example, an individual for whom physiological arousal is the motivational precursor will be characterized by excessive fantasy about the inappropriate sex object and conditioning of deviant arousal response over time. This subtype of offender will display aggression or violence during the sex offense only if the violence itself is sexually arousing (i.e., sexual sadism). For an individual who demonstrates a cognitive motivational precursor (i.e., cognitive justifications for the act), planning of the act and a lesser amount of deviant arousal would be most significant. Hall and Hirschman (1991) used acquaintance rape as an example for this particular type of offender. They posited that episodic affective dyscontrol as a motivational precursor will manifest itself in an individual who is more impulsive and predatory in nature. They hypothesized that offenses driven by poor affect modulation will be unplanned, violent, and opportunistic. Finally, if the motivational precursor is a developmentally related personality problem or disorder, the offender will likely have had chronic developmental problems and higher levels of general criminal and antisocial behaviors and will use violence in the commission of a sex offense. Hall and Hirschman believed that this last subtype will likely have the worst prognosis in terms of response to treatment.

When Hall and Hirschman (1991) initially developed this model, they based it on sound empirical evidence regarding the personality, cognitive, and physiological traits of sex offenders. However, despite their attempt to combine these features into a comprehensive theory, their hypothesized sex-offending process demonstrates a number of serious limitations. First, we address general limitations of the model's basic concepts and how they are arranged in an etiological format. Second, we review more specific difficulties with the four components presented by Hall and Hirschman. Finally, we describe problems inherent in their use of the "motivational precursor" as well as the typologies resulting from the four primary factors included in the model (see Ward, 2001, for additional critiques of the model relating to clinical and treatment implications).

Perhaps one of the most significant limitations of this model is its lack of explanation regarding external forces acting on the individual. The model is largely intrapersonal, assuming that internal forces are almost exclusively responsible for the initiation and maintenance of deviant sexual behaviors. Although it is likely true that the majority of sex offenders manifest these internal state and trait variables that Hall and Hirschman (1991, 1992) described, the research literature in this area regarding environmental contingencies, such as external reinforcements and punishments (e.g., threat of sanction, social acceptance of rape myths), interpersonal relationship variables, and social learning effects, cannot easily be discounted. Important intrapersonal variables may in fact predispose an individual to commit sexual offenses, but interpersonal and environmental factors may trigger or perpetuate certain behaviors beyond the internal motivators.

In fact, the state variables described in this theory are highly dependent on environmental factors that Hall and Hirschman (1991, 1992) did not specifically identify. A related problem, though, is the role given to these state features. Ward (2001) noted that a critical flaw in the basic premise of this model is the reliance on state variables as causal factors. State factors, such as cognitive distortions or affective dyscontrol, are typically viewed as the manifestation of other underlying causes. For example, individuals may experience affective dyscontrol because of a more fundamental difficulty with emotional regulation. It is this more consistent trait variable that is actually responsible for the negative affective response. In other words, the factors that Hall and Hirschman described as state dependent are likely manifestations of enduring characteristics that are more directly involved in the causation of sexually inappropriate behaviors. Because one must have these more fundamental causal characteristics to activate the state variables (e.g., self-regulatory deficits causing temporary affective dyscontrol), it is more appropriate to study the underlying characteristics than to simply describe the role of state factors as the primary causal variables.

A second limitation of this model is that Hall and Hirschman (1991, 1992) failed to adequately describe the interaction between the hypothesized variables. The authors presented examples in which each of the four factors is a primary cause of sex offending, but they did not state how these factors interact with one another (Ward, 2001); neither did they explain the causal mechanism behind each factor (e.g., how cognitive appraisals lead to direct behavior). For example, they noted that the cognitive appraisal of physiological sexual arousal is important, but they failed to describe the pathway that connects the arousal to cognitive appraisal to sexual behavior. The reader is left with the impression that important steps in the process have been omitted. How was the appraisal made? What made it specific to sexually deviant behavior? How did the individual move from cognitive appraisal to action?

Furthermore, it is unclear whether all or merely some of the four factors are required for a deviant sexual behavior to occur (Ward, 2001). Are each of these components both necessary and, at the same time, sufficient for a sex offense to occur? Hall and Hirschman (1991, 1992) stated, for example, that the underlying physiological mechanisms behind deviant sexual arousal and nondeviant sexual arousal are the same and that cognitive appraisal is in fact the critical variable. If cognitive appraisal, rather than the presence of deviant sexual arousal, is the necessary component, then why is deviant arousal a part of the model? From their explanation, deviant sexual arousal is not a necessary condition. Ward (2001) expanded on this idea, arguing that this lack of conceptual clarity makes this theory more of a framework, introducing important variables that play a role in the process without specifying which variables and specific pathways are necessary for the offense process to occur.

A third problem relates to ambiguity about the core constructs presented in the model (Ward, 2001). There is a great deal of conceptual overlap among the four factors. For example, Hall and Hirschman (1991, 1992) described affective dyscontrol as entirely separate from personality problems or disorders. However, from the research literature on personality disorders (e.g., Millon & Davis, 1996), it appears that difficulty with affective control may be a critical component of the majority of personality disorders. Describing these two variables as independent components may not be theoretically sound. Also, Ward (2001) described conceptual confusion created by Hall and Hirschman's use of *cognitive appraisal* as interchangeable with *cognitive distortions*. There are empirically derived differences among perception, information processing, and the formation of cognitive attitudes and beliefs. Hall and Hirschman failed to specify which of these cognitive traits or processes are included in the model and how they are differentiated from one another in the causal process.

A fourth limitation is that the role of volition is not described and is nearly absent in Hall and Hirschman's explanation of sexual deviance. *Volition*, or the process by which an offender makes a decision to commit an offense, is ultimately related to how much the individual desires sexual contact with an inappropriate victim or object. This underlying desire or need fueling volitional choice is also not addressed as a component of the process (Ward, 2001). Behavioral models that rely on the potential for punishment include volition as a major component of the process. Threat appraisal, which Hall and Hirschman (1991, 1992) briefly mentioned in terms of cognitive appraisal, is largely based on desire. It is desire or need that triggers the internal cost–benefit analysis. A sex offender must first have some desire to commit a deviant sexual act before he would then weigh potential benefits and potential costs, and it is volition that might drive him to commit a sexually inappropriate act in the face of potential punishment. Also, in their discussion of disinhibiting factors that may contribute to offending (e.g., mood, substance use), Hall and Hirschman did not address desire or a conscious overriding of volitional control. This is an important omission in that the idea of volitional control is such a fundamental aspect of many treatment (and punishment) programs aimed at sex-offending individuals.

A fifth limitation is the origin of the four factors described in this model. As we noted earlier in this section, three of these factors are described as state dependent and may in fact result from more underlying character traits. However, there is also the issue of how an individual reaches a point where he manifests these characteristics. Hall and Hirschman's (1991) description begins with the assumption that these components—deviant physiological arousal, specific types of cognitive appraisals, and affective dyscontrol—are inherent to the individual. They did not explain the etiology of these factors, and they did not adequately explain how these factors come to exist in a specific group of offenders. They did attempt to explain the appearance of personality disorders or problems that they believed were significant by describing various developmental and environmental factors that have been supported in the literature. Again, though, they did not comprehensively address how these background experiences ultimately led to the personality-disordered characteristics in their model. Without an explanation of why sex-offending individuals have these cognitive justifications and biased cognitive appraisal processes that are hypothesized to be so important in the offending process, the model lacks explanatory depth. One cannot assume that deviant sexual arousal is a given. This and other factors had to develop somehow. An understanding of that development is important to explain the full causal pathway leading to sexually aggressive and inappropriate behaviors.

A sixth problem is the assumption that these particular characteristics are specific to sex offenders. If one is arguing that these traits, or a combination of them, lead to sex-offending behaviors, then one must demonstrate that these traits are not common to other, non–sex-offending populations. However, the personality disordered characteristics that are described in this model are also seen in individuals with antisocial personality disorder (Millon & Davis, 1996) and psychopathy (e.g., Hare, 1999). Furthermore, several researchers have shown that cognitive distortions, such as rape myths, are believed by normal, nonoffending segments of the population (e.g., Briere, Malamuth, & Check, 1985; Malamuth, 1981) and cannot be ascribed to sex offenders alone. These examples illustrate the difficulty with linking these traits or state factors solely with sex offending. We are still left with the question of what characteristics of sex offenders differentiate them from those who do not commit sex offenses and how these characteristics ultimately lead to sexually deviant behavior.

A seventh problem area is the description of the motivational precursor. Hall and Hirschman (1991, 1992) introduced this concept to distinguish groups of offenders using the four components of the model. This is the one feature of the individual that is more prominent and "motivating" than the others and is responsible for driving the commission of a sex offense. It is unclear, however, how this motivational precursor initially develops and whether it changes over time. Not only did the authors fail to explain where all four of the model's components originate, but they also did not address how one factor in particular came to be so vitally important; neither did they provide insight into the development of the motivational precursor. Was it consciously selected? Was it simply stronger at the outset than the others, and, if yes, why it was stronger? Was it learned or acquired first? We also do not know whether the motivational precursor changes or develops over time. It might be that the motivational precursor varies significantly given different environmental conditions (e.g., involvement in delinquent behaviors).

On a related note, Ward (2001) questioned how this motivational precursor interacts with the other three components of the model. Hall and Hirschman (1991, 1992) claimed that this one crucial variable interacts with and intensifies the others, but they did not explain the mechanisms for this interaction; how does the activation of the one primary driving force then activate the other three and intensify or strengthen them? Without understanding this mechanism, we are left with a theory that has little predictive power in terms of etiology or prevention of sexual crime.

Finally, Hall and Hirschman (1991, 1992) used their quadripartite model to develop a typology of offenders, primarily based on the four potential motivational precursors. This is problematic in that they confused typology with etiological theory (Ward, 2001). Forming a typology based on certain descriptive characteristics can be useful in terms of identifying, treating, and making predictions about sex offenders; however, the same traits or variables used in forming a typology may not be significant or even relevant when forming an etiological theory. For example, sex offenders may commit offenses against specific victim groups (e.g., children, women in their 20s), but their choice of victim may play very little role in the actual formation of sexually deviant interests or arousal. Selection of a particular victim may simply reflect opportunity or reduced likelihood of detection rather than the culmination of a complex developmental process. Additionally, one could say that grouping offenders according to personality type might be useful for predicting treatment outcome or potential recidivism but, as has been demonstrated by conflicting results in personality research (see chap. 6, this volume), these same personality variables may not be developmental antecedents to specific sexual behaviors. If prevention is the primary goal, then the development of an etiological theory is critical.

MALAMUTH'S CONFLUENCE MODEL

Malamuth based his causal explanation of sexual aggression (Malamuth, 1996, 1998a) on an early study conducted by Malamuth, Sockloskie, Koss, and Tanaka (1991) that evaluated the roles of hostile attitudes and sexual promiscuity in producing sexually aggressive or coercive behaviors. In this study, early childhood experience was posited to significantly impact dominant and hostile attitudes toward women and mediate the relationship between sexually promiscuous and sexually aggressive behaviors. Malamuth (1996, 1998a) and others (Malamuth, Heavey, & Linz, 1993; Malamuth, Linz, Heavey, Barnes, & Acker, 1995) later expanded these findings to form a cohesive, integrative theory known as the *confluence model of sexual aggression*.

The core idea of the confluence model is that sexual aggression occurs through the synergistic convergence of several factors. Each of these factors is independently correlated with sexual coercion or aggression, but alone is not sufficient to produce sexual violence. Thus, the combination of these factors is what leads to sex-offending behaviors. These variables are viewed as potential motivators, disinhibitors, or predictors of opportunity (Malamuth et al., 1993). In other words, their effects vary significantly depending on changing conditions within the environment. Additionally, these factors are believed to uniquely predict sexual violence against women as opposed to generalized violence against any individual.

The first of these factors is *promiscuous or impersonal sexual style*, which is characterized by an immature and irresponsible approach to sexual activity, with a corresponding lack of desire for sexual intimacy or the formation of long-term sexual relationships. The relevance of sexual promiscuity is related to evolutionary theory, which was described at length in chapter 8. In brief, short-term sexual mating strategies are favored by some men who are at a competitive disadvantage for securing mate access or who have adopted coercive or aggressive sexual strategies to ensure female compliance in mating scenarios. Either way, engaging in sexual activity with a variety of women in a noncommittal and impersonal way is viewed as the result of an evolutionary strategy favoring short-term over long-term mating strategies.

As described by Malamuth (1998a), a relationship between an impersonal or promiscuous sexual style and sexually aggressive behaviors forms when the individual adopts this short-term mating strategy and uses whatever means necessary to achieve sexual mating goals. This may include coercive or aggressive sexual tactics. In this formulation, individuals who have an immature view of sexuality and an emphasis on short-term sexual goals (e.g., immediate sexual gratification) are those who are more prone to commit aggressive sexual behaviors.

This sexual style emerges from childhood environments that are harsh and exploitative (Malamuth, 1996, 1998a). These early experiences predispose the individual to develop goals oriented toward short-term gain, which may involve the exploitation of others and pose a risk to the development of stable intimate relationships. It is from this background that individuals develop coercive sexual strategies that will allow short-term success in obtaining sexual satisfaction. Also, young men who value sexual encounters as a source of self-esteem or social status may have a higher likelihood of exhibiting impersonal and promiscuous sexual behaviors (Malamuth et al., 1993).

The second of the three relevant factors or paths is *hostile masculinity*, defined as a hostile and defensive orientation toward others, particularly women, along with a hypersensitivity to perceived rejection. Hostile masculinity also includes a willingness to aggress against women and a sense of gratification from achieving domination over women (Malamuth, 1998a). This may also include an overt hostility toward characteristics that are seen as feminine (Malamuth et al., 1993).

Within this model, hostile masculinity appears to viewed as both a cognitive schema and a personality trait. It affects perceptions of environmental stimuli, information processing, and patterns of interpersonal responding. In this way, hostile masculinity is seen as a relatively stable construct, but it may be exacerbated in terms of behavioral responding by certain environmental events, such as perceived rejection by a woman. Sexual arousal may develop in response to increased hostility toward a target female and may disinhibit aggressive or dominant responding and thereby facilitate violence toward women (Malamuth et al., 1993).

This hostility purportedly develops in a number of ways. One such explanation is that early environmental messages conveying hostility, anger, and mistrust are integrated into the developing child's cognitive worldview and contribute to hostile schemas in adulthood. Another potential source of hostile masculinity is through perceived betrayal or rejection by women. Men who have been rejected or who perceive rejection or ridicule from women may develop anger, controlling and dominant attitudes, and beliefs supportive of aggression toward women (Malamuth, 1998a). This will then increase the likelihood of aggressive acting out toward women in an effort to control or dominate females and obtain desired outcomes (e.g., sexual intercourse). A final explanation for the development of hostile masculinity is that through an evolutionary need to ensure male parentage of a woman's offspring, men developed a need to control women's sexuality (Malamuth, 1996). From this, some men may be more dominant toward women when they feel that their sexuality or sexual prowess is in question, potentially leading to sexual assault or other coercive sexual behavior.

The third component of the confluence model was added by Dean and Malamuth (1997) to reflect another relevant contributor to sexually aggressive behavior. This final element is a *high-dominance, low-nurturance approach to interpersonal relationships*. A personality style that is high in dominance and low in nurturance is distinguished by self-interested motives and goals, a lack of compassion or sensitivity, and little concern for potential harm toward others (Malamuth, 1998a).

This factor was introduced not as an entirely separate pathway but as a moderating variable that affects the expression of sexually aggressive motives. The confluence model's original formulation included hostile masculinity and sexual promiscuity as interacting factors that would produce attitudes supportive of sexual violence, attraction or arousal to domination of women, and a short-term mating strategy that involved little investment in forming long-term intimate bonds. These characteristics combined would then predispose the individual to a greater likelihood of using coercive or aggressive sexual tactics to gain female compliance. However, research by Dean and Malamuth (1997) suggested that although these factors are likely necessary components of the process, they are not entirely sufficient in bridging the gap between willingness to commit sexual aggression or fantasy about sexualized violence and actually engaging in sexual aggression. Self-interested or dominant motives, and a corresponding lack of nurturance and compassion, are believed to moderate the impact of these variables on behavior and produce sex-offending outcomes.

The development of varying levels of dominance versus nurturance is posited to occur as a result of early childhood socialization and the incorporation of familial and cultural messages (Dean & Malamuth, 1997; Malamuth, 1998a, 1998b). For example, early socialization practices may instill values of dominance and control over women that carry over into intimate relationships in adulthood. Derogatory messages regarding nurturance and the male role in interpersonal relationships may have a similar effect. Malamuth (1998a) also believed that the development of a dominant personality style is due in part to evolutionary processes. Intense competition for resources in the environment, including mate access, may have led to the necessity for dominant or aggressive tactics to achieve important survival goals. The success of dominant traits over nurturant ones in environments requiring a competitive advantage may have then produced a strategic advantage for individuals who pursue more self-interested and high-risk goals.

Research on the confluence model has suggested that a number of important corollaries of the theory may hold true. For example, Malamuth (1998a) reported that high dominance relative to nurturance is correlated with sexual aggression and coercive sexual tactics, that those who use sexual coercion are more likely to endorse short-term mating strategies, and that hostile masculinity is related to perceptual biases against women and sexual arousal to perceived control over women. More extensive research on this model has attempted to prove the significant causal relationships between these pathways and resulting sexual aggression. Work by Malamuth et al. (1991) suggested that the combination of hostile masculinity and sexual promiscuity significantly causally predicted coercive sexual interactions. When these factors were evaluated singly, they were not independently sufficient to produce a causal effect. These findings were replicated later with the same sample after a 10-year period (Malamuth et al., 1995). Additional work by Dean and Malamuth (1997) extrapolated high dominance as an important causal factor in the process and demonstrated similar causal effects. Their work also demonstrated that high dominance relative to nurturance was an important factor for determining when individuals with hostility toward women and sexually aggressive thoughts or fantasies would turn to sexually coercive behaviors. Dean and Malamuth (1997) found that individuals with self-interested motives were far more likely to act on aggressive thoughts than those with similar hostile schemas or promiscuous sexual habits but more compassionate or empathic motivations.

Still, there are a number of limitations to the confluence model of sexual aggression. We refer the reader to chapter 8 of this volume, in which many of the important limitations of evolutionary theories are outlined and discussed. Given that Malamuth (1996, 1998a) based much of this model on evolutionary principles, this model is subject to many of the same criticisms, such as its reliance on evolutionary assumptions that stem from animal models, its focus on a narrow range of sexually deviant behavior (i.e., rape), and its emphasis on adolescent or adult female victims.

Other limitations are specific to this particular model. One such limitation is that the focus on relationships and interactions between two or three factors often overlooks potential underlying latent factors, which may be responsible for these relationships. Hostile masculinity and an emphasis on dominance and control in interpersonal relationships may not be distinct pathways or factors but instead indicators of a broader latent construct. For example, although Malamuth (1998a) argued that general hostility does not predict specific sexual aggression whereas hostility toward women does, this does not rule out the possibility that underlying hostile attitudes or beliefs may be the source of the interaction effect with other critical variables in the model. Similarly, hostility toward women and preferences for impersonal sexual interactions may not be separate causal effects but merely manifestations of other underlying causes, perhaps including difficulties with forming intimate bonds with others, especially women, or an inability to cope with situations involving potential rejection and hurt. The model does not fully account for underlying or latent relationships that may be the source of predictive power for the identified variables. This limits our ability to make useful predictions or treatment recommendations on the basis of only these factors. We must consider broader constructs that may represent greater sources of causal influence.

Another limitation of this model is that, although it notes that these factors may serve as facilitators, disinhibitors, or motivations for sex offending, it does not specify why these factors are not simply several among many potential disinhibitors, including substance intoxication, emotional dysregulation, or strong cognitive justifications. Other important variables that may also facilitate the sex-offending process have been neglected in this model. Their absence is not explained by the authors (i.e., Dean & Malamuth, 1997; Malamuth, 1996, 1998a); neither does the empirical research demonstrate efforts to disprove the important causal relationships of other potential factors. In sum, the model places certain factors above others but does not explain how they are uniquely causal or predictive in the sex-offending process.

Although limitations related to the development of these factors or traits through evolutionary processes are discussed in greater length in chapter 8 of this volume, another problem arises in the discussion of the link between rejection and the formation of hostile masculinity. In this model, hostile masculinity predicts sexually coercive tactics. Malamuth (1998a) indicated that hostile attitudes toward women may form in response to consistent rejection of sexual advances. He then posited that women may be rejecting because of the man's use of coercive sexual tactics. In other words, coercive sexual behaviors lead to rejection, which leads to hostile masculinity, which then causes coercive sexual behaviors. This circular reasoning is extremely problematic, making empirical evaluation of this process difficult.

Finally, the research studies conducted by Malamuth et al. (1991, 1995) rely exclusively on the responses and behaviors of college students. Although their research does suggest that these students engage in sexually coercive behaviors and manifest these particular traits, college samples may not be generalizable to sex offenders who commit more frequent acts of sexual aggression and violence. Individuals in these samples may be functioning at a higher level than the average individual who engages in sexual aggression. Therefore, the factors that would explain and predict such behavior may not appear as readily or significantly as they would in a sample more representative of the population of interest. Because of this, causal models tested on largely non–sex-offending individuals without sex-offender comparisons may not carry the explanatory power that is desired to make behavioral predictions.

WARD AND SIEGERT'S PATHWAYS MODEL

Ward and Siegert (2002b) introduced the *pathways model*, which combines some elements of the three previously discussed integrative theories and models with various empirically derived features of sex offenders to describe the etiology of child sexual abuse. The authors focused their attention on one particular type of sex offending, namely, that of adults sexually abusing children, noting that theories of etiology should be specific to a particular population of interest and avoid the problem of overgenerality.

Ward and Siegert (2002b) began their explanation by identifying useful features of three integrated models designed to explain sex-offending behaviors. They noted that Finkelhor's (1984) precondition model is important in that it outlines important connections between the psychological vulnerabilities of the offender and various aspects of the offense process, that Marshall and Barbaree (1990) described the potential link between early developmental difficulties and the predisposition to sexually abuse children, and that Hall and Hirschman (1991, 1992) introduced the role of typologies in etiological explanation. Taking these features into consideration, Ward and Siegert then developed a model using four symptom clusters typically identified in adults who commit sexually inappropriate acts with children: (a) intimacy and social skills deficits, (b) distorted sexual scripts, (c) emotional dysregulation, and (d) cognitive distortions (Beech & Ward, 2004; Ward & Beech, 2004; Ward & Siegert, 2002b). According to their model, all offenders will demonstrate these four problem clusters in some way. However, what makes each offender unique is the severity, direction, and pervasiveness of these difficulties, which will significantly vary from individual to individual on the basis of developmental characteristics and psychological vulnerabilities. The clinical features generated by each of these underlying deficits or difficulties also interact with one another to produce outcomes still more specific to the individual.

The first symptom cluster identified by Ward and Siegert (2002b) consists of *intimacy and social skills deficits*. They suggested that childhood environments characterized by abuse and neglect on the part of the child's primary caregivers will distort internal representations of functional relationships and bias the child's expectations of intimacy and emotional responsiveness from others in his environment. Resulting difficulties in forming secure attachments to others would then predispose the individual to a host of interpersonal problems, including poor emotional regulation, low self-esteem, and difficulty forming intimate bonds with others.

The second feature of this model relates to the *sexual scripts* or *sexual schemas* of these individuals. The authors defined a *sexual script* as a cognitive schema that cues an individual to various aspects of a potential sexual encounter, including "when sex is to take place, with whom, what to do, and how to interpret the cues or signals associated with different phases in a sexual encounter" (Ward & Siegert, 2002b, p. 332). The idea is that every individual forms sexual scripts based on the features within his environment, involving both culturally and socially learned messages. However, if something distorts or disrupts the typical learning process (e.g., childhood sexual abuse), some distortions of the sexual script may occur. These could take the form of distortions in the identification of appropriate sexual partners, interpretation of nonsexual cues as sexual ones, or even inappropriate behaviors related to sexual arousal (e.g., sadism).

The third feature Ward and Siegert (2002b) considered was the role of *emotional dysregulation*. Self-regulation in general and emotional regulation specifically are important in terms of controlling affective states, setting relevant goals, and activating behavior that is relevant to achieving specified goals. Emotional dysregulation may manifest itself on a variety of levels, each impacting the ultimate behavioral outcome. For example, setting dysfunctional goals might lead an individual to pursue sexual gratification regardless of the availability of an appropriate sexual partner. An inability to regulate affective states might similarly lead an individual to act in sexually deviant ways if that has been shown successful in the past at reducing negative affect.

Finally, *cognitive distortions* are also a central component of the pathways model. These have been described as maladaptive beliefs or attitudes that are supportive of particular types of behavior (see chap. 4). The cognitive distortions likely arise from underlying cognitive schemas and implicit theories of human behavior, which the individual uses to interpret the behavior of others, to make inferences regarding their emotional and mental states, and to predict others' future behaviors as well. Pedophiles, for example, might endorse offense-supportive cognitive distortions (e.g., sex is another way to show intimacy, regardless of whether it is with a child or an adult) that in fact stem from beliefs that children are appropriate and desirable sexual partners, which ultimately motivate behaviors associated with not only sexual satiation but also interactions with children.

From these four symptom clusters, Ward and Siegert (2002b) created five different pathways to describe the development of deviant sexual behaviors. They hypothesized that each offender fundamentally possesses each of these four clusters to some degree but that certain features in particular form a primary causal mechanism that ultimately determines a unique offense pathway and etiological profile. So even though all four mechanisms are present in the individual and factor into each offense, the primary mechanism impacts how these features will be manifested into specific offense behaviors.

Pathway 1, *intimacy deficits*, describes an offender who opportunistically offends if the preferred sexual partner is unavailable. This offender has normal sexual scripts and does not confuse sex and intimacy but instead has deeper problems with intimacy deficits and turns to a potential sexual relationship to ease feelings of loneliness. The most significant problem associated with this pathway is insecure attachment, which predisposes the individual to anticipate negative outcomes from intimate relationships with other adults. This will subsequently lead to deliberate attempts to avoid this outcome, which may include the substitution of other potential "partners" (e.g., children) in the place of adults.

Pathway 2 revolves around *deviant sexual scripts*, meaning that individuals following this developmental pathway are more likely to have distorted cognitive scripts guiding their sexual and intimate behaviors as well as more maladaptive and dysfunctional cognitive schemas motivating their behaviors. Ward and Siegert (2002b) posited that the nature of the distortions in the sexual script involves the context of sexual activity, meaning that the features of the sexual script related to determining when sexual contact is appropriate or desirable are distorted and represent a fundamental confusion between sex and intimacy. Offenders with these specific difficulties will misinterpret cues signaling affection or intimacy as interest in sexual activity. These individuals also have some degree of difficulty forming intimate relationships with appropriate partners (i.e., adults) and not only will seek out children to replace that intimacy but will also confuse affectionate behaviors by children as sexual invitations.

In Pathway 3, *emotional dysregulation* is the primary causal mechanism driving deviant sexual behavior with children. Much like those described in Pathway 1, these individuals have intact and functional sexual scripts, but instead of manifesting significant interpersonal and intimacy deficits these offenders manifest problematic emotion regulation mechanisms that may include difficulties identifying and modulating emotional states. In this pathway, the individual is faced with a strong negative mood state that he is unable to relieve. This could lead to a variety of potential outcomes, such as loss of control or disinhibition. Here, a sex offender might use sex with a child or other victim as a means by which to restore emotional balance and eliminate a negative mood state. Sexual activity then becomes a type of coping strategy, and over time sexual satisfaction and positive emotional valence become intricately linked (Ward & Siegert, 2002b). Once this connection has occurred, an individual who then needs a restoration to a positive or neutral mood state will opportunistically seek an outlet for sexual desire, which may lead to the selection of an inappropriate sexual partner.

Pathway 4 is characterized by *antisocial cognitions*, or attitudes and beliefs supportive of criminal behaviors. Ward and Siegert (2002b) believe individuals from this pathway are those who have intact and normal sexual scripts and who do not demonstrate deviant sexual arousal but instead embrace an antisocial lifestyle and have little regard for the emotional and psychological needs of others. In other words, these are individuals with significant feelings of entitlement who lack empathy for those in their social world. In terms of antisocial attitudes and beliefs, these individuals may endorse cultural beliefs consistent with their offending lifestyle (e.g., sense of superiority over others, attitude of power over children). Although these are not individuals who typically seek out opportunities to commit a sex offense, they have a high disregard for the needs of others and for socially normative behaviors and would offend against a child given the combination of intense sexual desire and limited opportunity with an appropriate partner.

Ward and Siegert (2002b) also considered a fifth pathway, which they described as one of *multiple dysfunctional mechanisms*. In Pathway 5, each of the four symptom clusters is evident, with no particular type of problem as the most prominent. This encompasses individuals who have distorted sexual scripts, dysfunctional cognitive beliefs about children and sexual activity, intimacy and interpersonal skills deficits, and emotional dysregulation. Because there is no one feature that may be more salient or observable than the others, it is a combination of opportunity to offend and the lack of conflicting goals or inhibitory mechanisms that will ultimately result in a sexual offense against a child.

This model was later applied to risk assessment variables to bridge the gap between risk assessment and etiological theory (Beech & Ward, 2004;

Ward & Beech, 2004). Risk assessment instruments are designed to offer probability estimates of the risk of reoffending. The assumption underlying the identification of significant risk variables is that these mechanisms play a role in maintaining the offending process. Beech and Ward (2004; Ward & Beech, 2004) suggested that not only are these mechanisms predictive of future offending but also that it is implicitly assumed that they are also causal. Therefore, they created an etiological model of risk using the basic tenets of Ward and Siegert's (2002b) pathways model. Here, various developmental factors (i.e., abuse, rejection, and attachment problems) lead to vulnerability and trait factors described in the pathways model (e.g., cognitive distortions, regulatory difficulties), which may combine with certain triggering events or risk factors (e.g., victim access, relationship conflict) to increase state factors associated with risk of reoffending (e.g., deviant fantasies, negative affective states). The combination of the symptom clusters identified in the pathways model with significantly predictive risk variables is meant to explain the initiation of sex offending and the maintenance of sexually deviant behaviors as well.

The pathways model was recently tested in a sample of adult sex offenders who self-reported various developmental and psychological experiences. Connolly (2004) conducted unstructured interviews with 13 incarcerated child molesters in an attempt to identify offending pathways consistent with Ward and Siegert's (2002b) model. This study matched 10 of the men to Pathways 1, 2, and 5 and failed to match the other 3 men to any one pathway in particular. Although this study may demonstrate some limited support for the pathways model, the sample ultimately did not conform to Ward and Siegert's model, because several men were unmatched to a pathway, and others were grouped to only three of the five. Attempting to conclude that the findings are valid, however, is impossible given the study's small sample size, qualitative analysis, and the use of unstructured interviews.

Although in their pathways model, Ward and Siegert's (2002b) addressed a wide range of psychological and developmental issues that have been empirically tied to sex offending, their etiological conceptualization possesses a number of limitations. Furthermore, the application of this model to a risk assessment framework by Beech and Ward (2004) and Ward and Beech (2004) is also problematic.

First, there are logical inconsistencies in Ward and Siegert's (2002b) explanation of the role of the four symptom clusters in the five pathways. The authors stated several times that offenders manifest all four of these symptom clusters before and during the offense process. They noted that sex offenders who sexually abuse children can therefore be expected to demonstrate dysfunctional emotion regulation, cognitive distortions, intimacy and social skills deficits, and distorted sexual scripts. However, in their description of each pathway, they began Pathways 1, 3, and 4 by noting that these offenders have normal sexual scripts, not distorted ones. This is directly contradictory to their earlier statements that these offenders will universally demonstrate distorted sexual scripts. They did not explain this inconsistency. Furthermore, they failed to address the role of each symptom cluster in each pathway, sometimes entirely leaving out how that particular vulnerability is related to the offense process in that specific pathway. For example, intimacy and social skills deficits and emotional dysregulation were completely omitted from Pathway 4. It is unclear, then, whether these two components of the model play a role in the offending process for the individuals associated with Pathway 4. These inconsistencies make the model incomplete and difficult to apply to a specific individual or situation.

Second, Ward and Siegert (2002b) failed to adequately describe the origins of each of these four symptom clusters. Their description leaves the reader with the impression that each of these factors was significantly and singly caused by poor attachment. They did not discuss at any length the role of social-learning processes, biological or genetic traits, or personality traits. These important etiological variables were not addressed; neither are they suggested as potential causal variables in the development of these developmental vulnerabilities. It is important to consider the origins of these factors, because any preventative or treatment-based interventions could then target the root cause of the problems. For example, understanding the development of cognitive distortions beyond assumptions of problematic attachment is necessary to treat or prevent these beliefs from forming in youthful offenders.

Third, Ward and Siegert (2002b) created the five pathways to explain various types of child sexual abusers. The groupings that they created are very specific—perhaps too much so. It seems problematic to separate offenders into such precise categories without an apparent empirical justification for doing so. For example, in Pathway 4 there are offenders who are antisocial and embrace a criminal lifestyle. However, research on sex offenders suggests that individuals in all five pathways are likely highly antisocial and endorse procriminal attitudes (e.g., Simon, 1997a, 1997b, 2000). This specific attribute is not characteristic of just one pathway. Additionally, one could examine Pathway 1, in which the offender is hypothesized to have intimacy and interpersonal skills deficits but normal sexual scripts and functional cognitive beliefs. It is likely, however, that this type of offender would be rare. Many research studies on the psychological and interpersonal characteristics of pedophiles and child molesters demonstrate not only significant interpersonal problems but also distorted cognitive beliefs (e.g., Blumenthal, Gudjonsson, & Burns, 1999; Neidigh & Krop, 1992; Sahota & Chesterman, 1998; Segal & Stermac, 1990). Pathway 5, which is a multifactor pathway of offending, probably accounts for the vast majority of offenders. In sum, the authors created very specialized offender groups that may not be supported by the available literature on sex offenders. There is likely more overlap among these pathways than they hypothesized.

Related to this is another concern regarding their assumptions about specialization and multiple trajectories of offending. The theoretical implication that a large portion of sex offenders are specialists in one type of offending (i.e., child molestation) is questionable when compared with research on multiple paraphilias (e.g., Abel, Becker, Cunningham-Rathner, & Mittelman, 1988) and the general criminal behaviors of many sex offenders (e.g., Simon, 1997a, 1997b, 2000). Ward and Siegert (2002b) implied that sex offenders have distinct trajectories from other, non–sex offenders, despite the research evidence demonstrating that sex offenders also commit many non–sex crimes during their offending careers. This idea, then, that only one pathway of sex offenders will manifest general criminal traits and behaviors, is not supported by the research. It is likely that nearly all of the sex offenders who match with the various pathways distinguished by Ward and Siegert will have these general criminal and antisocial traits. Furthermore, these offenders will also display other deviant sexual behaviors besides those specifically related to the sexual abuse of children. Although little empirical evidence has been provided in the literature regarding clear trajectories of sex offending as opposed to general offender trajectories, the problem with this model is that the pathways they hypothesized were not developed according to empirical research on differentiating sex-offender characteristics. The amount of overlap between these pathways and the assumptions about "specialized" sex offenders in Pathways 1, 2, and 3 make this model problematic if applied to a diverse sample of sex offenders.

Fourth, these pathways rely heavily on the role of cognitions, sexual scripts, and schemas related to deviant sexual attitudes and beliefs. However, as is the problem with many other cognitive theories of sex offending, Ward and Siegert (2002b) did not fully explain how one moves from cognition to behavior. Without a clear and comprehensive explanation of how one makes the leap from deviant sexual scripts or offense-supportive schemas to actually committing a sex offense, it is unclear how these pathways definitively lead to sexually deviant behavior. This should be further explained to make the pathways model more applicable in terms of treatment and prevention.

Fifth, the model lacks consideration for the role of pedophilia in the sexual abuse of a child. Ward and Siegert (2002b) noted that their model can explain child molestation that occurs in the absence of pedophilia (e.g., Pathway 4), yet they did not explain the development of this particular disorder and how it ultimately relates to offending when compared with those who do not manifest pedophilic interest. In the early part of their theoretical description, they stated that many offenders manifest deviant sexual arousal. However, they did not explain the exact origin of this arousal. Instead, they focused on important psychological mechanisms that interact with this arousal (if it is present in the individual) to lead to sex-offending behaviors. Furthermore, they did not describe any important differences between offending trajectories in those who have pedophilia and those who do not. It is unclear to the reader whether they were suggesting that individuals with consistent deviant sexual arousal (e.g., pedophilia) will be impacted differently by these psychological mechanisms (e.g., loneliness, poor attachment) than those without. Additionally, they did not address what specific variables drive those without deviant sexual arousal toward children to commit deviant sexual acts. It must be more than just opportunity and the promise of sexual satisfaction, or many more individuals who are similar to those in Pathway 4 (i.e., general criminals) would commit sex offenses against children.

Finally, the work of Beech and Ward (2004) and Ward and Beech (2004) attempts to combine an etiological model of sex offending with a risk assessment model of sexual recidivism. The problem with this, however, is that current measurements of risk implicitly, and sometimes explicitly, assume that a sex offense has already occurred. Thus, some risk variables (e.g., age and gender of victim) cannot logically be used to explain the causal mechanisms behind sex offending. Because of this, we also do not know whether other, less offense-related characteristics explain causation. For example, the cognitive distortions described by these authors as both etiological and risk factors may have not developed prior to the initiation of the first sex offense. Ward and Siegert (2002b) noted in their original conceptualization of the pathways model that it is possible that these distortions developed as post hoc justifications for a sexually deviant act. In addition, research has not yet demonstrated the mechanisms behind risk variables. In other words, we do not yet know why certain variables are more predictive of risk than others; we only know that they are. Because of this limitation, applying a model of risk assessment to an etiological framework may be interesting, but it ultimately is causally uninformative until we know how these risk variables truly interact to produce future offenses.

SUMMARY AND CONCLUSIONS

In this chapter, we have described and reviewed five integrative theories and models designed to explain sex-offending behaviors. In Finkelhor's (1984) precondition model, four conditions or factors purportedly lead to child sexual abuse: (a) motivation to offend, (b) overcoming internal inhibitors, (c) overcoming external inhibitors, and (d) overcoming the resistance of the child. In Marshall and Barbaree's (1990) integrative model, biological influences, childhood experiences, and cognitive–behavioral factors are combined, also taking into consideration the individual's sociocultural context, to explain child sexual abuse. Hall and Hirschman's (1991, 1992) quadripartite model attributes sex-offending outcomes to a combination of physiological arousal, cognitive appraisal, affective dyscontrol, and personality disorder traits. Malamuth's (1996, 1998a, 1998b) confluence model combines three variables within an evolutionary framework, emphasizing promiscuous or impersonal style, hostile masculinity, and high dominance–low nurturance. Finally, Ward and Siegert's (2002b) pathways model describes four primary pathways through which offending occurs, focusing on intimacy and social skills deficits, distorted sexual scripts, emotional dysregulation, and cognitive distortions.

The primary advantage of the models and theories described in this chapter is that they represent attempts at theoretical integration. The resulting theories and models are richer and more comprehensive than the single-faceted theories examined thus far in this book. They incorporate multiple causal factors and combine them in such a way as to provide a more detailed explanation of how the behavior might develop over time and in a variety of contexts. Instead of looking at one variable or set of variables and attempting to explain how that single factor impacts the individual on multiple levels and leads to the development of a very specific, yet rare behavior, the integrative theories incorporate a variety of factors, some of which have been identified as relevant to sex-offending populations in the larger body of research. The result is that we have an etiological perspective that views sexually deviant behavior as resulting from multiple factors; combined in specific and determinate ways; mediating and moderating the individual's functioning within environmental, interpersonal, and internal contexts. It is with the idea of integration and complex development that we turn to the final theory in this book.

10

MULTIMODAL SELF-REGULATION THEORY: A NEW INTEGRATION

Because each of the theories and models for the etiology of sex offenders considered in the prior chapters has a number of critical limitations that constrain their explanatory power and our ability to make useful predictions about sexually inappropriate behavior, we now present a new theory that focuses on important developmental antecedents to sex-offending behaviors and emphasizes ways in which they interact with internal and external events in childhood, adolescence, and adulthood to produce sexually deviant outcomes. This theory integrates a variety of psychosocial perspectives, drawing from theories of child development, emotional and self-regulatory capacities, personality influences, and conditioning paradigms. The primary driving force behind this etiological conceptualization is *self-regulation*. We suggest that significant self-regulatory deficits, emerging from early childhood experiences, shape the development of deviant sexual interest and arousal.

The idea that self-regulation is a key component of this process is not entirely new. Treatment models (e.g., Ward & Hudson, 1998, 2000; Ward, Polaschek, & Beech, 2006) have used the idea of profound deficits in the ability to self-regulate as a major factor in the maintenance of sex offending. These models have emphasized the goal-setting components and various drive pathways of self-regulation to assist in our conceptualization of relapse, treatment response, and recidivism. In addition, some etiological models (e.g., Burk & Burkhart, 2003; Cortoni & Marshall, 2000) emphasize the potential role of self-regulatory difficulty in creating sex as a reliable but inappropriate coping strategy for internal or interpersonal distress. However, these prior models lack an explanation for the scope of regulatory deficits, corresponding maladaptive regulatory strategies, and the specific formation of deviant sexual interests as opposed to hypersexual behavior or inappropriate sexual interests that are not vastly deviant from typical sexual expression (e.g., coercive sexual behavior instead of explicit sexual interest in prepubescent children or animals). Furthermore, these conceptualizations as a whole emphasize the immediate proximal events leading up to the offense rather than broadly considering distal developmental antecedents and ongoing interactional processes. Multimodal self-regulation theory not only explains these critical variables but also outlines the development of paraphilic sexual interests within a developmental framework.

Because a combination of factors influences the development of deviant sexual behaviors, we first discuss biological propensities that influence later outcomes. Second, we address childhood experiences with family and peers and the perceptions of these experiences that are unique to the individual. Because an extensive literature exists on the impact of biological predispositions, temperament, and childhood socialization on adult psychopathology and other potential negative outcomes, we only briefly describe these topics. Third, we describe the impact of these variables on the individual's ability to regulate emotions, followed by a description of how inappropriate and deviant sexual interests and behaviors form in light of these regulatory deficits and how personality factors may lead to variation of sexual interests. We also discuss how these strengthen over time and may lead to consistent or persistent sexually deviant behaviors. Important behavioral outcomes of dysregulation are considered, including personality and cognitive variables that interact with poor regulatory ability to drive specific regulatory behaviors, such as inappropriate sexual activity. The chapter concludes with three examples to illustrate how this process occurs. Before we begin, however, we refer the reader to Figure 10.1, which provides a graphic representation of the critical factors involved in our theoretical model. Although relevant research is discussed in this chapter, the need to fully explain the theory precludes considering all of the research or possible limitations. Chapter 11 is devoted to considering these issues in greater detail as well as considering the treatment implications of this theory.

TEMPERAMENT AND BIOLOGICAL PROPENSITIES

Any psychological theory designed to explain some important aspect of human behavior must first begin by addressing biological propensities and

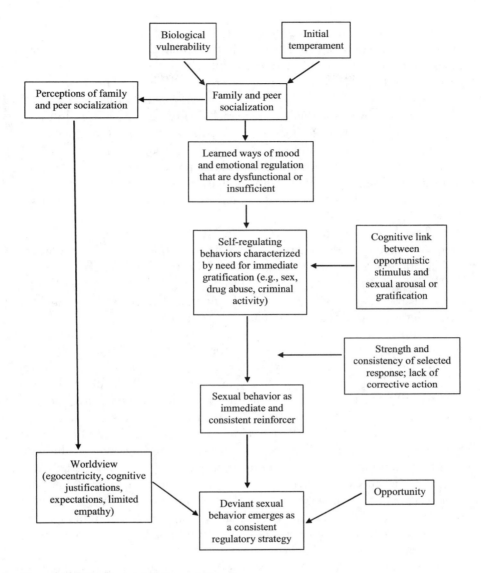

Figure 10.1. Multimodal self-regulation theory.

temperamental factors. Rather than being a "blank slate" at birth, each individual is born with certain biological features, including hereditary predispositions, temperament, and cognitive or neurological capacity (e.g., attention). These factors, in isolation, are not inherently positive or negative, but they significantly influence the way in which the individual interacts with and reacts to his or her environment. Depending on environmental conditions, the reaction may then be labeled as *adaptive* (positive) or *maladaptive* (negative). Maladaptive reactions are those that demonstrate poorness of fit with the environment and may lead to negative outcomes, manifested in the form of psychological or behavioral distress. In particular, these negative outcomes have implications for the individual's ability to regulate the self, modulate emotion, and function effectively in interpersonal relationships.

A number of these biological and temperamental variables have been identified as significant predictors of maladaptive behavioral and psychological development. These factors are definitively related to neither sex offending nor sexually deviant psychopathology, although they may play a role in the development of these and other related problems. Many of the characteristics discussed here apply to a wide variety of outcomes, including psychopathology, delinquency, and general distress in later life (e.g., Kubzansky, Martin, & Buka, 2004).

The developmental literature notes that some infants and young children are inherently more emotionally reactive than others (Davidson, Putnam, & Larson, 2000; Izard & Kobak, 1991; Linehan, 1993a; Malatesta-Magai, 1991; Scaramella & Leve, 2004). Mothers and other caregivers have described these infants as being more difficult to soothe, having lower frustration tolerance, and being more easily distressed by external stimuli (e.g., sudden noises; Malatesta-Magai, 1991; Scaramella & Leve, 2004). These infants perhaps have lower thresholds for emotional stimulation (Izard & Kobak, 1991), which results in greater reactivity and is manifested in the form of irritability, emotional lability, and increased tendencies to become more easily frustrated and emotionally overaroused (Shaw, Owens, Giovannelli, & Winslow, 2001). When faced with new environmental demands, these children will also demonstrate this heightened emotional reactivity in the form of distress or anxiety and will have greater difficulty returning to their emotional baseline after exposure to unexpected changes or novel stimuli (Cole, Martin, & Dennis, 2004; Linehan, 1993a; Malatesta-Magai, 1991; Scaramella & Leve, 2004). It is interesting that some research has also shown that male infants may show a greater vulnerability to environmental stressors, given these temperamental features, than their female counterparts (Scaramella & Leve, 2004).

Another consideration for these individuals is the nature of their "default" emotional experience. Some literature suggests that these infants and children show proneness to negative emotional experience (e.g., Hanish et al., 2004). Therefore, individuals with these temperamental features will not only demonstrate greater emotional sensitivity and reactivity, but they will also be more likely to experience negative emotionality, which may be related to the increased tendency to respond with frustration, aggression, or irritability, as has been shown in developmental research (Hanish et al., 2004; Kubzansky et al., 2004; Scaramella & Leve, 2004; Shaw et al., 2001). We again see gender as a potential mediator, with some evidence that young boys show more enduring negative emotionality than young girls (Hanish et al., 2004).

Specific areas of the brain have been implicated in these constitutional features of emotional experience. The structures and neural communication pathways of the limbic system are crucial for recognizing and reacting to emotional stimuli, and these areas are likely associated with greater emotional vulnerability (e.g., Izard & Kobak, 1991; Linehan, 1993a). The prefrontal cortex, which is involved in the interpretation of environmental stimuli and inhibition of impulses, has been related to intensity and regulation of angry and aggressive emotional expression in developmental research (Davidson et al., 2000; R. M. Ryan, Kuhl, & Deci, 1997). Context learning, which is associated with the hippocampus and related memory structures, may also contribute to a young child's ability to learn ways of responding to emotional experience in the context of environmental feedback (Izard & Kobak, 1991). Last, attentional capacity also has important implications for the child's ability to selectively attend to relevant stimuli, disengage attention from stimuli that may provoke negative affect, and anticipate environmental outcomes (Raver, 2004; Rothbart, Ziaie, & O'Boyle, 1992).

These biological and temperamental predispositions not only impact the way the individual experiences and responds to internal tension and distress but also shape the surrounding environment. This is discussed at greater length in the next section, but we must briefly consider how these traits are manifested in ways that interact with environmental agents. For instance, infants and children with higher distress, low frustration tolerance, and emotional vulnerability may require more parental attention. Parents may be incapable of responding to the child's needs, thereby increasing emotional distress. Additionally, the ways in which children manifest these emotions, such as irritability or aggression, might increase negative interactions with caregivers and peers. Continued failure to adapt to environmental contingencies might reinforce maladaptive ways of dealing with negative emotion, again increasing vulnerability to negative affect.

Unfortunately, it is difficult, if not impossible, at present to describe these characteristics within a sex-offending population. Developmental research includes longitudinal data on important outcomes for children with these predispositions, but none of the available literature notes the development of deviant sexual interests or behaviors in these groups. This is probably due to the low incidence of sex offending in the population as a whole, which would reduce the incidence of sexually deviant behaviors in these relatively small and selected samples. Other research on the emotionality and emotional experiences of sex offenders is available but has used post hoc methods to identify these traits in early childhood, which could be biased by recall or expectancy effects. Thus, more research in this particular area is needed to draw a clear connection between these given traits and sexually deviant behavior as one of several potential outcomes. We believe that individuals who have developed deviant sexual interests likely exhibited many of these biological and temperamental predispositions in their early development. Characteristics such as emotional vulnerability, proneness to negative emotion, and difficulty with learning to soothe negative affect importantly shaped their social interactions and the acquisition of maladaptive patterns of emotion and self-regulation.

PEER AND FAMILY SOCIALIZATION

As mentioned in the previous section, it is possible for the individual's biological and temperamental characteristics to shape and interact with those in the surrounding environment. The individual uses his or her available resources, such as emotional regulation and learned expectations, to understand and predict events in the world. The infant or young child who experiences emotions more intensely or more frequently than others may be treated differently by parents or other caregivers. In other cases, parents or caregivers may simply lack the resources to appropriately care for the needs of the developing infant. How individuals are treated by important others during critical periods of development and how they are socialized in the environment further determine how the child will be able to form relationships, regulate emotion, and function adaptively within the environment.

Parental and Family Socialization

A young child needs assistance from others in his or her environment to respond to emotional and physiological arousal. Negative emotions—how they are associated with the immediate environment and how environmental agents respond to them—are particularly salient to the developing child (Kopp, 1992). The parents or primary caregivers help the child cope with internal tension and adapt to changes within the environment, ultimately equipping him or her with patterns of emotional responding, including variation, intensity, and duration of emotional experience (Cicchetti, Ganiban, & Barnett, 1991).

Unfortunately, not all parents and caregivers appropriately socialize their children or respond to signals of emotional distress in consistent and effective ways. For example, a parent may create an unstable, inconsistent, and therefore unpredictable environment for the child. In this situation, the parent responds inconsistently to the needs of the child, perhaps failing to give clear feedback about emotional experience or behavior. This could be due to the parent's lack of ability to recognize the child's needs. Another possibility is that the parent lacks the resources necessary to modulate internal distress or tension, thereby making it difficult to consistently reinforce adaptive emotional responding in the child. Regardless, the child will have difficulty emulating effective regulation of behavior and adaptive responding to distressing emotion and will fail to develop a sense of internal control. Failure to do so may create a cycle in which the child expresses greater distress and behavioral dysregulation, which is met with more ineffective or inconsistent responding from the parent or caregiver.

A second type of ineffective or inappropriate socialization is overly harsh or punitive parental behavior. This would also include markedly abusive behaviors on the part of the parent. Here, the predominant response to a child's needs is critical, hostile, demanding, or harmful. An extensive literature documents the link between childhood maltreatment and negative outcomes such as emotional dysregulation, aggression and delinquency, and psychopathology (Calkins, 2004; Cicchetti et al., 1991; Granic & Patterson, 2006; Maughan & Cicchetti, 2002; McCabe, Cunnington, & Brooks-Gunn, 2004; Moffitt, 1993; Scaramella & Leve, 2004). Hostile or abusive parents may punish a child for emotional expression or minimize his or her emotional experience, thus interfering with the development of adaptive emotional responding (Eisenberg, Fabes, Carlo, & Karbon, 1992). Additionally, maltreated children may internalize hostile interpersonal behaviors or ineffective strategies for dealing with distressing emotion (Calkins, 2004; Eisenberg, Smith, Sadovsky, & Spinrad, 2004).

Temperament and harsh or demanding parenting strategies may interact to form a coercive interaction cycle between child and parents (Scaramella & Leve, 2004). Signals of distress from the child may elicit angry or coercive reactions from parents who are unable to understand or respond to the emotional needs of the child. In turn, the parental response will increase the child's distress and perhaps exacerbate behavioral problems related to that distress. Over time, these interactions produce lasting difficulties with self-regulation as well as poor inhibitory control and an inability to delay gratification (Eisenberg et al., 2004; Granic & Patterson, 2006; McCabe et al., 2004; Moffitt, 1993).

Important gender differences may contribute to differential functioning in males and females. For example, some evidence suggests that mothers show greater emotional expression to their daughters than to their sons (Malatesta-Magai, 1991). Other research suggests that mothers or caregivers in general may respond to their sons' emotional reactivity more harshly and with greater hostility (Scaramella & Leve, 2004). This may have a negative impact on the development of appropriate emotional expression in infants and youth with increased emotional sensitivity. McCabe et al. (2004) also posited that girls generally show more ability to self-regulate than boys, which could lead to poorer outcome for males in families with ineffective parental socialization.

Peer Socialization

Peers also play a valuable role for a young child in learning appropriate ways of adapting to environmental demands. Children with difficulty regulating emotions and behavior are typically less socially competent and experience difficulty in interacting appropriately with peers (Eisenberg et al., 1992; Hanish et al., 2004; Maughan & Cicchetti, 2002). These findings are also linked to the experiences of inconsistent or hostile parenting at home (Maughan & Cichetti, 2002), which further exacerbates the child's difficulty with identifying and modulating negative affect. Some research also suggests that self-regulatory skills are more difficult for the child to access in the presence of peers (e.g., McCabe et al., 2004), which could make it more difficult to deal with distressing emotion or negative interaction for the child who already has a tenuous hold on the ability to cope with internal tension.

Negative interactions with peers may further shape the emotionally dysregulated child in two important ways. For one, researchers have hypothesized that peer relationships and the experience of poorly regulated internal experiences may interact to influence the development of empathy in some children. Leary (2004) noted that children will be able to understand the internal and emotional states of others only so far as they are able to understand their own. Others have similarly noted that the ability to accurately infer the motives or intentions of other people, a critical feature of empathic understanding, comes from the ability to accurately identify and comprehend emotional responding (Vohs & Ciarocco, 2004). Children need not only appropriate regulatory skills to acquire empathy but also adult models of empathic responding. Without adequate socialization and capacity to cope with negative affect, emotionally dysregulated children might then focus primarily on the self and not others in social situations when negative emotions are high (Eisenberg et al., 1992).

A second critical result of negative social interactions and poorly internalized or nonexistent regulatory scripts is continuing victimization over time. A young child who expresses greater levels of negative emotion tends to elicit more negative responses from peers, including acts of victimization (Hanish et al., 2004). Specifically, researchers have identified specific negative emotional responses that correlate with greater levels of victimization by peers, including reactive aggression, anger, anxiety, and sadness (Hanish et al., 2004; Scaramella & Leve, 2004). This victimization by peers, coupled with a higher frequency of negative experiences within the home, often predicts poorer outcome for adult psychological functioning in these youth (Hanish et al., 2004).

Again, gender effects mediate children's relationships with peers and their functioning as adults. Male children who experience frequent emotional dysregulation are less popular and less socially competent than their similar female peers (Eisenberg et al., 1992). Males also experience higher rates of peer victimization and have a higher incidence of psychological dysfunction in adulthood than their female counterparts (Hanish et al., 2004). This adds to the growing research demonstrating that emotional reactivity and self-regulatory difficulties in early childhood have a more negative impact on future psychological and behavioral functioning for males than for females.

Perceptions of Peer and Family Socialization

Another potentially important variable in this framework is the individual's perception of socializing agents in his or her environment. Although this is not commonly discussed in the developmental literature, the idea that children's interpretations of early childhood experiences and their perceptions of how they are treated by others would shape later reactions to the environment is consistent with current cognitive models of development. From the cognitive literature described in chapter 4, we see that early experiences shape the development of cognitive schemas and the individual's ability to interpret and predict behavior. Similarly, it would make sense to say that the way an individual has interpreted these early experiences also contributes to his or her cognitive view of the world. An individual's interpretation of an event and the actual experience of the event are closely linked. However, it is important here to note that some individuals leave similar experiences with very different perceptions of and reactions to what happened.

Negative childhood experiences coupled with emotional vulnerability and distress might cause some individuals to adopt the perspective that the world is a hostile and uncaring place. These beliefs might continue into adolescence and adulthood, giving a negative cast to the individual's beliefs about relationships and the emotions of others. Others may react with a sense of entitlement, believing that the world owes them something that was never given during childhood. Another possibility is that the individual will normalize these experiences, believing that harsh treatment or victimization of others are appropriate ways to deal with internal or interpersonal tension. The relationship between empathy and emotion regulation in interpersonal contexts, which was mentioned previously, could also have important implications for how the person perceives his or her childhood experience. Beliefs centered on the self would limit the individual's ability to objectively evaluate past experiences and learn the difference between adaptive and maladaptive responding.

In this sense, the experience itself is important in determining future behavioral and emotional reactions, but perceptions of the experience may be equally critical in defining how that event will impact future functioning. The individual may adopt certain beliefs about the cause of an event, the motivations of others involved, the appropriateness or inevitability of the responses (both emotional and behavioral), and the impact that the event had on later outcomes. These variables are potentially important in creating a pattern of cognitive processing of information, establishing expectations and biases from environmental stimuli, and forming the way in which the person views his or her world.

Sex Offending and Early Socialization Effects

The available literature provides some information about sex offenders' early relationships with parents and peers. Research has shown that these individuals experienced greater familial turmoil during childhood and frequently had parents with high rates of substance abuse and psychopathology (e.g., Becker, 1988; Briggs & Hawkins, 1996; Seghorn, Prentky, & Boucher, 1987; Zgourides, Monto, & Harris, 1997). The majority of studies also note the presence of emotional, physical, and sexual abuse within this population. Reported rates of physical maltreatment in this population range from 17% to 58%, with 17% to 93% reporting incidents of sexual abuse during childhood and with additional findings of emotional or verbal abuse and neglect during this same developmental period (Briggs & Hawkins, 1996; Graham, 1996; Haapasalo & Kankkonen, 1997; Jonson-Reid & Way, 2001; Kobayashi, Sales, Becker, Figueredo, & Kaplan, 1995; Veneziano, Veneziano, & LeGrand, 2000; Worling, 1995; Zgourides et al., 1997). Although these data rely heavily on self-report and therefore must be interpreted with caution, we can say that sex-offending individuals consistently report negative experiences in childhood that likely affected the ability to self-regulate, learn appropriate regulation strategies from important others, and perceive events they experienced in an adaptive way.

There is a dearth of evidence regarding how sex offenders interacted with peers in the early childhood environment. However, evidence suggesting that these individuals may have offended against peers in early childhood and adolescence, or associated with other sex-offending youth, indicates that their peer relationships were not ideal (e.g., Blaske, Borduin, Henggeler, & Mann, 1989; Fehrenbach, Smith, Monastersky, & Deisher, 1986; Hanson & Scott, 1996). In addition, some offenders report having been victimized by peers, either sexually, physically, or verbally (e.g., Hendriks & Bijleveld, 2004; Langevin, Wright, & Handy, 1989; Miner & Munns, 2005), which would again indicate that they did not form healthy social relationships and were perhaps easily victimized by other youth.

In our etiological model, we suggest that sexually deviant individuals have early childhood experiences characterized by victimization and other negative experiences. These, coupled with biological and temperamental vulnerabilities, leave these individuals with self-regulatory skills that are either nonexistent, inadequate given their emotional sensitivity and distress proneness, or maladaptive. Experiences with inconsistent or ineffective parental socialization also affect these individuals, making it difficult for them to develop sufficient regulatory strategies and internalize important behavioral techniques that would help them tolerate frustration or distress (e.g., delay of gratification). Those who experience abusive parenting or abuse at the hands of peers or trusted others (e.g., teachers) are left with greater difficulty in regulating negative affect and internal tensions and begin to develop a distorted worldview and decreased ability to appropriately empathize with others. Perceptions of these childhood experiences also contribute to the lasting effect of these events on the individual. Beliefs that normalize negative experiences, or beliefs in the world as a hostile place, may in turn foster greater emotional distress and an inability to deal with that distress.

Gender may have a significant mediating effect on this developmental process. Male children or adolescents may have greater difficulty moderating internal tension and distress under these specified conditions. The compounded effect of these variables may not only make males more vulnerable to poor self-regulation but may also change the way in which they respond to states of dysregulation and tension. These factors give us a potential explanation for why males are more likely to develop and exhibit sexually deviant behaviors than females. Note that this explanation does not exclude women from engaging in sex-offending behaviors or developing paraphilic interests, but it does provide relevant information to explain the disproportionate prevalence of this behavior in men.

SELF-REGULATION

Self-regulation is commonly divided into four domains: (a) emotion regulation, (b) cognitive regulation, (c) behavioral regulation, and (d) interpersonal regulation. These processes, either separately or in combination, define the individual's ability to monitor, examine, interpret, and respond to internal and external stimuli in a way that is consistent with both immediate and delayed goals. The goal of self-regulation, then, is to modulate thoughts, behaviors, and emotions so that they meet specific, predetermined goals. These goals may include emotional homeostasis, interpersonal comfort, or behavioral gratification. Dysregulation occurs then when the individual is either unable to or incapable of performing any of these regulatory tasks in a manner that may be required in the moment. For the following discussion, we rely heavily on the concepts of emotional regulation and dysregulation, whereby internal distress or tension—as measured by individual emotional homeostasis—drives certain behaviors that are designed to reduce that internal discomfort (for lengthier literature on emotion regulation, see Baumeister & Vohs, 2004; Gross, 1998, 1999a, 1999b; Linehan, 1993a).

Much of the preceding discussion leads to the following point: Individuals with inadequate strategies for modulating overwhelming negative affect may adopt maladaptive or inappropriate means through which to regulate themselves. Individuals use a variety of strategies to maintain emotional homeostasis, meaning that they attempt to keep their mood regulated at a certain internal level of acceptable affect. Sudden and noticeable changes in emotion, whether positive or negative, will motivate the individual to engage in self-regulating behaviors to reestablish a comfortable emotional homeostasis (e.g., Carver, 2004). The methods by which an individual regulates emotion depend largely on the early experiences we have just outlined. For individuals with insufficient regulatory strategies, it may be difficult to return to a comfortable level of affect. Overwhelming emotion will cause increased distress, a concentrated focus on the self and internal tension, and may lead to rather desperate and perhaps maladaptive attempts to develop effective regulatory strategies.

Because overwhelming negative affect may be inherently more motivating than overwhelming positive affect (Larsen & Prizmic, 2004), individuals will more likely develop these maladaptive strategies in response to negative emotional states. Thus, we could reasonably expect that poorly regulated individuals would establish patterns of maladaptive responding when facing emotional distress. One strategy noted in the literature for reducing negative affect is self-reward or engaging in pleasurable activities, which is sometimes considered one of the most successful strategies for coping with negative emotional experience (e.g., Larsen & Prizmic, 2004). Using reinforcing activities is also a strategy that may not require extensive internal or cognitive resources and could potentially provide more immediate emotional relief.

In our model, we hypothesize that sex offenders are individuals who lack adaptive, internalized strategies for dealing with negative affect, which may lead to a number of internalizing problems, such as psychopathology and externalized behaviors characterized by aggression and impulsivity (e.g., Becker, 1998). The drive to diminish emotional or behavioral distress is very strong and thus motivates the individual to relieve that distress quickly and effectively. However, because these are individuals who have failed to internalize appropriate strategies for coping with this distress (e.g., social support; cognitive reframing, problem solving, or mood management), they must use external strategies that are easily accessible and require little effort. These externalized regulatory strategies are also those that promise immediate gratification, given that the individual is unable to tolerate distress for a prolonged period of time. For example, using a substance such as alcohol or marijuana to cope with distress is more immediately reinforcing and involves less effort than engaging in a long-term problem-solving strategy that would directly address the initial source of the distress.

Others have noted the tendency of sex offenders and offenders in general to use a variety of externalized strategies for self-regulation (e.g., Burk & Burkhart, 2003). We believe that sex-offending individuals use several maladaptive strategies that are characterized by immediate gratification and decreased personal effort. The strategies with which we are most concerned here include sexual activity, illicit substance use, and criminal or delinquent behaviors. We briefly provide examples of how each of these activities meets the criteria mentioned previously for immediately effective but maladaptive regulatory strategies.

First, sexual satisfaction is a readily available strategy that typically promises significant physiological reinforcement. Furthermore, sexual activity is often linked with intimacy and feelings of belongingness, which are also reinforcing. A strong biological drive for sexual activity coupled with the strong reinforcing properties of sex thereby make it an accessible and satisfying way to alleviate negative internal tension. It is not surprising that individuals would choose to engage in sexual activity to distract themselves from distressing events or emotions, increase positive mood, or fulfill self-esteem or identity needs. A substantial body of literature notes that sex offenders frequently used masturbation and other sexual practices as a means to "self-soothe" during childhood and adolescence as well as adulthood (e.g., Burk & Burkhart, 2003; Cortoni & Marshall, 2000; Marshall & Marshall, 2000). For example, a male adolescent who discovers that masturbation is a means through which he can cope with feelings of inadequacy and anger toward others may develop a pattern of masturbation or engaging in sexual fantasy whenever these feelings arise. Over time, this would become a consistent activity that would decrease internal distress through reinforcing physiological satiation and fantasies that promise acceptance and understanding from a sexual partner. A lack of equally effective and reinforcing means by which this male adolescent can tolerate these distressing emotions may drive the development of sexual coping mechanisms in times of dysregulation.

Second, the use of substances such as alcohol or narcotics almost always provides some kind of reinforcement for the individual because of the primary effects of these substances. Extensive research with human and animals models has consistently demonstrated that drugs and alcohol serve as positive reinforcers for neurochemical systems in the brain (Gardner, 1992; McKim, 2000). Some substances may elicit feelings of intense euphoria or elation, some may decrease awareness or change perceptions of environmental surroundings, and others will stimulate or disinhibit the body's systems. These effects lead to a pleasurable experience for the user, which may serve a variety of purposes. Here, we are concerned with the impact of these effects on an individual with limited or insufficient means to regulate negative internal states. For one who lacks the ability to self-generate mood regulation strategies, the reinforcing properties of mood-altering substances might be even more attractive and difficult to resist. These substances will artificially change the internal balance and provoke an altered sense of well-being. Combined with strong properties of psychological and physiological addiction (e.g., Childress, Ehrman, Rohsenow, Robbins, & O'Brien, 1992; Gardner, 1992), use of substances as a consistent but maladaptive self-regulation strategy may develop over time for individuals with poor internal regulatory controls. The high rates of substance abuse among sex offenders has been well documented in the literature, with rates of problematic substance use ranging from 60% to 90% in adult sex offenders and as high as 50% in adolescent samples (Abracen, Looman, & Anderson, 2000; Becker, Stinson, Tromp, & Messer, 2003; Noffsinger & Resnick, 2000).

Finally, criminal or delinquent acts may result as a maladaptive strategy for self-regulation because of the individual's inability to delay gratification and control his impulses. Gottfredson and Hirschi (1990) introduced this idea in their general theory of crime, suggesting that a fundamental problem with self-control or the lack of self-restraint is what drives an inability to delay gratification. They posited that this lack of self-control, combined with opportunity, leads to relatively unplanned and risky criminal activities. Furthermore, people with low self-control have a higher likelihood of engaging in other high-risk activities that provide quick benefit and require little effort or planning, such as substance abuse, gambling, and risky sexual behaviors, and they will also be limited in their ability to consider the potential costs of these behaviors (Gottfredson & Hirschi, 1990; Hirschi, 2004). We believe that low self-control is one of several indicators of difficulties with efficient and adaptive self-regulation. Again, individuals with some difficulty in generating successful internal means of regulating distress and desires will seek external ways of regulating emotion and behavior. Criminal or delinquent behaviors are also likely to serve as sources of external regulation because they will immediately gratify desires, require comparatively little effort, and may offer excitement or risk that are also reinforcing. As we mentioned in chapter 2, sex offenders are not specialists and engage in a wide variety of other criminal behaviors, often at a rate that far exceeds their illegal sexual behaviors (Simon, 1997a, 1997b, 2000).

Another important point relates to a possible interaction between the development of maladaptive external strategies for self-regulation and peer and family socialization. Some individuals may have negative experiences within the home and with their peers but will also learn offense-supportive beliefs and behaviors from these sources. As has been noted in the criminological literature (Akers, 1985, 1998, 2000; Gottfredson & Hirschi, 1990; Granic & Patterson, 2006; Moffitt, 1993), parents and important others may model inappropriate criminal or violent behaviors for the developing child, teaching him or her that these are appropriate and effective responses to internal distress or expressed needs. For a child or adolescent who has difficulty with regulation, further messages endorsing impulsive self-serving behaviors as a means through which to fulfill needs or improve functioning within the environment may exacerbate the individual's inability to develop adaptive internal regulation strategies.

DEVIANT SEXUALITY

Thus far, much of our etiological discussion has remained consistent with earlier findings in the literature. We have perhaps provided a more

comprehensive picture of how self-regulatory deficits develop in these offenders and how they are linked with sex offending and other related behaviors, but there is a major component missing in the process: If sex is used as a
coping strategy or externalized regulatory strategy, why is it that some individuals develop deviant sexual interests or behaviors? After all, it could be
argued that these individuals can meet their needs through engaging in acceptable and appropriate forms of sexual activity. Even if access to the more
traditional means of sexual satisfaction were blocked, individuals could engage in masturbation, use pornography, or pay for erotic materials and services. In other words, sexual gratification could still operate as a coping mechanism without the introduction of deviant sexual practices.

So how is it that some people develop sexual interest in children, animals, sadism, or fetish objects? And why is it that many individuals with a
history of sex offending and paraphilic sexual interest report not just one
paraphilia but many (e.g., Abel, Becker, Cunningham-Rathner, & Mittelman,
1988)? These are the questions that our model must address to fully explain
how sexually deviant interests develop. Our concern here is with individuals
who have repeatedly engaged in sexually deviant fantasies or behaviors. Although we understand that deviant sexual arousal is not a necessary or even
sufficient condition for sex-offending behavior to occur, at a minimum, some
process occurs through which individuals develop a willingness to engage in
deviant sexual behaviors. The theory being described here allows for individuals to use deviant sexual behaviors as a potential coping strategy through
several mechanisms, including one in which readily available and opportunistic resources are used to achieve sexual gratification and mediation of
internal distress and another mechanism whereby the individual seeks out
reinforced sexual coping strategies that have developed over time and may
reflect more enduring sexual interest or arousal patterns.

Again, some offenders use strategies based on available opportunities
that they perceive as potentially useful or helpful, without entrenched sexual
interests consistent with the selected strategy. Others develop deviant sexual
interests focused on one or more specific targets and are often classified as
those with paraphilic sexual interests. These are the offenders that are most
often being identified by recent sex offender legislation and are viewed as the
most complex treatment cases (e.g., Winick & La Fond, 2003). This is perhaps due to a perception that their deviant arousal patterns make them more
persistent sexual offenders, or at least those for whom short-term therapies
may be less successful. It is for this reason that we now consider the initial
moment during which deviant sexual interests are considered as potentially
useful or satisfying sexual strategies for these offenders.

Our basic premise is that sexual arousal becomes linked with a deviant
or inappropriate stimulus at some point during sexual development. The way
in which this occurs is through the mind's attempt to cognitively label the
experience of sexual arousal and locate a potential source for that arousal.

think of sexual excitement as a process that is first stimulated
age, or representation of some erotic or arousing stimulus that
physiological response. With this typical representation of
nd development, we are able to easily identify the source of
nd arousal as whatever stimulus directly preceded that arousal.
s describing the childhood sexual abuse of adult offenders
have noted the potential relationship between early deviant sexual experience and later deviant sexual behavior (e.g., Wiederman, 2004), which is discussed at length in chapter 6 of this volume. However, there may be instances in which sexual arousal is not so easily linked with an overt sexual stimulus. For example, a male adolescent who is in the early stages of puberty may experience rather spontaneous erections and pleasurable sexual sensations in the absence of a clear sexual stimulus. For males who understand this process, who are able to easily recognize physiological sensations and label them appropriately, and who have sufficient ability to regulate corresponding emotional states, the experience of this spontaneous sexual arousal is not a significant source of confusion or misunderstanding. However, adolescents who lack these abilities might have some difficulty identifying the source of this physiological sensation, or view it as an appropriate response to any emotional or behavioral distress that they are currently experiencing. In doing so, they will look for a reliable way to identify the source of that arousal in order to replicate the pleasurable sexual sensations in the future.

Within this framework, sexual arousal may become linked with a deviant stimulus because of the individual's interpretation of the initial arousal, regardless of whether that interpretation was an accurate or sexually appropriate source of the arousal. In some cases, the source of the arousal may be fairly obvious. In the examples provided at the end of this chapter, a young man becomes aroused while watching his female neighbor undress. He links the experience of the arousal with the neighbor but also makes a crucial connection to the experience of watching her, thus sparking voyeuristic sexual interests.

In other cases, an individual might experience nondirected sexual arousal during nonrelated physiological or psychological states, such as anxiety, anger, or humiliation. Because there is not a clear source of the arousal, these individuals will search for a potential cause in their environment. This will not only provide an explanation for their bodily sensations but will also give them the necessary information to induce a similar state of arousal in the future. An individual who is feeling angry and experiences spontaneous arousal may cognitively link the arousal with the target of his anger, which could possibly induce violent sexual thoughts. Another who experiences this unexplained arousal might attribute it to objects within the environment, such as shoes or a particular part of the body, thus forming an early fetish-like attachment to that object.

Because sexually deviant interests are still relatively rare within even a clinical or criminal population, it is understood that the events described previously are unlikely to occur. The majority of individuals do not form sexual interests in inappropriate or unusual nonsexual objects. Even early exposure to sexual arousal, linked with inappropriate stimuli, does not reliably result in a fixed pattern of sexual arousal. For example, we could hypothesize that a child who is abused might experience sexual arousal during the abuse process. It is possible, then, that the child could link sexual arousal to that abuse experience and seek a way (i.e., sexual fantasy or behavior involving sex between an adult and a child) to evoke that same arousal in the future. Similarly, the child may link the anxiety or fear associated with the abuse with subsequent sexual release, thereby perpetuating a link between negative emotion and externalized regulation (i.e., sexual behavior) in future circumstances (Wiederman, 2004). However, many other things are necessary for this connection to occur. The child would initially have to normalize this experience to some extent. Believing that this is normal sexual expression would foster a greater tendency to engage in the behavior later on or use this as a source of sexual fantasy. In addition, the child must lack other sources that would reliably reproduce the same or similar experiences, either emotionally or sexually. In other words, a child or adolescent with alternate and available sources of sexual arousal or gratification, and with intact emotional resources and regulation strategies, would not need to incorporate these unusual experiences into his behavioral repertoire.

These and other relevant environmental, interpersonal, affective, and cognitive factors all likely contribute to the individual's development of sexual interest. The majority of children and adolescents are able to appropriately and accurately identify the source of their sexual arousal and do not attribute the arousal to inappropriate or deviant sources. Similarly, most children who experience early sexual abuse, or other unusual sexual experiences, do not view these experiences as potential future sources of sexual gratification. However, for some, these early behavioral and cognitive events drive the development of their sexual interest. These early cues help them define and shape their sexual identity and help them seek reliable and effective ways to achieve sexual gratification. When these early misattributions as to the source of sexual arousal are combined with an inability to sufficiently regulate internal distress, sexually deviant coping mechanisms may result.

As mentioned previously, other individuals who commit sex offenses do not endorse reliable arousal to deviant sexual stimuli—yet they still commit these offenses. We believe that a similar process is at work in the development of these behaviors, despite their normal sexual arousal pattern. Some individuals in a state of dysregulation may seek out opportunistic strategies for regulating their distress, including those that involve sexual victimization of others. These individuals may have broadly developed a willingness to engage in a variety of deviant behaviors, including sexually deviant behaviors. Through the same process of adaptive strategy development, they are willing to engage in these behaviors in an attempt to regulate their internal state. Successful regulation, then, may lead them to engage in these behaviors repeatedly, much as one would expect with those who are consistently sexually aroused by deviant stimuli.

BEHAVIORAL CONDITIONING IN THE DEVELOPMENT OF MALADAPTIVE STRATEGIES

Several principles of behavioral conditioning are likely involved in the early stages of this process. Our central hypothesis is that poor self-regulation drives many of the behaviors we see in this population, including sexual deviance. Thus, a critical component of this process is how the individual learns to use these particular strategies (i.e., sexual activity, sexually deviant behaviors, substance abuse, and general criminal or risky behaviors) as external self-regulators. This model assumes that these strategies are more effective or available than other external or internal resources that the individual may have, and although they are maladaptive, they serve the ultimate purpose of restoring and regulating internal sensations.

To be adopted as a regulatory strategy, these self-regulating behaviors must meet several criteria. First, the selected self-regulating response (e.g., sexual gratification) must be stronger than others available within the internal or external world. As we discussed previously, sexual gratification is a strong physiological reinforcer. Sexual satisfaction and sexual arousal are also immediate reinforcements that require little effort. Therefore, because the selected self-regulating response is a powerful one that is likely to work with little personal effort, it will perhaps be a stronger regulator than those that are otherwise available to the individual.

Second, the response must be consistently reinforcing over time. Here we are hypothesizing that the selected regulatory strategy not only is effective in reducing emotional or interpersonal distress in the moment but that it is also reliable in producing this response. Any of the external regulatory strategies discussed thus far would need to meet this standard in order to persist over time. A regulatory strategy that works only once is not likely to become ingrained. This is not to say that it must work in every situation involving distress but only that it works often enough to produce a conditioned expectation of reinforcement or relief. Furthermore, the reliability of the reinforcement must be greater or equal to the potential reinforcement offered by other strategies. Otherwise, sexual and other external strategies would not be viewed as potentially helpful in the most distressing situations.

Third, a lack of corrective action in the early stages of behavioral adaptation is necessary. As discussed in chapter 5, behavioral learning requires not only reinforcement but also a lack of negative consequences in order to foster or maintain a specific learned behavior. This model assumes that individuals who develop deviant sexual practices in response to poorly regulated internal states are those who engaged in these maladaptive behaviors with little consequence or corrective action from their environment. In some cases, there might have been no negative response from the environment to counteract the reinforcing experience of the sexual act. This would be consistent with much of the literature indicating that many sex offenders admit to deviant sexual behaviors that were never brought to the attention of the authorities (e.g., A. J. L. Baker, Tabacoff, Tornusciolo, & Eisenstadt, 2001; Righthand & Welch, 2004). Another possibility is that there were some negative reactions to the behavior but that they were not strong enough or consistent enough to counteract the reinforcing effect of the actual behavior. In other words, these behaviors may become stronger over time not simply because they are reinforcing but also because for some individuals they will not be punished or extinguished by environmental sanctions.

During important developmental periods, individuals will develop a set of available and effective forms of self-regulatory practices. For some, these will be adaptive internal and external strategies (e.g., cognitive reframing, mood management, relaxation techniques) in response to temporary internal distress. For others, these practices will be maladaptive external strategies focused on alleviating overwhelming internal distress quickly and effortlessly. For the population of interest, those with paraphilic sexual interests or behaviors, our theory proposes that these external strategies will involve criminal behavior; substance abuse; and sexual activity, including deviant sexual activity. Over time, the reinforcing effects of these practices, combined with a lack of negative consequences, will produce deviant sexual desires or behaviors as an immediate and consistent response to internal dysregulation.

COGNITIVE BELIEFS AND PERSONALITY TRAITS AS MEDIATORS

In this process, certain cognitive beliefs and personality traits serve as critical mediating variables. The development of these maladaptive regulatory strategies is not exclusively attributable to behavioral principles. If it were simply a matter of pursuing options that combined opportunity with reinforced behavior, there would likely be more individuals who commit these types of offenses and develop deviant sexual interests. There are important cognitive attitudes and expectations that arise from early developmental experiences and perceptions that also feed into this process. Additionally, personality traits must be considered for their role in sustaining such a process. Here, we discuss these factors as they relate to our model and offer hypotheses regarding their impact on the escalation and expression of deviant sexual behaviors.

Egocentricity and Limited Perspective Taking

As we described earlier in the review of developmental literature, children and adolescents with emotional vulnerability and high internal distress often have a greater self-focus in interpersonal contexts. Perhaps it is because these overwhelming negative internal states are difficult to ignore. Regardless, the individual is more likely to focus on his own emotional state than that of others. Situations in which emotional dysregulation is high would then predispose the individual to give less attention to the needs or rights of others. For example, a poorly regulated youth who is experiencing intense anger or frustration might do whatever is necessary to diminish this negative mood state, regardless of how the resulting behaviors will impact others. He might physically lash out at a peer whom he perceives as the source of his anger, not considering how his violent action will affect his peer or their relationship.

Because of this predisposition to become more egocentric in situations involving intense dysregulation, it might be easier for these individuals to disregard others' needs, rights, or perspectives. This is a critical disinhibiting factor to be considered in the development of sexually inappropriate behaviors. At some point, the individual must be able to either overlook the potential harm to the victim or somehow justify the necessity of this harm. In the offender's mind, these actions are justified, or not harmful to others, because the needs of the self (i.e., restoration to emotional homeostasis) are more important and more salient than the needs of others.

Egocentricity and limited empathy may then resurface in similar situations characterized by emotional dysregulation, thus creating a pattern in which the individual disregards the broader impact of his behavior within the environment. Related beliefs or attitudes (e.g., "I didn't hurt anyone") may then become relatively fixed, forming cognitively distorted beliefs about victims, sexual activity, and the appropriateness of certain behaviors. Therefore, the interaction of distressing internal events, a focus on the self, and a driving need to regulate emotion may create for some individuals a willingness to engage in reinforcing behaviors that are harmful to others.

Sensation Seeking

Research regarding a need for excitement and sensation seeking has focused largely on psychopathic individuals (e.g., Hare, 1999) and individuals who engage in frequent criminal activity (e.g., Gottfredson & Hirschi, 1990). This personality feature is generally characterized as a drive to engage in new, exciting, and risky activities because of an inability to tolerate routine or monotony (Hare, 1999; Millon & Davis, 1996). An individual with a high threshold for excitement will seek new and exciting opportunities that typically carry a certain amount of risk. Again, to prevent these activities from becoming routine, we could expect that the amount of risk or thrill involved would need to incrementally increase over time.

In the proposed model, sensation seeking or increased risk taking to achieve excitement is one variable that mediates the selection of self-regulatory strategies. Individuals who have a high threshold for excitement will need variability and a certain amount of inherent risk in their strategies to achieve a consistent regulatory effect. We have already described potential external sources of regulation, including sexual activity, illicit substance use, and criminal behavior. For sensation seekers who use sexual activity as a way to cope with emotional dysregulation, new, unusual, and possibly risky sexual behaviors will be needed over time to achieve the same regulatory effect. Thus, a need for excitement may drive the individual to seek out new and forbidden sexual acts that promise sexual gratification, new sensations, or thrills. This, combined with other personality characteristics, such as low empathy or egocentricity, might substantially contribute to an individual's likelihood of engaging in inappropriate or deviant sexual opportunities.

Resentment and a Sense of Entitlement

Some features of the individual's cognitive worldview might also mediate the development and maintenance of deviant sexual interests and behaviors. Previously learned implicit beliefs that the world is a hostile or uncaring place have been linked with a greater propensity to engage in criminal activity (Lochman, 1987). One explanation for this effect is that those who see the world as unfair and hostile are more likely to resent the way that they have been treated by those in the environment. A feeling of entitlement or deservedness regarding how one should be treated might stem from this resentment.

It is clear that resentment about important developmental events (e.g., parental abuse or neglect, isolation from peers) and a sense that one deserves better treatment alone do not create sex-offending behaviors or even serious violations of societal norms. However, for one who already displays a propensity for the maladaptive regulatory strategies or other personality characteristics described here, an overdeveloped sense of deservedness or resentment might contribute to one's willingness to engage in such behaviors. For example, someone with a strong sense of entitlement combined with egocentricity might be all the more willing to violate the rights of others to achieve a personal goal, such as excitement, sexual thrill, or monetary gain. Therefore, the presence of these characteristics might interact with other important variables in our model to produce sex-offending behaviors over time.

Other Important Cognitive and Personality Variables

Impulsivity and irresponsibility are also factors that may interact with self-regulatory difficulties to create a willingness to engage in sexually inappropriate or other maladaptive forms of externalized self-regulation. Impulse control is a necessary factor in the ability to delay gratification, develop appropriate long-term strategies for emotional and behavioral regulation, and to resist opportunities for criminal or delinquent behaviors. Impulsivity thus increases one's likelihood of engaging in risky and poorly planned behaviors, including those that may be harmful to the self or others. Irresponsibility is a related factor that may contribute to an increased willingness to engage in relatively easy, short-term strategies to achieve specified goals. An irresponsible approach to life precludes serious consideration of long-term or potentially negative consequences of behavior that might produce short-term gain. In our model, these two characteristics also interact in the decision-making process that determines which regulatory strategies are tried and ultimately selected consistently across the life span.

Finally, the development of offense-supportive cognitive beliefs also must be addressed. As was discussed in chapter 4, many sex-offending individuals hold beliefs and attitudes that serve as justifications or explanations for their behaviors. However, it is still difficult to determine the extent to which these cognitions formed before or after the development of deviant sexual interest. Still, we can hypothesize that some of these beliefs or attitudes may have developed prior to offending if there was documented exposure to these cognitive beliefs by important others in the environment. For example, parental beliefs that are supportive of violence against women and a man's right to control a woman, including controlling her sexual behavior, might significantly influence a male adolescent's ability to accept the idea of rape. Similarly, experiences of sexual abuse that are either normalized by the offender or not communicated as a negative or inappropriate experience by others might reinforce ideas that sexual activity between adults and children is okay under certain circumstances. Again, this might influence the developing child's conceptualization of normative sexual activity. In these ways, early cognitive beliefs may lower inhibitions regarding sexual behavior or influence ideas about normative sexual experiences and then interact with the regulatory difficulties described at length in this model.

DEVIANT AROUSAL, FANTASY, AND MULTIPLE PARAPHILIAS

Up to this point, we have described a process through which individuals may seek sexual activity in response to internal distress or dysregulation. We have also described ways in which the individual chooses sexual opportunities that are deviant or inappropriate in nature. The continued use of externalized strategies, including those that involve sexual gratification, depend on a number of behavioral contingencies described previously. Some individuals will persist with these behaviors because they are reliable, effective, and available sources of self-regulation. These individuals may never develop measurable deviant sexual interests yet will continue to engage in deviant sexual behavior because of the other rewarding aspects of regulating internal distress. Other individuals will not only engage in these behaviors but will also engage in related fantasies and may demonstrate strong sexual arousal, because of either early development of deviant interests or later reinforcement of these interest patterns. Because the formation of the deviant interests requires greater explanation, we again focus on this aspect of the theory in greater detail.

In the early stages of this process, the individual may not have persistent or specific sexual arousal to the stimulus of concern. For example, on one occasion a male adolescent may become sexually aroused in the presence of a child. Even so, at this point he is not consistently or even frequently sexually aroused while in the presence of children. The youth's internal pairing of the arousal, which may alleviate internal distress, with the presence of a child later creates the regular occurrence of sexual arousal in response to children. Again, however, not all youth who have this experience may develop pedophilia or engage in sexual activity with children in the future. Here, we outline the factors that drive the development of a more persistent deviant arousal and the maintenance of sexual activity with the desired person or object after the initial exposure to sexually inappropriate stimuli.

Once the arousal has been cognitively associated with a given stimulus, such as a child, the individual might seek ways in which to evoke similar states of sexual arousal and gratification. The most reliable way to do so, without actually committing a sexual offense against a child, would be to fantasize about sexual activity with a child. Masturbation during the fantasy process would further reinforce the object of the fantasy as a source of sexual pleasure (McGuire, Carlisle, & Young, 1964). Therefore, the idea of sexual behavior involving a child becomes reliably associated with sexual gratification. In time, the individual is aroused by the thought of a child or the presence of a child, regardless of whether he is experiencing internal distress or tension at that moment. Although this does not mean that sexual regulation strategies or coping skills will not be used at times of dysregulation, it does mark the point at which the stimulus first associated with relief of distress becomes sexually arousing in and of itself, without antecedent emotional difficulty. Also, although normative sexual fantasies involving consenting, age-appropriate partners may be a part of the cognitive world of the offender, the deviant sexual fantasies must be pleasurable and reinforcing, if not more so, for the continued use of deviant fantasy material in the pursuit of sexual gratification.

For an individual to move from fantasized sexual interactions to real sexual interactions with the object of the fantasy involves several factors that have already been discussed briefly in this chapter. Egocentricity, lack of empathy, and entitlement all increase the probability of an individual engaging in the inappropriate sexual behaviors imagined in fantasies. Sensation seeking would drive the individual to move from fantasy to reality, in which the potential sexual gratification would be more exciting and reinforcing. Additionally, beliefs supportive of offending would disinhibit the individual and decrease internal barriers to victimization. Finally, the role of opportunity is important. The opportunity to engage in these behaviors must also be present in order for the individual to move from fantasy to sex-offending behaviors.

It is also our belief that the same factors that predispose individuals to develop one paraphilic sexual interest also predispose them to develop multiple paraphilias. The fact that many sex offenders with consistent deviant arousal or paraphilias in one domain endorse multiple deviant interests cannot be ignored. The existence of this phenomenon is suggestive of a greater underlying sexual or behavioral problem for these offenders. In our model, we suggest that the use of sexual activity or gratification as a regulatory strategy depends on opportunity and exposure to certain sexual stimuli, interpretations of sexual arousal, and important behavioral contingencies that would support the selected behavior. Given these conditions, it is also likely that an individual who is dysregulated, easily sexually aroused during times of dysregulation, and disinhibited in terms of willingness to engage in deviant sexual practices would engage in numerous inappropriate sexual behaviors, given the opportunity to do so.

A desire for new and exciting experiences, each greater than the last, would also drive the development of multiple paraphilic interests and behaviors. Although this is not as conscious a process as is described in our previous discussion, it makes sense to consider that individuals who find voyeurism a reliable outlet for sexual desires might also consider exhibitionism or other paraphilic behaviors in the search for equally available and satisfying experiences.

The literature on the incidence and prevalence of paraphilic interests suggests that sex offenders typically identify one paraphilia that was prominent before others developed or became strong components of sexual fantasy and behavior (Abel et al., 1988). This is supportive of the idea that the same processes that drove the development of the first paraphilia also likely predisposed the development of others, given the interaction between internal predisposing factors, opportunity, and the promise of additional positive reinforcement.

In sum, we have presented a model that explains the initiation of sex-offending behaviors in individuals both with and without persistent deviant sexual interests. We attribute much of the process to important developmental events that lead to poorly regulated internal states and difficulties with others in the environment (i.e., family and peers). The individual develops maladaptive regulatory strategies that rely on external sources of reinforcement, promising effortless, reliable, and immediate gratification. Sexual activity is adopted as a regulatory coping skill and reinforced over time. For some of these individuals, early attribution of physiological arousal to relevant stimuli in the environment may create deviant sexual interests, which are then reinforced through sexual fantasy. Personality traits, cognitive beliefs, and behavioral associations further entrench the sexual interests of the individual and may lead to behavioral expression of the deviant interest and the development of additional paraphilias.

We conclude this chapter by providing three hypothetical examples illustrating how the proposed model would apply to a real world setting. These examples are not clinical case studies meant to prove our theory; instead, they have each been designed to highlight the important features of the model in a contextual framework. Each of these examples includes a diagram of the model with specific factors included and a brief discussion of the critical variables that contribute to the development of the described paraphilia. In these examples, we have tried to incorporate as many of the potential factors mentioned in the model to facilitate understanding, but it is reasonable to assume that not all offenders would exhibit every behavior that we have described.

THREE CASE EXAMPLES

We now describe and discuss three hypothetical examples illustrating the application of the multimodal self-regulation theory to the development of several types of sex-offending behaviors: pedophilia, exhibitionism and voyeurism, and sexual sadism and rape. Each example concludes with a brief discussion of the specific components of the theory that are most relevant.

Pedophilia

John Smith was born to his 16-year-old mother after she had been impregnated by an unknown male at a friend's party. She had consumed a considerable amount of alcohol and passed out, only to discover later that she was pregnant. She did not disclose her pregnancy to her mother, who was single and raising five children, until she was well into her second trimester, and therefore she did not receive consistent prenatal care. Because of her pregnancy, Ms. Smith dropped out of high school and stayed home to take care of her four younger brothers and sisters.

When John was born, he was a colicky baby and difficult to soothe. Ms. Smith often found herself frustrated and desperate with his frequent crying, because her parenting skills were limited. She did not know how to calm his crying or respond to his needy behaviors, so she often yelled at him and resorted to physical punishment, such as hitting, to quiet him. Occasionally these reactions would work to temporarily cease his crying, but they usually only exacerbated his distress. During her child's infancy, Ms. Smith continued to care for not only her own child but also her younger siblings. The home environment was chaotic, with frequent fighting among the siblings and some neglect of young John. Because he was such a temperamentally difficult child, he was often picked on by his slightly older aunts and uncles. He was not placed in a preschool because of the family's financial difficulties, so all of his time was spent at home with his mother and the other children. His grandmother was the sole supporter of her large family and was generally absent from their home.

During his toddler years, John lagged in his language skills, but his mother did not notice these early problems. His limited communication skills were met with teasing and denigration from the rest of his family. They often made fun of him for using "baby talk." John found that to communicate his needs, he had to cry or throw a temper tantrum. As an adult, John reported that during this time in his life he felt unloved and unwanted by his family. He felt that he was a scapegoat for the family's problems, specifically, those of his mother, and resented the way he had been treated.

Ms. Smith later obtained work at a company that sold children's toys and moved out of the family home when her son was 6. She met a man at work, Mr. White, who was interested in pursuing a relationship with her. In retrospect, she was able to recall that Mr. White asked her many questions about young John and was particularly pleased that she had a son. He told her at the time that he had always wanted a boy. When they were out together, he insisted that John come along with them. She was pleased that John finally had a responsible male father figure in his life. She worried about the difficulties that he was having with other children in kindergarten and hoped that Mr. White would be a good influence on her son.

Mr. White moved into their residence after several months of dating Ms. Smith. Because Mr. White was concerned about John staying at home unsupervised, he arranged his shift at work so that he and Ms. Smith would not have to employ a child care provider. Ms. Smith watched John during the day, and Mr. White cared for him in the evenings. This afforded him the opportunity to begin grooming John. He started by giving John baths and letting him stay up past his bedtime. Over time, he spent more time focused on washing John's genitals and asking him whether it felt good. He told him that it was okay for "Daddy to make his son feel good" and for Daddy and son to have secrets from Mommy because this is what daddies and sons do. The behavior progressed from genital stimulation of the boy to oral stimulation and anal–digital penetration. Although John later reported that he felt strange about this because of a safety program at school called "Go Tell," he was hesitant to tell anyone else because this was the first time he felt loved. This was also the first time that an adult had wanted to spend time with him, and he felt a sense of loyalty to Mr. White, not wanting to end their time together.

This behavior went on for several years, but Mr. White abandoned the family after John turned 12 and entered puberty. Ms. Smith reacted to his abandonment badly and began drinking. John was very upset about this and did not understand why Mr. White left. He was angry at his mother, blaming her, but he was also angry at himself and wondered whether he had done something wrong. He became depressed, began fighting frequently at school, and withdrew to his room when he was at home. As a way of comforting himself, he masturbated to fantasies of the sexual activity between him and Mr. White. When he was most depressed and angry, this made him feel better. His mother was often drunk or absent from the home, so she was unaware of his behavior. While she was absent, he began drinking some of the alcohol that she left in their home. At this point, he used alcohol and masturbation whenever he was feeling low or bored, and he thought about how difficult his life had been. He was unconcerned about his mother or her behavior, instead focusing on how unfairly he had been treated and how he deserved a better life.

One weekend, when John was 14, one of his aunts asked him to watch her two young children, a girl, age 3, and a boy, age 5, while she was at work. He told himself that this would be an opportunity to regain a sense of love and intimacy that he had with Mr. White. He engaged in the same types of grooming behavior and later sexual contact with his nephew. This behavior alleviated some of the depression and anger that resulted from Mr. White's abandonment. He now had a sexual outlet for his fantasies and believed that he was once again in a relationship with someone who cared about him.

Discussion of Case Example 1

John Smith was an individual with pedophilic fantasies and behaviors. John clearly faced a number of challenges to adaptive development in early childhood. He was an emotionally sensitive and vulnerable child who lived in an environment that was unable to respond to his unique needs. He failed to learn appropriate and adaptive strategies to regulate feelings of depression, anger, and isolation. Inconsistent and harsh parenting strategies left him with inadequate resources to soothe himself. Furthermore, his difficulties with peers exacerbated feelings of isolation and the idea that the world was an unfair and uncaring place.

His primary exposure to feelings of love and affection from a caregiver came in the form of sexual abuse, which caused him to view sexual activity between a child and adult in the context of appropriate intimacy. This early experience with sexual arousal and sexual gratification was cognitively linked with adult–child sexual relations. In the absence of normal peer relationships and interventions that might disrupt his distorted views of sexual relationships, John grew to rely on consistent masturbatory fantasies to cope with distressing emotions. These fantasies and sexual behaviors were consistently rewarding, provided immediate gratification, and were not punished or extinguished by his environment. John also engaged in the use of alcohol, made available by his mother, to cope with his negative emotions. Over time, a desire to have another relationship, growing difficulties with depression and anger, and a need for new sexual experiences, combined with opportunity (his young nephew) to culminate in a sexual relationship between the adolescent, John, and his 5-year-old victim (see Figure 10.2).

Exhibitionism and Voyeurism

Jason Brown was born to upper middle class, college-educated parents. He was their second child, with a sister 3 years his senior. The mother had no mental health problems, and the father had some difficulties with anxiety as a child and adolescent. Jason's mother reported that the pregnancy was normal and the birth uncomplicated. He was a wanted child. He was slightly hyperactive as a child, and his hyperactivity increased on entering school. His teachers reported that he had a difficult time making friends because of his hyperactivity. Over time, his peer group began pulling away from him, and he felt fairly isolated from other children. Jason managed to make a few friends, but his friendships were not long in duration and often resulted in angry arguments and fights that would end the friendships.

Other than his hyperactivity, his childhood was rather uneventful. Jason's parents both worked, and although they spent time with their children, their time was limited by their work schedules, which also included frequent travel away from the home. His parents began drifting apart when he was approximately 7 years of age. The children felt a great deal of tension in the home, and their mother was under extreme stress and mildly dysthymic. She was dealing with her husband's frequent absences, her own busy work schedule, and the children, and she was angry at her husband for their current situation. This continued for 3 more years, with the relationship between Jason's parents becoming more strained. Jason's father began an extramarital affair, and his mother subsequently filed for divorce. The court awarded joint custody to the parents, with Jason spending weekdays with the mother and weekends with the father. Because his mother was so angry, she constantly denigrated her ex-husband in front of their children and made negative comments about men in general. On numerous occasions, she stated to Jason, "I hope you don't turn into your father. I wouldn't be able to live with that."

During the stressful period preceding the divorce, Jason experienced an increase in his hyperactivity and developed some depressive symptoms. He loved both his parents, but he felt pressured to take sides. He did not know how to react to his mother's anger, which sometimes seemed directed toward him. His older sister handled the tension by becoming more involved in her schoolwork and other activities. She spent more time with her friends. She excelled in school and in sports and was frequently held up to Jason as an example of how he should behave. This only exacerbated his existing feelings of isolation and low self-esteem, and he frequently retreated into a fantasy world in which he was powerful and people liked and respected him.

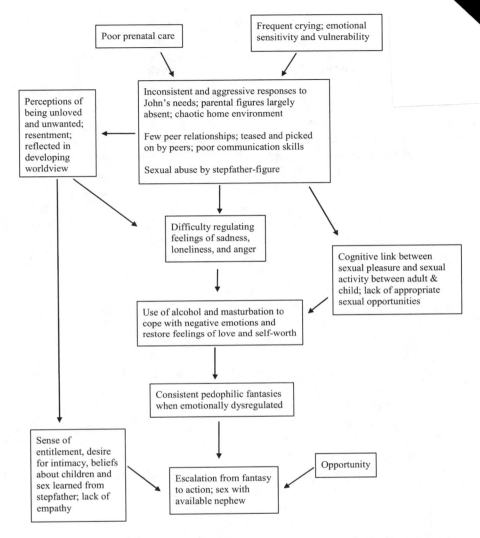

Figure 10.2. Case Example 1: Pedophilia.

When he was 13, Jason's father remarried a woman who had two daughters. Shortly thereafter, the stepmother became pregnant and gave birth to a son. Although Jason was happy to have a little brother, he was resentful of the attention given to his stepsisters and new baby brother. His father placed new restrictions on Jason because of the baby. He was no longer allowed to listen to his stereo or watch his favorite television shows at night because the baby would be sleeping. He decided he wanted to spend less time at his father's house, and his father and mother fought over this. His mother insisted that he stay with his father on the weekends, which made him angry at both of his parents.

Thereafter, when Jason went to visit his father, he retreated to his room and isolated himself from the family. He again fantasized about being important and being respected, which helped him cope with his feelings of anger and resentment. In his room at his father's house, there was a window that faced the house next door. From there, he could see the bedroom window of a teenage girl who was close to his older sister's age. One day, he was looking out the window and saw her undressing. He experienced a spontaneous erection and found it pleasurable. He masturbated, thinking about meeting this girl and being with her. Soon after that, he saw her in her front yard. She ignored him, leaving him humiliated and angry. He continued watching her window, remembering the pleasure associated with watching her. He fantasized about having intercourse with her and masturbated each time he saw her at her window. She later left for college, greatly upsetting Jason, who had come to rely on watching her and masturbating to deal with his normal adolescent sexual interest, his isolation, and his lack of a normative sexual relationship.

Jason began leaving both his parents' homes at night, looking for other young women he could watch. For him, this was a reliable way to become sexually aroused and alleviate his sadness and anger. This pattern continued, and on a number of occasions he was successful at finding adolescent and young adult girls in whom he was interested. While he was watching, he would rub his genitals through his clothing and then masturbate without being seen. At home, he fantasized about these experiences and imagined these women inviting him inside. On one occasion, he was seen masturbating by one of the women he was watching. She screamed, and Jason immediately fled. He very much enjoyed the sensation of having his penis out for a woman to look at. It also made him feel powerful to know that she had no control over his behavior. He found the sexual pleasure from exposure to be more gratifying than just watching from afar. He began seeking out locations where he could relive this experience without being caught. Although he had other types of fantasies, ones of him watching women and exposing himself to them were the most satisfying, and he could engage in these behaviors at almost any time.

Discussion of Case Example 2

Jason Brown began life with few adaptational problems, relative to the preceding case example. Still, his early difficulties with hyperactivity predisposed him to difficulties in relating to his peers, as has been noted in the literature (Campbell, 2000; B. B. Lahey, McBurnett, & Loeber, 2000). Early discord and tension within the home due to his parents' deteriorating relationship left Jason somewhat unable to cope with changes in the way his parents treated him, as well as one another. He lacked the social support network of friends that other children might have had in similar negative circumstances. Furthermore, Jason's mother focused much of her anger and depression on him, which he was not emotionally equipped to handle at such a young age. His father's subsequent remarriage and his feelings of resentment and anger toward his parents and his new siblings left him even more isolated and unable to deal with his emotional distress and difficulties at school.

Jason retreated into a fantasy world where he was powerful and respected by others. Within this context, he also experienced sexual arousal while viewing a female neighbor through his bedroom window. He linked the arousal and sexual gratification that he felt not only to the images of this young woman but also to the experience of having watched her without her knowledge. When she ignored him and, in his mind, humiliated him by rebuffing his advances at friendship, he retreated to his earlier fantasy of watching her. Maintaining that it was as arousing to watch her as being in a relationship with her helped him preserve his sense of self-esteem and gave him a readily available opportunity for sexual satisfaction. Perhaps because of his fantasies of control and importance, as well as his sense of entitlement and a desire for new sexual experiences, the opportunity to expose himself to the women he watched became gratifying and led him to continued voyeuristic and exhibitionistic behaviors (see Figure 10.3).

Sexual Sadism and Rape

Jake Williams was born to a working-class family in an urban area. His mother had a difficult pregnancy and died during childbirth. His father moved back into the family home with his new son. Present in the home was Jake's grandmother, who had a history of alcohol problems and resentment about her son moving in and the responsibility of having to care for an infant. She had encouraged her son to place the baby up for adoption, but he had refused. Jake's early experiences with his grandmother were negative. When he cried as an infant, she would ignore him and not respond. When his father was home, he was loving toward Jake, but his work schedule kept him away for most of Jake's early years. As he was developing, Jake's grandmother told him that he was responsible for his mother's death and that it was a burden for her to take care of him.

As Jake entered the toddler years, his grandmother did not child proof the home, so he sustained a number of minor injuries. When he misbehaved, or when she had been drinking, his grandmother hit him with a stick or belt. If he cried during these punishments, it made her angrier, and she punished him more severely. Jake's grandmother inconsistently toilet trained him, with the result that he was never fully toilet trained by her. When he entered school, he on occasion had accidents and also wet the bed at night. His grandmother responded by making him sit in scalding water and spanked him until he had bruises.

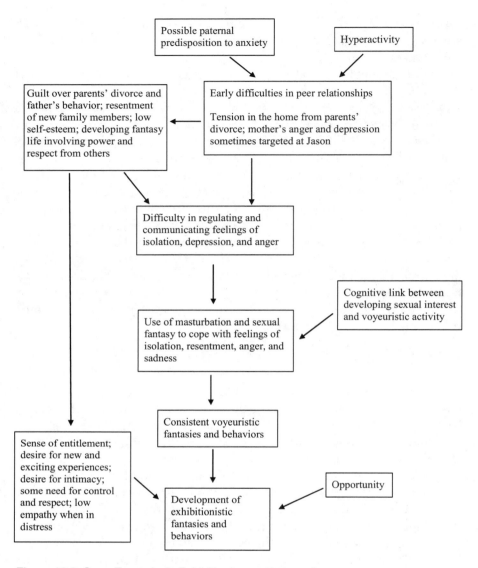

Figure 10.3. Case Example 2: Exhibitionism and voyeurism.

When he attended school, she did not allow him to bring any of his friends to the house. As a young child, he was depressed. When his father was home, he was loving, but Jake felt the inconsistency and was angry at his father for being away. Because he was now of school age, his father decided that he should have a pet to take care of. He hoped that the new pet—a puppy—would alleviate his son's isolation and sadness. Jake loved his new puppy, but having sole responsibility for taking care of it overwhelmed him. His grandmother told him that he must train the dog not to urinate or defecate inside the house. He did not know how to do this, and when the puppy had accidents inside the house, Jake's grandmother yelled at and hit him. He took his anger out on the puppy by yelling at it and hitting it with a stick. Although at first he felt sorry for the puppy, he later ruminated on how badly he had been treated and continued to take his anger out on his dog, often feeling that others should experience as much pain as he had.

When he was about 11 years old, Jake started a fire in a trash can in a park near his school. A teacher leaving school saw this and recognized Jake. The principal called Jake's father, who laughed off the incident and said that he also had started fires when he was young. He did not see this behavior as a concern. Jake was not punished for this and continued to set fires, but making sure that he was not seen. This behavior made him feel powerful and gave him a thrill. Other than the fire setting, however, he was a fairly passive child and ignored by most of his teachers.

As he was nearing puberty, he discovered sexually explicit magazines that his father had hidden in their home. He looked at the images and became aroused. He masturbated while thinking of the pornographic images and his desires for power and control, fusing sex with violence and humiliation. In his fantasies, he forced women to have sex with him and called them derogatory names, similar to what he would like to say to his grandmother when she was punishing him. He also sought out video games and music that were consistent with his fantasies, in which women were objects to be controlled. These media further fueled his fantasy life.

At age 14, there was a girl at school whom he liked, and he asked her to go to the movies with him. His father dropped him and his date off at the theater. During the movie, Jake tried to kiss her and grab her breasts. She became upset and pushed him away. Jake was angry and embarrassed, and for the remainder of the movie fantasized about forced sex with this girl. When his father came to pick them up, the girl was silent in the car and wouldn't look at Jake. After dropping her off at her house, Jake's father asked how the date went. Jake told him, "She's a bitch." The father did not explore Jake's response further but said, "Well, some girls are that way."

Jake continued to fantasize about forcing women to have sex, but his fantasies escalated over time to include images of him hurting the women as well. He found this to be a very exciting release for his angry thoughts toward others in his life. Once he was old enough to drive, Jake left the house at night and looked for women that he could follow. When he was 17, he was parked in the parking lot of a local community college when he spotted a woman walking alone to her car. He threatened her with a knife, forced her behind a building, raped her vaginally and anally, and punched her numerous times. He left her unconscious and bleeding and drove home. He was not caught and took delight in the news coverage about the incident. He fantasized about the incident, and over time began fantasizing about what it would have been like to kill the woman. His fantasies expanded to images of capturing women, tying them up, and torturing them until death. He was very angry at women and remembered being rejected by his grandmother and other girls at school. Now he had reached a point where whenever he saw an attractive woman, he became angry at her and started thinking about hurting and raping her.

Discussion of Case Example 3

Jake began his life under negative circumstances, with his mother's death and reliance on a primary caregiver (i.e., his grandmother) who did not want him. Inconsistent and physically and emotionally abusive disciplinary practices limited Jake's ability to develop in an adaptive and healthy manner. He became an angry and confused child and reacted to these feelings by inflicting pain on his puppy and setting fires. These activities provided him an outlet, even if maladaptive, through which he alleviated growing tensions. Once he was exposed to pornographic material, he became aroused by the images. Although his arousal to sexually explicit imagery may be normal for a boy his age, his incorporation of angry and hostile cognitions toward others is unusual. While viewing the images, he thought about his grandmother and others who had hurt him or aroused his anger. In this instance, it was likely that his poorly regulated emotions, such as anger and frustration, became easily confused with behavioral excitement (e.g., sexual arousal). Although he felt sexually excited, he also experienced intense emotional arousal, which typically had been linked with thoughts of violence or frustration in his mind.

Over time, these thoughts of sex and violence began to escalate, and he acted out with sexual aggressiveness while on a date with a female peer. Her response embarrassed him and perhaps fueled his anger and dislike for the women in his life. An inability to appropriately or adaptively deal with these feelings caused him to engage in further sexual fantasy, which had become more rewarding over time. Finally, through conditioning of the deviant arousal and a desire for new fantasy material or more exciting sexual experiences, he acted out on his fantasies and committed a rape against a local college student (see Figure 10.4).

SUMMARY AND CONCLUSIONS

Multimodal self-regulation theory combines elements from the developmental, cognitive, behavioral, and personality literatures. This theory offers a new integrative and conceptual framework, incorporating important developmental factors and describing their interactions and effects across the life span. Self-regulation, or the ability to modulate internal and external stimuli in a way that is consistent with identified goals, is a key component of this theory. Biological propensities and developmental antecedents are related to the development of self-regulatory functioning. For some individuals, early emotional vulnerabilities, ineffective responding from primary

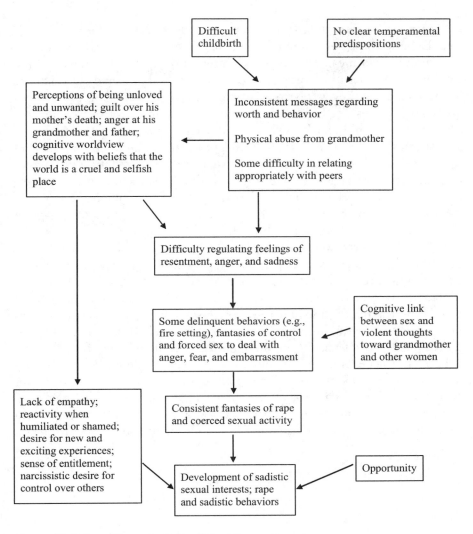

Figure 10.4. Case Example 3: Sexual sadism and rape.

caregivers, negative events in childhood, and difficulty with peers may contribute to difficulties with regulating or modulating negative affect, interpersonal distress, or behavioral impulses. The drive to maintain emotional or internal homeostasis may lead these individuals to develop dysfunctional or maladaptive strategies in an attempt to self-regulate.

Individuals with these difficulties may be driven to engage in seemingly impulsive or low-effort external regulatory strategies. Three such strategies may involve sexual and/or criminal activity and illicit substance use, all of which may promise short-term gratification or satisfaction with little effort or resources required. Early opportunity, perceptions, and interpretations of bodily sensations and environmental events may lead to a number of maladaptive outcomes, including involvement in risky or deviant sexual behaviors. Because these behaviors are immediately and consistently reinforcing (i.e., provide gratification and reduce internal distress or tension) and are not linked with negative consequences or sanctions that would outweigh the positive benefits, they will become strengthened over time. In terms of deviant sexual interests or behaviors, if they are reinforced in this manner it is likely that some individuals will maintain these behaviors and develop persistent sexual interest in deviant or inappropriate stimuli. These responses will then be used as consistent external sources of self-regulation in times of distress. Other variables are relevant to this process, including certain personality and cognitive variables that drive the development of multiple paraphilias and may contribute to an individual's willingness to engage in these behaviors and victimize others.

In this chapter, we have additionally discussed the literature that suggests that these processes may be relevant in a sex-offending population. Further empirical research, including future directions for this theory, are presented in chapter 11. We have concluded here with the presentation of three case examples that outline how these processes may occur in a developmental, social, and cognitive–behavioral context. In each of our case examples, difficulties with self-regulation and emotion modulation significantly contributed to the development of maladaptive sexual behaviors. These behaviors, formed in response to internal discomfort or tension, continued over time and resulted in patterns of deviant sexual activity. We must now consider how to evaluate these processes and apply them to broader, real world examples of individuals with paraphilias and deviant sexual interests and behaviors.

11
FUTURE DIRECTIONS FOR RESEARCH AND TREATMENT

Although the logic underlying multimodal self-regulation theory (see chap. 10) is persuasive, it is important to consider how the theory should be empirically tested with regard to its future use in assessment, treatment, and evaluation of risk. This chapter addresses this need. In the next section, we briefly address what previous research has taught us regarding the empirical basis of the new model, including a recent study assessing the impact of self-regulatory dysfunction on paraphilias, antisocial behaviors, and substance use in a sample of adult sex offenders. We then consider methodological issues and theoretical constructs that need to be resolved in order to fully validate this theory. Finally, we focus on the theory's clinical practice implications. Specifically, we consider how multimodal self-regulation theory can and should be applied to prevention and treatment efforts.

WHAT WE KNOW FROM PREVIOUS RESEARCH

In chapters 3 through 10, we summarized and critiqued the available literature on the etiology of sexually deviant behaviors. In describing the critical components of multimodal self-regulation theory, we included research findings that, although not carried out to test this theory, were nonetheless relevant to it and supported the theory's hypotheses. In this section, we explore how these past research findings can inform future research in this area.

For starters, the multimodal self-regulation theory assumes that important events in childhood, including potential abuse or neglect, shape the development of self-regulation, cognitive worldview, personality, and learned responses to internal and external stimuli. That adverse childhood experience can have a negative impact on developmental processes is not a new concept. However, as we found in chapter 6, the causal link between childhood abuse and delinquent or sexually deviant behaviors in adulthood is still somewhat unclear. Many individuals with experiences of sexual abuse in childhood do not go on to commit future offenses (e.g., Berliner & Elliot, 2002), and thus the role of sexual abuse in the development of deviant sexual interests in those who do commit later offenses is undetermined. Hence, there is no direct connection between childhood abuse and violent or deviant behavior in adulthood. However, consistent findings of abuse in the backgrounds of many of these offenders (Briggs & Hawkins, 1996; Graham, 1996; Haapasalo & Kankkonen, 1997; Jonson-Reid & Way, 2001; Kobayashi, Sales, Becker, Figueredo, & Kaplan, 1995; Veneziano, Veneziano, & LeGrand, 2000; Worling, 1995; Zgourides, Monto, & Harris, 1997) suggest that an indirect link likely exists between this early developmental event and sexually deviant outcomes.

In multimodal self-regulation theory, self-regulation has a mediating effect on this relationship, with adverse developmental experiences affecting individual regulatory functioning, which can have an impact on behavioral functioning given other intervening variables (e.g., opportunity, behavioral reinforcement). Therefore, our discussion of the empirical evidence that implies the existence of indirect relationships between childhood abuse and later offending behavior should be expanded to include the role of regulatory functioning in this process.

This leads us to another area of empirical support, which is the vast literature on self-regulatory functioning and the impact of dysregulation on a variety of other psychological factors and resulting behavioral outcomes. Evidence supporting a link between early childhood temperament, genetic factors, and later ability to regulate internal and external tension was summarized in chapter 10. These relationships are critical features of multimodal self-regulation theory, in which early temperamental and genetic characteristics shape regulatory functioning and indirectly impact regulatory strategies that are selected across the life span. We also relied on evidence that childhood socialization shapes the development of appropriate or inappropriate regulatory strategies. As already mentioned, ample research demonstrating patterns of negative childhood socialization (i.e., abuse) in sex offenders supports our hypothesis that this may play an early role in the formation of deviant sexual interests.

Additional research supports the connection between emotional dysregulation or affective instability and difficulty with interpersonal relationships. This relationship may exist because of a common underlying factor (i.e., self-regulatory deficits) that may produce both interpersonal skills deficits and emotional dysregulation. It may also be attributable to interactions between these two constructs, whereby extreme emotional lability and difficulty in regulating negative affect may impact the individual's ability to function in interpersonal relationships, or whereby social skills deficits exacerbate problems related to coping with emotional distress. Regardless, empirical research with children and adolescents has demonstrated a strong link between negative interpersonal interactions and high emotionality (e.g., Eisenberg, Fabes, Carlo, & Karbon, 1992; Hanish et al., 2004; Linehan, 1993a; Maughan & Cicchetti, 2002), with similar research demonstrating high rates of mood disorders, emotional distress, and inadequate relationships with others in sex-offending populations (e.g., Becker, Kaplan, Tenke, & Tartaglini, 1991; Marshall, 1993; Raymond, Coleman, Ohlerking, Christenson, & Miner, 1999).

There is also a strong relationship between dysregulation and impulsivity or impulsive behaviors (e.g., Baumeister & Vohs, 2004). This relationship is important in terms of multimodal self-regulation theory because the behaviors hypothesized to result from self-regulatory deficit are those that may involve some degree of impulsivity or disinhibition. The research on impulsivity (see chap. 7, this volume) was mixed as to the nature of the relationship between sex offending and impulsivity (Caputo, Frick, & Brodsky, 1999; Eher, Neuwirth, Fruehwald, & Frottier, 2003; Porter, Campbell, Woodworth, & Birt, 2001; Prentky & Knight, 1991). Impulsivity was found in a significant number of sex offenders but was not a significant predictor of sexually deviant behavior or a discriminating factor between sex offenders and non–sex offenders. However, when viewed in the context of this new model, it may be easier to understand the relationship between impulsive responding and the development of a very specific type of impulsive or disinhibited behavior. Self-regulatory deficits may produce more seemingly impulsive behaviors in order to achieve gratification or externally regulate internal tension. The opportunities available within the environment largely drive the type of impulsive behavior that is manifested, in addition to background experiences and the effects of conditioning processes. Therefore, self-regulatory abilities underlie this perceived relationship between impulsivity and sex-offending behaviors.

Another aspect of the theory, which already has some empirical support, is the role of conditioning processes in the development and maintenance of sex-offending behaviors. In chapter 5, we outlined a number of empirical studies of behavioral conditioning that demonstrate the effects of reinforcement and punishment on this behavior. One such early study, conducted by McGuire, Carlisle, and Young (1964), indicated that sexual fantasies reinforce the relationship between the sexual object and sexual satisfaction or pleasure. This is consistent with the ideas presented in our multimodal self-regulation theory, whereby the degree to which the selected source of sexual gratification is reinforced impacts the likelihood that this source of pleasure will reappear in fantasies or sexual behaviors in the future. Also per our discussion in chapter 5, the availability of the selected stimulus, the nature of reinforcement, and a lack of punishment or negative consequences associated with the fantasy or behavior will affect the relationship between selection of a self-regulatory strategy and its continued use over time.

Several factors also mediate the relationship between selection of a self-regulatory strategy (e.g., paraphilic behavior) and the proliferation of differing but still-similar strategies over time. The characteristics believed to mediate this effect are classified into clusters of selected personality traits and attitudes or beliefs reflecting an individual's cognitive worldview.

The empirical literature describing the relationships between certain personality traits and sex offending also was discussed previously, in chapter 7. Several of these traits reappear in the model described in out theory, including lack of empathy, egocentricity, sensation seeking, and impulsivity. We have hypothesized that these particular traits are relevant mediators in the process of developing sexually deviant interests and expanding these interests to include other categories of behavior that promise similar reinforcement and regulation. Evidence from the literature exploring psychopathy indicates that these traits are often present in individuals with a history of repeated sexual offenses (Holt, Meloy, & Strack, 1999; Porter et al., 2001). Although the empirical research up to this point has suggested that the nature of the relationship between these traits and the commission of sex offenses is largely unknown, we can still safely say that these personality characteristics are present and may play an important role in the process.

An additional mediating variable, discussed in chapter 10, is the cognitive worldview, including beliefs and attitudes about the self, interpersonal relationships, offending behaviors, and even the victim. In chapter 4, we introduced many of these concepts, as well as hypotheses about their relationship to sex-offending behaviors. In that chapter we discussed the fact that many sex offenders do evidence cognitive distortions related to their offending, skewed or nonnormal perceptions of interpersonal interactions, or generalized beliefs about the world that support their offending practices (e.g., Blumenthal, Gudjonsson, & Burns, 1999; Hanson, 1999; Hanson, Gizzarelli, & Scott, 1994; Johnston & Ward, 1996; Neidigh & Krop, 1992; Sahota & Chesterman, 1998; Segal & Stermac, 1990; Ward, 2000b). Specifically, beliefs of narcissistic entitlement (Hanson et al., 1994), external attributions that blame others for the behavior (e.g., Blumenthal et al., 1999; Geer, Estupinan, & Manguno-Mire, 2000; McKay, Chapman, & Long, 1996), and self-serving cognitive biases (Marshall, Anderson, & Champagne, 1997; Ward, Fon, Hudson, & McCormack, 1998) are all empirically supported characteristics of the cognitive worldview of these offenders.

Where the research on cognitive traits becomes less certain, however, is the point at which one must decide how these features are related to offense processes. Few would argue that cognitive beliefs alone are enough to precipitate offending. It appears that they most likely play a facilitating role in the process. What we have hypothesized in multimodal self-regulation theory is that certain cognitive characteristics, which are not necessarily offense specific (e.g., a sense of entitlement), develop through a parallel process and interact with self-regulatory needs and behavioral reinforcements to disinhibit the individual and facilitate the selection of successful externalized regulatory strategies that may include certain sexual behaviors.

Finally, some of the hypothesized relationships between outcomes (i.e., paraphilias, criminal behavior, and substance abuse) have already been identified as significant correlates within sex-offending populations. Many studies have noted the co-occurrence of sexually deviant interests, substance abuse problems, and antisocial or criminal behaviors (Abracen, Looman, & Anderson, 2000; Becker, Stinson, Tromp, & Messer, 2003; Burk & Burkhart, 2003; Noffsinger & Resnick, 2000; Simon, 1997a, 1997b, 2000). We believe that the reason for close relationships between these factors is because they are similarly driven by deficits in the individual's ability to regulate internal tension or distress. By this logic, they will not be perfect correlates because other unique factors determine which of these strategies are selected and preferred over time. We have additionally hypothesized that opportunity and relevant cognitive factors also determine which strategy will be used. This theory thus posits that they should be related in that they are attributable to a common underlying cause, but not perfectly so because of other contributing factors.

In a preliminary study evaluating several of the basic tenets of multimodal self-regulation theory, Stinson, Becker, and Sales (in press) examine the characteristics of 95 adult male sex offenders in a residential facility. The goal of this particular study was to demonstrate a causal relationship between indicators of self-regulatory dysfunction and the three predicted outcomes: (a) paraphilias, (b) antisocial behaviors, and (c) problems with substance use and dependence. The also authors tested relationships between negative childhood experience and the development of regulatory problems, as well as the impact of potential mediators such as personality traits or cognitive attitudes and beliefs.

Overall, this particular sample showed relatively high rates of negative childhood experience, with nearly 90% reporting either emotional–verbal, physical, or sexual abuse or neglect during childhood. Over half indicated that one or both parents had a substance abuse problem that was notable during their childhood. These characteristics were significantly correlated with later manifestations of self-regulatory difficulty.

Dysregulation in this sample was measured through a combination of symptoms of mood or emotional dysregulation and indicators of emotional neediness. These varying symptoms of underlying regulatory deficits and emotional distress correlated quite strongly with one another and the resulting self-regulation factor that was obtained. A path analysis was used to determine the causal impact of dysregulation on the severity and number of paraphilias, indicators of antisocial and criminal behavior, and history of substance abuse disorders. In this analysis, the proposed model demonstrated good fit with the data, $\chi^2(2, N = 95) = 1.312$, $p = .519$; root-mean-square error of approximation = .000; goodness-of-fit index = .993; adjusted goodness-of-fit index = .966; normed fit index = .982; comparative fit index = 1.000, with self-dysregulation significantly causally predicting both paraphilias and antisocial behaviors (see Figure 11.1). The model did not, however, show similar effects for substance abuse, which was discussed further by Stinson et al. (in press). It is interesting that the original three outcome variables were significantly correlated, as has been shown in previous research, but the correlation between paraphilias and antisocial behaviors disappeared once self-regulatory deficits were taken into account. In other words, the relationship between these two outcomes may be entirely due to their shared relationship with self-dysregulation.

On the basis of this study, we can determine that difficulties with self-regulation may in fact contribute to paraphilic or sexually deviant behaviors in a significant way. However, multimodal self-regulation theory also includes other factors that act on this process, such as behavioral reinforcement and opportunity, which probably would account for the remainder of the variance in severity and number of paraphilias that was not explained by self-regulatory deficits. Additional variables tested here were sadistic and narcissistic characteristics, traits associated with Factor 1 of the Hare Psychopathy Checklist—Revised (Hare, 1991; e.g., egocentricity, sensation seeking), and cognitive distortions related to offending behaviors. Although these factors were related to self-regulatory deficits, they did not offer any additional explanatory power when assumed as additional causal factors for paraphilias. However, their relationships with self-regulatory deficit and early childhood experience imply a need for further understanding of these variables.

An obvious limitation of multimodal self-regulation theory is a lack of empirical research evaluating the validity of the theory in its entirety. However, this preliminary evaluation demonstrates empirical support for several of the core predictions of this theory. Self-regulatory deficits are related to adverse childhood events for a sample of adult male sex offenders with repeated paraphilic behaviors. Additionally, these self-regulatory problems are causally related to the development of paraphilias and patterns of antisocial behavior, and they explain the shared variance between these factors. These important findings provide the basis for future research in this area, allowing us to expand on these basic concepts of the model and criti-

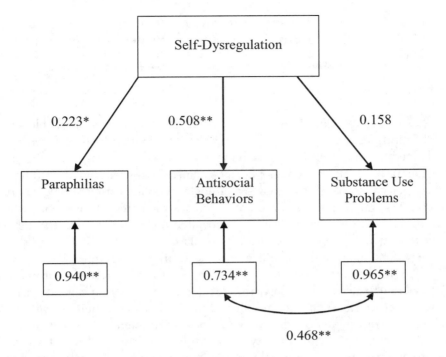

Figure 11.1. Self-regulation deficits predicting paraphilias, antisocial behaviors, and substance use. From "Self-Regulation and the Etiology of Sexual Deviance: Evaluating Causal Theory," by J. D. Stinson, J. V. Becker, and B. D. Sales, in press, *Violence and Victims.* Printed with permission.
*p < .05. **p < .001.

cally evaluate the remaining factors that have yet to be tested or fully explained by research.

WHAT WE STILL NEED FROM THE RESEARCH

Despite early findings that are supportive of multimodal self-regulation theory, we still need to know much more to demonstrate the accuracy of this theory. This is typically true of any new theory; time is needed to subject its basic tenets to rigorous research. In this section, we describe the research still needed in this area, including definitions, methodology, and important comparisons with other samples. We primarily restrict this discussion to practical methods of testing the theory, although at times we also include seemingly idealized measurements or research designs that would offer us the most information about this theory. Given the limitations of current research in this field (see chap. 2), some of these hypothesized methods will not be possible with current technologies and measurement instruments. However, we still discuss ways the research could be improved, so that this theory and other empirical research will receive the most fair, accurate, and rigorous testing available.

Definitions

One of the primary things still needed in this area is a set of reliable and valid definitions for many of our key variables. For example, *self-regulation* can be defined in a number of ways, each tapping into a different aspect of regulatory functioning, such as behavioral, emotional, or cognitive regulation. These concepts, although often categorized as a single group indicating self-regulatory functioning, might produce different outcomes when tested independently. Although these constructs have been separated out conceptually, they have not been studied independently in this population. Thus, it is important that future research address this significant oversight in the literature.

Another concept that must be defined for this research to continue is *emotional vulnerability*. Although the developmental and self-regulation research often refers to emotional vulnerability as both an inherent trait and one that is continually interacting with the environment, clear methods of measuring emotional vulnerability and defining it for the purposes of consistent research application are lacking. We must further differentiate between or effectively combine related concepts, such as emotional sensitivity and emotional durability (i.e., return to baseline after an emotional event) to know their impact on relevant outcomes.

A third concept needing additional clarification is *impulsivity*, which has been linked with deficits in behavioral regulation or difficulty in delaying gratification. *Impulsivity* may be defined as either behavioral, which would include engaging in acts that seem impulsive and involve little forethought or planning, or cognitive, which might describe the lack of cost–benefit analysis that is presumed to occur before planned action. Many theorists and researchers in the sex-offender literature assume that impulsive behavior arises from impulsive thinking and that this is due to a generally impulsive personality style. However, we have not been rigorous enough in testing these conceptualizations of impulsivity and determining how they relate to other concepts of self-regulation. One of the reasons this is so important is that in this model, impulsive behaviors are an outcome of an impulsive cognitive or emotional style. We must be able to better differentiate the two to test this hypothesis. Therefore, to say that we need clearer definitions of our concepts does not simply refer to semantics or differentiating related constructs. It also describes a need for measurable or operational definitions of variables.

Fourth, we need to define the role of *opportunity* for sexual arousal during development, as well as opportunistic strategies that may be used to regulate internal tension or distress. Opportunity variables present a variety of problems for the researcher who is trying to operationally define available opportunities and retrospectively measure them. One of the primary limitations to our conceptualization of opportunity is defining the moment at which something is first perceived as an available opportunity, which may significantly differ from person to person. For example, in cases in which the offender has committed incest against a younger sibling, we do no know why the presence of the sibling was perceived as a potential sexual opportunity for this individual, when other individuals with siblings have never viewed them as opportunities for sexual gratification. Even after we have been able to define one's perceptions of available opportunities, we must also have a way of measuring whether the perceived opportunity was realistic given the context in which it occurred or could have occurred. Some individuals, for example, might not offend against a sibling despite clear perceptions of opportunity because of close supervision by an adult, whereas others might engage in deviant behavior regardless of supervision or likelihood of being caught. These examples demonstrate the types of difficulties that need to be addressed in future empirical studies using this and other similar variables.

Another variable for which we must create measurable definitions is *behavioral reinforcement*. Multimodal self-regulation theory also relies on conditioning principles from the environment to determine which regulatory strategies will be either abandoned as ineffectual or inappropriate or maintained as successful and rewarding alternatives. As we discussed in chapter 5, because of the idiosyncratic nature of an individual's responses to potential punishments or reinforcements, it is difficult to develop a measure or definition of punishments or reinforcements that will be consistent across individuals. Some might respond to external punishments (e.g., incarceration), whereas others seemingly do not. Therefore, how do we define these punishing events when attempting to determine the conditioning principles at work in the development of the behavior? Furthermore, how do we measure or identify cognitive factors, such as guilt, that may also play a role in shaping relevant behavior? The problem here is not simply that we must rely on self-report for manifestations of guilt, which are subject to social bias, but also because these involve retrospective reports of experience. We do not yet know from the sex-offender literature whether people are more likely to remember reinforcements or punishments for their behavior, or whether they remember the actual impact that these contingencies had. An offender reporting an early response to his deviant sexual behavior might say that he "got into trouble," but the reality might be that any punishment or embarrassment related to being caught for his behavior had no effect on his thoughts or feelings about himself at the time it occurred.

These issues related to definitions and empirical measurement of key constructs should be taken into consideration for future research. Because we do not have the ability to read minds or ensure that self-report is always valid, truthful, and not tainted by the effects of memory, we cannot expect that researchers will be able to offer perfect solutions to the problems previously outlined. However, to truly understand how this process works, we must address these issues and strive to create instruments that are as accurate and meaningful as possible within the limits of our current technologies and abilities.

Methodology

A second major focus for future research should be refining methodological strategies for testing multimodal self-regulation theory, as well as other etiological hypotheses that arise within the field. As we discussed in chapter 2, current research has been limited by retrospective reports of experiences, some of which occurred during childhood, and post hoc measurement of critical factors or variables. One possible way to circumvent some of these limitations is through use of longitudinal research, which is becoming increasingly used to explore antecedents to sex offending and other antisocial behaviors, as well as developmental changes in these behaviors and the long-term impact of treatment (e.g., Nisbet, Wilson, & Smallbone, 2004; Parkinson, Shrimpton, Oates, Swanston, & O'Toole, 2004; van Wijk et al., 2005; White & Smith, 2004). This method allows researchers to learn of critical events and test variables at different points through the developmental process without relying too heavily on outdated or poorly remembered information. There is still the problem of reliance on self-report, but the aim of many longitudinal studies is to collect self-report data that capture events in the immediate as opposed to remote past and verify this information with other available sources (e.g., parents, teachers). This would also allow for information to be gathered prior to any sexually inappropriate behavior, which might prevent biased recollection of early experiences. The reader should be aware that this type of research raises serious ethical dilemmas that we will not address in this book but that should be considered in other venues.

Longitudinal research techniques would also need to incorporate ongoing assessment of personality and cognitive factors that have been hypothesized here as contributing factors in the development of paraphilic sexual interests. Furthermore, researchers could then continually track self-regulatory ability, environmental events that impact self-regulation, and the selection of regulatory strategies. This would of course require reliable and consistent measures of self-regulation and its various components, as discussed in the preceding section. In this way, however, we could more firmly establish links between self-regulatory deficits and the selection of strategies to reduce distress, which may include externalized means of immediate gratification that are available within the individual's environment. Additional variables to be measured during childhood and adolescence would include opportunities for appropriate and inappropriate regulation strategies as well as the content of, and reinforcement offered by, sexual fantasy.

Although longitudinal data would perhaps offer insights into the clearest connections in a causal sequence for our variables of interest, there are some limitations. Because of the low base rate of paraphilias in the population, even large samples might not provide very many individuals who manifest both self-regulatory difficulty and the outcome variable of the most interest (i.e., paraphilias). Despite this problem, we believe that longitudinal research is probably the most effective means we currently have to track these variables in a population and empirically relate them to the predicted outcomes of multimodal self-regulation theory.

Empirical tests of this model should also include a variety of comparison samples. Although we can learn a great deal about the characteristics of sex offenders in an exploratory analysis, what will demonstrate the predictive power of this model is comparison with groups who have similar characteristics, because of either early developmental experience or similar behavioral outcomes. One important sample that should be included in a comparison study is sex-offending individuals without paraphilias. The preliminary research by Stinson et al. (in press) demonstrated significant causal relationships within one group of paraphilic offenders. However, future research should compare samples like this with samples of sex offenders who have not committed as many offenses, despite being given similar opportunity, and who do not have paraphilias. We expect that the results of this comparison will reveal significantly higher self-regulatory difficulties in the group with paraphilic and repeated sex offenses, while the nonparaphilic sex-offender group will likely still manifest some of the regulatory difficulties described here.

Another sample that should be considered for comparison is one made of individuals who have marked problems with self-dysregulation but who have not committed sex offenses and who deny sexually deviant fantasy content. In comparing these two groups, researchers could determine other factors at work in our model that differentially predict paraphilic behaviors as external forms of self-regulation. These comparisons could include non–sex-offender samples, substance-abusing samples, or individuals with personality disorders with extreme emotional dysregulation. Theoretically, factors such as cognitive labeling of arousal during sexual development, specific perceptions of early childhood experience, personality variables, and reinforcement contingencies might contribute to the differing outcomes in these groups.

Even more generally, research needs to continue focusing on the contribution of biological predispositions and negative experiences in childhood to further strengthen our understanding of the link between these factors and poor self-regulation. Again, longitudinal research would allow us to compare the temperamental features and childhood experiences of children who later develop problems with self-regulation and those who do not. Other factors that occur during critical stages of development may be identified so that we can better understand how one's self-regulatory abilities develop and how children may adopt dysfunctional regulatory strategies compared with their peers.

Relationships Between Variables

Other aspects of this model that must be explored and clarified are the assumed relationships between causal and outcome variables. For example, personality variables included in the model may be highly correlated with self-regulatory deficits (e.g., Stinson et al., in press), which makes it difficult to determine the extent to which these factors may independently impact the development of sexually deviant interests and behaviors. The same factors that drive the development of these traits will also drive patterns of dysregulation. Therefore, we must find a way to separate these variables and confirm their role, possibly as mediators, in this process.

Additionally, we must enhance our understanding of the relationship between childhood experience and the perceptions of that experience, because each of these are important in the early stages of this process. Some additive or synergistic effect of these two variables leads to relevant outcomes for the individual's cognitive worldview, personality structure, and acceptance of certain behaviors as regulatory strategies. We must gain knowledge about not only how these two variables affect one another but also how they interact to produce the hypothesized results.

We also see a need for additional research into the relationships between our measures of outcome. As mentioned earlier in this chapter, paraphilias, antisocial or criminal behaviors, and substance abuse or dependence are all highly correlated in sex-offender samples. What we need to establish is the reason for this relationship, beyond the simple explanation that sexually deviant behaviors or use of illicit substances are themselves criminal activities. Although we have noted several times that sex offenders, like many other, non–sex offenders, do not specialize in their offenses and instead commit a variety of criminal acts, there are still groups of these offenders who commit seemingly frequent sex offenses that may be disproportionate to their non–sex offenses and who profess continued interest in deviant sexual stimuli (i.e., paraphilias). This suggests that there is something more to the relationships between outcomes than just an extension of one type of behavior. This idea is supported by the finding that the relationship between paraphilias and antisocial behaviors was no longer relevant once a common underlying factor, self-regulation, was accounted for in the first empirical study of this model (Stinson et al., in press). Thus, we need additional research verifying this relationship and seeking other common factors that may link these outcomes in these individuals, such as shared personality characteristics, opportunity, and similar behavioral reinforcement pathways.

IMPLICATIONS FOR PREVENTION AND TREATMENT

Once a theory, designed to explain the development of sexually deviant interests and sex-offending behaviors, has been introduced and subjected to empirical scrutiny, the next logical step is to study its implications for prevention and treatment. It is clear that sex offending has become a growing societal concern because of the increasing number of incarcerated or hospitalized sex offenders who typically require some form of treatment before they can be integrated back into our communities. In this final section, we briefly discuss the etiological limitations of current treatment and then turn to the prevention and treatment strategies that may be suggested by the tenets of multimodal self-regulation theory. We also include evidence of current treatments that may already include these components and thus provide a framework for future endeavors.

Theory of Problem, Theory of Change

A recent article by Kirsch and Becker (2006) outlined several problematic assumptions that have characterized sex-offender treatment over the past several decades. These researchers related limitations in treatment to a large disconnect between etiological theory and treatment implementation. One source of this disconnect is the largely atheoretical approach that has been used to develop treatment programs within this area. The sex-offending literature is replete with different theories, many of which have critical and often-overlooked flaws. In addition, prevention and treatment programs are not fundamentally based on any one unified theory. Instead, those who design treatment programs often take elements from a variety of these etiological approaches, including cognitive, personality, and behavioral theories, and simply address each of them as separate elements in the sex-offending process. This is problematic not only because of the weak theoretical foundation for many of the independent treatment components but also because it is inconsistent with generally accepted clinical practice within psychology. A core idea behind mental health treatment is that strategies for change should be driven by a defined theory of what first caused the disorder. Culling together treatment techniques and goals from a broad spectrum of etiological possibilities, without regard to a unified causal theory, weakens the effectiveness of treatment because it is not based on an understanding of how the change process should address the causal factors.

Another source of disconnect between etiology and treatment is that causal and maintenance factors are treated interchangeably in research and practice (Kirsch & Becker, 2006). Etiological theories should concentrate on what initially caused the behavior and what specific variables or circumstances led to the development of deviant sexual interests. Although it is possible that many of these factors also maintain the behavior over time, this is not clearly addressed in etiological theory or research for the majority of these models. Treatment practices are broadly concerned with the prevention of continued sexual violence, which necessitates a focus on those factors that maintain the behavior once it has already been initiated. Therefore, when treatment interventions are derived, if they are in any way based on etiological theory they often modify the causal variables to fit the treatment framework. In other words, etiological ideas, which were created to explain the first offense, are modified so that they can explain the next offense, with little empirical basis for doing so.

Examples of this disparity between etiology and treatment can be found throughout the treatment literature. For example, cognitive–behavioral interventions for sex offenders target various aspects of the cognitive schema, such as rationalizations or justifications for offending, victim empathy, and other cognitive distortions related to offending. These factors are treated as causal within the intervention framework, with the idea that modifying these variables or responses will change offense patterns. However, the etiological literature suggests that cognitive schemas and dysfunctional information-processing systems are to blame for offending and that cognitive distortions are merely reflections of this. It does not offer hypotheses about the impact of modification of these beliefs on future offending. Furthermore, as we presented in chapter 4, there is some debate as to whether these factors formed prior to offending or after it, which complicates the use of these factors in a treatment program.

Another example is relapse prevention, which has been gaining popularity within the sex-offender treatment community. Relapse prevention is entirely based on the idea that certain variables or situations perpetuate offending and should be targeted by treatment interventions. Within this model there is no clear assumption of causality. Proponents of this model suggest not that these circumstances or factors are what initially caused the problem, but instead what maintain it. The question then arises as to whether it is more effective in the long term to treat what may have caused the problem or what maintains it. At this point, studies indicating limited effectiveness of relapse prevention would suggest that focusing entirely on the maintenance factors is ineffective at preventing future sex crimes (e.g., Marques, Wiederanders, Day, Nelson, & van Ommeren, 2005). An additional concern with the etiological soundness of relapse prevention is its origin. This treatment was derived from the addictions literature and modified for use with sex offenders. This carries an implicit assumption that the causal origins of sex offending are similar to those for substance abuse (Marlatt & Gordon, 1985). As we discussed in chapter 5, there are substantial limitations to the application of etiological explanations for addiction to sex-offending behaviors, which again suggests that the focus of relapse prevention is perhaps inappropriate for our treatment goals with this population.

A related problem also noted by Kirsch and Becker (2006) is the failure of many treatment models to integrate new empirical findings that would impact the way treatment is conceptualized or delivered. As was mentioned previously, research questioning the etiological role of cognitive distortions or victim empathy has not been incorporated into treatment interventions (for more, see Kirsch & Becker, 2006). Not only should interventions be developed on the basis of a sound etiological framework, but also they should also be continually revised when new information about their validity becomes available.

With multimodal self-regulation theory, we hope to provide a sound etiological basis from which prevention and treatment interventions may be derived. Our goal is to inform research and shape the direction of treatment development, but more empirical research is needed to firmly establish links between this theory and the interventions that may follow from its major tenets. Once these have been validated, we will then have a better idea of which components are most critical for treatment. Until then, we can merely hypothesize treatment goals that would be consistent with multimodal self-regulation theory. We may also look to current treatment models that have some relationship to the causal pathways in multimodal self-regulation theory. We will now devote the remainder of this chapter to these tasks.

Prevention, Treatment, and Multimodal Self-Regulation Theory

The first way that this theory can inform the development of prevention and treatment interventions is to recognize its core features. Prevention and treatment should focus on each of the major components of self-regulatory functioning: emotional regulation, cognitive regulation, behavioral regulation, and interpersonal regulation. These four areas of regulatory functioning have been defined in a variety of works dedicated to understanding dysregulation and its impact on the individual's ability to function adaptively in his or her environment (e.g., Baumeister & Vohs, 2004; Linehan, 1993a, 1993b). Improvement strategies should independently focus on each of these areas to ensure optimal regulatory functioning in a variety of domains. The reason for this multifaceted attention to self-regulatory ability is straightforward: Some individuals are so profoundly impaired in their self-regulatory ability that their deficits are noticeable across all domains. However, what may be more common is for an individual to demonstrate selective skills in these areas, provided that distress or tension has not reached a critical threshold. For example, an individual may demonstrate reasonably adaptive interpersonal regulation in the absence of emotional distress but be unable to cope with interpersonal stress when under high amounts of emotional distress or tension. Therefore, a tentative grasp on interpersonal regulation weakens in the face of emotional dysregulation. Thus, it is important to focus on each of these areas to ensure that the individual learns to self-monitor and form adaptive responding across a variety of situations.

This model also assumes a critical relationship between self-dysregulation and the development of maladaptive regulatory skills. Thus, another target for intervention is the need to increase one's capacity to regulate internal distress through adaptive and appropriate regulatory strategies. This would include a need to extinguish those maladaptive strategies that may have already developed or are in the early stages of development. The key components of enhancing regulatory capacity involve learning to recognize and label internal tension; cope with distressing emotions or thoughts; monitor interpersonal feedback and incorporate it into appropriate emotional, cognitive, and behavioral responding; and learn and internalize appropriate skills that allow for adaptive self-regulation. The presumption of the model is that these skills either were never learned or were insufficiently used during critical periods of development. Therefore, interventions that teach and enhance self-regulatory skills at a basic level are needed for these individuals to ensure that they are successful. Asking the individual to start at a high level of regulation, such as learning to delay gratification for a highly desired object, will most likely leave the individual frustrated and unable to cope. Our discussion in chapter 10 noted that the strategies must be both available and potentially effective in order to be considered as options. Therefore, to promote long-term regulatory skills, therapists need to focus on basic regulatory abilities, such as labeling internal emotional and physical states and attributing these feelings to an appropriate source, and then build toward more complicated tasks.

The other component of this intervention effort is to decrease the use of maladaptive regulatory skills. In the case of treatment for individuals who have already committed sex offenses, we know that these maladaptive strategies are in place and have been reinforced over time. For prevention strategies that focus on high-risk individuals, the presence of maladaptive regulatory techniques may be less obvious. Regardless, in attempting to facilitate the development of appropriate and adaptive strategies, we must eliminate the strategies that are ultimately harmful toward to the individual and other people in the environment. To do so takes a very motivated individual who is willing not only to report the use of maladaptive techniques but also to engage in attempts to stop using these techniques or strategies. This may involve intensive self-monitoring of behavior or urges to engage in the behavior, development of satisfactory alternatives to the behavior, using strategies to decrease the reinforcing nature of the behavior, and attempts to reinforce alternative behaviors.

Often, individuals who have committed sex offenses are already aware of some of the negative consequences of their behavior. An exclusive focus on these negative outcomes is unlikely to result in behavioral change unless reinforcing alternatives are discovered and made available for the individual. This is where the adaptive strategies become important. These two areas of treatment are closely intertwined. To promote adaptive strategies, one must reduce the maladaptive ones, but to decrease the maladaptive strategies over time, the individual must have access to adaptive and appropriate alternatives. Prevention and treatment programs must incorporate these strategies into a comprehensive program to promote the individual's capacity for adaptive self-regulation.

Interventions aimed at self-regulatory functioning should also involve several core components that were briefly introduced in the previous discussion. The ability to monitor emotions, thoughts, physiological sensations, and behavioral urges is a critical part of this process. It is likely that the individual acts impulsively on these internal sensations with little regard to their origin or adaptive function. Because of this disconnect, the individual is perceived as dysregulated and impulsive in his behavioral responding. The ability to monitor these internal states and recognize them as independent from action are important targets for change. Treatment should also prioritize skill development, whereby the individual can learn to cope with these internal states or sensations through adaptive skills that can be applied in a variety of situations. Finally, learning to recognize the relationship between these internal states and previous maladaptive coping behaviors may also be beneficial for reducing the use of maladaptive strategies in the motivated individual.

As a corollary to these interventions targeting self-regulation, prevention and treatment efforts should also focus on other, related behaviors that emerge. Substance abuse treatment, for example, must also be incorporated into the treatment program. We believe that extensive substance abuse and dependence likely results from the same drive for external regulation that produces sexually deviant interests and sex-offending behaviors. Similarly, antisocial or criminal behaviors should also be treated as a comparable treatment target. These and other maladaptive regulatory behaviors should be addressed within the context of increasing adaptive regulatory strategies, and identifying and decreasing those that are precipitated by states of internal dysregulation.

A second major area of treatment intervention that is presumed by multimodal self-regulation theory relates to adverse experiences in childhood and adolescence. As we discussed in chapter 10, negative childhood experiences, including abuse, neglect, and poor support from family and peers, often impact the developing child's views of the self and the world as well as self-regulatory ability. We have previously mentioned several times that there is no definitive link between childhood abuse and later perpetration of offenses against others. However, some individuals who have experienced abuse develop difficulties with self-regulation and go on to commit crimes against others, including sex crimes. Therefore, we cannot ignore the potential role of negative childhood experience and the way that it shapes later emotions, cognitions, and behaviors.

Because of this indirect relationship, we must consider treatment interventions that deal with childhood abuse and neglect. These interventions would ideally target affective sequelae, including depression, anxiety, guilt, or anger, as well as self-destructive behaviors, difficulties with interpersonal relationships, and mistrust of others (Berliner & Elliot, 2002; Lusk & Waterman, 1986). These potential effects of childhood abuse, specifically sexual abuse, may have a lasting impact on the child's ability to regulate emotion and behavior, as well as negative effects on cognition and worldview. This would also be an area for subsequent intervention, with a focus on perceptions of self, interpersonal relationships, and appropriate means for coping with negative emotions and meeting needs.

Another goal for treatment and prevention is to alter learned patterns of reinforcement. This may seem redundant given the focus on extinguishing maladaptive behaviors that have been reinforced over time and reinforcing new, adaptive behavioral strategies. However, there is a broader need for developing internalized reinforcement and provoking a form of cost–benefit analysis that may be vastly different than that which the individual has used thus far. One of the characteristics noted in our theory is the tendency to engage in high-risk behaviors and thrill-seeking activities. Here, the promise of temporary but immediate gratification is favored over long-term gain that may require dedication or effort. In this case, we must devote intervention efforts to revising the individual's perceptions and values so that these high-risk, minimal (but immediate) benefit goals are no longer seen as desirable. Reinforcing goals that promise long-term benefit, but require greater effort (e.g., learning appropriate self-regulation skills), should also be a target of treatment for these individuals.

In chapter 10, we also discussed the nature of peer relationships for individuals who have marked difficulties with self-regulation in childhood and adolescence. The developmental literature suggests that peer interactions are often negative and serve to heighten the individual's interpersonal and emotional dysregulation. Because of this, treatment practices consistent with multimodal self-regulation theory would also support efforts to enhance social support networks for these individuals. This emphasis on social relationships is all the more necessary once a sex offense has been committed, because the very nature of the crime often leads to further alienation and ostracism of the offender. Interventions devoted to forming appropriate and rewarding relationships, though not directly related to preventing future sexual violence, could provide a healthy outlet in which to experience internal distress or tension. The overall impact of this intervention might be limited for people with extreme difficulty in forming close relationships or those who have little desire to do so.

Sex education is the final prevention or treatment component that emerges from our conceptualization of sexual deviance. We have proposed in our theory that early cognitive links between stimuli and physiological sexual arousal, if reinforced, may create a more lasting sexual response. Individuals who are poorly regulated, and at high risk for a variety of developmental outcomes, could be targeted with sex education and information regarding culturally normative sexual behaviors, with the idea that it will provide them appropriate information about sexual stimuli and encourage healthy rather than unhealthy or inappropriate sexual relationships. Additionally, education about sexuality and sexual relationships could strengthen an individual's ability to effectively cope in interpersonal sexual situations. The youth described in chapter 10 to illustrate multimodal self-regulation theory were all young men who lacked appropriate understanding of their sexuality and the nature of sexual relationships. Education for these youth could have provided them with the means to engage in appropriate sexual fantasy and relationships.

Sex education is also important as a treatment strategy, in that many sex offenders demonstrate limited knowledge of these topics (e.g., Becker, Harris, & Sales, 1993; Quayle, Deu, & Giblin, 1998; Sahota & Chesterman, 1998). Exposure to information about normative sexual expression and the role of sexual arousal could impact the way these individuals view their sexuality. Many offenders who have engaged in a variety of inappropriate sexual behaviors may have also engaged in appropriate sexual relationships, but because of the immediate gratification promised by their inappropriate behaviors, they may not have found the normative relationships as rewarding or readily available. Treatment should therefore focus on establishing realistic expectations related to sexual arousal and gratification and coping with sexual urges.

Current Interventions and Multimodal Self-Regulation Theory

Although a discussion of a new treatment program based on this theory is beyond the scope of this book, we have noted several components that may be important in developing a more comprehensive treatment program based on the ideas described here. A number of current prevention and treatment programs already use some of the principles that we outlined previously. We briefly discuss three of these programs, highlighting the components that are most relevant to the hypotheses that we have proposed in multimodal self-regulation theory of sexual deviance.

The first of these models is dialectical behavior therapy, a cognitive behavior therapy designed for individuals with borderline personality disorder (Linehan, 1993a, 1993b). Although this treatment program was originally designed, implemented, and tested for individuals with this personality disorder, its primary focus is on self-injurious, harmful, or impulsive behaviors in those who are extremely dysregulated. Components of this approach, including monitoring urges and emotions, skills training, and behavioral techniques such as chain analysis and solution analysis, could be translated into effective treatments for sex offenders. Furthermore, the emphasis that is placed on modulating distressing emotion and interpersonal conflict would be beneficial for these offenders, who manifest dysregulation and limited self-control across several domains.

A second treatment model that is consistent with the aims of multimodal self-regulation theory is multisystemic therapy, which was developed for adolescents who have engaged in antisocial and criminal behaviors (Henggeler, Schoenwald, Borduin, Rowland, & Cunningham, 1998) and has been applied in the treatment of juvenile sex offenders (Borduin, Henggeler, Blaske, & Stein, 1990; Borduin & Schaeffer, 2002). The core hypothesis underlying multisystemic therapy is that antisocial behavior by youth is driven by a number of determining characteristics within the family, peer, community, and school contexts. The focus of treatment is on strengthening protective factors (e.g., appropriate disciplinary practices at home, prosocial interactions with peers) in this array of environments with the goals of reducing antisocial and delinquent behavior, improving family communication and relationships, and decreasing the occurrence of future mental health or behavioral problems for the adolescent. The emphasis placed on enhancing parental effectiveness and forming relationships with prosocial peers are factors that would be consistent with treatments derived from multimodal self-regulation theory. We believe that monitoring and treating at-risk youth and their families in this manner will not only reduce antisocial behaviors but could also lower or prevent the incidence of future sex-offending behaviors by addressing some of the developmental factors that are critical in the etiological process. Furthermore, the focus on developmental antecedents and early childhood contexts in multisystemic therapy is also critical for identifying early problems in development and intervening before they could lead to more serious problems in the future, including antisocial behaviors, substance use, and sexual acting out.

Finally, the current sex-offender treatment literature does describe a treatment emphasizing self-regulation as a target for reducing sexual recidivism: the *self-regulation model* of the relapse process (Ward et al., 2004; Ward & Hudson, 2000; Ward, Polaschek, & Beech, 2006), which applies self-regulatory goals to a relapse prevention framework. This treatment model defines self-regulation in terms of the approach and avoidance goals that would immediately precede relapse (i.e., a sex offense). The regulatory goals are then described in terms of four pathways, each of which involve immediate proximal events that could potentially trigger a sex-offending incident. However, limited definitions of *self-regulation* and *self-regulatory processes*, insufficient consideration or acknowledgement of other relevant factors, such as the influence of behavioral reinforcement (Yates, 2005), and an exclusive focus on immediately proximal events in a maintenance of offending prevent complete compatibility between multimodal self-regulation theory and the self-regulation model as applied to treatment. And although this treatment model may have some value in describing the effects of self-regulatory goals and feedback loops in the offense process, it relies too heavily on the relapse prevention model, which has been the subject of recent criticism (Laws, 2003; Marques et al., 2005; Ward & Hudson, 1996).

We include this model here as a current treatment with promise because it does acknowledge the important role played by self-regulatory deficits in the maintenance of sexually deviant behaviors. However, because of the confusing manner in which treatment for self-regulatory difficulties is described (Yates, 2005), as well as the other limitations mentioned previously, more work would be required to incorporate some of these ideas into a more comprehensive treatment plan based on multimodal self-regulation theory.

CONCLUDING THOUGHTS

As we have discussed in this chapter, further research on multimodal self-regulation theory is needed to ensure the validity of its important constructs and hypotheses and explore potential uses of this theory for prevention and treatment of sexual crimes. We again stress the necessity of additional study of this theory, because too many other theories already described in this book have lacked the empirical scrutiny that might have led to earlier advancements in our understanding of sex offending. A firm etiological basis for designing prevention and treatment interventions will allow for adequate and accurate testing of intervention assumptions in a cohesive etiological framework. We can expect to make advances in our field only if we are willing to devote ourselves to the level of empiricism that is required for scientific discovery.

REFERENCES

Abel, G. G., Becker, J. V., & Cunningham-Rathner, J. (1984). Complications, consent, and cognitions in sex between children and adults. *International Journal of Law and Psychiatry, 7,* 89–103.

Abel, G. G., Becker, J. V., Cunningham-Rathner, J., & Mittelman, M. (1988). Multiple paraphilic diagnoses among sex offenders. *Bulletin of the American Academy of Psychiatry and the Law, 16,* 153–168.

Abel, G. G., Osborn, C. A., Anthony, D., & Gardos, P. (1992). Current treatments of paraphiliacs. *Annual Review of Sex Research, 3,* 255–290.

Abracen, J., Looman, J., & Anderson, D. (2000). Alcohol and drug abuse in sexual and nonsexual violent offenders. *Sexual Abuse: A Journal of Research and Treatment, 12,* 263–274.

Aigner, M., Eher, R., Fruehwald, S., Forttier, P., Gutierrez-Lobos, K., & Dwyer, S. M. (2000). Brain abnormalities and violent behavior. *Journal of Psychology and Human Sexuality, 11,* 57–64.

Ainsworth, M. D. S. (1963). The development of infant–mother interaction among the Ganda. In B. M. Foss (Ed.), *Determinants of infant behavior* (pp. 67–104). New York: Wiley.

Ainsworth, M. D. S. (1967). *Infancy in Uganda.* Baltimore: Johns Hopkins University Press.

Ainsworth, M. D. S., Bell, S. M., & Stayton, D. J. (1974). Infant–mother attachment and social development. In M. P. Richards (Ed.), *The introduction of the child into a social world* (pp. 99–135). London: Cambridge University Press.

Ainsworth, M. D. S., Blehar, M. C., Waters, E., & Wall, S. (1978). *Patterns of attachment.* Hillsdale, NJ: Erlbaum.

Ajzen, I., & Fishbein, M. (1980). *Understanding attitudes and predicting social behavior.* Englewood Cliffs, NJ: Prentice Hall.

Akers, R. L. (1985). *Deviant behavior: A social learning approach.* Belmont, CA: Wadsworth.

Akers, R. L. (1998). *Social learning and social structure: A general theory of crime and deviance.* Boston: Northeastern University Press.

Akers, R. L. (2000). *Criminological theories: Introduction and evaluation* (3rd ed.). Los Angeles: Roxbury.

Akins, K. A., & Windham, M. W. (1992). Just science? *Behavioral and Brain Sciences, 15,* 376–377.

Allgeier, E. R., & Wiederman, M. W. (1992). Evidence for an evolved adaptation to rape? Not yet. *Behavioral and Brain Sciences, 15,* 377–379.

American Psychiatric Association. (1987). *Diagnostic and statistical manual of mental disorders* (3rd ed., rev.). Washington, DC: Author.

American Psychiatric Association. (2000). *Diagnostic and statistical manual of mental disorders* (4th ed., text rev.). Washington, DC: Author.

Anderson, W. P., Kunce, J. T., & Rich, B. (1979). Sex offenders: Three personality types. *Journal of Clinical Psychology, 35,* 671–676.

Armentrout, J. A., & Hauer, A. L. (1978). MMPIs of rapists of adults, rapists of children, and non-rapist sex offenders. *Journal of Clinical Psychology, 34,* 330–332.

Awad, G. A., & Saunders, E. G. (1989). Adolescent child molesters: Clinical observations. *Child Psychiatry and Human Development, 19,* 195–206.

Bailey, K. G. (1988). Phylogenetic regression–progression and the problem of rape motivation. *New Trends in Experimental and Clinical Psychiatry, 4,* 235–251.

Bain, J., Langevin, R., Dickey, R., & Ben-Aron, M. (1987). Sex hormones in murderers and assaulters. *Behavioral Science and the Law, 5,* 95–101.

Bain, J., Langevin, R., Hucker, S., Dickey, R., Wright, P., & Schonberg, C. (1988). Sex hormones in pedophiles: I. Baseline values of six hormones; II. The gonadotropin releasing hormone test. *Annals of Sex Research, 1,* 443–454.

Baker, A. J. L., Tabacoff, R., Tornusciolo, G., & Eisenstadt, M. (2001). Calculating the number of offenses and victims of juvenile sexual offending: The role of posttreatment disclosures. *Sexual Abuse: A Journal of Research and Treatment, 13,* 79–90.

Baker, E., & Beech, A. R. (2004). Dissociation and variability of adult attachment dimensions and early maladaptive schemas in sexual and violent offenders. *Journal of Interpersonal Violence, 19,* 1119–1136.

Baldwin, K., & Roys, D. T. (1998). Factors associated with denial in a sample of alleged adult sexual offenders. *Sexual Abuse: A Journal of Research and Treatment, 10,* 211–226.

Bandura, A. (1969a). *Principles of behavior modification.* New York: Holt, Rinehart & Winston.

Bandura, A. (1969b). Social learning of moral judgments. *Journal of Personality and Social Psychology, 11,* 275–279.

Bandura, A. (1977). *Social learning theory.* Englewood Cliffs, NJ: Prentice Hall.

Barbaree, H. E., & Cortoni, F. A. (1993). Treatment of the juvenile sex offenders within the criminal justice and mental health systems. In H. E. Barbaree & W. L. Marshall (Eds.), *The juvenile sex offender* (pp. 243–263). New York: Guilford Press.

Barbaree, H. E., Marshall, W. L., & McCormick, J. (1998). The development of deviant sexual behaviour among adolescents and its implications for prevention and treatment. *Irish Journal of Psychology, 19,* 1–31.

Barker, M. (1993). What do we know about the effectiveness of cognitive–behavioral treatment for sex offenders? *Journal of Mental Health, 2,* 97–103.

Barlow, D. H. (2002). *Anxiety and its disorders: The nature and treatment of anxiety and panic* (2nd ed.). New York: Guilford Press.

Barnard, G. W., Hankins, G. C., & Robbins, L. (1992). Prior life trauma, post-traumatic stress symptoms, sexual disorders, and character traits in sex offenders: An exploratory study. *Journal of Traumatic Stress, 5,* 393–420.

Barrett, L., Dunbar, R., & Lycett, J. (2002). *Human evolutionary psychology.* Princeton, NJ: Princeton University Press.

Barrios, J. (2004a, October 1). New victim trauma. *Arizona Daily Star.* Retrieved from http://www.azstarnet.com

Barrios, J. (2004b, April 15). Rapist can be own lawyer in 5 attack cases, judge says. *Arizona Daily Star.* Retrieved from http://www.azstarnet.com

Barrios, J. (2004c, September 27). Selby trial starts today with jury selection. *Arizona Daily Star.* Retrieved from http://www.azstarnet.com

Barth, R. J., & Kinder, B. N. (1987). The mislabeling of sexual impulsivity. *Journal of Sex and Marital Therapy, 13,* 15–23.

Baumeister, R. F., Catanese, K. R., & Wallace, H. M. (2002). Conquest by force: A narcissistic reactance theory of rape and sexual coercion. *Review of General Psychology, 6,* 92–135.

Baumeister, R. F., & Vohs, K. D. (2004). *Handbook of self-regulation: Research, theory, and applications.* New York: Guilford Press.

Bauserman, R. (1996). Sexual aggression and pornography: A review of correlational research. *Basic and Applied Social Psychology, 18,* 405–427.

Beail, N. (2002). Interrogative suggestibility, memory, and intellectual disability. *Journal of Applied Research in Intellectual Disabilities, 15,* 129–137.

Beccaria, C. (1963). *On crimes and punishments* (H. Paolucci, Trans.). Englewood Cliffs, NJ: Prentice Hall. (Original work published 1764)

Beck, A. T. (2002). Cognitive models of depression. In R. L. Leahy & E. T. Dowd (Eds.), *Clinical advances in cognitive psychotherapy: Theory and application* (pp. 29–61). New York: Springer Publishing.

Becker, J. V. (1988). The effects of child sexual abuse on adolescent sex offenders. In G. E. Wyatt & G. J. Powell (Eds.), *Lasting effects of child sexual abuse* (pp. 193–207). Newbury Park, CA: Sage.

Becker, J. V. (1998). What we know about the characteristics and treatment of adolescents who have committed sexual offenses. *Child Maltreatment: Journal of the American Professional Society on the Abuse of Children, 3,* 317–329.

Becker, J. V., Hall, S. R., & Stinson, J. D. (2001). Female sexual offenders: Clinical, legal, and policy issues. *Journal of Forensic Psychology Practice, 1,* 29–50.

Becker, J. V., Harris, C. D., & Sales, B. D. (1993). Juveniles who commit sexual offenses: A critical review of the research. In G. C. N. Hall, R. Hirschman, J. R. Graham, & M. S. Zaragoza (Eds.), *Sexual aggression: Issues in etiology, assessment, and treatment* (pp. 215–228). Philadelphia: Taylor & Francis.

Becker, J. V., Hunter, J. A., Stein, R. M., & Kaplan, M. S. (1989). Factors associated with erection in adolescent sex offenders. *Journal of Psychopathology and Behavioral Assessment, 11,* 353–362.

Becker, J. V., & Kaplan, M. S. (1993). Cognitive–behavioral treatment of the juvenile sex offender. In H. E. Barbaree & W. L. Marshall (Eds.), *The juvenile sex offender* (pp. 264–277). New York: Guilford Press.

Becker, J. V., Kaplan, M. S., Tenke, C. E., & Tartaglini, A. (1991). The incidence of depressive symptomatology in juvenile sex offenders with a history of abuse. *Child Abuse & Neglect, 15,* 531–536.

Becker, J. V., Stinson, J. D., Tromp, S., & Messer, G. (2003). Characteristics of individuals petitioned for civil commitment. *International Journal of Offender Therapy and Comparative Criminology, 47,* 185–195.

Beckmann, J., Dupont, A., Erling, I., Jacobsen, P., Mikkelsen, M., & Theilgaard, A. (1974). Report of sex chromosome abnormalities in mentally retarded male offenders including a psychological study of patients with XYY and XXYY karyotypes. *Journal of Mental Deficiency Research, 18,* 331–353.

Beech, A. R., & Mitchell, I. J. (2005). A neurobiological perspective on attachment problems in sexual offenders and the role of selective serotonin re-uptake inhibitors in the treatment of such problems. *Clinical Psychology Review, 25,* 153–182.

Beech, A. R., & Ward, T. (2004). The integration of etiology and risk in sexual offenders: A theoretical framework. *Aggression and Violent Behavior, 10,* 31–63.

Bem, D. J., & Allen, A. (1974). On predicting some of the people some of the time: The search for cross-situational consistency in behavior. *Psychological Review, 81,* 506–520.

Benoit, J. L., & Kennedy, W. A. (1992). The abuse history of male adolescent sex offenders. *Journal of Interpersonal Violence, 7,* 543–548.

Bergen, R. K., & Bogle, K. A. (2000). Exploring the connection between pornography and sexual violence. *Violence and Victims, 15,* 227–234.

Berger, P., Berner, W., Bolterauer, J., Gutierrez, K., & Berger, K. (1999). Sadistic personality disorder in sex offenders: Relationship to antisocial personality disorder and sexual sadism. *Journal of Personality Disorders, 13,* 175–186.

Berlin, F. S. (1988). Issues in the exploration of biological factors contributing to the etiology of the "sex offender," plus some ethical considerations. In R. A. Prentky & V. L. Quinsey (Eds.), *Annals of the New York Academy of Sciences: Vol. 528. Human sexual aggression: Current perspectives* (pp. 183–192). New York: New York Academy of Sciences.

Berliner, L., & Elliot, D. M. (2002). Sexual abuse of children. In J. E. B. Meyers, L. Berliner, J. Briere, C. T. Hendrix, C. Jenny, & T. A. Reid (Eds.), *The APSAC handbook on child maltreatment* (2nd ed., pp. 55–78). Thousand Oaks, CA: Sage.

Berner, W., Berger, P., Gutierrez, K., Jordan, B., & Berger, K. (1992). The role of personality disorders in the treatment of sex offenders. *Journal of Offender Rehabilitation, 18*(3/4), 26–37.

Berntsen, D., & Rubin, D. C. (2002). Emotionally charged autobiographical memories across the life span: The recall of happy, sad, traumatic, and involuntary memories. *Psychology and Aging, 17,* 636–652.

Bixler, R. H. (1992). Men: A genetically invariant predisposition to rape? *Behavioral and Brain Sciences, 15*(2), 381.

Blanchard, G. (1990). Differential diagnosis of sex offenders. *American Journal of Preventive Psychiatry and Neurology, 2*(3), 45–47.

Blanchard, R., Watson, M. S., Choy, A., Dickey, R., Klassen, P., Kuban, M., & Ferren, D. J. (1999). Pedophiles: Mental retardation, maternal age, and sexual orientation. *Archives of Sexual Behavior, 28*, 111–127.

Blaske, D. M., Borduin, C. M., Henggeler, S. W., & Mann, B. J. (1989). Individual, family, and peer characteristics of adolescent sex offenders and assaultive offenders. *Developmental Psychology, 25*, 846–855.

Blumenthal, S., Gudjonsson, G., & Burns, J. (1999). Cognitive distortions and blame attribution in sex offenders against adults and children. *Child Abuse & Neglect, 23*, 129–143.

Bogaerts, S., Vervaeke, G., & Goethals, J. (2004). A comparison of relational attitude and personality disorders in the explanation of child molestation. *Sexual Abuse: A Journal of Research and Treatment, 16*, 37–48.

Bootzin, R. R. (1975). *Behavior modification and therapy: An introduction.* Cambridge, MA: Winthrop.

Borduin, C. M., Henggeler, S. W., Blaske, D. M., & Stein, R. (1990). Multisystemic treatment of adolescent sexual offenders. *International Journal of Offender Therapy and Comparative Criminology, 34*, 105–114.

Borduin, C. M., & Schaeffer, C. M. (2002). Multisystemic treatment of juvenile sexual offenders: A progress report. *Journal of Psychology and Human Sexuality, 13*, 25–42.

Bostic, P. A. (2004, April 16). Twins banned from Spring Hill campuses. *Longview (Texas) News-Journal.* Retrieved from http://www.news-journal.com

Bowlby, J. (1958). The nature of the child's tie to his mother. *International Journal of PsychoAnalysis, 39*, 350–373.

Bowlby, J. (1969). *Attachment and loss.* New York: Basic Books.

Bowlby, J. (1977). The making and breaking of affectional bonds: I. Aetiology and psychopathology in light of attachment theory. *British Journal of Psychiatry, 130*, 201–210.

Bowlby, J. (1979). *The making and breaking of affectional bonds.* London: Tavistock.

Bowlby, J. (1988). Developmental psychiatry comes of age. *American Journal of Psychiatry, 145*, 1–10.

Bradford, J. M. (1983). Research on sex offenders: Recent trends. *Psychiatric clinics of North America, 6*, 715–731.

Brennan, P. A., Mednick, S. A., & Volavka, J. (1995). Biomedical factors in crime. In J. Q. Wilson & J. Petersilia (Eds.), *Crime* (pp. 65–90). San Francisco: ICS Press.

Bretherton, I. (1995). The origins of attachment theory: John Bowlby and Mary Ainsworth. In S. Goldberg, R. Muir, & J. Kerr (Eds.), *Attachment theory: Social, developmental, and clinical perspectives* (pp. 45–84). Hillsdale, NJ: Analytic Press.

Briere, J., Malamuth, N. M., & Check, J. V. (1985). Sexuality and rape-supportive beliefs. *International Journal of Women's Studies, 8*, 398–403.

Briggs, F., & Hawkins, R. M. F. (1996). A comparison of the childhood experiences of convicted male child molesters and men who were sexually abused in childhood and claimed to be non-offenders. *Child Abuse & Neglect, 20*, 221–233.

Brown, G. R. (2000). Can studying non-human primates inform us about human rape? A zoologist's perspective. *Psychology, Evolution, & Gender, 2*, 321–324.

Brown, H., & Stein, J. (1997). Sexual abuse perpetrated by men with intellectual disabilities: A comparative study. *Journal of Intellectual Disability Research, 41*, 215–224.

Brownmiller, S., & Mehrhof, B. (1992). A feminist response to rape as an adaptation in men. *Behavioral and Brain Sciences, 15*, 381–382.

Burge, K. (2002, February 22). Geoghan sentenced to 9–10 years. *The Boston Globe*, p. A1.

Burgess, A. W., Hartman, C. R., & McCormack, A. (1987). Abused to abuser: Antecedents of socially deviant behaviors. *American Journal of Psychiatry, 144*, 1431–1436.

Burk, L. R., & Burkhart, B. R. (2003). Disorganized attachment as a diathesis for sexual deviance: Developmental experience and the motivation for sexual offending. *Aggression and Violent Behavior, 8*, 487–511.

Burton, D. L. (2000). Were adolescent sexual offenders children with sexual behavior problems? *Sexual Abuse: A Journal of Research and Treatment, 12*, 37–48.

Burton, D. L., Miller, D. L., & Shill, C. T. (2002). A social learning theory comparison of the sexual victimization of adolescent sexual offenders and nonsexual male delinquents. *Child Abuse & Neglect, 26*, 893–907.

Bushman, B. J., Bonacci, A. M., van Dijk, M., & Baumeister, R. F. (2003). Narcissism, sexual refusal, and aggression: Testing a narcissistic reactance model of sexual coercion. *Journal of Personality and Social Psychology, 84*, 1027–1040.

Buss, D. M. (1998). The psychology of human mate selection: Exploring the complexity of the strategic repertoire. In C. Crawford & D. L. Krebs (Eds.), *Handbook of evolutionary psychology: Ideas, issues, and applications* (pp. 405–429). Mahwah, NJ: Erlbaum.

Butcher, J. N., Graham, J. R., Ben-Porath, Y. S., Tellegen, A., Dahlstrom, W. G., & Kaemmer, B. (2001). *Minnesota Multiphasic Personality Inventory—2: Manual for administration and scoring* (2nd ed.). Minneapolis: University of Minnesota Press.

Calkins, S. D. (2004). Early attachment processes and the development of emotional self-regulation. In R. F. Baumeister & K. D. Vohs (Eds.), *Handbook of self-regulation: Research, theory, and applications* (pp. 324–339). New York: Guilford Press.

Campbell, S. M. (2000). Attention-deficit/hyperactivity disorder: A developmental view. In A. J. Sameroff, M. Lewis, & S. M. Miller (Eds.), *Handbook of developmental psychopathology* (2nd ed., pp. 383–401). New York: Kluwer Academic/ Plenum.

Caputo, A. A., Frick, P. J., & Brodsky, S. L. (1999). Family violence and juvenile sex offending: The potential mediating role of psychopathic traits and negative attitudes toward women. *Criminal Justice and Behavior, 26*, 338–356.

Carey, G. (1996). Family and genetic epidemiology of aggressive and antisocial behavior. In D. M. Stoff & R. B. Cairns (Eds.), Aggression and violence: Genetic, neurobiological, and biosocial perspectives (pp. 3–22). Mahwah, NJ: Erlbaum.

Carnes, P. J. (1983). *Out of the shadows: Understanding sexual addiction.* Minneapolis, MN: CompCare.

Carnes, P. J. (1990). Sexual addiction. In A. L. Horton, B. L. Johnson, L. M. Roundy, & D. Williams (Eds.), *The incest perpetrator: A family member no one wants to treat* (pp. 126–143). Thousand Oaks, CA: Sage.

Carnes, P. J. (1994). Editorial: Addicts vs. offenders. *Sexual Addiction and Compulsivity, 1*, 195–197.

Carpenter, D. R., Peed, S. F., & Eastman, B. (1995). Personality characteristics of adolescent sexual offenders: A pilot study. *Sexual Abuse: A Journal of Research and Treatment, 7*, 195–203.

Carver, C. S. (2004). Self-regulation of action and affect. In R. F. Baumeister & K. D. Vohs (Eds.), *Handbook of self-regulation: Research, theory, and applications* (pp. 13–39). New York: Guilford Press.

Carver, C. S., & Scheier, M. F. (2001). Optimism, pessimism, and self-regulation. In E. C. Chang (Ed.), *Optimism and pessimism: Implications for theory, research, and practice* (pp. 31–51). Washington, DC: American Psychological Association.

Caspi, A., Moffitt, T. E., Silva, P. A., Stouthamer-Loeber, M., Krueger, R. F., & Schmutte, P. S. (1994). Are some people crime-prone? Replications of the personality–crime relationship across countries, genders, races, and methods. *Criminology, 32*, 163–196.

Catalano, S. M. (2005). *Criminal victimization, 2004* (Bureau of Justice Statistics, National Crime Victimization Survey NCJ 210674). Washington, DC: U.S. Government Printing Office.

Chantry, K., & Craig, R. J. (1994a). MCMI typologies of criminal sexual offenders. *Sexual Addiction and Compulsivity, 1*, 215–226.

Chantry, K., & Craig, R. J. (1994b). Psychological screening of sexually violent offenders with the MCMI. *Journal of Clinical Psychology, 50*, 430–435.

Check, J. V. P., & Guloien, T. H. (1989). Reported proclivity for coercive sex following repeated exposure to sexually violent pornography, nonviolent dehumanizing pornography, and erotica. In D. Zillman & J. Bryant (Eds.), *Pornography: Research advances and policy considerations* (pp. 159–184). Hillsdale, NJ: Erlbaum.

Childress, A. R., Ehrman, R., Rohsenow, D. J., Robbins, S. J., & O'Brien, C. P. (1992). Classically conditioned factors in drug dependence. In J. H. Lowinson, P. Ruiz, R. B. Millman, & J. G. Langrod (Eds.), *Substance abuse: A comprehensive textbook* (2nd ed., pp. 56–69). Baltimore: Williams & Wilkins.

Christiansen, A. R., & Thyer, B. A. (2003). Female sexual offenders: A review of empirical research. *Journal of Human Behavior in the Social Environment, 6*(3), 1–16.

Cicchetti, D., Ganiban, J., & Barnett, D. (1991). Contributions from the study of high-risk populations to understanding the development of emotion regulation. In J. Garber & K. A. Dodge (Eds.), *The development of emotion regulation and dysregulation* (pp. 15–48). Cambridge, England: Cambridge University Press.

CNN. (2002, January 18). *Priest found guilty of molestation.* Retrieved March 16, 2006, from http://archives.cnn.com/2002/LAW/01/18/priest.verdict/index.html

CNN. (2003, August 23). *Timeline: Key dates in Geoghan's life.* Retrieved March 16, 2006, from http://www.cnn.com/2003/US/08/23/geoghan.chronlogy/index.html

Coccaro, E. F., & Kavoussi, R. J. (1996). Neurotransmitter correlates of impulsive aggression. In D. M. Stoff & R. B. Cairns (Eds.), *Aggression and violence: Genetic, neurobiological, and biosocial perspectives* (pp. 67–85). Mahwah, NJ: Erlbaum.

Cohen, L. J., & Galynker, I. I. (2002). Clinical features of pedophilia and implications for treatment. *Journal of Psychiatric Practice, 8,* 276–289.

Cohen, L. J., Gans, S. W., McGeoch, P. G., Poznansky, O., Itskovitch, Y., Murphy, S., et al. (2002). Impulsive personality traits in male pedophiles versus healthy controls: Is pedophilia an impulsive–aggressive behavior? *Comprehensive Psychiatry, 43,* 127–134.

Cohen, L. J., McGeoch, P. G., Watras-Gans, S., Acker, S., Poznansky, O., Cullen, K., et al. (2002). Personality impairment in male pedophiles. *Journal of Clinical Psychiatry, 63,* 912–919.

Cole, P. M., Martin, S. E., & Dennis, T. A. (2004). Emotion regulation as a scientific construct: Methodological challenges and directions for child development research. *Child Development, 75,* 317–333.

Coles, E. M. (1997). Impulsivity in major mental disorders. In C. D. Webster & M. A. Jackson (Eds.), *Impulsivity: Theory, assessment, and treatment* (pp. 180–194). New York: Guilford Press.

Connolly, M. (2004). Developmental trajectories and sexual offending: An analysis of the pathways model. *Qualitative Social Work, 3,* 39–59.

Cooke, D. J., & Michie, C. (2001). Refining the construct of psychopathy: Towards a hierarchical model. *Psychological Assessment, 13,* 171–188.

Coolidge, F. L., Segal, D. L., & Pointer, J. C. (2000). Personality disorders in older adult inpatients with chronic mental illness. *Journal of Clinical Geropsychology, 6,* 63–72.

Cooper, C. L., Murphy, W. D., & Haynes, M. R. (1996). Characteristics of abused and non-abused adolescent sexual offenders. *Sexual Abuse: A Journal of Research and Treatment, 8,* 105–119.

Corley, A., Corley, M. D., Walker, J., & Walker, S. (1994). The possibility of organic left posterior hemisphere dysfunction as a contributing factor in sex-offending behavior. *Sexual Addiction and Compulsivity, 1,* 337–346.

Cortoni, F. A., & Hanson, R. K. (2005). *A review of the recidivism rates of adult female sexual offenders.* Ottawa, Ontario, Canada: Correctional Service of Canada.

Cortoni, F. A., & Marshall, W. L. (2000). *Coping, attachment, and juvenile sexual history in sexual offenders.* Unpublished manuscript.

Costa, Jr., P. T., & McCrae, R. R. (1992). *Revised NEO Personality Inventory and Five-Factor Inventory professional manual*. Odessa, FL: Psychological Assessment Resources.

Cox-Lindenbaum, D. (2001). Group therapy for mentally retarded sex offenders. In A. Dosen & K. Day (Eds.), *Treating mental illness and behavior disorders in children and adults with mental retardation* (pp. 341–357). Washington, DC: American Psychiatric Press.

Coyne, J. A. (2003). Of vice and men: A case study in evolutionary psychology. In C. Travis (Ed.), *Evolution, gender, and rape* (pp. 171–190). Cambridge, MA: MIT Press.

Craissati, J., McClurg, G., & Browne, K. (2002). Characteristics of perpetrators of child sexual abuse who have been sexually victimized as children. *Sexual Abuse: A Journal of Research and Treatment, 14*, 225–240.

Cramer, E., McFarlane, J., Parker, B., Soeken, K., Silva, C., & Reel, S. (1998). Violent pornography and abuse of women: Theory to practice. *Violence and Victims, 13*, 319–332.

Crawford, C., & Galdikas, B. M. F. (1986). Rape in non-human animals: An evolutionary perspective. *Canadian Psychology, 27*, 215–230.

Cummings, J. L. (1999). Neuropsychiatry of sexual deviations. In R. Osview (Ed.), *Neuropsychiatry and mental health services* (pp. 363–384). Washington, DC: American Psychiatric Press.

Curnoe, S., & Langevin, R. (2002). Personality and deviant sexual fantasies: An examination of the MMPIs of sex offenders. *Journal of Clinical Psychology, 58*, 803–815.

Dalton, J. E. (1996). Juvenile male sex offenders: Mean scores on the Basic Self-Report of Personality. *Psychological Reports, 79*, 634.

Davidson, R. J., Putnam, K. M., & Larson, C. L. (2000, November 10). Dysfunction in the neural circuitry of emotion regulation: A possible prelude to violence. *Science, 289*, 591–594.

Day, K. (1994). Male mentally handicapped sex offenders. *British Journal of Psychiatry, 165*, 630–639.

Dean, K., & Malamuth, N. M. (1997). Characteristics of men who aggress sexually and of men who imagine aggressing: Risk and moderating variables. *Journal of Personality and Social Psychology, 72*, 449–455.

de Decker, A., Hermans, D., Raes, F., & Eelen, P. (2003). Autobiographical memory specificity and trauma in inpatient adolescents. *Journal of Clinical Child and Adolescent Psychology, 32*, 22–31.

Dennison, S. M., Stough, C., & Birgden, A. (2001). The Big 5 dimensional personality approach to understanding sex offenders. *Psychology, Crime, and Law, 7*, 243–261.

Denov, M. S. (2003). The myth of innocence: Sexual scripts and the recognition of child sexual abuse by female perpetrators. *Journal of Sex Research, 40*, 303–314.

Dienstbier, R. A. (1977). Sex and violence: Can research have it both ways? *Journal of Communication, 27*, 176–188.

Dobson, J. C. (1995). *Life on the edge*. Nashville, TN: Word Publishing.

Donnerstein, E., Linz, D., & Penrod, S. (1987). *The question of pornography: Research findings and policy implications*. New York: Free Press.

Donnerstein, E., & Malamuth, N. (1997). Pornography: Its consequences on the observer. In L. B. Schlesinger & E. Revitch (Eds.), *Sexual dynamics of anti-social behavior* (2nd ed., pp. 30–49). Springfield, IL: Charles C Thomas.

Donnerstein, E., Slaby, R. G., & Eron, L. D. (1995). The mass media and youth aggression. In L. D. Eron, J. H. Gentry, & P. Schlegel (Eds.), *Reason to hope: A psychosocial perspective on violence & youth* (pp. 219–250). Washington, DC: American Psychological Association.

Duthie, B., & McIvor, D. L. (1990). A new system for cluster-coding child molester MMPI profile types. *Criminal Justice and Behavior, 17,* 199–214.

Dwyer, S. M. (1990). Reduction of sex offender paraphilic fantasies: 6 month and 1 year follow-up. *Journal of Psychology and Human Sexuality, 3,* 57–65.

Dwyer, S. M., & Amberson, J. I. (1989). Behavioral patterns and personality characteristics of 56 sex offenders: A preliminary study. *Journal of Psychology and Human Sexuality, 2,* 105–118.

Eagle, M. (1995). The developmental perspectives of attachment and psychoanalytic theory. In S. Goldberg, R. Muir, & J. Kerr (Eds.), *Attachment theory: Social, developmental, and clinical perspectives* (pp. 123–150). Hillsdale, NJ: Analytic Press.

Earle, R. H., Earle, M. R., & Osborn, K. (1995). *Sex addiction: Case studies and management*. Philadelphia: Brunner/Mazel.

Edwards, D. W., Scott, C. L., Yarvis, R. M., Paizis, C. L., & Panizzon, M. S. (2003). Impulsiveness, impulsive aggression, personality disorder and spousal violence. *Violence and Victims, 18,* 3–14.

Edwards, V., Fivush, R., Anda, R. F., Felitti, V. J., & Nordenberg, D. F. (2001). Autobiographical memory disturbances in childhood abuse survivors. *Journal of Aggression, Maltreatment, and Trauma, 4,* 247–263.

Eher, R., Neuwirth, W., Fruehwald, S., & Frottier, P. (2003). Sexualization and lifestyle impulsivity: Clinically valid discriminators in sexual offenders. *International Journal of Offender Therapy and Comparative Criminology, 47,* 452–467.

Eisenberg, N., Fabes, R. A., Carlo, G., & Karbon, M. (1992). Emotional responsivity to others: Behavioral correlates and socialization antecedents. *New Directions for Child Development, 55,* 57–73.

Eisenberg, N., Smith, C. L., Sadovsky, A., & Spinrad, T. L. (2004). Effortful control: Relations with emotion regulation, adjustment, and socialization in childhood. In R. F. Baumeister & K. D. Vohs (Eds.), *Handbook of self-regulation: Research, theory, and applications* (pp. 259–282). New York: Guilford Press.

Eisenman, R. (2000). Explaining sex offenders: The concept of imprinting. *International Journal of Adolescence and Youth, 8,* 1–9.

Epps, K. J., Haworth, R., & Swaffer, T. (1993). Attitudes toward women and rape among male adolescents convicted of sexual versus nonsexual crimes. *Journal of Psychology, 127,* 501–506.

Erber, R., & Erber, M. W. (2001). Mood and processing: A view from a self-regulation perspective. In L. L. Martin & G. L. Clore (Eds.), *Theories of mood and cognition: A user's guidebook* (pp. 63–84). Mahwah, NJ: Erlbaum.

Evans, G. (2004, July 1). Peeping suspect begs jury for help. *Longview (Texas) News-Journal*. Retrieved from http://www.news-journal.com

Exner, J. E. (1974). *The Rorschach: A comprehensive system* (Vol. 1). New York: Wiley.

Extradition awaits Colorado sentencing. (2003, July 30). *Arizona Daily Star*. Retrieved from http://www.azstarnet.com

Eysenck, H. J. (1971). Personality and sexual adjustment. *British Journal of Psychiatry, 188*, 593–608.

Eysenck, H. J., & Eysenck, S. B. G. (1975). *Manual of the Eysenck Personality Inventory*. London: Hodder & Stoughton.

Fagan, P. J., Wise, T. N., Schmidt, C. W., Jr., Ponticas, Y., Marshall, R. D., & Costa, P. T., Jr. (1991). A comparison of five-factor personality dimensions in males with sexual dysfunction and males with paraphilia. *Journal of Personality Assessment, 57*, 434–448.

Farragher, T., & Paulson, M. (2003, August 24). Former priest slain: A troubled life spent exploiting vocation. *The Boston Globe*, p. B6.

Fazel, S., Hope, T., O'Donnell, I., & Jacoby, R. (2002). Psychiatric, demographic, and personality characteristics of elderly sex offenders. *Psychological Medicine, 32*, 219–226.

Fehrenbach, P. A., Smith, W., Monastersky, C., & Deisher, R. W. (1986). Adolescent sexual offenders: Offender and offense characteristics. *American Journal of Orthopsychiatry, 56*, 225–233.

Figueredo, A. J., Sales, B. D., Russell, K. P., Becker, J. V., & Kaplan, M. (2000). A Brunswikian evolutionary–developmental theory of adolescent sexual offending. *Behavioral Sciences and the Law, 18*, 309–329.

Finkelhor, D. (1984). *Child sexual abuse: New theory and research*. New York: Free Press.

Finkelhor, D. (1994). Current information on the scope and nature of child sexual abuse. *Future of Children, 4*, 31–53.

Finlay, W. M. L., & Lyons, E. (2001). Methodological issues in interviewing and using self-report questionnaires with people with mental retardation. *Psychological Assessment, 13*, 319–335.

Finlay, W. M. L., & Lyons, E. (2002). Acquiescence in interviews with people who have mental retardation. *Mental Retardation, 40*, 14–29.

Fishbein, M., & Ajzen, I. (1975). *Belief, attitude, intention, and behavior: An introduction to theory and research*. Boston: Addison-Wesley.

Fishbein, M., Hennessy, M., Yzer, M., & Douglas, J. (2003). Can we explain why some people do and some people do not act on their intentions? *Psychology, Health, and Medicine, 8*, 3–18.

Fisher, W. A., & Grenier, G. (1994). Violent pornography, antiwoman thoughts, and antiwoman acts: In search of reliable effects. *Journal of Sex Research, 31*, 23–38.

Fiske, S. T., & Taylor, S. E. (1991). *Social cognition* (2nd ed.). New York: McGraw-Hill.

Flor-Henry, P., Lang, R. A., Koles, Z. J., & Frenzel, R. R. (1988). Quantitative EEG investigations of genital exhibitionism. *Annals of Sex Research, 1,* 49–62.

Fonagy, P., & Target, M. (1996). Personality and sexual development, psychopathology and offending. In C. Cordess & M. Cox (Eds.), *Forensic psychotherapy: Crime, psychodynamics, and the offender patient: Vol. I. Mainly theory* (pp. 117–151). London: Jessica Kingsley.

Forbes, G. B., & Adams-Curtis, L. E. (2001). Experiences with sexual coercion in college males and females: Role of family conflict, sexist attitudes, acceptance of rape myths, self-esteem, and the Big-Five personality factors. *Journal of Interpersonal Violence, 16,* 865–889.

Foster, J. D., Campbell, W. K., & Twenge, J. M. (2003). Individual differences in narcissism: Inflated self-views across the lifespan and around the world. *Journal of Research in Personality, 37,* 469–486.

Freeman-Longo, R. E. (1986). The impact of sexual victimization on males. *Child Abuse & Neglect, 10,* 411–414.

Freud, S. (1962). *Three essays on the theory of sexuality* (J. Strachey, Trans.). New York: Avon Books. (Original work published 1905)

Freund, K. (1990). Courtship disorder. In W. L. Marshall, D. R. Laws, & H. E. Barbaree (Eds.), *Handbook of sexual assault: Issues, theories, and treatment of the offender* (pp. 195–207). New York: Plenum Press.

Freund, K., & Blanchard, R. (1986). The concept of courtship disorder. *Journal of Sex and Marital Therapy, 12,* 79–92.

Freund, K., & Kolarsky, A. (1965). Grundzuege eines einfachen Bezugsystems für die analyse sexualler Deviationen [Basic features of a reference system for considering anomalous erotic preferences]. *Psychiatrie, Neurologie, und medizinische Psychologie, 17,* 221–225.

Freund, K., & Kuban, M. (1994). The basis of the abused abuser theory of pedophilia: A further elaboration on an earlier study. *Archives of Sexual Behavior, 23,* 553–563.

Freund, K., Scher, H., & Hucker, S. (1983). The courtship disorders. *Archives of Sexual Behavior, 12,* 369–379.

Freund, K., Scher, H., & Hucker, S. (1984). The courtship disorders: A further investigation. *Archives of Sexual Behavior, 13,* 133–139.

Freund, K., & Seto, M. C. (1998). Preferential rape in the theory of courtship disorder. *Archives of Sexual Behavior, 27,* 433–443.

Freund, K., Seto, M. C., & Kuban, M. (1997). Frotteurism: Frotteurism and the theory of courtship disorder. In D. R. Laws & W. O'Donohue (Eds.), *Sexual deviance: Theory, assessment, and treatment* (pp. 111–130). New York: Guilford Press.

Freund, K., & Watson, R. (1990). Mapping the boundaries of courtship disorder. *Journal of Sex Research, 27,* 589–606.

Futterman, A., & Zirkel, S. (1992). Men are not born to rape. *Behavioral and Brain Sciences, 15,* 385–386.

Gabbard, G. O. (1994). *Psychodynamic psychiatry in clinical practice: The DSM–IV edition.* Washington, DC: American Psychiatric Press.

Gaffney, G. R., & Berlin, F. S. (1984). Is there hypothalamic–pituitary–gonadal dysfunction in pedophilia? A pilot study. *British Journal of Psychiatry, 145,* 657–660.

Gaffney, G. R., Lurie, S. F., & Berlin, F. S. (1984). Is there familial transmission of pedophilia? *Journal of Nervous and Mental Disease, 172,* 546–548.

Galski, T., Thornton, K. E., & Shumsky, D. (1990). Brain dysfunction in sex offenders. *Journal of Offender Rehabilitation, 16,* 65–79.

Gangestad, S. W., & Simpson, J. A. (2000). The evolution of human mating: Trade-offs and strategic pluralism. *Behavioral and Brain Sciences, 23,* 573–644.

Garb, H. M., Lilienfeld, S. O., & Wood, J. M. (2004). Projective techniques and behavioral assessment. In S. N. Haynes & E. M. Heiby (Eds.), *Comprehensive handbook of psychological assessment: Vol. 3. Behavioral assessment* (pp. 453–469). Hoboken, NJ: Wiley.

Gardner, E. L. (1992). Brain reward mechanisms. In J. H. Lowinson, P. Ruiz, R. B. Millman, & J. G. Langrod (Eds.), *Substance abuse: A comprehensive textbook* (2nd ed., pp. 70–99). Baltimore: Williams & Wilkins.

Gariepy, J. L., Lewis, M. H., & Cairns, R. B. (1996). Genes, neurobiology, and aggression: Time frames and functions of social behaviors in adaptation. In D. M. Stoff & R. B. Cairns (Eds.), *Aggression and violence: Genetic, neurobiological, and biosocial perspectives* (pp. 41–63). Mahwah, NJ: Erlbaum.

Garland, R. J., & Dougher, M. J. (1990). The abused/abuser hypothesis of child sexual abuse: A critical review of theory and research. In J. R. Feierman (Ed.), *Pedophilia: Biosocial dimensions* (pp. 488–509). New York: Springer-Verlag.

Geer, J. H., Estupinan, L. A., & Manguno-Mire, G. M. (2000). Empathy, social skills, and other relevant cognitive processes in rapists and child molesters. *Aggression and Violent Behavior, 5,* 99–126.

Gingrich, T. N., & Campbell, J. B. (1995). Personality characteristics of sexual offenders. *Sexual Addiction and Compulsivity, 2,* 54–61.

Glueck, S., & Glueck, E. (1950). *Unraveling juvenile delinquency.* Cambridge, MA: Harvard University Press.

Gold, S. N., & Heffner, C. L. (1998). Sexual addiction: Many conceptions, minimal data. *Clinical Psychology Review, 18,* 367–381.

Goldman, D. (1996). The search for genetic alleles contributing to self-destructive and aggressive behaviors. In D. M. Stoff & R. B. Cairns (Eds.), *Aggression and violence: Genetic, neurobiological, and biosocial perspectives* (pp. 23–40). Mahwah, NJ: Erlbaum.

Goodman, A. (1992). Sexual addiction: Designation and treatment. *Journal of Sex and Marital Therapy, 18,* 303–314.

Gottfredson, M. R., & Hirschi, T. (1990). *A general theory of crime*. Stanford, CA: Stanford University Press.

Gottfredson, M. R., & Hirschi, T. (1993). A control theory interpretation of psychological research on aggression. In R. B. Felson & J. T. Tedeschi (Eds.), *Aggression and violence: Social interactionist perspectives* (pp. 47–68). Washington, DC: American Psychological Association.

Gottfredson, M. R., & Hirschi, T. (1994). A general theory of adolescent problem behavior: Problems and prospects. In R. D. Ketterlinus & M. E. Lamb (Eds.), *Adolescent problem behaviors: Issues and research* (pp. 41–56). Hillsdale, NJ: Erlbaum.

Gottfredson, M. R., & Polakowski, M. (1995). Determinants and prevention of criminal behavior. In N. Brewer & C. Wilson (Eds.), *Psychology and policing* (pp. 63–79). Hillsdale, NJ: Erlbaum.

Graham, K. R. (1996). The childhood victimization of sex offenders: An underestimated issue. *International Journal of Offender Therapy and Comparative Criminology, 40*, 192–203.

Granic, I., & Patterson, G. R. (2006). Toward a comprehensive model of antisocial development: A dynamic systems approach. *Psychological Review, 113*, 101–131.

Grayston, A. D., & De Luca, R. V. (1999). Female perpetrators of child sexual abuse: A review of the clinical and empirical literature. *Aggression and Violent Behavior, 4*, 93–106.

Greenfield, L. A. (1997). *Sex offenses and offenders: An analysis of data on rape and sexual assault* (U.S. Department of Justice Report NCJ-163392). Washington, DC: U.S. Government Printing Office.

Grier, P. E., Clark, M., & Stoner, S. B. (1993). Comparative study of personality traits of female sex offenders. *Psychological Reports, 73*, 1378.

Gross, J. J. (1998). The emerging field of emotion regulation: An integrative review. *Review of General Psychology, 2*, 271–299.

Gross, J. J. (1999a). Emotion and emotion regulation. In L. A. Pervin & O. P. John (Eds.), *Handbook of personality: Theory and research* (2nd ed., pp. 225–252). New York: Guilford Press.

Gross, J. J. (1999b). Emotion regulation: Past, present, future. *Cognition & Emotion, 13*, 551–573.

Groth, A. N., & Hobson, W. F. (1997). The dynamics of sexual assault. In L. B. Schlesinger & E. Revitch (Eds.), *Sexual dynamics of anti-social behavior* (2nd ed., pp. 158–170). Springfield, IL: Charles C Thomas.

Gudjonsson, G. H. (1990). Self-deception and other-deception in forensic assessment. *Personality and Individual Differences, 11*, 219–225.

Haapasalo, J., & Kankkonen, M. (1997). Self-reported childhood abuse among sex and violent offenders. *Archives of Sexual Behavior, 26*, 421–431.

Hall, G. C. N., Graham, J. R., & Shepherd, J. B. (1991). Three methods of developing MMPI taxonomies of sexual offenders. *Journal of Personality Assessment, 56*, 2–13.

Hall, G. C. N., & Hirschman, R. (1991). Toward a theory of sexual aggression: A quadripartite model. *Journal of Consulting and Clinical Psychology, 59,* 662–669.

Hall, G. C. N., & Hirschman, R. (1992). Sexual aggression against children: A conceptual perspective of etiology. *Criminal Justice and Behavior, 19,* 8–23.

Hall, G. C. N., Shepherd, J. B., & Mudrak, P. (1992). MMPI taxonomies of child sexual and nonsexual offenders: A cross-validation and extension. *Journal of Personality Assessment, 58,* 127–137.

Hanish, L. D., Eisenberg, N., Fabes, F. A., Spinrad, R. L., Ryan, P., & Schmidt, S. (2004). The expression and regulation of negative emotions: Risk factors for young children's peer victimization. *Development and Psychopathology, 16,* 335–353.

Hanson, R. K. (1999). Working with sex offenders: A personal view. *Journal of Sexual Aggression, 4,* 81–93.

Hanson, R. K., Gizzarelli, R., & Scott, H. (1994). The attitudes of incest offenders: Sexual entitlement and acceptance of sex with children. *Criminal Justice and Behavior, 21,* 187–202.

Hanson, R. K., & Scott, H. (1995). Assessing perspective-taking among sexual offenders, nonsexual criminals, and nonoffenders. *Sexual Abuse: A Journal of Research and Treatment, 7,* 259–277.

Hanson, R. K., & Scott, H. (1996). Social networks of sexual offenders. *Psychology, Crime, and Law, 2,* 249–258.

Happe, F., & Frith, U. (1996). Theory of mind and social impairment in children with conduct disorder. *British Journal of Developmental Psychology, 14,* 385–398.

Happel, R. M., & Auffrey, J. J. (1995). Sex offender assessment: Interrupting the dance of denial. *American Journal of Forensic Psychology, 13*(2), 5–22.

Hare, R. D. (1991). *The Hare Psychopathy Checklist—Revised.* Toronto, Ontario, Canada: Multi-Health Systems.

Hare, R. D. (1999). *Without conscience: The disturbing world of the psychopaths among us.* New York: Guilford Press.

Hare, R. D., Cooke, D. J., & Hart, S. D. (1999). Psychopathy and sadistic personality disorder. In T. Millon & P. H. Blaney (Eds.), *Oxford textbook of psychopathology* (pp. 555–584). Oxford, England: Oxford University Press.

Hare, R. D., Forth, A. E., & Hart, S. D. (1989). The psychopath as prototype for pathological lying and deception. In J. C. Yuille (Ed.), *Credibility assessment* (pp. 25–49). New York: Kluwer Academic/Plenum Publishers.

Harrison, L. E., Clayton-Smith, J., & Bailey, S. (2001). Exploring the complex relationship between adolescent sexual offending and sex chromosome abnormality. *Psychiatric Genetics, 11,* 5–10.

Hart, S. D., & Dempster, R. J. (1997). Impulsivity and psychopathy. In C. D. Webster & M. A. Jackson (Eds.), *Impulsivity: Theory, assessment, and treatment* (pp. 212–232). New York: Guilford Press.

Heal, L. W., & Sigelman, C. K. (1995). Response biases in interviews of individuals with limited mental ability. *Journal of Intellectual Disability Research, 39,* 331–340.

Heersink, N., & Strassberg, D. S. (1995). A normative and descriptive study of the MMPI with acknowledged child molesters. *Journal of Psychopathology and Behavioral Assessment, 17,* 377–391.

Hendricks, S. E., Fitzpatrick, D. F., Hartmann, K., Quaife, M. A., Stratbucker, R. A., & Graber, B. (1988). Brain structure and function in sexual molesters of children and adolescents. *Journal of Clinical Psychiatry, 49,* 108–112.

Hendriks, J., & Bijleveld, C. C. J. H. (2004). Juvenile sexual delinquents: Contrasting child abusers with peer abusers. *Criminal Behavior and Mental Health, 14,* 238–250.

Henggeler, S. W., Schoenwald, S. K., Borduin, C. M., Rowland, M. D., & Cunningham, P. B. (1998). *Multisystemic treatment of antisocial behavior in children and adolescents.* New York: Guilford Press.

Henn, F. A., Herjanic, M., & Vanderpearl, R. H. (1976). Forensic psychiatry: Profiles of two types of sex offenders. *American Journal of Psychiatry, 133,* 694–696.

Herkov, M. J., Gynther, M. D., Thomas, S., & Myers, W. C. (1996). MMPI differences among adolescent inpatients, rapists, sodomists, and sexual abusers. *Journal of Personality Assessment, 66,* 81–90.

Herman, J. L. (1988). Considering sex offenders: A model of addiction. *Signs, 13,* 695–724.

Hicks, S. J., & Sales, B. D. (2006). *Criminal profiling: Developing an effective science and practice.* Washington, DC: American Psychological Association.

Hirschi, T. (2004). Self-control and crime. In R. F. Baumeister & K. D. Vohs (Eds.), *Handbook of self-regulation: Research, theory, and applications* (pp. 537–552). New York: Guilford Press.

Hirschi, T., & Gottfredson, M. R. (1995). Control theory and the life-course perspective. *Studies on Crime and Crime Prevention, 4,* 131–142.

Hirschi, T., & Stark, R. (1969). Hellfire and delinquency. *Social Problems, 17,* 202–212.

Holmes, J. (1995). "Something there is that doesn't love a wall": John Bowlby, attachment theory, and psychoanalysis. In S. Goldberg, R. Muir, & J. Kerr (Eds.), *Attachment theory: Social, developmental, and clinical perspectives* (pp. 19–43). Hillsdale, NJ: Analytic Press.

Holt, S. E., Meloy, J. R., & Strack, S. (1999). Sadism and psychopathy in violent and sexually violent offenders. *Journal of the American Academy of Psychiatry and the Law, 27,* 23–32.

Howells, K. (1981). Adult sexual interest in children: Considerations relevant to theories of aetiology. In M. Cook & K. Howells (Eds.), *Adult sexual interest in children* (pp. 55–98). London: Academic Press.

Howells, K. (1994). Child sexual abuse: Finkelhor's precondition model revisited. *Psychology, Crime, and Law, 1,* 201–214.

Howitt, D. (1995). Pornography and the paedophile: Is it criminogenic? *British Journal of Medical Psychology, 68,* 15–27.

Hucker, S., & Bain, J. (1990). Androgenic hormones and sexual assault. In W. L. Marshall & D. R. Laws (Eds.), *Handbook of sexual assault: Issues, theories, and treatment of the offender* (pp. 93–102). New York: Plenum Press.

Hucker, S., Langevin, R., Dickey, R., Handy, L., Chambers, J., Wright, S., et al. (1988). Cerebral damage and dysfunction in sexually aggressive men. *Annals of Sex Research, 1,* 33–47.

Hucker, S., Langevin, R., Wortzman, G., Bain, J., Handy, L., Chambers, J., & Wright, S. (1986). Neuropsychological impairment in pedophiles. *Canadian Journal of Behavioral Science, 18,* 440–448.

Hudson, S. M., Marshall, W. L., Wales, D., McDonald, E., Bakker, L. W., & McLean, A. (1993). Emotional recognition skills of sex offenders. *Annals of Sex Research, 6,* 199–211.

Huesmann, L. R., Moise-Titus, J., Podolski, C. L., & Eron, L. D. (2003). Longitudinal relations between children's exposure to TV violence and their aggressive and violent behavior in young adulthood: 1977–1992. *Developmental Psychology, 29,* 201–221.

Hummel, P., Thomke, V., Oldenburger, H. A., & Specht, F. (2000). Male adolescent sex offenders against children: Similarities and differences between those offenders with and those without a history of sexual abuse. *Journal of Adolescence, 23,* 305–317.

Hunsley, J., Lee, C. M., & Wood, J. M. (2003). Controversial and questionable assessment techniques. In S. O. Lilienfeld, S. J. Lynn, & J. M. Lohr (Eds.), *Science and pseudoscience in clinical psychology* (pp. 39–76). New York: Guilford Press.

Hunter, J. A., Jr., & Becker, J. V. (1994). The role of deviant sexual arousal in juvenile sexual offending: Etiology, evaluation, and treatment. *Criminal Justice and Behavior, 21,* 132–149.

Hunter, J. A., Jr., & Figueredo, A. J. (2000). The influence of personality and history of sexual victimization in the prediction of juvenile perpetrated child molestation. *Behavior Modification, 24,* 241–263.

Isaac, J. (2006, January 7). Probation revoked for man who admits to sex acts in car. *Longview (Texas) News-Journal.* Retrieved from http://www.news-journal.com

Itzin, C. (2002). Pornography and the construction of misogyny. *Journal of Sexual Aggression, 8*(3), 4–42.

Izard, C. E., & Kobak, R. R. (1991). Emotions system functioning and emotion regulation. In J. Garber & K. A. Dodge (Eds.), *The development of emotion regulation and dysregulation* (pp. 303–321). Cambridge, England: Cambridge University Press.

Johansson-Love, J., & Fremouw, W. (2006). A critique of the female sexual perpetrator research. *Aggression and Violent Behavior, 11,* 12–26.

Johnson, B. E., Kuck, D. L., & Schander, P. R. (1997). Rape myth acceptance and sociodemographic characteristics: A multidimensional analysis. *Sex Roles, 36,* 693–707.

Johnston, L., & Ward, T. (1996). Social cognition and sexual offending: A theoretical framework. *Sexual Abuse: A Journal of Research and Treatment, 8*, 55–80.

Joireman, J., Anderson, J., & Strathman, A. (2003). The aggression paradox: Understanding links among aggression, sensation seeking, and the consideration of future consequences. *Journal of Personality and Social Psychology, 84*, 1287–1302.

Jones, O. D. (1999). Sex, culture, and the biology of rape: Toward explanation and prevention. *California Law Review, 87*, 829–941.

Jonson-Reid, J., & Way, I. (2001). Adolescent sexual offenders: Incidence of childhood maltreatment, serious emotional disturbance, and prior offenses. *American Journal of Orthopsychiatry, 71*, 120–130.

Kafka, M. P. (1995). Sexual impulsivity. In E. Hollander & D. J. Stein (Eds.), *Impulsivity and aggression* (pp. 201–228). Chichester, England: Wiley.

Kafka, M. P. (1997). A monoamine hypothesis for the pathophysiology of paraphilic disorders. *Archives of Sexual Behavior, 26*, 343–358.

Kafka, M. P. (2003). Sex offending and sexual appetite: The clinical and theoretical relevance of hypersexual desire. *International Journal of Offender Therapy and Comparative Criminology, 47*, 439–451.

Kafka, M. P., & Prentky, R. A. (1994). Preliminary observations of *DSM–III–R* Axis I comorbidity in men with paraphilias and paraphilia-related disorders. *Journal of Clinical Psychiatry, 55*, 481–487.

Kaplan, M. S., & Becker, J. V. (1992). Adolescent perpetrators of incest. In R. T. Ammerman & M. Hersen (Eds.), *Assessment of family violence: A clinical and legal sourcebook* (pp. 332–347). Oxford, England: Wiley.

Kaufman, K. L., Hilliker, D. R., Lathrop, P., & Daleiden, E. L. (1993). Assessing child sexual offenders' modus operandi: Accuracy in self-reported use of threats and coercion. *Annals of Sex Research, 6*, 213–299.

Kaufman, K. L., Hilliker, D. R., Lathrop, P., & Daleiden, E. L. (1996). Sexual offenders' modus operandi: A comparison of structured interview and questionnaire approaches. *Journal of Interpersonal Violence, 11*, 19–34.

Keenan, T., & Ward, T. (2000). A theory of mind perspective on cognitive, affective, and intimacy deficits in child sexual offenders. *Sexual Abuse: A Journal of Research and Treatment, 12*, 49–60.

Kenan, M. M., Kendjelic, E. M., & Molinari, V. A. (2000). Age-related differences in the frequency of personality disorders among inpatient veterans. *International Journal of Geriatric Psychiatry, 15*, 831–837.

Kennair, L. E. O. (2003). Evolutionary psychology and psychopathology. *Current Opinions in Psychiatry, 16*, 691–699.

Kennedy, H. G., & Grubin, D. H. (1992). Patterns of denial in sex offenders. *Psychological Medicine, 22*, 191–196.

Kernberg, O. F. (1976). *Object-relations theory and clinical psychoanalysis*. New York: Jason Aronson.

Kernberg, O. F. (1995). *Love relations: Normality and pathology*. New Haven, CT: Yale University Press.

Kimmel, M. (2003). An unnatural history of rape. In C. Travis (Ed.), *Evolution, gender, and rape* (pp. 219–233). Cambridge, MA: MIT Press.

Kirsch, L. G., & Becker, J. V. (2006). Sexual offending: Theory of problem, theory of change, and implications for treatment effectiveness. *Aggression and Violent Behavior, 11*, 208–224.

Klinteberg, B. A. (1996). Biology, norms, and personality: A developmental perspective. *Neuropsychobiology, 34*, 146–154.

Knight, R. A., & Prentky, R. A. (1990). Classifying sexual offenders. In W. L. Marshall, D. R. Laws, & H. E. Barbaree (Eds.), *Handbook of sexual assault* (pp. 23–52). New York: Plenum Press.

Knudsen, D. D. (1988). Child sexual abuse and pornography: Is there a relationship? *Journal of Family Violence, 3*, 253–267.

Kobayashi, J., Sales, B. D., Becker, J. V., Figueredo, A. J., & Kaplan, M. S. (1995). Perceived parental deviance, parent–child bonding, child abuse, and child sexual aggression. *Sexual Abuse: A Journal of Research and Treatment, 7*, 25–44.

Kopp, C. B. (1992). Emotional distress and control in young children. *New Directions for Child Development, 55*, 41–56.

Koss, M. P. (2003). Evolutionary models of why men rape: Acknowledging the complexities. In C. Travis (Ed.), *Evolution, gender, and rape* (pp. 191–205). Cambridge, MA: MIT Press.

Krafft-Ebing, R. F. von (1997). *Psychopathia sexualis* (D. Falls, Trans.). London: Velvet Publications. (Original work published 1886)

Kubzansky, L. D., Martin, L. T., & Buka, S. L. (2004). Early manifestations of personality and adult emotional functioning. *Emotion, 4*, 364–377.

La Fond, J. Q. (2005). *Preventing sexual violence: How society should cope with sex offenders.* Washington, DC: American Psychological Association.

Lahey, B. B., McBurnett, K., & Loeber, R. (2000). Are attention-deficit/hyperactivity disorder and oppositional defiant disorder developmental precursors to conduct disorder? In A. J. Sameroff, M. Lewis, & S. M. Miller (Eds.), *Handbook of developmental psychopathology* (2nd ed., pp. 431–446). New York: Kluwer Academic/PlenumPublishers.

Lahey, K. A. (1991). Pornography and harm: Learning to listen to women. *International Journal of Law & Psychiatry, 14*, 117–131.

Lalumiere, M. L., Chalmers, L. J., Quinsey, V. L., & Seto, M. C. (1996). A test of the mate deprivation hypothesis of sexual coercion. *Ethology and Sociobiology, 17*, 299–318.

Lalumiere, M. L., Harris, G. T., Quinsey, V. L., & Rice, M. E. (2005). *The causes of rape: Understanding individual differences in male propensity for sexual aggression.* Washington, DC: American Psychological Association.

Lalumiere, M. L., & Quinsey, V. L. (1994). The discriminability of rapists from non-sex offenders using phallometric measures: A meta-analysis. *Criminal Justice and Behavior, 21*, 150–175.

Lalumiere, M. L., & Quinsey, V. L. (1996). Sexual deviance, antisociality, mating effort, and the use of sexually coercive behaviors. *Personality and Individual Differences, 21,* 33–48.

Lang, R. A. (1993). Neuropsychological deficits in sexual offenders: Implications for treatment. *Sexual and Marital Therapy, 8,* 181–200.

Lang, R. A., Flor-Henry, P., & Frenzel, R. R. (1990). Sex hormone profiles in pedophilic and incestuous men. *Annals of Sex Research, 3,* 59–74.

Langevin, R., Bain, J., Wortzman, G., Hucker, S., Dickey, R., & Wright, P. (1988). Sexual sadism: Brain, blood, and behavior. In R. A. Prentky & V. L. Quinsey (Eds.), *Annals of the New York Academy of Sciences: Vol. 528. Human sexual aggression: Current perspectives* (pp. 163–171). New York: New York Academy of Sciences.

Langevin, R., & Lang, R. A. (1990). Substance abuse among sex offenders. *Annals of Sex Research, 3,* 397–424.

Langevin, R., Lang, R., Reynolds, R., Wright, P., Garrels, D., Marchese, V., et al. (1988). Personality and sexual anomalies: An examination of the Millon Clinical Multiaxial Inventory. *Annals of Sex Research, 1,* 13–32.

Langevin, R., Lang, R. A., Wright, P., Handy, L., Frenzel, R. R., & Black, E. L. (1988). Pornography and sexual offenses. *Annals of Sex Research, 1,* 335–362.

Langevin, R., Paitich, D., Freeman, R., Mann, K., & Handy, L. (1978). Personality characteristics and sexual anomalies in males. *Canadian Journal of Behavioral Science, 10,* 222–238.

Langevin, R., Wortzman, G., Dickey, R., Wright, P., & Handy, L. (1988). Neuropsychological impairment in incest offenders. *Annals of Sex Research, 1,* 401–415.

Langevin, R., Wortzman, G., Wright, P., & Handy, L. (1989). Studies of brain damage and dysfunction in sex offenders. *Annals of Sex Research, 2,* 163–179.

Langevin, R., Wright, P., & Handy, L. (1989). Characteristics of sex offenders who were sexually victimized as children. *Annals of Sex Research, 2,* 227–253.

Larsen, R. J., & Buss, D. M. (2002). Personality psychology: Domains of knowledge about human behavior. New York: McGraw-Hill.

Larsen, R. J., & Prizmic, Z. (2004). Affect regulation. In R. F. Baumeister & K. D. Vohs (Eds.), *Handbook of self-regulation: Research, theory, and applications* (pp. 40–61). New York: Guilford Press.

Laws, D. R. (2003). The rise and fall of relapse prevention. *Australian Psychologist, 38,* 22–30.

Leary, M. R. (2004). The sociometer, self-esteem, and the regulation of interpersonal behavior. In R. F. Baumeister & K. D. Vohs (Eds.), *Handbook of self-regulation: Research, theory, and applications* (pp. 373–391). New York: Guilford Press.

Leguizamo, A. (2002). The object relations and victimization histories of juvenile sex offenders. In B. K. Schwartz (Ed.), *The sex offender: Current treatment modalities and systems issues* (Vol. IV, pp. 4-1–4-39). Kingston, NJ: Civic Research Institute.

Levin, S. M., & Stava, L. (1987). Personality characteristics of sex offenders: A review. *Archives of Sexual Behavior, 16,* 57–79.

Lewis, C. F., & Stanley, C. R. (2000). Women accused of sexual offenses. *Behavioral Sciences and the Law, 18,* 73–81.

Lilienfeld, S. O., Wood, J. M., & Garb, H. M. (2000). The scientific status of projective techniques. *Psychological Science in the Public Interest, 1,* 27–66.

Linehan, M. M. (1993a). *Cognitive–behavioral treatment of borderline personality disorder.* New York: Guilford Press.

Linehan, M. M. (1993b). *Skills training manual for treating borderline personality disorder.* New York: Guilford Press.

Linz, D. G., Donnerstein, E., & Penrod, S. (1988). Effects of long-term exposure to violent and sexually degrading depictions of women. *Journal of Personality and Social Psychology, 55,* 758–768.

Lloyd, E. A. (2003). Violence against science: Rape and evolution. In C. Travis (Ed.), *Evolution, gender, and rape* (pp. 235–261). Cambridge, MA: MIT Press.

Lochman, J. E. (1987). Self and peer perceptions and attributional biases of aggressive and nonaggressive boys in dyadic interactions. *Journal of Consulting and Clinical Psychology, 55,* 404–410.

Lockhart, L. L., Saunders, B. E., & Cleveland, P. (1988). Adult male sexual offenders: An overview of treatment techniques. *Journal of Social Work and Human Sexuality, 7*(2), 1–32.

Looman, J., & Marshall, W. L. (2005). Sexual arousal in rapists. *Criminal Justice and Behavior, 32,* 367–389.

Losada-Paisey, G. (1998). Use of the MMPI–A to assess personality of juvenile male delinquents who are sex offenders and nonsex offenders. *Psychological Reports, 83,* 115–122.

Lundy, J. P. (1994). Behavior patterns that comprise sexual addiction as identified by mental health professionals. *Sexual Addiction and Compulsivity, 1,* 46–56.

Lusk, R., & Waterman, J. (1986). Effects of sexual abuse on children. In K. MacFarlane, J. Waterman, S. Conerly, L. Damon, M. Durfee, & S. Long (Eds), *Sexual abuse of young children: Evaluation and treatment* (pp. 101–120). New York: Guilford Press.

Lussier, P., Proulx, J., & McKibben, A. (2001). Personality characteristics and adaptive emotional states and deviant sexual fantasies in sexual aggressors. *International Journal of Offender Therapy and Comparative Criminology, 45,* 159–170.

Lyn, T. S., & Burton, D. L. (2004). Adult attachment and sexual offender status. *American Journal of Orthopsychiatry, 74,* 150–159.

Lynch, J. (2004a, April 17). Gladewater twins behind bars again. *Longview (Texas) News-Journal.* Retrieved from http://www.news-journal.com

Lynch, J. (2004b, April 15). Man accused of peeping at teen in dressing room. *Longview (Texas) News-Journal.* Retrieved from http://www.news-journal.com

Lynch, J. (2004c, May 7). Registered sex offender accused of molestation. *Longview (Texas) News-Journal.* Retrieved from http://www.news-journal.com

Malamuth, N. M. (1981). Rape proclivity among males. *Journal of Social Issues*, *37*, 138–157.

Malamuth, N. M. (1996). The confluence model of sexual aggression: Feminist and evolutionary perspectives. In D. M. Buss & N. M. Malamuth (Eds.), *Sex, power, conflict: Evolutionary and feminist perspectives* (pp. 269–295). New York: Oxford University Press.

Malamuth, N. M. (1998a). The confluence model as an organizing framework for research on sexually aggressive men: Risk moderators, imagined aggression, and pornography consumption. In R. G. Geen & E. Donnerstein (Eds.), *Human aggression: Theories, research, and implications for social policy* (pp. 229–245). San Diego, CA: Academic Press.

Malamuth, N. M. (1998b). An evolutionary-based model integrating research on the characteristics of sexually coercive men. In J. G. Adair, D. Belanger, & K. L. Dion (Eds.), *Advances in psychological science: Vol. 1. Social, personal, and cultural aspects* (pp. 151–184). Hove, England: The International Union of Psychological Science.

Malamuth, N. M., & Brown, L. M. (1994). Sexually aggressive men's perceptions of women's communications: Testing three explanations. *Journal of Personality and Social Psychology*, *67*, 699–712.

Malamuth, N. M., & Check, J. V. P. (1980). Penile tumescence and perceptual responses to rape as a function of victim's perceived reactions. *Journal of Applied Social Psychology*, *10*, 528–547.

Malamuth, N. M., & Check, J. V. P. (1981). The effects of mass media exposure on acceptance of violence against women: A field experiment. *Journal of Research in Personality*, *15*, 436–446.

Malamuth, N. M., & Check, J. V. P. (1985). The effects of aggressive pornography on beliefs in rape myths: Individual differences. *Journal of Research in Personality*, *19*, 299–320.

Malamuth, N. M., Heavey, C. L., & Linz, D. (1993). Predicting men's antisocial behavioral against women: The interaction model of sexual aggression. In G. C. N. Hall, R. Hirschman, J. R. Graham, & M. S. Zaragoza (Eds.), *Sexual aggression: Issues in etiology, assessment, and treatment* (pp. 63–97). Philadelphia: Taylor & Francis.

Malamuth, N. M., & Heilmann, M. F. (1998). Evolutionary psychology and sexual aggression. In C. Crawford & D. L. Krebs (Eds.), *Handbook of evolutionary psychology: Ideas, issues, and applications* (pp. 515–542). Mahwah, NJ: Erlbaum.

Malamuth, N. M., Linz, D., Heavey, C. L., Barnes, G., & Acker, M. (1995). Using the confluence model of sexual aggression to predict men's conflict with women: A 10-year follow-up study. *Journal of Personality and Social Psychology*, *69*, 353–369.

Malamuth, N. M., Sockloskie, R. J., Koss, M. P., & Tanaka, J. S. (1991). Characteristics of aggressors against women: Testing a model using a national sample of college students. *Journal of Consulting and Clinical Psychology*, *59*, 670–681.

Malatesta-Magai, C. (1991). Development of emotion expression during infancy: General course and patterns of individual difference. In J. Garber & K. A. Dodge (Eds.), *The development of emotion regulation and dysregulation* (pp. 49–68). Cambridge, England: Cambridge University Press.

Maletzky, B. M. (1993). Factors associated with success and failure in the behavioral and cognitive treatment of sexual offenders. *Annals of Sex Research, 6,* 241–258.

Mann, J., Sidman, J., & Starr, S. (1973). Evaluating social consequences of erotic films: An experimental approach. *Journal of Social Issues, 29,* 113–131.

Marieb, E. N. (2001). *Human anatomy and physiology* (5th ed.). New York: Addison Wesley Longman.

Marlatt, G. A., Baer, J. S., Donovan, D. M., & Kivlahan, D. R. (1988). Addictive behaviors: Etiology and treatment. *Annual Review of Psychology, 39,* 223–252.

Marlatt, G. A., & Gordon, J. R. (Eds.). (1985). *Relapse prevention.* New York: Guilford Press.

Marques, J. K., Day, D. M., & Nelson, C. (1994). Effects of cognitive–behavioral treatment on sex offender recidivism: Preliminary results of a longitudinal study. *Criminal Justice & Behavior, 21,* 28–54.

Marques, J. K., Wiederanders, M., Day, D. M., Nelson, C., & van Ommeren, A. (2005). Effects of a relapse prevention program on sexual recidivism: Final results from California's Sex Offender Treatment and Evaluation Project (SOTEP). *Sexual Abuse: A Journal of Research and Treatment, 17,* 79–107.

Marshall, W. L. (1988). The use of sexually explicit stimuli by rapists, child molesters, and nonoffenders. *Journal of Sex Research, 25,* 267–288.

Marshall, W. L. (1989). Intimacy, loneliness, and sexual offenders. *Behaviour Research and Therapy, 27,* 491–504.

Marshall, W. L. (1993). The role of attachments, intimacy, and loneliness in the etiology and maintenance of sex offending. *Sexual and Marital Therapy, 8,* 109–121.

Marshall, W. L. (1997). The relationship between self-esteem and deviant sexual arousal in nonfamilial child molesters. *Behavior Modification, 21,* 86–96.

Marshall, W. L. (2000). Revisiting the use of pornography by sexual offenders: Implications for theory and practice. *Journal of Sexual Aggression, 6,* 67–77.

Marshall, W. L., Anderson, D., & Champagne, F. (1997). Self-esteem and its relationship to sexual offending. *Psychology, Crime, & Law, 3,* 161–186.

Marshall, W. L., Anderson, D., & Fernandez, Y. M. (1999). *Cognitive behavioural treatment of sexual offenders.* Chichester, England: Wiley.

Marshall, W. L., & Barbaree, H. E. (1990). An integrated theory of the etiology of sexual offending. In W. L. Marshall, D. R. Laws, & H. E. Barbaree (Eds.), *Handbook of sexual assault: Issues, theories, and treatment of the offender* (pp. 257–275). New York: Plenum Press.

Marshall, W. L., & Eccles, A. (1993). Pavlovian conditioning processes in adolescent sex offenders. In H. E. Barbaree & W. L. Marshall (Eds.), *The juvenile sex offender* (pp. 118–142). New York: Guilford Press.

Marshall, W. L., & Eccles, A. (1996). Cognitive–behavioral treatment of sex offenders. In V. B. Van Hasselt & M. Hersen (Eds.), *Sourcebook of psychological treatment manuals for adult disorders* (pp. 295–332). New York: Plenum Press.

Marshall, W. L., & Fernandez, Y. M. (1998). Cognitive–behavioral approaches to the treatment of the paraphilias: Sexual offenders. In V. E. Caballo (Ed.), *International handbook of cognitive and behavioral treatments for psychological disorders* (pp. 281–312). Oxford, England: Pergamon/Elsevier Science.

Marshall, W. L., Hudson, S. M., Jones, R., & Fernandez, Y. M. (1995). Empathy in sex offenders. *Clinical Psychology Review, 15*, 99–113.

Marshall, W. L., Laws, D. R., & Barbaree, H. E. (1990). *Handbook of sexual assault: Issues, theories, and treatment of the offender.* New York: Plenum Press.

Marshall, W. L., & Marshall, L. E. (2000). The origins of sex offending. *Trauma, Violence, and Abuse, 1*, 250–263.

Marshall, W. L., & Mazzucco, A. (1995). Self-esteem and parental attachments in child molesters. *Sexual Abuse: A Journal of Research and Treatment, 7*, 279–285.

Masterson, J. (1984). The effects of erotica and pornography on attitudes and behavior: A review. *Bulletin of the British Psychological Society, 37*, 249–252.

Maughan, A., & Cicchetti, D. (2002). Impact of child maltreatment and interadult violence on children's emotion regulation abilities and socioemotional adjustment. *Child Development, 73*, 1525–1542.

McCabe, L. A., Cunnington, M., & Brooks-Gunn, J. (2004). The development of self-regulation in young children: Individual characteristics and environmental contexts. In R. F. Baumeister & K. D. Vohs (Eds.), *Handbook of self-regulation: Research, theory, and applications* (pp. 340–356). New York: Guilford Press.

McCreary, C. P. (1975). Personality differences among child molesters. *Journal of Personality Assessment, 39*, 591–593.

McElroy, S. L., Soutullo, C. A., Taylor, P., Nelson, E. B., Beckman, D. A., Brusman, L. A., et al. (1999). Psychiatric features of 36 men convicted of sexual offenses. *Journal of Clinical Psychiatry, 60*, 414–420.

McFall, R. M. (1990). An enhancement of social skills: An information-processing analysis. In W. L. Marshall, D. R. Laws, & H. E. Barbaree (Eds.), *Handbook of sexual assault: Issues, theories, and treatment of the offender* (pp. 311–329). New York: Plenum Press.

McGrath, R. J., Cumming, G., & Livingston, J. A. (2003). Outcome of a treatment program for adult sex offenders: From prison to community. *Journal of Interpersonal Violence, 18*, 3–17.

McGrath, R. J., Hoke, S. E., & Vojtisek, J. E. (1998). Cognitive–behavioral treatment of sex offenders. *Criminal Justice & Behavior, 25*, 203–225.

McGuire, R. J., Carlisle, J. M., & Young, B. G. (1964). Sexual deviations as conditioned behaviour: A hypothesis. *Behaviour Research and Therapy, 2*, 185–195.

McKay, M. M., Chapman, J. W., & Long, N. R. (1996). Causal attributions for criminal offending and sexual arousal: Comparison of child sex offenders with other offenders. *British Journal of Clinical Psychology, 35*, 63–75.

McKim, W. A. (2000). *Drugs and behavior: An introduction to behavioral pharmacology* (4th ed.). Upper Saddle River, NJ: Prentice Hall.

Meesters, C., Merckelbach, H., Muris, P., & Wessel, I. (2000). Autobiographical memory and trauma in adolescents. *Journal of Behavior Therapy and Experimental Psychiatry, 31,* 29–39.

Melton, A. W. (1964). *Categories of human learning.* Oxford, England: Academic Press.

Miller, G. F. (1998). How mate choice shaped human nature: A review of sexual selection and human evolution. In C. Crawford & D. L. Krebs (Eds.), *Handbook of evolutionary psychology: Ideas, issues, and applications* (pp. 87–129). Mahwah, NJ: Erlbaum.

Millon, T., & Davis, R. D. (1996). *Disorders of personality: DSM–IV and beyond* (2nd ed.). New York: Wiley.

Millon, T., Davis, R. D., & Millon, C. (1997). *Millon Clinical Multiaxial Inventory—III manual* (2nd ed.). Minneapolis, MN: NCS Pearson.

Miner, M. H., & Munns, R. (2005). Isolation and normlessness: Attitudinal comparisons of adolescent sex offenders, juvenile offenders, and nondelinquents. *International Journal of Offender Therapy and Comparative Criminology, 49,* 491–504.

Mio, J. S., Nanjundappa, G., Verleur, D. E., & de Rios, M. D. (1986). Drug abuse and the adolescent sex offender: A preliminary analysis. *Journal of Psychoactive Drugs, 18,* 65–72.

Moffitt, T. E. (1993). Adolescence-limited and life-course-persistent antisocial behavior: A developmental taxonomy. *Psychological Review, 100,* 674–701.

Molinari, V., Kunik, M. E., & Snow-Turek, A. L. (1999). Age-related personality differences in inpatients with personality disorder: A cross-sectional study. *Journal of Clinical Geropsychology, 5,* 191–202.

Moody, E. E., Jr., Brissie, J., & Kim, J. (1994). Personality and background characteristics of adolescent sexual offenders. *Journal of Addictions and Offender Counseling, 14,* 38–48.

Morey, L. C. (1991). *Personality Assessment Inventory: Professional manual.* Odessa, FL: Psychological Assessment Resources.

Murphy, W. D. (1990). Assessment and modification of cognitive distortions in sex offenders. In W. L. Marshall, D. R. Laws, & H. E. Barbaree (Eds.), *Handbook of sexual assault: Issues, theories, and treatment of the offender* (pp. 331–342). New York: Plenum Press.

Murray, G. C., McKenzie, K., Quigley, A., Matheson, E., Michie, A. M., & Lindsay, W. R. (2001). A comparison of the neuropsychological profiles of adult male sex offenders and non-offenders with a learning disability. *Journal of Sexual Aggression, 7,* 57–64.

Nadler, R. D. (1988). Sexual aggression in the great apes. In R. A. Prentky & V. L. Quinsey (Eds.), *Annals of the New York Academy of Sciences: Vol. 528. Human* sexual aggression: Current perspectives (pp. 154–162). New York: New York Academy of Sciences.

Nathan, P., & Ward, T. (2002). Female sex offenders: Clinical and demographic features. *Journal of Sexual Aggression, 8,* 5–21.

National Clearinghouse on Family Violence. (1998). *Addressing the needs of developmentally delayed sex offenders: A guide.* Ottawa, Ontario, Canada: Minister of Public Works and Government Services.

Neidigh, L., & Krop, H. (1992). Cognitive distortions among child sexual offenders. *Journal of Sex Education and Therapy, 18,* 208–215.

Nelson, C. (1993). The hierarchical organization of behavior: A useful feedback model of self-regulation. *Current Directions in Psychological Science, 2,* 121–126.

Nelson, C., Miner, M., Marques, J., Russell, K., & Achterkirchen, J. (1989). Relapse prevention: A cognitive–behavioral model for treatment of the rapist and child molester. *Journal of Social Work and Human Sexuality, 7,* 1–32.

Nestor, P. G. (2002). Mental disorder and violence: Personality dimensions and critical features. *American Journal of Psychiatry, 159,* 1973–1978.

Newell, L. A. (2002a, September 25). Rape suspect Selby arrested in Colorado. *Arizona Daily Star.* Retrieved from http://www.azstarnet.com

Newell, L. A. (2002b, September 26). States sprint for extradition. *Arizona Daily Star.* Retrieved from http://www.azstarnet.com

Nisbet, I. A., Wilson, P. H., & Smallbone, S. W. (2004). A prospective longitudinal study of sexual recidivism among adolescent sexual offenders. *Sexual Abuse: A Journal of Research and Treatment, 16,* 223–234.

Noffsinger, S. G., & Resnick, P. J. (2000). Sexual predator laws and offenders with addictions. *Psychiatric Annals, 30,* 602–608.

Norris, J. (1991). Social influence effects on responses to sexually explicit material containing violence. *Journal of Sex Research, 28,* 67–76.

Nugent, P. M., & Kroner, D. G. (1996). Denial, response styles, and admittance of offenses among child molesters and rapists. *Journal of Interpersonal Violence, 11,* 475–486.

Nussbaum, D., Collins, M., Cutier, J., Zimmerman, W., Farguson, B., & Jacques, I. (2002). Crime type and specific personality indicia: Cloninger's TCI impulsivity, empathy, and attachment subscales in non-violent, violent, and sexual offenders. *American Journal of Forensic Psychology, 20,* 23–56.

O'Callaghan, D. (1998). Practice issues in working with young abusers who have learning disabilities. *Child Abuse Review, 7,* 435–448.

Oliver, L. L., Hall, G. C. N., & Neuhaus, S. M. (1993). A comparison of the personality and background characteristics of adolescent sex offenders and other adolescent offenders. *Criminal Justice and Behavior, 20,* 359–370.

Palermo, G. B. (2002). A dynamic formulation of sex offender behavior and its therapeutic relevance. *Journal of Forensic Psychology Practice, 2,* 25–51.

Palmer, C. T. (1991). Human rape: Adaptation or by-product? *Journal of Sex Research, 28,* 365–386.

Palmer, C. T. (1992). The use and abuse of Darwinian psychology: Its impact on attempts to determine the evolutionary basis of rape. *Ethology and Sociobiology, 13*, 289–299.

Parkinson, P. N., Shrimpton, S., Oates, R. K., Swanston, H. Y., & O'Toole, B. I. (2004). Nonsex offences committed by child molesters: Findings from a longitudinal study. *International Journal of Offender Therapy and Comparative Criminology, 48*, 28–39.

Parks, E. D., & Balon, R. (1995). Autobiographical memory for childhood events: Patterns of recall in psychiatric patients with a history of alleged trauma. *Psychiatry: Interpersonal and Biological Processes, 58*, 199–208.

Pavlov, I. (1927). *Conditioned reflexes.* New York: Oxford University Press.

Pearson, M. M., & Little, R. B. (1969). The addictive process in unusual addictions: A further elaboration of etiology. *American Journal of Psychiatry, 125*, 1166–1171.

Piaget, J. (1977). *The essential Piaget.* New York: Basic Books.

Ponseti, J., Vaih-Koch, S. R., & Bosinski, H. A. G. (2001). On the etiology of sexual delinquency: Neuropsychological parameters and co-morbidity. *Sexuologie, 8*, 65–77.

Porter, S., Campbell, M. A., Woodworth, M., & Birt, A. R. (2001). A new psychological conceptualization of the sexual psychopath. In F. Columbus (Ed.), *Advances in psychology research* (Vol. 7, pp. 21–36). Huntington, NY: Nova Science.

Prentky, R. A., & Knight, R. A. (1991). Identifying critical dimensions for discriminating among rapists. *Journal of Consulting and Clinical Psychology, 59*, 643–661.

Prescott, L., Harley, J. P., & Klein, D. A. (2005). *Microbiology.* New York: McGraw-Hill.

Price, M., Gutheil, T. G., Commons, M. L., Kafka, M. P., & Dodd-Kimmey, S. (2001). Telephone scatologia: Comorbidity and theories of etiology. *Psychiatric Annals, 31*, 226–232.

Purves, D., Augustine, G. J., Fitzpatrick, D., Katz, L. C., LaMantia, A. S., & McNamara, J. O. (Eds.). (1997). *Neuroscience.* Sunderland, MA: Sinauer Associates.

Putnam, F. W. (2003). Ten-year research update review: Child sexual abuse. *Journal of the American Academy of Child and Adolescent Psychiatry, 42*, 269–278.

Quayle, M., Deu, N., & Giblin, S. (1998). Sexual knowledge and sex education in a secure hospital setting. *Criminal Behaviour and Mental Health, 8*(Suppl.), 66–76.

Quinsey, V. L., & Lalumiere, M. L. (1995). Evolutionary perspectives on sexual offending. *Sexual Abuse: A Journal of Research and Treatment, 7*, 301–315.

Racey, B. D., Lopez, N. L., & Schneider, H. G. (2000). Sexually assaultive adolescents: Cue perception, interpersonal competence, and cognitive distortions. *International Journal of Adolescence and Youth, 8*, 229–239.

Raes, F., Hermans, D., Williams, J., & Eelen, P. (2005). Autobiographical memory specificity and emotional abuse. *British Journal of Clinical Psychology, 44*, 133–138.

Raine, A., & Buchsbaum, M. S. (1996). Violence, brain imaging, and neuropsychology. In D. M. Stoff & R. B. Cairns (Eds.), *Aggression and violence: Genetic, neurobiological, and biosocial perspectives* (pp. 195–217). Mahwah, NJ: Erlbaum.

Raver, C. C. (2004). Placing emotional self-regulation in sociocultural and socioeconomic contexts. *Child Development, 75*, 346–353.

Raymond, N. C., Coleman, E., Ohlerking, F., Christenson, G. A., & Miner, M. (1999). Psychiatric comorbidity in pedophilic sex offenders. *American Journal of Psychology, 156*, 786–788.

Reid, W. H. (1995). Impulsivity and aggression in antisocial personality. In E. Hollander & D. J. Stein (Eds.), *Impulsivity and aggression* (pp. 175–182). Chichester, England: Wiley.

Rhee, S. H., & Waldman, I. D. (2002). Genetic and environmental influences on antisocial behavior: A meta-analysis of twin and adoption studies. *Psychological Bulletin, 128*, 490–529.

Rice, M. E., Chaplin, T. C., Harris, G. T., & Coutts, J. (1994). Empathy for the victim and sexual arousal among rapists and nonrapists. *Journal of Interpersonal Violence, 9*, 435–449.

Righthand, S., & Welch, C. (2004). Characteristics of youth who sexually offend. *Journal of Child Sexual Abuse, 13*, 15–32.

Rind, B., Tromovitch, P., & Bauserman, R. (1998). A meta-analytic examination of assumed properties of child sexual abuse using college samples. *Psychological Bulletin, 124*, 22–53.

Rogers, R., & Cruise, K. R. (2000). Malingering and deception among psychopaths. In C. B. Gacono (Ed.), *Clinical and forensic assessment of psychopathy: A practitioner's guide* (pp. 269–284). Mahwah, NJ: Erlbaum.

Roshier, B. (1989). *Controlling crime: The classical perspective in criminology.* Chicago: Lyceum Books.

Rothbart, M. K., Ziaie, H., & O'Boyle, C. G. (1992). Self-regulation and emotion in infancy. *New Directions for Child Development, 55*, 7–23.

Ryan, G. (2002). Victims who go on to victimize others: No simple explanations. *Child Abuse & Neglect, 26*, 891–892.

Ryan, R. M., Kuhl, J., & Deci, E. L. (1997). Nature and autonomy: An organizational view of social and neurobiological aspects of self-regulation in behavior and development. *Development and Psychopathology, 9*, 701–728.

Sahota, K., & Chesterman, P. (1998). Mentally ill sex offenders in a regional secure unit: II. Cognitions, perceptions, and fantasies. *Journal of Forensic Psychiatry, 9*, 161–172.

Salekin, R. T., Ziegler, T. A., Larrea, M. A., Anthony, V. L., & Bennett, A. D. (2003). Predicting dangerousness with two Millon Adolescent Clinical Inventory psychopathy scales: The importance of egocentric and callous traits. *Journal of Personality Assessment, 80*, 154–163.

Scaramella, L. V., & Leve, L. D. (2004). Clarifying parent–child reciprocities during early childhood: The early childhood coercion model. *Clinical Child and Family Psychology Review, 7*, 89–107.

Schilling, R. F., & Schinke, S. P. (1989). Mentally retarded sex offenders: Fact, fiction, and treatment. *Journal of Social Work and Human Sexuality, 7*, 33–48.

Schoen, J., & Hoover, J. H. (1990). Mentally retarded sex offenders. *Journal of Offender Rehabilitation, 16*, 81–91.

Schwartz, B. K., & Cellini, H. R. (1995). Female sex offenders. In B. K. Schwartz & H. R. Cellini (Eds.), *The sex offender: Corrections, treatment, and legal practice* (pp. 5-1–5-22). Kingston, NJ: Civic Research Institute.

Schwartz, M. F., & Brasted, W. S. (1985). Sexual addiction: Self-hatred, guilt, and passive rage contribute to this deviant behavior. *Medical Aspects of Human Sexuality, 19*, 103–107.

Segal, Z. V., & Stermac, L. E. (1990). The role of cognition in sexual assault. In W. L. Marshall, D. R. Laws, & H. E. Barbaree (Eds.), *Handbook of sexual assault: Issues, theories, and treatment of the offender* (pp. 161–174). New York: Plenum Press.

Seghorn, T. K., Prentky, R. A., & Boucher, R. J. (1987). Childhood sexual abuse in the lives of sexually aggressive offenders. *Journal of the American Academy of Child and Adolescent Psychiatry, 26*, 262–267.

Seligman, M. E., & Johnston, J. C. (1973). A cognitive theory of avoidance learning. In F. J. McGuigan & D. B. Lumsden (Eds.), *Contemporary approaches to conditioning and learning* (pp. 69–110). New York: Wiley.

Seto, M. C., Cantor, J. M., & Blanchard, R. (2006). Child pornography offenses are a valid diagnostic indicator of pedophilia. *Journal of Abnormal Psychology, 115*, 610–615.

Seto, M. C., Khattar, N. A., & Lalumiere, M. L. (1997). Deception and sexual strategy in psychopathy. *Personality and Individual Differences, 22*, 301–307.

Sewell, K. W., & Salekin, R. T. (1997). Understanding and detecting dissimulation in sex offenders. In R. Rogers (Ed.), *Clinical assessment of malingering and deception* (2nd ed., pp. 328–350). New York: Guilford Press.

Shaffer, H. J. (1994). Considering two models of excessive sexual behavior: Addiction and obsessive–compulsive disorder. *Sexual Addiction and Compulsivity, 1*, 6–18.

Shaw, D. S., Owens, E. B., Giovannelli, J., & Winslow, E. B. (2001). Infant and toddler pathways leading to early externalizing disorders. *Journal of the American Academy of Child and Adolescent Psychiatry, 40*, 36–43.

Shealy, L., Kalichman, S. C., Henderson, M. C., Szymanowski, D., & McKee, G. (1991). MMPI profile subtypes of incarcerated sex offenders against children. *Violence and Victims, 6*, 201–212.

Shields, S. A., & Steinke, P. (2003). Does self-report make sense as an investigative method in evolutionary psychology? In C. Travis (Ed.), *Evolution, gender, and rape* (pp. 87–104). Cambridge, MA: MIT Press.

Shields, W. M., & Shields, L. M. (1983). Forcible rape: An evolutionary perspective. *Ethology and Sociobiology, 4*, 115–136.

Siegert, R. J., & Ward, T. (2002). Evolutionary psychology: Origins and criticisms. *Australian Psychologist, 37*, 20–29.

Sigelman, C. K., Budd, E. C., Spanhel, C. L., & Schoenrock, C. J. (1981). When in doubt, say yes: Acquiescence in interviews with mentally retarded persons. *Mental Retardation, 19*, 53–58.

Simmons, J. (2002). *Doctors and discoveries: Lives that created today's medicine.* Boston: Houghton Mifflin.

Simon, L. M. J. (1997a). Do criminal offenders specialize in crime types? *Applied and Preventative Psychology, 6*, 35–53.

Simon, L. M. J. (1997b). The myth of sex offender specialization: An empirical analysis. *New England Journal on Criminal and Civil Commitment, 23*, 387–403.

Simon, L. M. J. (1999). Are the worst offenders the least reliable? *Studies on Crime and Crime Prevention, 8*, 210–224.

Simon, L. M. J. (2000). An examination of the assumptions of specialization, mental disorder, and dangerousness in sex offenders. *Behavioral Sciences and the Law, 18*, 275–308.

Simons, D., Wurtele, S. K., & Heil, P. (2002). Childhood victimization and lack of empathy as predictors of sexual offending against women and children. *Journal of Interpersonal Violence, 17*, 1291–1307.

Simonson, S., Machelor, P., & Pallack, B. (2004, November 23). Serial rapist Selby hangs himself in jail. *Arizona Daily Star.* Retrieved from http://www.azstarnet.com

Sinclair, R. C., Lee, T., & Johnson, T. E. (1995). The effect of social-comparison feedback on aggressive responses to erotic and aggressive films. *Journal of Applied Social Psychology, 25*, 818–837.

Skinner, B. F. (1932). On the rate of formation of a conditioned reflex. *Journal of General Psychology, 7*, 274–286.

Smallbone, S. W., & Milne, L. (2000). Associations between trait anger and aggression used in the commission of sexual offenses. *International Journal of Offender Therapy and Comparative Criminology, 44*, 606–617.

Smith, W. R., Monastersky, C., & Deisher, R. M. (1987). MMPI-based personality types among juvenile sexual offenders. *Journal of Clinical Psychology, 43*, 422–430.

Smuts, B. (1992). Psychological adaptations, development, and individual differences. *Behavioral and Brain Sciences, 15*, 401–402.

Smuts, B. (1996). Male aggression against women: An evolutionary perspective. In D. M. Buss & N. M. Malamuth (Eds.), *Sex, power, conflict: Evolutionary and feminist perspectives* (pp. 231–267). New York: Oxford University Press.

Smuts, B., & Smuts, R. W. (1993). Male aggression and sexual coercion of females in nonhuman primates and other mammals: Evidence and theoretical implications. *Advances in the Study of Behavior, 22*, 1–63.

Snyder, H. N. (2000). *Sexual assault of young children as reported to law enforcement: Victim, incident, and offender characteristics* (Report NCJ 182990). Washington, DC: U.S. Government Printing Office.

Stamps, V. R., Abeling, N. G. G. M., Van Gennip, A. H., Van Cruchten, A. G., & Gurling, H. M. D. (2001). Mild learning difficulties and offending behaviour—

Is there a link with monoamine oxidase A deficiency? *Psychiatric Genetics, 11*, 173–176.

Stermac, L., & Sheridan, P. (1993). The developmentally disabled adolescent sex offender. In H. E. Barbaree, W. L. Marshall, & S. M. Hudson (Eds.), *The juvenile sex offender* (pp. 235–242). New York: Guilford Press.

Stinson, J. D., Becker, J. V., & Sales, B. D. (in press). Self-regulation and the etiology of sexual deviance: Evaluating causal theory. *Violence and Victims.*

Stoff, D. M., & Vitiello, B. (1996). Role of serotonin in aggression of children and adolescents: Biochemical and pharmacological studies. In D. M. Stoff & R. B. Cairns (Eds.), *Aggression and violence: Genetic, neurobiological, and biosocial perspectives* (pp. 101–123). Mahwah, NJ: Erlbaum.

Stoller, R. J. (1975). *Perversion: The erotic form of hatred.* New York: Pantheon Books.

Stoller, R. J. (1987). Perversion and the desire to harm. In R. Stern (Ed.), *Theories of the unconscious and theories of the self* (pp. 221–234). Hillsdale, NJ: Analytic Press.

Stoller, R. J. (1991). The term perversion. In G. I. Fogel & W. A. Myers (Eds.), *Perversions and near-perversions in clinical practice: New psychoanalytic perspectives* (pp. 36–56). New Haven, CT: Yale University Press.

Sutherland, E. H., & Cressey, D. R. (1966). *Principles of criminology* (7th ed.). Philadelphia: Lippincott.

Thompson, B. (2004, July 8). 22-year-old Gladewater man sentenced to prison. *Longview (Texas) News-Journal.* Retrieved from http://www.news-journal.com

Thornhill, R., & Palmer, C. T. (2000). *A natural history of rape: Biological bases of sexual coercion.* Cambridge, MA: MIT Press.

Thornhill, R., & Palmer, C. T. (2004). Evolutionary life history perspective on rape. In C. Crawford & C. Salmon (Eds.), *Evolutionary psychology, public policy, and personal decisions* (pp. 249–274). Mahwah, NJ: Erlbaum.

Thornhill, R., & Sauer, K. P. (1991). The notal organ of the scorpionfly (*Panorpa vulgaris*): An adaptation to coercive mating duration. *Behavioral Ecology, 2*, 156–154.

Thornhill, R., & Thornhill, N. W. (1983). Human rape: An evolutionary analysis. *Ethology and Sociobiology, 4*, 137–173.

Thornhill, R., & Thornhill, N. W. (1992). The evolutionary psychology of men's coercive sexuality. *Behavioral and Brain Sciences, 15*, 363–421.

Tomie, A. (1996). Self-regulation and animal behavior. *Psychological Inquiry, 7*, 83–85.

Travis, C. B. (2003). *Evolution, gender, and rape.* Cambridge, MA: MIT Press.

U.S. Department of Justice. (2006). *Crime in the United States, 2004.* Washington, DC: U.S. Government Printing Office.

Valliant, P. M., & Blasutti, B. (1992). Personality differences of sex offenders referred for treatment. *Psychological Reports, 71*, 1067–1074.

van Wijk, A., Loeber, R., Vermeiren, R., Pardini, D., Bullens, R., & Doreleijers, T. (2005). Violent juvenile sex offenders compared with violent juvenile nonsex offenders: Explorative findings from the Pittsburgh Youth Study. *Sexual Abuse: A Journal of Research and Treatment, 17*, 333–352.

Veneziano, C., Veneziano, L., & LeGrand, S. (2000). The relationship between adolescent sex offender behaviors and victim characteristics with prior victimization. *Journal of Interpersonal Violence, 15*, 363–374.

Virkkunen, M., & Linnoila, M. (1996). Serotonin and glucose metabolism in impulsively violent alcoholic offenders. In D. M. Stoff & R. B. Cairns (Eds.), *Aggression and violence: Genetic, neurobiological, and biosocial perspectives* (pp. 87–99). Mahwah, NJ: Erlbaum.

Vohs, K. D., & Ciarocco, N. J. (2004). Interpersonal functioning requires self-regulation. In R. F. Baumeister & K. D. Vohs (Eds.), *Handbook of self-regulation: Research, theory, and applications* (pp. 392–407). New York: Guilford Press.

Walker, W. D., Rowe, R. C., & Quinsey, V. L. (1993). Authoritarianism and sexual aggression. *Journal of Personality and Social Psychology, 65*, 1036–1045.

Waller, J. (2002). *The discovery of the germ.* Cambridge, England: Icon.

Ward, T. (2000a). Relapse prevention: Critique and reformulation. *Journal of Sexual Aggression, 5*, 118–133.

Ward, T. (2000b). Sexual offenders' cognitive distortions as implicit theories. *Aggression and Violent Behavior, 5*, 491–507.

Ward, T. (2001). A critique of Hall and Hirschman's quadripartite model of child sexual abuse. *Psychology, Crime, and Law, 7*, 333–350.

Ward, T. (2002). Marshall and Barbaree's integrated theory of child sexual abuse: A critique. *Psychology, Crime, and Law, 8*, 209–228.

Ward, T., & Beech, A. R. (2004). The etiology of risk: A preliminary model. *Sexual Abuse: A Journal of Research and Treatment, 16*, 271–284.

Ward, T., Bickley, J., Webster, S. D., Fisher, D., Beech, A., & Eldridge, H. (2004). *The self-regulation model of the offense and relapse process: Vol. 1. Assessment.* Victoria, British Columbia, Canada: Pacific Psychological Assessment Corporation.

Ward, T., Fon, C., Hudson, S. M., & McCormack, J. (1998). A descriptive model of dysfunctional cognitions in child molesters. *Journal of Interpersonal Violence, 13*, 129–155.

Ward, T., & Hudson, S. M. (1996). Relapse prevention: A critical analysis. *Sexual Abuse: A Journal of Research and Treatment, 8*, 177–200.

Ward, T., & Hudson, S. M. (1998). A model of the relapse process in sexual offenders. *Journal of Interpersonal Violence, 13*, 700–725.

Ward, T., & Hudson, S. M. (2000). A self-regulation model of relapse prevention. In D. R. Laws, S. M. Hudson, & T. Ward (Eds.), *Remaking relapse prevention with sex offenders: A sourcebook* (pp. 79–101). Newbury Park, CA: Sage.

Ward, T., & Hudson, S. M. (2001). Finkehor's precondition model of child sexual abuse: A critique. *Psychology, Crime, and Law, 7*, 291–307.

Ward, T., Hudson, S. M., Johnston, L., & Marshall, W. L. (1997). Cognitive distortions in sex offenders: An integrative review. *Clinical Psychology Review, 17,* 479–507.

Ward, T., Hudson, S. M., & Keenan, T. (1998). A self-regulation model of the sexual offense process. *Sexual Abuse: A Journal of Research and Treatment, 10,* 141–157.

Ward, T., Hudson, S. M., & Marshall, W. L. (1996). Attachment style in sex offenders: A preliminary study. *Journal of Sex Research, 33,* 17–26.

Ward, T., Hudson, S. M., Marshall, W. L., & Siegert, R. (1995). Attachment style and intimacy deficits in sexual offenders: A theoretical framework. *Sexual Abuse: A Journal of Research and Treatment, 7,* 317–335.

Ward, T., Polaschek, D. L. L., & Beech, A. R. (2006). *Theories of sexual offending.* Chichester, England: Wiley.

Ward, T., & Siegert, R. (2002a). Rape and evolutionary psychology: A critique of Thornhill and Palmer's theory. *Aggression and Violent Behavior, 7,* 145–168.

Ward, T., & Siegert, R. J. (2002b). Toward a comprehensive theory of child sexual abuse: A theory knitting perspective. *Psychology, Crime, and Law, 8,* 319–351.

Watzlawick, P., & Beavin, J. (1967). Some formal aspects of communication. *American Behavioral Scientist, 10*(8), 4–8.

Weiner, B. (1986). *An attributed theory of motivation and emotion.* New York: Springer-Verlag.

White, J. W., & Smith, P. H. (2004). Sexual assault perpetration and reperpetration: From adolescence to young adulthood. *Criminal Justice and Behavior, 31,* 182–202.

Wiederman, M. W. (2004). Self-control and sexual behavior. In R. F. Baumeister & K. D. Vohs (Eds.), *Handbook of self-regulation: Research, theory, and applications* (pp. 525–536). New York: Guilford Press.

Wilson, J. Q. (2003). On deterrence. In E. McLaughlin, J. Muncie, & G. Hughes (Eds.), *Criminological perspectives: Essential readings* (2nd ed., pp. 333–340). Thousand Oaks, CA: Sage.

Winick, B. J., & La Fond, J. Q. (2003). *Protecting society from sexually dangerous offenders: Law, justice, and therapy.* Washington, DC: American Psychological Association.

Worling, J. R. (1995). Sexual abuse histories of adolescent male sex offenders: Differences on the basis of the age and gender of their victims. *Journal of Abnormal Psychology, 104,* 610–613.

Worling, J. R. (2001). Personality-based typology of adolescent male sex offenders: Differences in recidivism rates, victim-selection characteristics, and personal victimization histories. *Sexual Abuse: A Journal of Research and Treatment, 13,* 149–166.

Wright, P., Nobrega, J., Langevin, R., & Wortzman, G. (1990). Brain density and symmetry in pedophilic and sexually aggressive offenders. *Annals of Sex Research, 3,* 319–328.

Yanagida, E. H., & Ching, J. W. J. (1993). MMPI profiles of child abusers. *Journal of Clinical Psychology, 49,* 569–576.

Yates, P. M. (2005, Summer). Book review: The self-regulation model of the offense and relapse process: A manual: Vol. I. Assessment. *Association for the Treatment of Sexual Abusers Newsletter, 17.*

Zgourides, G., Monto, M., & Harris, R. (1997). Correlates of adolescent male sexual offense: Prior adult sexual contact, sexual attitudes, and use of sexually explicit materials. *International Journal of Offender Therapy and Comparative Criminology, 41,* 272–283.

Zillman, D., & Bryant, D. (1989). *Pornography: Research advances and policy considerations.* Hillsdale, NJ: Erlbaum.

AUTHOR INDEX

SUBJECT INDEX

267

Fantasy, 6, 100, 189–190
Fear of negative consequences, 66
Fear of rejection, 48–49
Feedback loops, 68–69
Female sexual offenders, 16, 133
Fetish objects, 95, 97
Finkelhor, D., 137–141
Follicle stimulating hormone (FSH), 33, 34
Force, amount of, 82
Freud, Sigmund, 93–96, 114, 115
Frontal lobe abnormality, 31
Frotteurism, 131
FSH. See Follicle stimulating hormone
Future directions of research, 203–223
    needed research, 209–214
    prevention/treatment implications, 214–223
    previous research, knowledge from, 203–209

Gender differences
    in mating decisions, 123
    in reproductive capabilities, 122
Gender identity, 99–100
Gene–environment interactions, 125
Genetic defects, 36–37
Genetic predispositions, 5
Genital phase (of sexual development), 94
Geoghan, John, 4–6
GnRH. See Gonadotropic releasing hormone
Goal-directed behavior, 68–70
Goals, of researcher, 23
Goal-setting bias, 52
Gonadotropic releasing hormone (GnRH), 34–35
Guilt feeling attribution, 51

Hall, G. C. N., 147–153
Happenstance, 64–65
Harty, Randal, 4, 5
Harty, Russel, 4, 5
Heterogeneous groups of offenders, 16
High-dominance, low-nurturance approach to interpersonal relationships, 155–157
Hippocampus, 171
Hirschman, R., 147–153
Historical accuracy, of recall, 19
Honest courtship, 126
Hormones, 32–35
Hormone-secreting mechanisms, 34–35
Hostile masculinity, 155–158

Hypothalamus–pituitary regulation systems, 35

Id, 94–96
Illegal yet anonymous sexual behaviors, 72
Immediate gratification, 66
Impersonal sexual style, 154–155
Impulsive aggression, 35
Impulsivity, 187–188, 205
    and antisocial/psychopathic traits, 105–106
    definitions of, 210
    and mental retardation, 39
    and psychoanalytic theory, 95
Incentives, 79
Incest
    and left temporal lobe abnormalities, 29
    as nonreproductively driven sexual assault, 132
Incest offenders
    personality characteristics of, 101–102
    personality traits of, 104
    sexual entitlement in, 52
Inclusion criteria, 13–14
Information-processing models, 54–57
    empathy and theory of mind, 56–57
    social information-processing dysfunction, 54–56
Information-processing strategies, 58–59
Inhibitions, 145–146
Inhibitory mechanisms, 142
Inhibitory system, 35–36
Insect studies, 126
Instinct, 134
Institutionalization, 20–21
Instrumental anger, 106, 107
Intact regulation, 70
Integrative theories and models, 137–166
    Finkelhor's precondition model, 137–141
    Hall and Hirschman's quadripartite model, 147–153
    Malamuth's confluence model, 153–158
    Marshall and Barbaree's integrative theory, 142–147
    Ward and Siegert's pathways model, 158–165
Intellectual functioning, 20, 28
Intellectual impairment. See Mental retardation
Internal inhibitors, overcoming, 138–139
Internalized regulatory strategies, 178

Interpersonal relationships, 205
Interpersonal skills, 39, 40, 128
Interpersonal violence, 143
Interspecies rape, 130
Intimacy deficits (pathway 1), 159, 160
Intimidation, 66–67
Involuntary sexual responses, 70
Irresponsibility, 187–188

Judgment, 39

Klinefelter's syndrome, 37
Koch, Robert, 7
Krafft-Ebing, Richard von, 3, 93

Latency phase (of sexual development), 94
Learned behavior patterns, 55
Learning, context, 171
Left temporal lobe abnormalities, 29–30
Leydig cells of testes, 32, 33
LH. See Luteinizing hormone
Locus of control, 50
Loneliness, 46–48
Longitudinal research, 23, 212–213
Luteinizing hormone (LH), 33–35

Maladaptive reactions, 169–170
Malamuth, N. M., 153–158
Male dominance, 143
Male–male sexual abuse, 82
Male offenders, 82
Males, competitively disadvantaged, 127–128
Male victims, 82
Manipulation, 18
Manipulative courtship, 126
Marine mammals, 130
Marshall, W. L., 142–147
Masturbation, 65, 179, 189
Mate deprivation hypothesis, 127–128
Mate selection, 122–123
Mating effort, 125
MCMI. See Millon Clinical Multiaxial Inventory
Mediators
    defined, 73
    in multimodal self-regulation theory, 185–188
    personality traits as, 104–113
Memory(-ies)
    of childhood, 19–20
    impairment of, 19

recall of, 19, 21
and social information-processing dysfunction, 55
Men
    mating decisions of, 123
    reproductivity of, 122
Mental age, 40–41
Mental element attribution, 51
Mental retardation, 38–41
Methamphetamine, 36
Methodological limitations of relevant research, 13–25
    post hoc nature of research, 23–24
    sampling effects as, 13–16
    selection of comparison groups, 21–23
    self-report as, 17–21
Methodology, for future research, 212–213
Millon Clinical Multiaxial Inventory (MCMI), 101, 102, 104
Minnesota Multiphasic Personality Inventory (MMPI), 101, 102, 104
Minors, as victims of sexual assault, 3
Misregulation, 69–70
MMPI. See Minnesota Multiphasic Personality Inventory
Moderating variables, 73
Monoamine oxidase, 35
Mood
    and addiction, 71
    and deviant sexual arousal, 65–66
    and self-regulation, 177–178
Moral standards, 95
Motivational precursor, 149–150, 152–153
Motivation to sexually abuse, 138, 141
Multimodal self-regulation theory, 167–202, 204, 207, 208
    behavioral conditioning in development of maladaptive strategies, 184–185
    case examples, 191–201
    cognitive beliefs and personality traits as mediators, 185–188
    and current interventions, 221–223
    deviant arousal/fantasy/multiple paraphilias, 188–191
    deviant sexuality, 180–184
    peer and family socialization, 172–177
    and prevention/treatment, 217–221
    self-regulation, 177–180
    temperament and biological propensities, 168–172
Multiple dysfunctional mechanisms (pathway 5), 161

and multimodal self-regulation theory,
217–221
Primates, 128, 130
Prisons, 4
Projection, 114
Prolactin, 33, 34
Promiscuous sexual style, 154–155
Psychoanalytic theory, 94–96
Psychodynamic personality theory, 94–101
    attachment theory, 98–99
    classical psychoanalysis/ego psychology,
        94–96
    object relations theory, 96–98
    Robert Stoller's contributions to, 99–
        101
Psychopathia Sexualis (Richard von Krafft-
    Ebing), 3
Psychopathic traits, 7, 105–108
Psychopathology, 15
Psychopathy, 112
Psychosexual stages, 94, 115
Psychotic individuals, 15–16
Punishment
    in development of maladaptive strate-
        gies, 184–185
    and deviant sexual behavior, 66–68
    idea of, 74
    observed, 83
    parental, 173

Quadripartite model, 147–153

Rape(s)
    as adaptation, 129
    as by-product of other adaptations, 129–
        130
    case example of, 197–201
    by competitively disadvantaged males,
        127–128
    control used in, 65
    narcissistic reactance theory of, 109–110
    number of, 3
    as primitive sexual strategy, 124, 126
    and risk taking, 125
    and sadism, 111
Rape myths, 85
Rape pornography, 85–88
Rapists
    and anger, 107
    attributions of, 51
    and impulsivity, 106
    personality characteristics of, 102

personality disorders in, 113
personality traits of, 104
and right temporal lobe abnormalities,
    30–31
and social information-processing dys-
    function, 56
socioeconomically disadvantaged, 128
Rationalizations, 17–18, 23
Reactive–expressive anger, 106–107
Recall, 19, 21
Reinforcement(s), 6
    as coping strategy, 178
    definitions of, 211
    in development of maladaptive strate-
        gies, 184
    for deviant sexual arousal, 65–66, 68
    and multimodal self-regulation theory,
        220
    and self-regulation, 69
    and sexually violent pornography, 86
Rejection, fear of, 48–49
Relapse prevention, 216
Relationship(s)
    between self and objects, 96–97
    between variables, 214
    between victim and offender, 82
Reproduction, 122–123
Reproductive costs, 125
Reproductive opportunity, 127
Research
    knowledge from previous, 203–209
    needed future, 209–214
Resentment, 187
Resistance of child, overcoming, 139
Response, to sexual abuse, 83
Reward, 69
Right temporal lobe abnormalities, 30–31
Risk assessment, 161–162
Risk prediction, 8–9
Risk taking, 125, 180, 186–187
Role models
    characteristics of, 78
    of inappropriate behavior, 180
    and integrative theory, 143
    social learning from, 88
Rorschach Inkblot Test, 114
"Rules of behavior," 47

Sadism, 6–7, 111–112
Sadistic sexual offenses, 30
Sampling effects, 13–16
Scatologia, 131

ABOUT THE AUTHORS

Jill D. Stinson, PhD, formerly of the University of Arizona, is a clinical psychologist and researcher at Fulton State Hospital, a maximum-security forensic institution in Missouri. Her recent work includes examinations of mood disorders and emotional regulation in sex offenders, sexual behavior problems in offenders with intellectual–developmental disabilities, the prediction of sexual and institutional violence, the development and evaluation of a new treatment method for sex offenders, and the use of functional behavioral analysis to assess sexual behavior. Dr. Stinson is a member of the American Psychological Association, American Psychology–Law Society, Association for the Treatment of Sexual Abusers, and Association for Psychological Science.

Bruce D. Sales, JD, PhD, is a professor of psychology, sociology, psychiatry, and law at the University of Arizona, where he also directs its psychology, policy, and law program. His recent books include *Scientific Jury Selection* (with J. Lieberman, 2007); *Criminal Profiling: Developing an Effective Science and Practice* (with S. J. Hicks, 2006); *Experts in Court: Reconciling Law, Science, and Professional Knowledge* (with D. Shuman, 2005); *More Than the Law: Social and Behavioral Knowledge in Legal Decision-Making* (with P. English, 2005); *Family Mediation: Facts, Myths, and Future Prospects* (with C. Beck, 2001); and *Treating Adult and Juvenile Offenders With Special Needs* (coedited with J. Ashford and W. Reid, 2001). Dr. Sales, the first editor of the journals *Law and Human Behavior* and *Psychology, Public Policy, and Law,* is a Fellow of the American Psychological Association (APA) and the Association for Psychological Science. He is an elected member of the American Law Institute and twice served as president of the American Psychology–Law Society (AP-LS). He received the Award for Distinguished Contributions to Psychology and Law from the AP-LS, the Award for Distinguished Professional Contributions to public service from APA, and an honorary doctor of science degree from the City University of New York for being the "founding father of forensic psychology as an academic discipline."

Judith V. Becker, PhD, is a professor of psychology and psychiatry at the University of Arizona. She is the former president of both the International Academy of Sex Research and the Association for the Treatment of Sexual Abusers. She is also the past editor of *Sexual Abuse: A Journal of Research and Treatment* and currently serves on a number of editorial boards. Dr. Becker has authored or coauthored more than 100 journal articles and chapters on adult and juvenile sex offenders, sexual abuse, and victimization. She also consults on forensic cases.